Anthropological Theory Today

Anthropological Theory Today

Edited by Henrietta L. Moore

Polity Press

Copyright © this collection Polity Press 1999

First published in 1999 by Polity Press in association with Blackwell Publishers Ltd.

Editorial office:
Polity Press
65 Bridge Street
Cambridge CB2 IUR
UK

Marketing and production:
Blackwell Publishers Ltd
108 Cowley Road
Oxford OX4 1JF
UK

Published in the USA by
Blackwell Publishers Inc.
Commerce Place
350 Main Street
Malden, MA 02148
USA

ISBN 0-7456-2022-1
ISBN 0-7456-2023-X (pbk)

A catalogue record for this book is available from the British Library.

Library of Congress Cataloging-in-Publication Data

Anthropological theory today / edited by Henrietta L. Moore.
     p.   cm
    ISBN 0–7456–2022–1 (b.). — ISBN 0–7456–2023–X (p.)
    1. Anthropology—Philosophy.   2. Ethnology—Philosophy.
I. Moore, Henrietta L.
GN33.A445   1999
301′.01—dc21   99–26798
                                                                                    CIP

Typeset in 10 on 12 pt Sabon
by Ace Filmsetting Ltd, Frome, Somerset
Printed in Great Britain by T. J. International, Padstow, Cornwall

This book is printed on acid-free paper.

Contents

The Contributors

Debbora Battaglia is Professor of Anthropology at Mount Holyoke College. Her publications include *On the Bones of the Serpent: Person, Memory, and Mortality in Sabari Island Society* and *Rhetorics of Self-Making* (an edited anthology), as well as articles and chapters on the subject of self and identity in Melanesia. She is currently researching the discourse of human cloning.

Pascal Boyer is a Senior Researcher at the Centre National de la Recherche Scientifique, Lyon, and is a former Fellow of King's College, Cambridge. His work focuses on cognitive constraints on cultural transmission, particularly in the domain of religious concepts, using both anthropological and experimental techniques. Recent books include *Tradition as Truth and Communication* (1990) and *The Naturalness of Religious Ideas* (1994).

James G. Carrier teaches anthropology at Durham University. He has worked extensively on Western economy, and has written, edited and co-edited books such as *Gifts and Commodities: Exchange and Western Capitalism since 1700* (1995), *Meanings of the Market: The Free Market in Western Culture* (1997) and *Virtualism: A New Political Economy* (1998). He is starting to work on aspects of the effects of neo-liberalism in the Caribbean.

Thomas J. Csordas is Professor of Anthropology at Case Western Reserve University. He has conducted ethnographic research on ritual in the

Catholic Charismatic Renewal movement and on the Navajo Indian reservation. He is author of *The Sacred Self: A Cultural Phenomenology of Charismatic Healing* (1994), *Language, Charisma, and Creativity: The Ritual Life of a Religious Movement* (1997), and editor of *Embodiment and Experience: The Existential Ground of Culture and Self* (1994).

Catherine Lutz is Professor of Anthropology at University of North Carolina at Chapel Hill. She is the author of *Unnatural Emotions* (1988) and co-author, with Jane Collins, of *Reading National Geographic* (1993). She is currently writing an historical ethnography of Fayetteville, North Carolina, to be titled *War's Wages: A Military City and the American 20th Century*.

Daniel Miller is Professor of Material Culture at the Department of Anthropology, University College London. He also holds the appointment of British Academy Research Reader (1998–2000). His current interests are in consumption, political economy and Internet use in Trinidad. Recent publications include *A Theory of Shopping* (1998), *Virtualism* (1998, ed. with J. Carrier), *Material Cultures* (1998) and *Capitalism: An Ethnographic Approach* (1997).

Henrietta Moore is Professor of Social Anthropology and Director of the Gender Institute at the London School of Economics. Her interests include East and West Africa and the Anthropology of Gender. Her most recent books include *A Passion for Difference* (1994) and *The Future of Anthropological Knowledge* (1996).

Donald M. Nonini is Associate Professor of Anthropology at the University of North Carolina at Chapel Hill. His research interests include the cultural politics of the Chinese diaspora of the Asia Pacific region, and globalization, democracy and race relations in the southern United States. He is the co-editor, with Aihwa Ong, of *Ungrounded Empires: The Cultural Politics of Modern Chinese Transnationalism* (1997), and is currently writing an ethnographic and historical study entitled *"Getting through Life": The Cultural Politics of the Chinese Diaspora in Malaysia*; he is also co-author of a book in progress (with Dorothy Holland, Catherine Lutz et al.), entitled *Downsizing Democracy*, on the practices and discourses of local politics in the southern US and their relation to globalization.

Aihwa Ong is Professor of Anthropology at the University of California, Berkeley. She is the author of *Spirits of Resistance and Capitalist Discipline* (1987) and *Flexible Citizenship: The Cultural Logics of Trans-*

nationality (1999). She is co-editor of *Bewitching Women, Pious Men: Gender and Labor Politics in Southeast Asia* (1995), and of *Ungrounded Empires: The Cultural Politics of Modern Chinese Transnationalism* (1997). Her research and teaching are in critical globalization, capitalist transition, and sovereignty. She is completing a book on Asian diasporas and citizenship.

Nicholas Thomas is Director of the Centre for Cross-Cultural Research at the Australian National University. He has written widely on colonial histories, the anthropology of Oceania and contemporary art. His publications include *Entangled Objects* (1991), *Colonialism's Culture* (1994), *Oceanic Art* (1995), *In Oceania* (1997) and *Possessions: Indigenous Art/ Colonial Culture* (1999).

James F. Weiner is Senior Fellow in the Department of Anthropology, Research School of Pacific and Asian Studies, Australian National University, Canberra. He previously taught at the Universities of Manchester and Adelaide. His field of interests include myth, poetry, language, art, and (more recently) indigenous landowner politics, identity and representational practices in contemporary Australia and Papua New Guinea. Dr Weiner is also currently engaged as a consultant on several Native Title claims in the state of Queensland and is about to embark on a long-term research project centring on the proposed Papua New Guinea–Queensland gas pipeline. His most recent book is *The Lost Drum: The Myth of Sexuality in Papua New Guinea and Beyond* (1995).

1 Anthropological Theory at the Turn of the Century

Henrietta L. Moore

What is anthropological theory?

It is very tempting to begin a book of this kind with the statement that there is no such thing as anthropological theory. This temptation is not simply an idle or mischievous one, but stems from three interrelated problems: what is anthropological about anthropological theory?; what do anthropological theories theorize about?; and why have so many anthropologists in the last ten years repudiated theory in favour of ethnography? These questions are further complicated by the fact that anthropologists are often very unclear about the distinction between a generalization and a theory, and thus confusions arise about degrees of abstraction or, more precisely, about the relationship between observations, normative assumptions and theoretical propositions.[1] Such confusions have only been deepened by debates in the last ten years or so about the purpose and pretexts of anthropological knowledge. The inclusion of the anthropologist and their role in knowledge construction within the parameters of theoretical critique has had the effect, among other things, of linking anthropology as a practice to questions of power, domination and discrimination in ways that have highlighted moral and ethical dilemmas for practitioners individually and collectively. The results have been diverse, but in some sense have involved not only a retreat from theory, but even from the project of anthropology itself (Moore, 1997). However, the situation as the millennium approaches has improved with several calls for a renewal of theoretical thinking in the discipline and an emerging note of optimism about the future of anthropology (cf. Knauft, 1996 and 1997; Hastrup, 1995 and 1997; Moore, 1996a and 1997; Reyna, 1997; Benthall, 1995; Strathern, 1995).[2] It would probably be wise to retain a degree of scepticism about a sense of progress and renewal occurring at such a conveniently millennial moment, but nonetheless anthropology as a discipline and a practice has faced new challenges in the last two decades and new theories and new forms of theorizing have emerged and are taking discernible shape in response.

Anthropology as discipline and practice

In order to characterize this response, it is first necessary to say something about the nature of anthropological theory. One way to do this is to try and formulate a reply to the question 'What do anthropological theories theorize about?' Standard rejoinders usually include 'culture', 'other cultures', 'cultural difference', 'ways of life', 'social systems' and 'world views'; more abstract formulations might include power, difference, diversity, agency and representation; while more concrete responses might list, for example, family forms, political structures, livelihoods and forms of faith. The question 'What is anthropological theory?' is demonstrably tied to the question 'What is anthropology?', as all these responses indicate. The problem here is that none of the things included in such lists, whether as empirical entities or as theoretical concepts, are exclusively the domain of anthropology (see Thomas, chapter 10 below), and this immediately raises difficulties of how to delineate and specify the anthropological object of study. Such difficulties are, of course, common to all the other disciplines in the social sciences whose domains of enquiry not only overlap, but are implicated in each other. What makes anthropology anthropology is not a specific object of enquiry, but the history of anthropology as a discipline and a practice.

In this sense anthropology is anthropology because it is a specific formal mode of enquiry, and one which deals not just with 'cultural difference', 'other cultures' and 'social systems', but with how those differences and social systems are embedded in hierarchical relations of power. Anthropological discourses have determinate historical conditions which provide the wider institutional and discursive spaces in which its theories and practices are inscribed (Scott, 1992: 372–3). This was true of anthropology in the past and is true of the discipline now. However, to make this point is not just to subscribe to simplistic versions of this view, such as anthropology in the past was 'the handmaiden of colonialism'. There are many instances in anthropology's history when individuals and anthropological practices and discourses were co-opted for political ends –

this is true of all academic disciplines – but to understand anthropology as a disciplinary project within determinate historical conditions requires more insight than simply cataloguing such abuses. The fundamental point is that anthropology as a discipline and a practice is part of an imaginary that helps to shape the relationship between the West and its Others (Scott, 1992: 387–8). This relationship is not a static one, and has undergone considerable changes in the last few decades (see below). These historical changes have had a profound impact on the theory and practice of anthropology.

One consequence has been a reconfiguration of the boundaries between academic and non-academic practice. Anthropology is no longer, if it ever was, confined within the academy, but is increasingly part of the practice and theory of development agencies, voluntary organizations, international organizations and governments (cf. Karim, 1996). In short, it is part of the practice of governmentality (Moore, 1996b). Again, this observation has to be distinguished from more simplistic versions of the utility argument; in other words that anthropology has a long history of wanting to make itself useful to governments and that this inspired the rise of a specific sub-field called development anthropology (cf. Grillo and Rew, 1985). The more pertinent point is that anthropology as theory and practice cannot be confined within the academy, but neither can the academy be insulated from the uses to which anthropological theorizing, data and practice are put in other contexts. This is not only true with regard to the practices of government, but also in relation to such things as popular culture, consumption practices and body art (see Moore, chapter 6 below).

'Neither a borrower nor a lender be'

If the development of the discipline of anthropology is not immune to the material and imaginary purposes anthropological data and theory serve elsewhere, then how are we to respond to the question 'What is anthropological about anthropological theory?' Anthropological theories are clearly not unique to anthropology. This is obvious both from the fact that most anthropological theory courses begin by teaching students the basics of Marx, Weber and Durkheim, and from the extensive theoretical borrowing anthropology engages in, the most recent examples include the work of Bourdieu, Foucault, Bakhtin and Gramsci. When Clifford Geertz (1983) referred nearly twenty years ago to 'the blurring of genres', he had in mind not only the breakdown of disciplinary boundaries, but anthropology's adoption of concepts and theories from philosophy and the humanities. This process of adoption and incorporation has never been new –

after all Lévi-Strauss's structuralism was based on the borrowing of theories from structural linguistics – but it has arguably increased over the last twenty years, and has been accompanied by greater specialization. Thus, if once anthropological enquiry could be divided into the domains of kinship, politics, economics and religion, or into archaeology, socio-cultural anthropology, biological anthropology and linguistics, the present situation is considerably more diverse, with a proliferation of specialist sub-fields, such as the anthropology of development, organizations, education, theatre and performance, nutrition, cognition, psychoanalysis, psychology, gender and medical anthropology, to mention only a few. All these sub-fields borrow theories extensively from other disciplines and require degrees of theoretical specialism. In addition, the study of various 'topics' in anthropology also requires specialist theoretical knowledge and typically involves borrowing from other disciplines or from particular intellectual traditions or critiques that cross-cut the disciplines of the humanities and the social sciences (e.g. feminist theory or political economy). Such topics include – to list only a few – the body, memory, the household, the person, land, consumption, nationalism, violence and art. The boundaries between 'sub-fields' and 'topics' are never fixed and are a matter of contestation within the discipline, where proponents constantly announce the arrival of a new sub-field of 'anthropology of . . .'.

This new degree of theoretical specialization has increased diversity within the discipline and is thought by some to have begun its fragmentation. Thus we cannot speak of 'anthropological theory' because anthropology is both everything and nothing. Sherry Ortner described the discipline fifteen years ago as 'a thing of shreds and patches' (1984: 126) with regard to theory. She discussed the impact of Marxism, structuralism and symbolic interpretativism on the discipline and identified varieties of practice theory as the way forward. The theories she was referring to – while not confined to anthropology – were larger intellectual trends or approaches that cross-cut and informed, albeit to different degrees, the various 'sub-fields' or 'topics' of the discipline. Is it currently possible to identify such larger trends in contemporary anthropology? The straightforward answer is 'yes' (cf. Knauft, 1996). Practice theories continue to inform many theoretical projects across the range of anthropological endeavours, and much of this work draws implicitly and explicitly on the work of Bourdieu, De Certeau and Giddens, as well as making use of phenomenological theories. Issues of power and domination continue to be central to the discipline, and while being post-Marxist in the straightforward sense of the term, just as practice theories are post-structuralist, much work draws directly on Foucault, Gramsci and Bakhtin.[3] A key concern with subjectivities, their lived constructions and resistances to forms of power and control is evident in the way scholars draw on the work of Foucault, subaltern theories and feminist theory. Broad trends are in evidence, but even since 1984, when Sherry Ortner published her article, it has become clear that it is no longer possible to speak of coherent theoretical approaches that are neatly delineated from others. Theories are themselves more composite, more partial and more eclectic.

Post-modernism and the crisis of representation

There is a tremendous irony here because one of the reasons why this is so is because of the impact of one particular set of theories on the humanities and social sciences in the last two decades (cf. Grossberg, Nelson and Treichler, 1992; Seidman, 1994).[4] This set of theories was variously labelled deconstructionist, post-structuralist and post-modernist, and in anthropology these theories inaugurated a critique of languages of representation, and insisted on the partiality and partialness of observations and locations, and the contingency and fragmentation of cultures, selves and histories. Their benefits and shortcomings for anthropology were vigorously debated by a relatively small group of scholars in the discipline in the 1980s and early 1990s (e.g. Clifford and Marcus, 1986; Marcus and Fischer, 1986; Clifford, 1988; Kapferer, 1988; Ulin, 1991; Polier and Roseberry, 1989; Sangren, 1988; Gellner, 1992; Roth, 1989). These debates, which had continuities with earlier disputes about the relative merits of interpretative versus scientific approaches in the discipline, focused on issues of the politics and pragmatics of representation replayed as antinomies between objectivism and subjectivism, and empiricism and social construction. However, the consequences of these debates were important for theoretical development in anthropology in a number of ways, all of which relate to the larger question 'What is anthropological about anthropological theory?'

One of the most notable features of the post-modernist/deconstructionist debate in anthropology, as elsewhere, was that it was anti-theory, in the sense that it provided a critique of the exclusionary practices of Western theorizing and explicitly eschewed 'grand theories' and 'meta-narratives' on the grounds that they homogenized differences. This had two consequences in anthropology: the first may be characterized in general terms as a reformulation of anthropological practices, and the second as a redefinition of the notion of theory itself. What connected these two processes was an emerging critique of the authority of the anthropologist as author, an insistence on the partiality and partialness of all interpretations, and a profound questioning of the assumptions and techniques used to develop and convey cultural representations and interpretations. This 'crisis of representation' was experienced by all the disciplines of the human sciences, but its particular inflection within anthropology was specifically tied to the geopolitics of West/Other relations and to anthropology's own fraught, but essential engagement with those relations. Anthropology occupies a discursive and practical space defined by West/Other relations, and no amount of critiques of 'othering' will ever alter that fact. Anthropology must on no account vacate that space because to do so would be to give up on the possibility of a critical politics and a critical ethics linked to an understanding of the way the world currently is and to the multifarious ways in which people are living out their lives.

However, at the beginning of the debate on the 'crisis of representation' in the 1980s, this point did not seem to be evident in anthropology, but what was clear was that anthropology's largely unquestioned and unexamined liberal values were being revealed as ethnocentric. This situation was a profoundly uncomfortable one for many anthropologists who tried, in vain, to resolve what was a political dilemma, albeit reconfigured as a moral one and often intensely felt on a personal level, through modifying their forms of writing and forms of fieldwork practice. In a sense this project was doomed to failure because modifications in rhetorical and personal praxis were insufficient to the larger task of developing a critical politics for the discipline (Moore, 1997: 129).

Why should this be so? The answer is really that although the postmodernist/deconstructionist debate in the discipline was of immense benefit and did result in changes in disciplinary practice and the textual representation of that practice – even in the work of anthropologists who were avowedly unsympathetic to the principles of the critique – the initial protagonists in the debate failed to acknowledge adequately that ethics is a matter of theory as well as of method (Moore, 1997: 126).[5] The critique of representation and the accompanying repudiation of 'grand theory' led to some practitioners in the discipline of anthropology apparently eschewing theory and generalization, and turning definitively to ethnography and the practice of fieldwork: empiricism and experience as solutions to the problems of representation and theory. Ethnography was the way out for anthropologists because it is the space in which we remain committed to a shared dialogue with the subjects of our enquiry and in which we have an opportunity to practice a personal ethics that can be dissociated to a degree from anthropology's complicitous history with the exclusionary practices and sanctioned ignorances of Western theorizing.

The turn to ethnography was a defensive gesture, but its benefits were illusory, in the sense that it could only displace, not resolve, the problem. The vituperative debate between the social constructionists – ethnography is fiction – and the ethnographic empiricists – anthropology is a science – often caricatured the careful way in which many anthropologists were trying to theorize not only anthropology's history and disciplinary assumptions, but the role of the anthropologist in knowledge construction. The fundamental tension within anthropology is that it is equally reliant on interpretative representation and on ethnography. This tension constitutes the discipline, and thus cannot be resolved either through a turn to ethnography or through a turn to interpretation. Anthropology is based on the irresolvable tension between 'the need to separate oneself from the world and render it up as an object of experience, and the desire to lose oneself within this object world and experience it directly' (Mitchell, 1988: 29). This tension is encapsulated in the method of participant-observation, and has been clearly demonstrated in the anthropological theorizing over the last twenty years which has given increasing emphasis to cultural construction, while simultaneously emphasizing praxis and phenomenology (see Csordas, chapter 7 below).

The problem for anthropology then is that a retreat to ethnographic particularism could never be an appropriate response to the charge that modernist meta-theories were exclusionary, hierarchical and homogenizing. Valuing cultural difference requires theory; assessing the connections between forms of cultural difference and hierarchical relations of power requires theory; linking personal experiences to processes of globalization and fragmentation requires theory. That is why anthropological theories, while they must be grounded in the particularities of lives lived, can never be isomorphic with them.

If the post-modernist/deconstructionist debate forced anthropology to rethink aspects of its practice, but did so in ways that encouraged a retreat from theory, then in what sense could this debate also be said to have brought about a redefinition of the notion of theory itself? The first point, of course, is that the retreat from theory was only ever a partial one and was, like the retreat to ethnography, somewhat illusory. During the whole period when anthropology was apparently eschewing theory, it was in fact continuing to produce theories. The post-modernists and/or deconstructionists were certainly producing theory, since they were introducing these ideas into anthropology.[6] Many other anthropologists were influenced by such theories, but continued to apply specific theoretical questions to fine-grained ethnographic data, as part of a process both of developing new insights into specific questions and of interrogating disciplinary concepts and assumptions.[7] This is very much in the historical tradition of anthropology which has in various periods subjected its own disciplinary assumptions and concepts to anthropological scrutiny. Anthropologists have long been aware that one of the goals of anthropological theorizing is to scrutinize our constructions via the detour of the other.[8] This is not a cynical use of other people's perspectives, but a mechanism for bringing cultures into relation with each other, within a critical framework. This process was intensified by the post-modernist/

deconstructionist debate in anthropology because of the emphasis placed on the role of the anthropologist in knowledge construction, the importance of positionality, and the partialness of interpretations. The result, however, was not just that key concepts like culture came under renewed scrutiny, but that the very conditions of possibility of anthropology itself were interrogated, what we might better call the pre-theoretical assumptions and values that make the discipline and its practice possible. The idea, for example, that cultures can be compared because they have independent existences.

The interrogation of the discipline's pre-theoretical assumptions and values did not take place in a vacuum, and two particular developments are of importance here. The first is that in the last twenty years or so anthropology has 'come home': it has increasingly turned to the study of communities in Western nations, and thus the pronouncements of the academy have been less and less isolated from the communities studied. But, processes of globalization and population movements have meant that communities 'at home' are increasingly culturally diverse: 'other cultures' are no longer confined to 'other parts' of the world. These changes in anthropology's object of study have been paralleled by a second development, and that is a change in the nature of the academy itself. If some of the cultures and communities studied by anthropologists are now transnational and translocational, then so too are anthropologists. It is the anthropologists and not just the informants who are post-colonials. This has had a major impact on debates on the role of the anthropologist in knowledge construction and on the development of a critical politics in the discipline. Issues of hybridity and positionality have been largely forced onto the agenda in anthropological theorizing by feminist, native and minority scholars in the discipline, and by those anthropologists who live the hybridity of multiple locations and subjectivities most acutely. As the world is simultaneously globalized and localized, so too is the discipline and practice of anthropology.

The post-modernist/deconstructionist debate in anthropology might have had a marked influence on the discipline, but it has done so under determinate historical conditions and in the context of the emergence of new discursive spaces. These new discursive spaces are both inside and outside anthropology itself. A number of commentators (e.g. Knauft, 1996 and 1997; Scott, 1992) have pointed out that as anthropology responded to post-modernist theories arriving from literary studies and the humanities and began the process of deconstructing anthropological texts, scholars from the humanities and literary studies moved into the domain of culture and from this emerged cultural studies, cultural criticism, post-colonial studies, multi-culturalism, black cultural studies, queer theory and other hybrid enquiries into forms of culturalism and things cultural (see the chapters by Thomas, Battaglia and Moore below). These approaches have as many differences as they share similarities, but they all in one way or another draw on difference theories, on issues surrounding the politics of identity, as well as engaging with processes of globalization, hybridity and cultural transformation. Anthropology's relation to these intellectual developments has been mixed (see Thomas, chapter 10 below). The discipline has remained both nervous and cautious about these 'newcomers' into the area of its traditional domain of enquiry 'culture' (Rosaldo, 1994; Turner, 1993; Harvey, 1996). New understandings of culture assert not just its contested nature, but the fact that cultures are mobile, unbounded, open-ended and hybrid. It is not just that anthropology can no longer be defined as the discipline that studies 'other cultures' and cultural forms – because so many others do too – but also that its very object of study, culture, is rapidly transforming.

How this book works

The changing nature of anthropology and of anthropological theory thus poses particular challenges for a book entitled *Anthropological Theory Today*. It is not just that there is no longer, if there ever was, a single anthropology, and that there are no coherent sets of uniquely anthropological theories, but rather that the nature of the theoretical is itself in question.[9] Theory is now a diverse set of critical strategies which incorporates within itself a critique of its own locations, positions and interests: that is, it is highly reflexive. This notion of theory – which is the legacy of a moment of high post-modernism/deconstruction – underpins multifarious intellectual projects across a range of disciplines. It self-identifies as the meta-critique of all critiques, as a field of nomadic critical operations that undermines any attempt to authenticate cultures, selves and histories. This view of theory is itself a myth or rather only a moment in a larger critical strategy. It too can be critiqued, as it acknowledges, for its own pre-theoretical assumptions: its constituting concepts and values. What this book attempts is not a comprehensive theoretical overview of the field of anthropology – such a task would be impossible, as well as undesirable. Rather, it sets out through a series of essays to demonstrate the ways in which anthropology and anthropological theorizing are changing in response to changes inside and outside the academy. It locates anthropological theorizing within a set of determinate historical conditions, but does not do so through an overview or synthesis of those conditions. It attempts instead to provide examples of anthropologists working theory in response to their readings of those conditions and their positions within them. It discusses the use of some of the key concept metaphors that organize critique within the discipline – such as gender, self and body – but chooses to demonstrate how theory works with certain concept metaphors rather than providing a synthesis of all concept metaphors within the discipline – another impossible task in any event. It examines the question of how anthropology borrows, appropriates and transforms theories from other disciplines and/or from broader intellectual critiques through examples of how this works in certain contexts, as seen from the perspective of particular authors, and not as part of a huge list or extensive genealogy of such borrowings and relations. Through the range of theoretical thinking they present, the essays in this volume demonstrate the composite nature of anthropological theorizing, and show how different kinds of theories work at different levels of scope and abstraction. The guiding principle of this book – if it can be said to have one – is that it is not a synthesis, it is an intervention in a debate, as well as in a set of practices labelled anthropology.

The landscape of debate: A contested terrain

The global and the local: culture and political economy

Many anthropologists have emphasized the importance of locating ethnography within a globalized world, and have stressed that this involves documenting the impact of large-scale processes on subjectivities and communities, but doing so in a way that demonstrates the specific and evolving nature of local responses (cf. Strathern, 1995; James, 1995; Miller, 1995). In contrast to a post-modern perspective that hyper-valorizes difference, and in counterpoint to the anti-theory stance of the post-modern critique in anthropology, this approach insists that documenting political and economic struggles, changing livelihoods, individual and collective identities, experiences of disempowerment, spiritualities and world views demands a commitment both to detailed scholarship (ethnography) and to analytical rigour (critical theory). There is a generally acknowledged view in anthropology that the context in which the discipline is operating has changed and is continuing to change. As a number of commentators have made clear, there are identifiable features of a late modern and globalized world (Giddens, 1991 and 1994; Waters, 1995; Kearney, 1995), all of which have had a major impact not just on anthropology's practice, but on the discipline's pre-theoretical commitments. These changes may be broadly characterized as:[10]

- Increasing articulation of industrialization with domestic commodity production, with service and marketing industries, and with electronic and mass media economy

- Political and economic shifts from centralization to decentralization, post-Fordist or flexible accumulation, and trans-national influence at the expense of nation-state autonomy
- Increasing disparities of wealth, health and well-being both within and across communities articulated with race, class, ethnic, gender and religious difference
- Increasing communities of identity and imagination across space and time, often involving huge movements of people and the development of diasporic (trans-national or trans-locational) communities
- Increase of information, information flow and communication speed, associated with time-space compression and the increased movement of people and ideas
- Increase in conflict, violence and warfare, associated with a nexus of poverty, discrimination and cultural politics.

These features of globalization are well reconized, but they have prompted new work in anthropology on the cultural dimensions of globalization, and thus on two old questions: 'What is culture?' and 'How does one study the relation between cultures?' (Friedman, 1994; Appadurai, 1996; Hannerz, 1992). There is general agreement that globalization has not produced cultural homogenization, but is creating new cultural configurations through which people are living out new subjectivities and social relations. As Kearney says (1995: 551) 'contemporary anthropological global theory is innovating theories of culture, social organization, and identity for global and transnational persons and communities'. Diversity and difference are being given new meaning, and whereas once we might have been able to align cultural and other differences with the spatial metaphors of centre/periphery, us/them, processes of production, consumption and identity formation that were once the result of capitalism's impact on the periphery have now flowed back and transformed the so-called centre (Kearney, 1995: 554). Cultures are becoming both deterritorialized and reterritorialized: they are no longer predicated on particular spatial co-ordinates, but neither are they adrift from the particularities of lives lived. Cultures are extended across space and time, and formed through new media and coalitions of shifting identities and understandings. The anthropological terrain of culture has shifted: new forms of public culture are emerging, as are new ideas about what it means to be 'modern', a citizen, an individual.

Such new work in anthropology figures culture as a series of sites of contested representation and resistance within fields of power. The notion of culture as an autonomous entity has been undermined, and that critique has inevitably resulted in a challenge to other spatialized entities and the identities predicated upon them: for example, the nation-state (cf. Ong and Nonini, 1997). Aihwa Ong takes up this theme in her chapter in this volume and discusses how the traditional anthropological notion of culture encouraged a view of non-Western societies as communitarian in character as opposed to the individualistic values of Western cultures. She argues that understanding the relationship between cultural values and societal forms requires a notion of cultural politics premised on revisions of the notions of culture, state and citizen. The hierarchical dualisms of earlier forms of analysis – modern/non-modern, individualistic/communitarian, secular/religious, state/kin-based societies – which are implicit in the traditional anthropological notion of culture and a defining feature of a traditional political anthropology are inappropriate for understanding forms of political control, economic development and cultural values in the contemporary societies of South-East Asia.

James Carrier and Daniel Miller discuss the relationship between the global and the local, between macro- and micro-processes, from the perspective of a reformulated economic anthropology. They reaffirm the importance of anthropology's commitment both to theoretical models and to the particularities of individual and collective agency. They point out that a particular notion of 'the economy' is a defining feature of how Westerners understand themselves as Westerners, and view themselves as 'moderns'. Contemporary anthropology needs to deconstruct this notion of the economy, and Carrier and Miller proceed to do this through a repositioning of the relationship between economy and morality in the context of an anthropological critique of the discipline of economics.

The chapters by Ong and Carrier and Miller critique the spatialization implicit in the pre-theoretical commitments of the notions of the political and the economic, and show how those notions are tied to Western understandings of Western societies in ways that threaten to occlude how others in other contexts conceptualize and operationalize the relationship between cultural values, local identities and economic and political processes (cf. Ong, 1996). The chapter by Lutz and Nonini addresses the relationship between the local and the global from yet another perspective. Their concern is with how trans-national economic and political processes have transformed people's livelihoods and increased levels of conflict, violence and warfare. They too demonstrate the necessity of a commitment both to theoretical models that can make sense of the specifics in each locality and to the ethnographic specifics upon which generalizations must be based. Their work shows how aspects of identities and subjectivities – gender, race and class – are co-opted, inflected and intensified through the operations of power constitutive of economic and political processes (cf. Yanagisako and Delaney, 1995; Ginsburg and Rapp, 1995; Alexander and Mohanty, 1997).

Social justice and cultural relativism

Lutz and Nonini's chapter raises the question of anthropology's commitment to documenting forms of social, economic and political exploitation and discrimination and their consequences for people's lives and aspirations. Such a commitment is of long standing in anthropology and is an inevitable part of the history of a discipline concerned with understanding cultural and social difference in the context of hierarchical power relations and the inequalities of geopolitics. Knauft has recently called for a 'critical humanism', which he defines both as a commitment to document the richness of people's lives and to 'expose, analyze, and critique human inequality and domination' (Knauft, 1996: 50). Forms of inequality and domination are intertwined, not always hegemonic and sometimes conflicting. This means that the specifics of inequality – race, gender, class, ethnicity, nationality, caste – have to be studied on the ground, and that the material dimensions of inequality and domination have to be linked to forms of knowledge, discourse and representation (Knauft, 1996: 50–1; Scheper-Hughes, 1992). This is a goal with which many practitioners can identify, but within the complex political and ethical field in which anthropology as a practice and a discourse is located, good intentions do not always produce good results.

Recent debate on this point has been heated, with some anthropologists calling for high-quality, objective ethnography on the grounds that the role of the anthropologist as scientist is to speak truth to power. In this context D'Andrade argues that any claim anthropology might have to moral authority 'rests on knowing *empirical* truths' (D'Andrade, 1995: 403), and thus one should keep objective and moral models separate. This is because the aim of a moral model is to allocate praise or blame and this shapes its cognitive character, while the purpose of an objective model is to gain a surer understanding of what is actually happening (D'Andrade, 1995: 408). Other anthropologists decry this suggestion and point out that there is no such thing as value-free enquiry, and therefore it is impossible to keep moral and objective models separate. This debate is, of course, a version of an older debate in anthropology about interpretation versus science, what gives it new impetus is a renewed interest in the thorny problem of cultural relativism.

In some sense, the recent debate on cultural relativism is a reaction to what many practitioners now feel was the apoliticism of post-modern theories. Such theories theorized difference, but effectively gave equal value to all differences. The result was a form of general political paralysis. In order to understand what is happening to people's lives, it is not enough to focus on fragmentation and particularism; there has to be some acknowledgement that hierarchical relations of power and domination set a larger context within which the particularities of lives are lived. If individuals and collectivities are to challenge relations of power, they cannot do so by asserting that each situation is unique and that there are no common discourses or understandings to link experiences and situations. Thus the politics of a 'critical humanism' or what Scheper-Hughes (1995) has called a 'militant anthropology' is closely allied to recent theoretical trends in anthropology that call for a marriage of detailed ethnography and robust theory (see above).

Scheper-Hughes argues that anthropological work must be based on an explicit ethical orientation to 'the other', and that the role of the anthropologist is not to stand on the side-lines, but to witness, to speak out about what is going on (Scheper-Hughes, 1995: 418–19). Again, this is a position with which many anthropologists can identify; the problem comes in the recognition that the practice of anthropology is always an intervention, and that speaking out involves not just witnessing, but intervening. Anthropologists, like others, cannot control the effects of their interventions, and good intentions do not always produce good results. To say this is to say little more than that moral action is always flawed, and the fact that something is flawed is not necessarily a reason for abandoning it. However, it is a reason for subjecting it to sustained critical reflection. Moral convictions always have to be tempered with a relativist stance in anthropology – albeit a temporary one – because if they are not then understanding is precluded in favour of judgement.

However, whenever we engage in discussion about morality and engagement in anthropology, we need to maintain a critical awareness of the cultural values that underpin the pre-theoretical commitments implicit in such discussions. Terms like objectivity and morality imply universal attributes which are part not only of liberal Western discourses, but are also a constitutive factor in the making of Western culture in its distinction from other cultures, and thus, of course, a constitutive part in the creation of the possibility of anthropology as a discipline and a practice (Ong, 1995 and 1996; chapter 3 below). Anthropology's engagement with 'other cultures' means an engagement with other values and pre-theoretical commitments, it does not mean a collapsing of distinctions between value frames or the permanent withdrawal of the possibility of value judgement.

These are not issues on which there is ever likely to be complete agreement in anthropology, and in fact one should not wish for agreement in these areas if one is in favour of a self-reflexive and critical anthropology. Such an anthropology must necessarily be plural and partial, but one should not mistake either position for disengagement.

Agency and self-reflexivity

In her chapter in this volume, Debbora Battaglia argues – not unlike Scheper-Hughes (1995) – that the ethics of anthropology is bound up with ethnography as a discourse of responsibility, in the sense of a discourse of reflexive awareness achieved across difference. This proposition finds resonances for many anthropologists, some of whom have pointed out that the alternative to attention to difference is indifference, and that forms of indifference are at the root of murderous assertions of cultural and individual particularity. Battaglia's chapter opens up questions of agency and self-reflexivity from the point of view both of the anthropologist and the anthropological subject. Her argument thus situates the discourse of anthropology within the wider context of anthropology understood as cultural practice. Her questioning focuses on the notion of self as a grounding concept-metaphor both for the anthropologist and the anthropological subject as agent. Her position is that the self is always a representational economy, an image of integration that strives, but fails, to encompass the diversity of experiences and subject positions. Battaglia's chapter demonstrates how a concept-metaphor like the self informs the agency of subjects – including that of the anthropologist – and yet is not a given, a stable and natural entity. Understanding the agency of others and how they act in the contemporary world is thus a matter of comprehending the spaces and oscillations between integrating notions and diverse experiences. Selfhood is a situationally, not essentially, defined project.

The question of how identities and subjectivities are formed in diverse situations is one of the major challenges of contemporary ethnography, and in a sense it is a continuation of older debates about the relationship between structure and agency. What is different is the way in which anthropological theory now tries to locate the agency of the anthropologist within the same frame as the agency of others, and thus to develop new forms of social engagement that ensure a radical departure from the earlier situations of anthropologists speaking for others. This extends the ethical grounding of anthropology in a way that does not presume that the anthropologist is a white, Western individual (cf. Moore, 1997), and thus it de-essentializes the anthropological/informant dyad so as to permit a more detailed and nuanced understanding of how subject positions and identities are shaped within anthropological encounters – encounters understood as determinate forms of cultural and social practice.

One of the facts of anthropological practice and theory is that the grounding concept-metaphors of the discipline are also deployed in specific projects by those who are the subjects of anthropological enquiry. The result is that these concept-metaphors – the body, the self, gender, mind – are never free of the uses to which they are put in various social contexts. In the chapter on gender in this volume, I discuss how anthropologists and feminists have subjected the notion of gender to critique and questioned its validity for understanding the projects and practices of others. My argument has certain continuities with that of Battaglia, in that I show how anthropology needs to deploy the concept-metaphor of gender to analyse continuities across space, time and experience, and yet simultaneously work against the integratory capacity of the concept to reveal alternative experiences and the pre-theoretical commitments that underpin the notion of gender in the social sciences.

Thomas Csordas reviews the history of the body in anthropological thought in his contribution to this volume, but does so from the perspective of the work that the concept-metaphor of the body has performed for anthropological theory over time. The present concern with theories of embodiment – which draw, among other things, on earlier theories of practice – demonstrates the way in which the concept-metaphor of the body has become bound up with issues of identity, subjectivity and agency in contemporary anthropological theorizing. The body is now understood in theoretical terms both as representation and as experience, and in this sense is a microcosm for the body of anthropological theory itself.

What this alerts us to is that concept-metaphors in anthropology are not foundational, but partial, and that their work is both to allow comparison and to open up spaces in which their meanings – in daily practice, in local discourses and in academic theorizing – can be interrogated (cf. Moore, 1997). What is clear is that however globalized and fragmented the contemporary world is or is said to be, individuals and collectivities still engage with it and live meaningful lives, they hack a sense of self and meaning out of disparate circumstances, and remain committed to various projects and relationships. There is a fundamental sense in which anthropology needs to remain aware of its historical determinations and the limitations of its own theoretical projects (Scott, 1992: 376–7). When we write of cultures being mobile and unbounded, or selves as contingent and multiply positioned, or communities as being dispersed and global, we need to be certain that we are not unintentionally cutting people off from their aspirations to the universal within their own particularities. Most people in the world – if we are speaking in absolute numbers – do still live in what they see as recognizable communities, believe themselves to be individuals, and think of their values and way of life as relatively coherent. They may not, of course, think this all the time or every day, but whatever the contingencies of life may be they remain in some relation to integratory concepts and practices that help to make life meaningful.

What it is to be human or what is it to be human?

It is held to be axiomatic in anthropology that humans make meaning out of life, indeed this is one of the features – if not the defining feature – of being human. To discuss the capacity for meaning creation – as I have in the previous paragraphs – as a determining characteristic of social agents around the world is, of course, to make a theoretical claim. This theoretical claim, however, does not operate on the same analytic level as standard generalizations based on ethnographic observations. It is certainly true that we can observe people everywhere making sense of their lives, and that one of the aims of anthropology should be to examine the way people conceive the world and reason upon it. Theories of agency, motivation and intention are all important here. But, a theoretical claim that people everywhere have the capacity to create meaning and that this is a defining feature of human agency is based on a pre-theoretical commitment. This pre-theoretical commitment is of a very particular kind in the sense that it is ontological rather than epistemological: in other words, it implies something about the nature of being human that is believed to be universally true. The problem for anthropology is that in spite of the impact of post-modern theorizing on the discipline and a political commitment to eschew homogenizing and exclusionary meta-theories, the discipline still has to engage with theories that are about the commonalities – and not just the differences – between all human beings. The impetus for this is not just the dialogue that must exist between socio-cultural anthropology, biological anthropology, psychology, linguistics and other cognate endeavours in recognition of the fact that humans have biological capacities and an evolutionary history, but also the political and humanist project of recognizing and valorizing the fact that humans everywhere are human. For this to be the case, there must be something shared about being human. This does not, of course, imply that those things that are shared are realized in the same way.

Contemporary socio-cultural anthropology has had a stormy relationship with the 'biological' in the form of socio-biology and evolutionary psychology. The general mistrust of universal theories has created something of a theoretical and political impasse, as well as a kind of misrecognition of the role of ontological theories in the discipline. It is evident from a review of recent work in anthropology that when we speak of or try to describe such processes as how humans acquire a body image or how symbolism works, or assert that the unconscious monitoring of human action is at the basis of human agency or that language brings humans into a relation with time, we are describing processes and making assertions that we imagine to be universally true, in that they apply to all humans. The role of ontological presuppositions is the subject of the chapters by James Weiner and Pascal Boyer.

Boyer discusses cognitive theories and their relevance for anthropology. He argues that cultural representations are informed by tacit principles or intuitive ontologies that are common to all humans. These cognitive capacities are evolved properties of the mind – all humans have these capacities – but they do not directly determine the content of cultural representations. Cultural theories of the person, for example, vary widely and are local enrichments of intuitive ontologies. What Boyer reminds us of then is that theories can be composite – the theory that accounts for intuitive ontologies is not of the same order or kind as the theory that accounts for variation in the content of cultural representations – and that theories can have ontological and epistemological components. Indeed, certain kinds of questions, such as 'Do all humans think in the same way?', require theories that have universal and particular elements and pretensions. This is why it is not true to say that anthropology has done away with universal or 'grand theories' (cf. Moore, 1997). What it has done is to recognize the composite nature of theorizing.

Part of what is at issue here is the relationship between the individual and the social or the self and the symbolic. Boyer argues that intuitive ontologies are fragmented systems of domain-specific expectations, thus placing agency in context at the heart of anthropological theories of cognition. He also maintains that any individual mind entertains a huge number of mental representations, but only a few of these are shared in roughly similar forms among members of a group. In other words, only a few can be thought of as 'cultural'. The question of how we relate to the experiences and interpretations of others is one of the questions underpinning Weiner's chapter on anthropology and psychoanalysis. Here Weiner points out that as anthropologists we cannot ignore the issue of the subjective perception of the world or the fact that we develop a sense of self through engagement with others, with their experiences and interpretations.

What psychoanalytic anthropology stresses is the similarity in the symbolic capacity of humans, and the fact that agency is never a matter of voluntarism. In other words, any serious theory of human agency must take account of desire and of unconscious motivation. Psychoanalysis is a theory about what it is to be human and as such it is premised on a number of ontological presuppositions, the most famous of which is the existence of the unconscious. In any consideration of the relationship between psychoanalysis and anthropology, the question of universals always get raised: 'Is the Oedipus complex universal?', for example. However, what Weiner draws our attention to is that a psychoanalytic anthropology must needs be based on composite theories. Theories that are context dependent and are related to a specific time and place, and theories that incorporate forms of ontological thinking. Weiner demonstrates this most directly in his discussion of the parallels between psychoanalysis's critique of the Western theory of the individual and Melanesian views of the acting person.

The relationship between the different elements in a composite theory is a complex and historically determined one. What contemporary anthropology and psychoanalysis share is a recognition that the self is not distinct from the relations into which it enters. From the anthropological point of view, this is not just true of 'other selves' – alternative understandings of self and person – but also of the anthropological self. The anthropologist as subject is encompassed within the same frame as the subjects of anthropological enquiry, is coeval with them, and is constituted through relations with them. This view of the framing of anthropological enquiry depends upon a much more nuanced recognition of locations, positionings and subjectivities than a previous view of anthropologist/informant relations as simply an interaction of autonomous selves, a relation of us and them separated by cultural difference.

Conclusion

The central traditional concepts of anthropology have changed in the face of globalization and changes in the forms of political economy, the nation-state, violence, the media and cultural identities. Diversity and difference have taken on new meanings in anthropology and the major controversies and debates can no longer be approached satisfactorily through traditional dualisms. However, contemporary questions are in some important ways reforged continuities of older questions, such as 'What is culture'; what is the relationship between social values and the material world, between structure and agency, between the individual and the symbolic; is anthropology a science or a moral project; and what is the role of the anthropologist? The major change in anthropological theorizing has come about through placing the anthropologist within the same frame of reference as the subjects of anthropology; through responding to the changing nature of anthropology inside and outside the academy; and through recognizing that anthropology is part of the world it studies.

Notes

1 Theories are, of course, types of generalization. However, much of the recent confusion about theory in anthropology could have been avoided by emphasizing the differences in scope and level of abstraction of various gener-

alizations. Generalizations, for the purposes of my point here, are relatively low in abstraction and scope and are derived from observations. Theories are higher in abstraction and scope and are induced from generalizations. Some anthropologists in the last decade or so, while wanting to critique meta-narratives and exclusionary theory, have been forced into the wholly unnecessary position of disavowing the validity of any generalizations and rejecting all forms of generalization as essentialist (Knauft, 1997: 283).

2   This new found optimism is in sharp contrast to the much-cited pessimism of some of anthropology's elder statesmen: Sahlins has characterized the discipline as being 'in the twilight of its career' (Sahlins, 1995: 14), while Geertz's more precise claim is that the discipline will disappear in about fifty years (Handler, 1991: 612).

3   I use the terms post-Marxist and post-structuralist here to mean theoretical positions and concepts that would not be possible in the discipline if previous Marxist and structuralist theories had not produced the theoretical critiques and detailed analyses that they did.

4   For discussions of the history of the introduction of these theories into anthropology, see Knauft, 1996 and 1997; Pool, 1991; Scott, 1992; Coombe, 1991.

5   Knowledge construction is necessarily linked to theories of the good life (see Taylor, 1991 and 1995). Knauft also asserts a necessary connection between ethics and theory in anthropology through his notion of 'critical humanist sensibilities' (Knauft, 1996).

6   Rather ironically, the existence of post-modernist or deconstructionist anthropologists is somewhat in doubt. There certainly were proponents of various related theoretical positions, camp followers and others who used the terms in their writings, but very few anthropologists have ever 'come out' and said that they are a post-modernist or deconstructionist anthropologist. Knauft (1997: 282) notes the limited present use of the term post-modernist in anthropology, except 'as an epithet against those charged with New Age navel-gazing'.

7   This is evident, apart from anything else, in the proliferation and development of sub-fields and topics in the last decades, as discussed above.

8   My use of 'our' in this context refers to the collectivity of anthropologists. This collectivity is inevitably imaginary, but it is not to be confused with the West or white or first world scholars; it refers to those people who share a disciplinary training and an engagement with anthropological discourses. Such an engagement or relation is obviously a contestatory one, and thus it is not assumed that all anthropologists share similar views or experiences.

9   Certain commentators might be moved to remark that anthropological theories do exist, in the sense of comparative kinship, for example. This is true in so far as anthropology courses in many universities continue to teach such theories and ethnographers continue to document kin ties and draw kinship diagrams, but the main point is that such theories no longer operate as the basic organizing principles of anthropological descriptions and explanations. Indeed, kinship still exists, people still live their kin relations, but kinship is no longer a grounding trope of anthropological enquiry.

10   I have developed this list from Knauft, 1997: 283–4.

Bibliography

Alexander, J., and C. Mohanty, eds, 1997. *Feminist Genealogies, Colonial Legacies, Democratic Futures*. London: Routledge.

Appadurai, A., 1996. *Modernity at Large: Cultural Dimensions of Globalisation*. Minneapolis: University of Minnesota Press.

Benthall, J., 1995. 'From self-applause through Self-Criticism to Self-Confidence', in *The Future of Anthropology. Its Relevance to the Contemporary World*, ed. A. Ahmed and C. Shore. London: Athlone Press.

Clifford, J., 1988. *The Predicament of Culture: Twentieth-Century Ethnography, Literature and Art*. Cambridge, MA: Harvard University Press.

Clifford, J., and G. Marcus, eds, 1986. *Writing Culture: The Poetics and Politics of Ethnography*. Berkeley: University of California Press.

Coombe, R., 1991. 'Encountering the Postmodern: New Directions in Cultural Anthropology', *Canadian Review of Anthropology and Sociology* 28: 188–205.

D'Andrade, R., 1995. 'Moral Models in Anthropology', *Current Anthropology* 36(3): 399–408.

Friedman, J., 1994. *Cultural Identity and Global Process*. London: Sage.

Geertz, C., 1983. *Local Knowledge: Further Essays in Interpretive Anthropology*. New York: Basic Books.

Gellner, E., 1992. *Postmodernism, Reason and Religion*. London: Routledge.

Giddens, A., 1991. *Modernity and Self-Identity*. Cambridge: Polity Press.

Giddens,. A., 1994. *Beyond Left and Right*. Cambridge: Polity Press.

Ginsburg, F., and R. Rapp, eds, 1995. *Conceiving the New World Order: The Global Politics of Reproduction*. Berkeley: University of California Press.

Grillo, R., and A. Rew, eds, 1985. *Social Anthropology and Development Policy*. London: Tavistock.

Grossberg, L., C. Nelson, and P. Treichler, eds, 1992. *Cultural Studies*. London: Routledge.

Handler, R., 1991. 'An Interview with Clifford Geertz', *Current Anthropology* 32: 603–13.

Hannerz, U., 1992. *Cultural Complexity: Studies in the Social Organisation of Meaning*. New York: Columbia University Press.

Harvey, P., 1996. *Hybrids of Modernity: Anthropology, the Nation State and the Universal Exhibition*. London: Routledge.

Hastrup, K., 1995. *A Passage to Anthropology: Between Experience and Theory*. London: Routledge.

Hastrup, K., 1997. 'The Dynamics of Anthropological Theory', *Cultural Dynamics* 9(3): 351–71.

James, W., ed., 1995. *The Pursuit of Certainty: Religious and Cultural Formations*. London: Routledge.

Kapferer, B., 1988. 'The Anthropologist as Hero: Three Exponents of Postmodernist Anthropology', *Critique of Anthropology* 8(2): 77–104.

Karim, W. J., 1996. 'Anthropology without Tears: How a "Local" sees the "Local" and the Global', in Moore, 1996a.

Kearney, M., 1995. 'The Local and the Global: The Anthropology of Globalisation and Transnationalism', *Annual Review of Anthropology* 24: 547–65.

Knauft, B., 1996. *Genealogies for the Present in Cultural Anthropology*. London: Routledge.

Knauft, B., 1997. 'Theoretical currents in Late Modern Cultural Anthropology', *Cultural Dynamics* 9(3): 277–300.

Marcus, G., and M. Fischer, 1986. *Anthropology as Cultural Critique: An Experimental Moment in the Human Sciences*. Chicago: University of Chicago Press.

Miller, D., ed., 1995. *Worlds Apart: Modernity through the Prism of the Local*. London: Routledge.

Mitchell, T., 1988. *Colonizing Egypt*. Cambridge: Cambridge University Press.

Moore, H. L., ed., 1996a. *The Future of Anthropological Knowledge*. London: Routledge.

Moore, H. L., 1996b. 'The Changing Nature of Anthropological Knowledge: An Introduction', in Moore, 1996a.

Moore, H. L., 1997. 'Interior Landscapes and External Worlds: The Return of Grand Theory in Anthropology', *The Australian Journal of Anthropology* 8(2): 125–44.

Ong, A., 1995. 'Comment on "Objectivity and Militancy: A Debate" ', *Current Anthropology* 36(3): 428–30.

Ong, A., 1996. 'Anthropology, China and Modernities: The Geopolitics of Cultural Knowledge', in *The Future of Anthropological Knowledge*, ed. H. L. Moore. London: Routledge.

Ong, A., and D. Nonini, eds, 1997. *Underground Empires: The Cultural Politics of Modern Chinese Nationalism*. London: Routledge.

Ortner, S., 1984. 'Theory in Anthropology since the Sixties', *Comparative Studies in Society and History* 26: 126–66.

Polier, N., and W. Roseberry, 1989. 'Tristes Tropes: Postmodern Anthropologists Encounter the Other and Discover Themselves', *Economy and Society* 18: 245–64.

Pool, R., 1991. 'Postmodern Ethnography?', *Critique of Anthropology* 11(4): 309–31.

Reyna, S., 1997. 'Theory in Anthropology in the Nineties', *Cultural Dynamics* 9(3): 325–50.

Rosaldo, R., 1994. 'Whose Cultural Studies', *American Anthropologist* 96: 524–9.

Roth, P., 1989. 'Ethnography without Tears', *Current Anthropology* 39: 555–69.

Sahlins, M., 1995. *How Natives Think: About Captain Cook, For Example*. Chicago: University of Chicago Press.

Sangren, P., 1988. 'Rhetoric and the Authority of Ethnography: Postmodernism and the Social Reproduction of Texts', *Current Anthropology* 29(3): 405–35.

Scheper-Hughes, N., 1992. 'Hungry Bodies, Medicine and the State: Toward a Critical Psychological Anthropology', in *New Directions in Psychological Anthropology*, ed. T. Schwartz, G. White, and C. Lutz. Cambridge: Cambridge University Press.

Scheper-Hughes, N. 1995. 'The Primacy of the Ethical: Propositions for a Militant Anthropology', *Current Anthropology* 36(3): 409–20.

Scott, D., 1992. 'Criticism and Culture: Theory and Post-colonial Claims on

Anthropological Disciplinarity', *Critique of Anthropology* 12(4): 371–94.

Seidman, S., ed., 1994. *The Postmodern Turn: New Perspectives on Social Theory.* Cambridge: Cambridge University Press.

Strathern, M., ed., 1995. *Shifting Contexts: Transformations in Anthropological Knowledge.* London: Routledge.

Taylor, C., 1991. *The Ethics of Authenticity.* Cambridge, Mass.: Harvard University Press.

Taylor, C., 1995. *Philosophical Arguments.* Cambridge, Mass.: Harvard University Press.

Turner, T., 1993. 'Anthropology and Multiculturalism: What is Anthropology that Multiculturalists should be Mindful of it?', *Cultural Anthropology* 8: 411–29.

Ulin, R., 1991. 'Critical Anthropology Twenty Years Later: Modernism and Postmodernism in Anthropology', *Critique of Anthropology* 11(1): 63–89.

Waters, M., 1995. *Globalisation.* London: Routledge.

Yanagisako, S., and C. Delaney, eds, 1995. *Naturalising Power: Essays in Feminist Cultural Analysis.* London: Routledge.

2 From Private Virtue to Public Vice

James G. Carrier and Daniel Miller

Economy and anthropology

Anthropology cannot be defined by any one agenda or ambition, but one of the critical criteria by which it is likely to be judged is how well it deals with the relationship between the private and the public, between the agency of individuals, households and small groups on the one hand, and on the other the behaviour of transnational and global institutions and forces. This relationship is a fundamental element in the struggle by anthropology to influence the discipline of economics. For much of the twentieth century the social sciences, including anthropology, have seen themselves as engaged in a fight with economics over the academic representation of social relations. So far, this has been a losing battle. In the mass media, the rhetoric, discourse and models of economists stand in apparently unassailable dominance in defining what is important in the contemporary world.

Our argument is that the birth of modern economics rested upon the discovery of a paradox in the relationship of the private and the public, the microscopic and the macroscopic, in which a vice in one was seen to produce a virtue in the other. This was a radical departure from previous versions of economics, which were based on the idea that the microscopic and the macroscopic were simply smaller or larger versions of each other. Mandeville's famous observation that private vice could yield public benefit because the common good would be built on the satisfaction of individual greed encapsulates that paradoxical relationship. Although the idea was seen as a scandalous condoning of modern consumption when it was first mooted (Sassatelli, 1997) it came to justify the methodical lack of empirical interest in motivation by economists, who became increasingly focused upon macroscopic aggregates and their relationships: demand, supply, price, savings and the like. In stark contrast, anthropologists are deeply concerned with individual and small-scale social agents, but often have problems articulating these with larger historical processes. This increases the chance that the discipline will be ignored as parochial and naive. Equally, however, an anthropology that creates universalist models but disdains subjective perception and agency is one that has lost touch with its own primary mode of encounter with the world, empathetic ethnography. Anthropology's most important strength against economics is its claim that it can rearticulate models of economic processes with the lives of economic agents.

Anthropologists and economists

Historically, anthropologists working on economy have found themselves working in the shadow of academic economics, and particularly reigning marginalist and neo-classical economic theory, that part of economics that is most influential in the discipline and is most invoked in public debate. For example, in one of the founding works in the sub-discipline, *Argonauts of the Western Pacific*, Malinowski looked not just forward to Trobriand Islanders or sideways to other anthropologists, but also back over his shoulder, to the models and understandings of the discipline of economics. The same is true of the debate between substantivists and formalists, which is probably the best-known event in the history of economic anthropology (LeClair and Schneider, 1968). More recently, the distinction between gifts and commodities that was so fruitful in the 1980s sprang from works by Mauss (1990 [1925]) and by C. A. Gregory (1982) that were intended as criticisms of the predominant renderings and presuppositions of neo-classical economics.

All the branches of anthropology investigate areas of life that are salient to people in Western societies, and the anthropologists and anthropological knowledge of some of those branches may attract the interest of managers in advertising agencies and in the personnel offices of large corporations, and even of consultants to advising firms on how to conduct business in strange places. As such, students of semiotics or cosmology may find themselves consumed and used by such groups in much the same way, and in direct complement to, the ideas of economists. However, it is economic anthropology that investigates the area that is probably most salient to the way that Westerners understand themselves as Westerners, economy (Dumont, 1977). As popularly conceived, the genius of the West lies not in its religious or kinship organization, in its ritual practices or linguistic forms, but in its economy. When the latest figures on national well-being are reported, after all, those figures describe the economy.

Anthropologists concerned with economy, then, carry out their work in the face of two powerful potential audiences, academic economists and the general public. This very statement, of course, reveals its own presumption. Academic economists do not eagerly follow debates in economic anthropology, nervously awaiting the next issue of the *Journal of the Royal Anthropological Institute* or the *American Ethnologist*. Journalists do not report the scholarly findings of the sub-discipline to a public anxious to learn how best to secure and improve the wealth of nations. No one listens; few care.

We find this situation worrisome, because of the growing power and breadth of academic economics. The discipline has acquired influence in public thought and debate, and increasingly has been able to shape government policies and procedures (MacLennan, 1997) and so make the world conform to the discipline's image of it (see generally Carrier and Miller, 1998). Similarly, important economists like Gary S. Becker (e.g. 1991 and 1996; see Fine, 1998) and Oliver Williamson (e.g. 1975; see Chapman and Buckley, 1997) have broadened their area of interest to include more and more spheres of life beyond commodity markets, such as kinship relations and value systems. Because the discipline has become so influential and so broad, it is important that it be scrutinized and challenged. Anthropologists interested in economy may be reluctant to challenge economics and may be reluctant to engage in public debate. However, if members of the discipline are concerned about the ways in which their world is being shaped, they must recognize both the influence of academic economics and the need for critical public discussion of its premises and prescriptions.

While we find this situation worrisome, we also find it provocative, for it leads us to consider the different ways that economists and economic anthropologists go about their respective tasks. Given that the two sets of people are concerned with the same thing, economic life, those differences are striking and diverse. We think, however, that there is a core divergence in approach that can illuminate and make sense of many of the differences, the degree to which members of the two disciplines are willing to make abstract generalizations about the nature and systemic consequences of human behaviour.

Economists have long been happy to describe and present tendencies in economic life, as they have long been happy to infer general consequences from these tendencies. Anthropologists, on the other hand, are prone to resist statements of regularities in human life that sacrifice the particular.

Their concern is more often with the differences between one society and another (Morauta, 1979); or in differences among individuals that make up a society (Clifford and Marcus, 1986). This concern with difference need not, of course, dominate the discipline. Radcliffe-Brown, for example, said that the particularism of intense ethnography needs to be complemented by what he called 'comparative sociology' (1952: 2), which seeks more general regularities within regions or in social life more generally. But while a concern with general processes and regularities has deep roots in the discipline, it began to lose legitimacy in the 1960s and 1970s, and Marxism was probably the last widespread anthropological approach that was overtly concerned with generalization and certainly the last that was concerned especially with economy.

While anthropologists recently have been prone to deal with the distinction between the specific and the general by abandoning concern with the general, economists have produced models that have dealt with the distinction. Most commonly they have done so by seeing the order and structure of the general as the consequence of the aggregate of individual particularities. For them, the macroscopic emerges out of the microscopic, and in turn constrains it. A simple example will illustrate this. The organization of a competitive market emerges from the aggregate of the individuals who transact within it. Equally, however, that organization constrains individuals, leading them to behave in appropriate ways by punishing those who do not.

While economists' solutions to the problems of the relationship between the general and the particular have many weaknesses, the sheer fact that they have accepted particular models has one great strength. It allows them to put forward a coherent view of how economic life operates at different levels, and so proceed, if they wish, to compare their models with reality, clarify them and refine them (this is a task that relatively few economists wish, in fact, to pursue; see McCloskey, 1986 and 1990). Anthropologists need to put forward their own practical solutions to these problems, ones that allow them to speak, even if only tentatively, about the general nature of economic life (a recent attempt by an economic anthropologist is Narotzky, 1997). Until they do so, it is unlikely that they will be able to criticize academic economics with any effect.[1]

The articulation between the microscopic and the macroscopic is the focus of our consideration and criticism of economics here. Because of the strong, recent anthropological aversion to seeing the macroscopic as anything much more than the environment in which local processes are played out, our focus may cause unease. However, anthropologists need to remember that even work that is resolutely focused on the microscopic is likely to have embedded in it, usually not articulated, a set of assumptions about the macroscopic. As we have noted, anthropologists' methodical ignorance of the macroscopic seems to come and go in disciplinary fashion. Fashionable or not, however, we need to keep both ends of the spectrum in view: slighting either side produces analyses that are only partial. We begin our consideration by sketching the emergence of the relationship between the microscopic and the macroscopic as it exists in modern economics.

From private vice to public virtue

Aristotle's is perhaps the earliest Western work that has interested anthropologists concerned with economic thought (e.g. Gudeman and Rivera, 1991: 145–9, 166–8; Polanyi, 1957), and his economic writings are concerned with the proper, which is to say ethical, management of the household. Households should be modest in their needs and should be able to generate their own subsistence. If they must trade, they should trade with like households in a spirit of generosity and favour. This self-reliance and generosity, this private virtue, celebrates and solidifies civic virtues and helps maintain the just society. This concern with local self-reliance was important in village England through to the eighteenth century (Carrier, 1994: 363–4). The values, policies and practices of localism and selfsufficiency were part of a moral economy (Thompson, 1971), in which trade was coupled with and subordinated to social relations more generally. In this construction, as in Aristotle's, the just society was based in part on just personal practice of the sort that J. E. Crowley (1974: 6) described for early colonial America: 'It was the traditional view that exchange . . . was a social matter involving reciprocity and redistribution: competition, in the sense of one man's gaining at the expense of another, was a violation of this traditional ethic' (see also Everitt, 1967: 569–70). For this period in England, then, as was the case for Aristotle, the public and the private are distinct, but their moralities were seen to march together. Virtuous dealings between individuals produce and are part of the virtuous public realm.

A different strand of economic thought, emerging from Plato's consideration of political leaders, remained significant until late in the eighteenth century. It addressed a question central to our consideration of the relationship between the macroscopic and the microscopic, 'why would an individual choose to act in the public interest when his own private interest might be advanced at the public expense?' (Lowry, 1991: 42). This strand also distinguishes private and public interests, and also assumes that private morality and public benefit go together. To assure that leaders were moral, there developed a long tradition of books of advice, much of it drawing from a compilation by Xenophon in the fourth century BC (1991: 43). However, in the seventeenth century commentators began to argue that the powers of the prince were becoming diffused, part of a general movement that rejected 'sovereign administrative authority in favour of a popular individualism' (1991: 45). The result was that by about 1700 there had emerged in England the view that the landed classes were distinctly able to contemplate and act for the public good, because their ownership of inalienable land both gave them a direct interest in the nation and secured their personal well-being. 'The landed man, successor to the master of the classical *oikos*, was permitted the leisure and autonomy to consider what was to others' good as well as his own' (Pocock, 1975: 464). This echoes the Platonist recognition of a potential tension between private interest and the common weal, but argues that this conflict was not realized among the landed class. It was, however, realized among those who were dependent, which included merchants, who were pressed by necessity to pursue narrower interest. (This was part of a broader understanding of the nature of autonomy and virtue; see Carrier, 1995: 161–4.)

Notions about the landed and the merchants were linked because the landed were distinguished in public thought from those engaged in exchange:

> the individual engaged in exchange could discern only particular values Ω that of the commodity which was his, that of the commodity for which he exchanged it. His activity did not oblige or even permit him to contemplate the universal good as he acted upon it, and he consequently continued to lack classical rationality
>
> *(Pocock, 1975: 464),*

the rationality that the prince was supposed to possess. Part of the reason for this was that those who engaged in exchange, merchants and those who traded in the financial instruments that were beginning to appear (de Bolla, 1989, chapter 4), were seen to be operating not autonomously, but as 'dependent on the executive power and hence incapable of virtue' (Pocock, 1975: 450). Merchants and brokers sought in various ways to demonstrate that they could be virtuous citizens. Ultimately, however, the solution to their problem lay in a reformation of the understanding of economy (see below).

The older civic view of economy and morality was associated with an economic policy that also was distinctly civic, mercantilism (Viner, 1969 [1948]; cf. Judges, 1969 [1939]). For our purposes, it is important that when mercantilist writers considered the relationship between the common weal and the actions of individuals or groups within society, their arguments resembled those relating to the civic morality of the landed.

That is, they stressed the 'possibility of lack of harmony between the special economic interests of the individual merchants or particular business groups or economic classes, on the one hand, and the economic interests of the commonwealth as a whole, on the other' (Viner, 1969 [1948]: 81). The assumption was, then, that there was the risk that uncivil private interests would hinder the civil good. Thus, for instance, in Parliamentary debate at the time of James I, speakers warned that merchants were prone to conflate their personal or commercial interest with the common weal, and so bring pressure on government to subvert the common weal to protect or extend the particular interest (Viner, 1969 [1948]: 82).

Writers on mercantilism addressed issues different from writers on the landed classes. However, they shared with them, and with Plato and Xenophon, the view that the relationship between the microscopic and the macroscopic was fairly straightforward: self-regard, uncivil behaviour, harms the common weal. Thus, they shared a common problem, that of assuring that people in their private actions would act in a civil way (see generally Myers, 1983). While the advocates of the landed class argued that possession of independence and an inalienable stake in the nation produced a harmony of private and public interest, mercantilists adopted the Hobbesian solution, a strong state, for only it could enforce and ensure the public interest in private life. Around 1700 Lord Shaftesbury provided yet another answer, that people had an intuitive sense of right and wrong, and an innate desire to do the right and avoid the wrong.

For Shaftesbury, right behaviour did not depend upon a mighty prince or upon the special concatenation of circumstances that prevailed among the landed. However, as the landed were able to be virtuous because they were autonomous, so Shaftesbury's argument implied that constraint could only hinder the exercise of innate moral sensibility. As Colin Campbell puts it in his discussion of Shaftesbury, 'virtuous behaviour can only be conduct which is freely chosen, arising directly out of one's very being' (1987: 150). Campbell illustrates this new morality with Shaftesbury's *Characteristics of Man, Manners, Opinions, Times*, published in 1711. There, Shaftesbury says of the good man: 'He never deliberates . . . or considers the matter by prudential rules of self-interest and advantage. He acts from his nature, in a manner necessarily, and without reflection; and if he did not, it were impossible for him to answer his character' (in Campbell, 1987: 150).

In the absence of constraint, then, there is a harmony of interest between the individual and the commonality, guaranteed by innate moral sense. This view was challenged almost at the moment that it was propounded, by Bernard Mandeville, in *The Fable of the Bees*, published in 1714. For him, there was no harmony of interest, and in his formulation we get the first clear, modern enunciation of a problematic, indeed paradoxical, relationship between the private and the public. Mandeville argued that modesty and restraint were private virtues, but that they did not, in fact, benefit the community. Rather, the pursuit of luxury and excess, private vices, did. It was through them that wealth was circulated and general prosperity furthered. This position is stated concisely in the sub-title of Mandeville's book, *Private Vices, Public Benefits*. Mandeville's polemical formulation is echoed by Adam Smith. He too held that people's private interests often are not beneficent, as indicated by a famous passage from *The Wealth of Nations*: 'It is not from the benevolence of the butcher, the brewer, or the baker, that we expect our dinner, but from their regard to their own interest' (Smith, 1976 [1776]: 18). More, Smith clearly takes up Mandeville's point that the private vices of self-indulgence and luxury facilitate the general welfare. Thus, in *The Theory of Moral Sentiments*, Smith (1976 [1759]: 184) chastizes the rich for distinctly uncivil behaviour, when he points to 'their natural selfishness and rapacity' and their concern for 'only their own convenience'. Yet in the pursuit of their private vice, 'the gratification of their own vain and insatiable desires, they divide with the poor the produce of all their improvements'. The result is, 'without intending it, without knowing it, [to] advance the interest of the society' (1976 [1759]: 185).[2]

We have arrived, then, at the core of the modern formulation of the relationship between the microscopic and the macroscopic that characterizes academic economics, one 'in which the exchange of goods and the division of labor operated to turn universal selfishness to universal benefit' (Pocock, 1975: 465). This is only the core, because Smith, in both *The Theory of Moral Sentiments* and *The Wealth of Nations*, explains the concordance of private vice and public benefit by a divine invisible hand, 'the operation of instincts planted in men by Providence. This providence was assumed to be benign and the order so established was favourable to the welfare of men' (Habakkuk, 1971: 45; see also Lubasz, 1992). Over the course of the nineteenth century, beneficent Providence was replaced by an equally beneficent logic of capital investment, but the outcome remained the same.

This formulation did not immediately sweep all before it. Early in the nineteenth century, for instance, Thomas Malthus argued for the concordance of the private and the public, saying that the private vice of sexual incontinence leads to the public wrong of excess population, misery and starvation. Around the same time, Jeremy Bentham argued that there was no reason to assume that private interest would lead to public benefit. More in the tradition of Hobbes, he developed his utilitarian calculus in order that a strong state would be able to enforce an order that produced the greatest good for the greatest number.

Even though it did not do so immediately, Mandeville's and Smith's answer to the question of the relationship of private and public interest ultimately triumphed. The key implication of this triumph is not that it distinguished the microscopic and the macroscopic realms, for such a distinction was common currency. Rather, their answer construed the relationship between these two realms as being problematic in a way that it had not commonly been seen previously. The public and the private no longer mimicked each other, virtue in one being associated with or indistinguishable from virtue in the other. Rather, their answer invoked the idea of the unintended consequence, familiar to anthropologists and sociologists of an earlier generation (e.g. Kluckhohn, 1982 [1944]), the idea that we cannot assume that macroscopic consequences echo in any straightforward way the microscopic social practices that we observe. And this, of course, required a fundamental revision of the ways that social practices are judged. It was no longer enough to argue that they are good in themselves or because they conform to a moral standard. Rather, ethical judgement must be concerned with consequences: if private vice can lead to public benefit, then even actions that induce present misery can be good if they lead to future happiness.

Private vice and public vice

The economists' disjunction of public and private that we have sketched has two implicit corollaries. The first is that portentous events, processes and consequences cannot necessarily be discerned at the level of the local. The second is that those portentous things may, in fact, appear to contradict what happens locally. Put in Mandeville's terms, the public virtue not only contradicts the private vice, it is not visible at the local level, where the vice reigns. These corollaries pose a problem for anthropologists, rooted as they are in ethnographic particularity. How do they justify their concern with the particular as anything other than parochial and insignificant? Anthropologists could, as they do, argue that their local studies show the relative nature of abstract generalizations, and hence their limitations. However, this is only a partial justification, as it does not offer any alternative link between the local and the general. Anthropologists could only engage with economists if they had a powerful alternative model of the nature of macroscopic economic behaviour. This alternative arrived eventually in the form of Marxism. To understand both the nature and limitations of anthropological Marxism, it is necessary to begin with Marx himself.

Marx took his stance from the original Hegelian concern with the way that objects and institutions tended to follow their own logic, and so to lose touch with their foundations as human creations. A consequence of this tendency is that institutions lose their original potential to enhance the human condition and, instead, turn against and oppress us through their increasingly abstract and autonomous logic. It is hardly surprising that Marx's sustained critique of abstraction had tremendous appeal to anthropologists, concerned both to criticize the less salubrious aspects of capitalism and to chart the local and the contextual. Indeed, for much of the 1970s and 1980s variants of Marxist economics dominated anthropology, and even today the assumption underlying much anthropological economics is that it must be a critique of capitalist economics, even if its source is now more likely to be Mauss than Marx. However, we suggest that anthropological Marxism conflated two different problems of abstraction and therefore failed to offer a powerful understanding of the relationship between the macroscopic and the microscopic.

Central to Marxist anthropology was the critique of what can be called a commodity culture, in which the abstraction of capital diminished the humanity of workers by reducing them to mere pawns in the strategies by which capital reproduced itself. The more that dominant thought within a society construed capital as an organic force with its own growth, agency and reproduction, the more that actual humanity was understood to lose those qualities and become merely the means for capital development (e.g. Taussig, 1977). This central critique led anthropologists to attend to the effects of macro-economic structures, and writers developed theories of a global system that articulated the economic trajectory of a given region and the larger development of capitalism and the market (e.g. Clammer, 1978; Frank, 1971; Wallerstein, 1974–80). This work proved immensely influential, since suddenly anthropology could graft its own putative critique of economics onto models that incorporated their particular ethnographic contexts as integral parts of systematic linkages. Underdevelopment was now the other side of development.

While this marked an improvement on a resolute anthropological localism, it is important to note that the articulation between the macroscopic and the microscopic contained in these theories abandoned the paradox that underpinned the economics that they criticized. In anthropological Marxism, the large-scale effects of economic behaviour were understood as relatively straightforward reflections of the direct interests of a specific class, capitalists. So, the private vice of the rapacity of particular capitalists led to the range of public vice associated in the Marxist model with capitalist domination.

As most of the societies that anthropologists studied did not have economies that were fully capitalist, this model had to be applied in modified form. For instance, Marxist anthropologists such as Gough (1981) could analyse villages largely on the basis of the social relations of landholding and the way that economic activity fostered the interests of the dominant landholding group. To this Meillassoux (1973), writing of India, could add that it was legitimate to ignore the phenomenological world of social relations, here dominated by caste, since caste was only the local manifestation of the general principle of ideology which meant that the mass of the population wilfully participated in their own exploitation. In this particular case the populations studied understood themselves in terms of the false categories of caste rather than the true categories of class.

The Marxists' main target was the abstract nature of capital and the consequent de-humanizing of people directly or indirectly caught up in capitalist economies, which reduced worker-producers to wage labourers and so allowed the ascendancy of the strategies for the reproduction and growth of capital (e.g. Meillassoux, 1981). This critique of capitalism remains a valid one and most anthropologists, including ourselves, would still wish to subscribe to it. Marxist models also provided an effective bridge which allowed anthropologists to articulate their own traditional concerns with areas such as kinship and the household and link these directly to ideas on modes of production that situated them within much larger social and historical processes. This was accomplished in different ways, ranging from Sahlins (1972) writing on the domestic mode of production to Godelier's (1972) renewal of the substantivist project to determine the specific rationality of diverse economic systems and Meillassoux's (1981) linkage between the control over people and the control over resources. Combined with more recent socialist feminist studies of topics such as the household, this tradition continues to influence attempts to develop economic anthropology in new areas such as the consideration of the relationship between consumption and production at the domestic level and within the larger economy (Narotzky, 1997).[3]

However, during his life Marx moved between two rather different approaches to the problem of capitalism. The early Marx was the more Hegelian, more humanistic and philosophical, more concerned with the alienation of people from the world of labour and the need to find a means to re-humanize economic relations. The later Marx, particularly in *Capital*, was a political economist, striving to create models of economic activity that were better than those generated by the dominant economic traditions of his day, the political economy that was the precursor to modern marginalist economics. Most of Marx's later work was based on economic modelling of the relationship between abstracted concepts, modelling apparently motivated by the hope that he could integrate the humanity of labour in a way that would allow terms like 'value' to retain their moral dimension, rather than being just another abstract element in an equation. If this is what he hoped, then Marx was probably wrong.

When anthropology appropriated Marxist perspectives it struggled at first between the earlier and later version of Marxist thought. However, writers such as Godelier, concerned more with the issues addressed by the early Marx, were overtaken by writers like Althusser, who followed the later Marx. Just as Marx himself increasingly became involved in macroscopic models of economy, so the Marxist anthropologists, detailing a whole litany of categories of modes of production, took on the economists largely through proposing models of economic relations that often differed only because they incorporated factors such as labour value that were not included in other economists' accounts. The result was an alternative version of economic analysis rather than an alternative to economic analysis. What began as a critique of the abstraction created by capital came to be expressed within the idiom of another abstraction, that of the economic modelling of modes of production.

In the end this could not be sustained within an anthropology that was founded in empathetic ethnography. The history of anthropological fashion is instructive here. In the early 1980s two scholarly approaches went quite dramatically out of fashion: structuralism, with its cognitive concerns; and Marxist anthropology, with its economic concerns. Although they were radically different modes of thinking about the world, they were linked by critics, who saw both as rationalist grand narratives that ignored the humanity (usually simplified as the subjectivity) of the ethnographic subject. Both approaches had responded to the parochialism of ethnography through attempts to grasp global and universal formations. Both, however, were castigated as esoteric models that had lost touch with the ultimate source of anthropological authenticity.

Private virtue to public vice

If the disciplinary rejection of Marxism was based on the belief that it abstracted too much from the experiences of social life and fieldwork, then that rejection is ironic, because the original core of Marx's work was a critique of abstraction. As Stallybrass has shown in his superb essay (1998), for Marx the central problem of capitalism was that the specificity of objects and people was lost in the abstract calculation of profit. The formalism of some of the later Marxists sought to address this problem. However, to borrow a point made by E. P. Thompson (1968), it focused on the structure of capitalism rather than its dynamics. As a result, it tended to ignore the ways that people sought to resist the forces that lead to their own reduction to mere pawns within capitalist calculation, the ways that they sought to recover the humanity that, Stallybrass shows, Marx expressed in the intimate relation he had with his own coat, and with material goods in general. We suggest that a return to this concern can help us build a framework that links the microscopic and the macroscopic, a framework that differs from the economistic model in that it takes the microscopic seriously and engages with it ethnographically. We show what such a framework might look like by summarizing some of the arguments that we have made recently that deal with consumption in Western capitalist societies.

In beginning with consumption, we start with people's immediate experience with objects, precisely the area that economists have failed to treat in an empirical, rather than an a priori, way (Douglas and Isherwood, 1978). In beginning with consumption we also start with an area that Marxist anthropologists generally ignored. In their attention to the public conflict between labour and capital, those anthropologists slighted the realm of private consumption, and so slighted what might in the long term be the more effective site of recovering human specificity. The Marxists acted as though the spread of the commodity form with the rise of capitalism fatally tainted all objects in all situations, and certainly the mundane objects of mass consumption. It was as though these objects were reduced to bearers of exchange value in capitalist production and reproduction, use value in the reproduction of the proletariat, and ideological lures that deflected the working class from attending to their position in the socio-economic order. Carrier (1995) has disputed this tendency, pointing out the inadequacy of the simplistic assumption that Western societies are simply capitalist and that consumption within them is simply the consumption of commodities. Equally, Miller (1987) has argued that this tendency is short-sighted. He suggests instead that the palpable popular concern with objects under advanced capitalism springs not from the false consciousness of hedonistic consumption, but from another aspect of capitalism. As the orders of production and commercial circulation become increasingly abstracted from social relationships, people turn more to objects in consumption as a way to create a sense of themselves through relationships with specific people and with specific things.

Both of us have attended to an important aspect of this process of using objects to create specific social relations, the ways in which people appropriated goods from the abstract nexus of commercial exchange. It is in this appropriation that people can negate the mass scale and impersonality of the state (Miller, 1988) and the market, a negation which occurs in terms of the specificity of the things that people purchase and of the specificity of the relationships expressed through those things. These strategies of appropriation appear sufficiently visible that some businesses have come to mimic them in their advertising. Attempting to make their commodities more attractive to purchasers, some mail-order companies portray their wares in highly personalized situations (Carrier, 1990). (This commercial attempt to pre-empt the logic of appropriation illustrates the complexity and dynamic nature of the processes that concern us here.)

Marking a parallel point, Miller (1998) has described the nuances of intimate relations of care and love within families and how these are developed through the sheer diversity of the commodities found within affluent capitalist societies. Certainly this sort of appropriation of commodities is neither free of conflict nor uniformly benign (Carrier and Heyman, 1997). However, it is important to recognize that it does occur and is significant, and hence that it is wrong to assume that significant appropriation is possible only at the site of production.

A concern with appropriation and localization has one key advantage over the formalism that preceded it: it is more compatible with the practice of anthropology as empathetic ethnography. The fieldwork that has been influenced by this approach (e.g. Herrmann, 1997; Miller, 1998; Watson, 1997) has returned to the ethnographic encounter with people in a wide variety of economic conditions. Such work documents how people construct relationships with objects and each other, and in so doing it helps show how people's confrontation with impersonal markets and multinational brands is manifest in their everyday attempts to construct social relations and to objectify moralities. Society is seen to be constructed through consumption in the teeth of what would reduce people to autonomous, amoral and purely self-interested individuals.

This thread within the anthropology of consumption also contains a logic of articulation between the private and public that was previously absent from both economic and political-economic models. In examining the intimate worlds within which the desires and demands of consumption are constructed and fulfilled, this thread replaces the economistic assumption of private vice leading to private virtue. More particularly, Miller (1998) has shown how consumption can be a vehicle by which people objectify virtue in everyday life. In the act of shopping, the image of hedonistic and self-regarding consumption is negated through an emphasis upon saving and thrift. Consequently, the person experiences the shopping as a virtuous action motivated by and realizing the larger and longer-term aims and needs of the household as a whole, as well as a sensitivity to the needs and desires of the individuals within it.

If these observations are put back into the larger context of the articulation between private worlds and their public effects, the consequence is to return us to the paradox at the centre of economic theory, though with the terms of the original equation reversed. Instead of the structures of the market miraculously transforming the avarice of individual economic desire into the larger public good of economic growth, what has become evident today is that it is the global market that, more than anything else, transforms the virtuous activity of household moralities into the cruelty and degradation of global poverty and inequality. We need to explain how this is so.

The effects of capitalist firms in creating inequalities were clearly analysed by Marx. But over the last hundred years various forces have attempted to ameliorate these consequences and work for the furtherance of the rights and rewards of labour. But just as these have achieved some positive effects, at least within social-democratic regimes, the increasing power of economists has curtailed both such reforms and the capacity of capitalist firms to accord with them. This more recent push towards purer market principles has largely been justified by the claims made by economists that the market will ultimately benefit everyone in their other economic role as consumers. But to achieve this influence they have replaced the study and interests of real consumers with the 'virtual' consumers they invented for their own purposes of economic modelling, though justified by reference to the realities of consumer thrift (see Carrier and Miller, 1998). Certainly global and national inequalities continue to result from the activities of capitalist firms. However, we suggest that these inequalities increasingly are sustained and protected by regional and global economic institutions like the North American Free Trade Agreement, the World Bank and the World Trade Organization, that insist upon structural adjustment and pure market relations (Carrier, 1997; McMichael, 1998; Miller, 1997). It is these institutions that have been most effective in advancing the kind of abstraction of people from social relations that, Marx argued, characterizes capitalism. We have argued that these institutions are virtualizers (Carrier and Miller, 1998). That is, they do not merely promulgate a particular view of the world, by their actions they seek to bring the world into conformity with the virtual reality defined by that view.

Such powerful institutions and systems need powerful legitimation, more than can be offered by the argument that what we are experiencing is merely the inevitable outcome of an autonomous logic of market competition. This leads to the second foundation for their claims. The expansion of the concept of the pure market has been sustained by representing it as the authentic expression of the population at large, in their role as consumers. For economists, consumers do indeed act as economically virtuous shoppers, for they attempt to obtain the best quality goods at the lowest prices that they can find. Economists completely misunderstand the form and nature of this thrift, for they cast it as self-seeking and self-regarding financial calculation of benefit and cost. Of course, this hardly matters to economists. They can argue that only the workings of the market can convert that thrift into the assurance that all goods are guaranteed to be the highest quality at the lowest prices. In this way, the latest twist to our story of articulations between the private and the public has led us to the contemporary narrative, where private virtue becomes public vice. The morality that, as Miller (1998) has argued, sustains thrift among shoppers, becomes transmuted by economists into the excuse for exploitation and growing inequality.

Conclusion

In this chapter we have been concerned to show the ways in which the relationship between the microscopic and macroscopic realms, the private and the public, is treated. We stated that this is one of the important elements of the long-running anthropological criticism of economics. Anthropologists have argued that, however much economists have claimed a clear conception of the microscopic and its relationship with the macroscopic, economists are much more willing to posit a microscopic realm than they are to investigate and analyse it. The result is that the private has been effectively excluded from their consideration. The consequence has been an ideological economics, one that has increased its claims to the status of a science of almost mathematical purity at the same time that it has reduced its empirical investigation of people's daily lives.

We have traced the different ways that economists and anthropologists have dealt with the private and the public realms and the relationship between them. We have also presented in crude form an anthropological approach to consumption that, we think, can address this relationship in a fruitful way that slights neither the microscopic nor the macroscopic. This approach attends to the everyday activity of consumption within households, but it also encourages us to see how household consumption is linked to that which seems to spiral upwards out of reach. Acts which within households are devoted to the expression of intimate relations, become, when transmuted within the political economy, acts that be detrimental to the interests of that household, in the same manner that in the contemporary political economy it is the virtuous act of saving for a pension that provides the largest single resource (as pension funds) for a world of high finance whose developments often include the destruction of those properties that are needed by the pensioner in favour of wealthier tenants.

In keeping with the orientation of the early Marx, this model reflects a concern for the larger historical development of oppressive, abstract forces that constrain the constant struggle for the re-humanizing of social life. As we have noted, these forces are not only manifest as capitalist firms. In addition, and perhaps more importantly, they are manifest in the conception of the pure, free market; they are manifest in the work of academic economists, who construct a virtual reality that is based on that conception; they are manifest in the virtualizing governments and global institutions that see the world in terms of that virtual reality and that implement policies that seek to make our world conform to it.

In making this point, we are a long way from the manifestations of abstraction that concerned Marx nearly a century and a half ago. However, we hold that a critical perspective cannot be a conservative perspective, one concerned more to be 'true to Marx' than to be true to the realities of the present day. If the target has moved, so the direction of our aim must move. If Marx saw capital as standing in a particular dialectical relation to the struggle of the species being in its quest to create itself as humanity, we see virtualizing institutions as standing in an analogous relationship today (Carrier and Miller, 1998). Like the forms of organization that came to represent capitalism, these institutions were originally developed as human creations intended to better all people's lives, not to constrain and impoverish so many of them.

It remains to suggest ways that anthropology can hope to persevere in its historical task of ensuring that the microscopic and the private are not reduced to a set of economists' a priori assumptions. Anthropology needs to be true to its history of immersion in ethnography. But equally, it needs to continue to develop its own alternative readings of the articulation between what can be observed and what can be theorized about macroeconomic change. To abandon the former is to embrace the shortcomings of economics; to abandon the latter is to perpetuate anthropology's current position as a discipline complementary to economics rather than critical of it. What are some of the ways that anthropologists might remain true to empathetic ethnography, yet address directly the relationship between what they observe in their fieldwork and macroscopic processes?

One such way is through the investigation of commodity circuits (or chains). While both economics and its critics deal with processes that involve the circulation of concrete things, the tendency to abstraction that reduces people to aggregate effects also commonly means that academics ignore the fact that those things are concrete. Tracing the often tortuous routes by which components from different parts of the world come together to produce a commodity and how these in turn are marketed and distributed sheds considerable light on the articulation between macroscopic social and economic relations and microscopic social and economic relations.

Inspired by Mintz's (1985) historical work on sugar, some of the most interesting early writing on commodity chains has come from human geography, especially through research on the food industry. The aim of this work has been to follow things sold in ordinary supermarkets, such as tropical fruits, and so help us to understand the relationship between their origin in Caribbean plantation systems and their place in global markets, retail trade and consumption (e.g. Cook, 1994; Jackson and Thrift, 1995: 215–17). Similar concern with tracing the implications of consumption is developing in other disciplines, such as history (Goodman,

1993; Orlove, 1997), anthropology (Appadurai, 1986; Morphy, 1995; Roseberry, 1996; Weiss, 1996), cultural studies (Du Gay et al., 1997) and sociology (Gereffi, 1994). Such studies challenge anthropologists to take seriously Marcus's (1995) call for multi-sited ethnography.

The study of commodity chains can reveal a range of important articulations. For instance, these commodities are items of production, and an empathetic ethnography of that production could lead to a more adequate understanding of the labour costs involved, costs that would include the experience of the labourers in question. They are also a good way to establish costs to the environment, such as are imposed by transportation. They can be used to trace back the constituent parts of goods to check if they include problematic ingredients such as genetically modified plants. Similarly, as many of the commodities that end up in the households of wealthier countries begin as the produce of poorer ones, the study of these chains can encourage a consideration of the relationship of the chains themselves, which are the substance of international trade, to the economic policies imposed upon and the economic practices that occur within those poorer countries. A concern with commodity chains encourages us to look into the forms of economic and political power that shape economic action, the ways that large corporations are governed, the relationship between forms of corporate finance and firms' financial horizons. It can also reveal conflicts between the interests that are generated by the commercial tasks of production, circulation and retail and the interests that tend to develop at the level of higher financial concerns that may become parasitic upon commerce.

At the same time, and at a more microscopic level, the study of commodity chains encourages us to consider the consequences these commodities have as items of consumption, whether as purchased by households or as delivered as state services. We can examine whether a better knowledge of the origins of a commodity would influence their consumption in the way both 'green' and 'red' activitists would hope. Such a study contributes also to the recent work on consumption, for example, when multinational goods consumed within particular localities turn out unexpectedly to enhance rather than detract from cultural diversity, because of the particular ways they are appropriated. More generally, the analysis of commodity chains has considerable potential for creating the kinds of narrative that would make commodities less abstract, and would allow consumers a much fuller understanding of the broader context and consequences of their actions.

A second way that anthropologists might address the relationship between what they observe in their fieldwork and macroscopic processes is through an ethnography of commercial institutions. Such research would help de-mystify those institutions, by relating their operations to the experience of humanity and social relations that goes on within them. Ethnographic studies of advertising and marketing have developed in recent years (e.g. Lien, 1997; Miller, 1997; Moeran, 1996), and both anthropologists and human geographers have worked on government and private financial institutions (e.g. MacLennan, 1997; O'Barr and Conley, 1992; Leyshon and Thrift, 1997). Goods become futures become bonds become derivatives; agricultural products become production quotas and those quotas become commodities that can be traded in their own right (Helgason and Pálsson, 1998). Especially with the rise of new technologies and financial instruments, the global finance that flows through the City looks ever more abstract. Field research in the City of London led Leyshon and Thrift to conclude that if the importance of face-to-face interaction between key individuals has changed, it has become more important rather than less. Chapman and Buckley (1997) came to similar conclusions in their study of the ways that corporate managers decided whether to produce things internally or buy them from other firms. Many economists, following Williamson (1975), argue that such decisions reflect the abstract and formal logic of transaction-cost analysis. Chapman and Buckley found, however, that decisions were made on the basis of informal and uncertain criteria, much more likely to be social and symbolic than economic. Studies such as these raise familiar anthropological questions about the relationship among formal cultural models, norms and practical action. Indeed, it would be intriguing to pursue these questions by studying economists themselves, who exhibit a noticeable gap between the models that they formulate about economic action and their own economic acts as, for example, consumers.

We have mentioned very briefly only two of the ways that anthropology can continue to ensure that the microscopic and the private are taken seriously, rather than being reduced to a set of a priori assumptions by economics, and are rearticulated with the macroscopic processes of which they are a part. Our intention is not to dictate the nature of future anthropological projects. Rather, we present these as examples of new directions that lead us beyond an anthropology lurching between being a science of universal or global structures as in the 1970s to a discipline that buries its head in the sands of 'native subjectivities' in the 1990s. Such a discipline has very little chance of offering an effective criticism of economics and its view of the world, the power of which is already extraordinary and seems set to continue to grow; and, we argue, such criticism is necessary to any anthropology that is serious about its own vision of being in the world.

No one who works in an anthropology department is likely to be without colleagues who are frustrated because of the ways in which what they have learned through their sensitivity to the microscopic, to the people among whom they conduct fieldwork, has been thwarted and denied by the greater power of economic structural insensitivity. The lesson of the 1990s is that a stance of pure relativism and parochialism, a celebration of anthropological marginality, is little more than a surrender to economics. For us, the way out of this impasse is for anthropologists to achieve what economists have not, a rearticulation of the private and the public through a clear understanding and portrayal of the consequences of each of these for the other. In the contemporary world this is our best chance, and perhaps our only chance, to generate what the older political economy sought to deliver, a portrait of the world in which human welfare is inextricably an element of that act of representation.

Notes

Our thanks to Henrietta Moore for editorial suggestions.

1   One of the main fields within which anthropologists are currently struggling with this articulation is that of development studies. Indeed, this seems to be the one area where anthropologists, however parochial their concerns, cannot help trying to understand economic policy and institutions such as aid agencies, since they see the direct effects of these policies and institutions upon the people whom they study. We have chosen not to discuss this field, however, since doing so would require a paper in itself and neither of us have sufficient knowledge or experience in this area.
2   Heinz Lubasz (1992) presents an analysis of Smith's work that qualifies and complicates what we say here, pointing out the ways that Smith reflects some of the older assumptions about inherent or natural morality. He does not, however, contradict our basic points.
3   There is a subsequent literature which has developed around the concept of the household, in which the concern is not to isolate a bounded unit, but rather in the spirit of the arguments of this chapter, to integrate kinship with macro processes. For relevant discussions see Moore, 1994, ch. 5; and Wilk, 1989 and 1996.

Bibliography

Appadurai, Arjun, ed., 1986. *The Social Life of Things: Commodities in Cultural Perspective*. Cambridge and New York: Cambridge University Press.
Becker, G. S., 1991. *A Treatise on the Family*. Enlarged edition. Cambridge, Mass: Harvard University Press.
——1996. *Accounting for Tastes*. Cambridge, Mass: Harvard University Press.
Campbell, C., 1987. *The Romantic Ethic and the Spirit of Modern Consumerism*. Oxford: Basil Blackwell.

Carrier, J. G., 1990. 'The Symbolism of Possession in Commodity Advertising', *Man* 25: 190–207.

——1994. 'Alienating Objects: The Emergence of Alienation in Retail Trade', *Man* 29: 359–80.

——1995. *Gifts and Commodities: Exchange and Western Capitalism since 1700*. London: Routledge.

——ed., 1997. *Meanings of the Market: The Free Market in Western Culture*. Oxford: Berg.

Carrier, J. G., and J. McC. Heyman, 1997. 'Consumption and Political Economy', *Journal of the Royal Anthropological Institute* 2: 355–73.

Carrier, J. G., and D. Miller, eds, 1998. *Virtualism: A New Political Economy*. Oxford: Berg (forthcoming).

Chapman, M., and P. J. Buckley, 1997. 'Markets, Transaction Costs, Economists and Social Anthropologists', in *Meanings of the Market: The Free Market in Western Culture*, ed. J. G. Carrier. Oxford: Berg, 225–50.

Clammer, J., ed., 1978. *The New Economic Anthropology*. London: Macmillan.

Clifford, J., and G. Marcus, eds, 1986. *Writing Culture: The Poetics and Politics of Ethnography*. Berkeley: University of California Press.

Cook, I., 1994. 'New Fruits and Vanity: Symbolic Production in the Global Food Economy', in *From Columbus to ConAgra: The Globalization of Agriculture and Food*, ed. A. Bohanno et al. Lawrence: University Press of Kansas, 232–48.

Crowley, J. E., 1974. *This Sheba, Self: The Conceptualization of Economic Life in Eighteenth Century America*. Baltimore: Johns Hopkins University Press.

De Bolla, P., 1989. *The Discourse of the Sublime: Readings in History, Aesthetics and the Subject*. Oxford: Basil Blackwell.

Douglas, M., and B. Isherwood, 1978. *The World of Goods*. Harmondsworth: Penguin.

Du Gay, P., et al., 1997. *Doing Cultural Studies*. London: Sage.

Dumont, L., 1977. *From Mandeville to Marx: The Genesis and Triumph of Economic Ideology*. Chicago: University of Chicago Press.

Everitt, A., 1967. 'The Marketing of Agricultural Produce', in *The Agrarian History of England and Wales, vol. IV: 1500–1640*, ed. Joan Thirsk. Cambridge: Cambridge University Press, 466–592.

Fine, B., 1998. 'The Triumph of Economics; Or, "Rationality" Can Be Dangerous to Your Reasoning', in *Virtualism: A New Political Economy*, ed. J. G. Carrier and D. Miller. Oxford: Berg (forthcoming).

Frank, Andre Gunder, 1971. *Sociology of Development and Underdevelopment of Sociology*. London: Pluto Press.

Gereffi, G., 1994. 'Capitalism, Development and Global Commodity Chains', in *Capitalism and Development*, ed. L. Sklair. London: Routledge, 211–31.

Godelier, M., 1972. *Rationality and Irrationality in Economics*. London: New Left Books.

Goodman, J., 1993. *Tobacco in History: The Cultures of Dependence*. London: Routledge.

Gough, K., 1981. *Rural Society in Southeast India*. Cambridge: Cambridge University Press.

Gregory, C. A., 1982. *Gifts and Commodities*. London: Academic Press.

Gudeman, S., and A. Rivera, 1991. *Conversations in Colombia: The Domestic Economy in Life and Text*. New York: Cambridge University Press.

Habakkuk, H. J., 1971. 'Population, Commerce and Economic Ideas', in *The New Cambridge Modern History*, VIII: *The American and French Revolutions, 1763–93*, ed. A. Goodwin. Cambridge: Cambridge University Press, 25–54.

Helgason, A., and G. Pálsson, 1998. 'Cash for Quotas: Disputes over the Legitimacy of an Economic Model of Fishing in Iceland', in *Virtualism: A New Political Economy*, ed. J. G. Carrier and D. Miller. Oxford: Berg (forthcoming).

Herrmann, G., 1997. 'Gift or Commodity: What Changes Hands in the U.S. Garage Sale?', *American Ethnologist* 24: 910–30.

Jackson, P., and N. Thrift, 1995. 'Geographies of Consumption', in *Acknowledging Consumption*, ed. D. Miller. London: Routledge, 204–37.

Judges, A. V., 1969 (1939). 'The Idea of a Mercantile State', in *Revisions in Mercantilism*, ed. D. C. Coleman. London: Methuen, 35–60.

Kluckhohn, C., 1982 (1944). 'Navaho Witchcraft', in *Witchcraft and Sorcery*, ed. M. Marwick. Second edition, Harmondsworth: Penguin, 246–62.

LeClair, E., and H. Schneider, eds, 1968. *Economic Anthropology*. New York: Holt, Rinehart and Winston.

Leyshon, A., and N. J. Thrift, 1997. *Money/Space: Geographies of Monetary Transformation*. London: Routledge.

Lien, M., 1997. *Marketing and Modernity*. Oxford: Berg.

Lowry, T., 1991. 'Understanding Ethical Individualism and the Administrative Tradition in Pre-Eighteenth Century Political Economy', in *Perspectives on the History of Economic Thought*, vol. V: *Themes in pre-Classical, Classical and Marxian Economics*, ed. W. J. Barber. Aldershot: Edward Elgar, 39–46.

Lubasz, H., 1992. 'Adam Smith and the Invisible Hand Ω of the Market?' in *Contesting Markets: Analyses of Ideology, Discourse and Practice*, ed. R. Dilley. Edinburgh: Edinburgh University Press, 37–56.

McCloskey, D. N., 1986. *The Rhetoric of Economics*. Brighton: Wheatsheaf.

——1990. *If You're so Smart: The Narrative of Economic Expertise*. Chicago: University of Chicago Press.

MacLennan, C. A., 1997. 'Democracy under the Influence: Cost-Benefit Analysis in the United States', in *Meanings of the Market: The Free Market in Western Culture*, ed. J. G. Carrier. Oxford: Berg, 195–224.

McMichael, P., 1998. 'Development and Structural Adjustment', in *Virtualism: The New Political Economy*, ed. J. G. Carrier and D. Miller. Oxford: Berg (forthcoming).

Malinowski, B., 1922. *Argonauts of the Western Pacific*. London: Routledge & Kegan Paul.

Marcus, G., 1995. 'Ethnography in/of the World System: The Emergence of Multi-Sited Ethnography', *Annual Review of Anthropology* 14: 95–117.

Mauss, M., 1990 (1925). *The Gift: The Form and Reason for Exchange in Archaic Societies*, trans. W. D. Halls. London: Routledge.

Meillassoux, C., 1973. 'Are there Castes in India?', *Economy and Society*, 2: 89–111.

——1981. *Maidens, Meal and Money*. Cambridge: Cambridge University Press.

Miller, D., 1987. *Material Culture and Mass Consumption*. Oxford: Basil

Blackwell.

——1988. 'Appropriating the State on the Council Estate', *Man* 23: 353–72.

——1997. *Capitalism: An Ethnographic Approach*. Oxford: Berg.

——1998. *A Theory of Shopping*. Cambridge: Polity Press.

Mintz, S. W., 1985. *Sweetness and Power: The Place of Sugar in Modern History*. New York: Viking.

Moeran, B., 1996. *A Japanese Advertising Agency*. Richmond: Curzon.

Moore, H., 1994. *A Passion for Difference*. Cambridge: Polity Press.

Morauta, L., 1979. 'Indigenous Anthropology in Papua New Guinea', *Current Anthropology* 20: 561–76.

Morphy, H., 1995. 'Aboriginal Art in a Global Context', in *Worlds Apart*, ed. D. Miller. London: Routledge, 211–39.

Myers, M. L., 1983. *The Soul of Modern Economic Man: Ideas of Self-Interest, Thomas Hobbes to Adam Smith*. Chicago: University of Chicago.

Narotzky, S., 1997. *New Directions in Economic Anthropology*. London: Pluto Press.

O'Barr, W. M., and J. M. Conley, 1992. *Fortune and Folly: The Wealth and Power of Institutional Investing*. Homewood, Ill.: Business One Irwin.

Orlove, B., ed., 1997. *The Allure of the Foreign*. Ann Arbor: University of Michigan Press.

Pocock, J. G. A., 1975. *The Machiavellian Moment*. Princeton: Princeton University Press.

Polanyi, K. 1957. 'Aristotle Discovers the Economy', in *Trade and Market in the Early Empires: Economies in History and Theory*, ed. K. Polanyi, C. M. Arensberg and H. W. Pearson. Glencoe, Ill.: The Free Press, 64–94.

Radcliffe-Brown, A. R., 1952. *Structure and Function in Primitive Society*. London: Routledge & Kegan Paul.

Roseberry, W., 1996. 'The Rise of Yuppie Coffees and the Reimagination of Class in the United States', *American Anthropologist* 98: 762–75.

Sahlins, M., 1972. *Stone Age Economics*. London: Tavistock.

Sassatelli, R., 1997 'Consuming Ambivalence: Eighteenth-century Public Discourse on Consumption and Mandeville's Legacy', *Journal of Material Culture* 2: 339–60.

Smith, A., 1976. (1759). *The Theory of Moral Sentiments*, ed. David D. Raphael and Alec L. Macfie. Oxford: Oxford University Press (reprinted 1984, Indianapolis: Liberty Fund).

——1976 (1776). *An Inquiry into the Nature and Causes of the Wealth of Nations*, ed. Edwin Cannan, Chicago: University of Chicago Press.

Stallybrass, Peter, 1998. 'Marx's Coat', in *Border Fetishisms*, ed. Patricia Speyr. London: Routledge, 183–207.

Taussig, M., 1977. 'The Genesis of Capitalism amongst a South American Peasantry: Devil's Labor and the Baptism of Money', *Comparative Studies in Society and History* 19: 130–55.

Thompson, E. P., 1968. *The Making of the English Working Class*. Harmondsworth: Penguin.

——1971. 'The Moral Economy of the English Crowd in the Eighteenth Century', *Past and Present* 50: 76–136.

Viner, J., 1969. (1948). 'Power versus Plenty as Objectives of Foreign Policy in the Seventeenth and Eighteenth Centuries', in *Revisions in Mercantalism*, ed. D. C. Coleman. London: Methuen, 61–91.

Wallerstein, I., 1974–80. *The Modern World System*. Two volumes. New York: Academic Press.

Watson, J., 1997. *Golden Arches East: McDonalds in East Asia*. Stanford: Stanford University Press.

Weiss, B., 1996. 'Coffee Breaks and Coffee Connections: The Lived Experience of a Commodity in Tanzanian and European Worlds', in *Cross Cultural Consumption*, ed. D. Howe. London: Routledge, 93–101.

Wilk, R., ed., 1989. *The Household Economy: Reconsidering the Domestic Mode of Production*. Boulder: Westview.

Wilk, R., 1996. *Economies and Cultures*. Boulder: Westview.

Williamson, O., 1975. *Markets and Hierarchies*. New York: The Free Press.

Clash of Civilizations or Asian Liberalism? An Anthropology of the State and Citizenship

3

Aihwa Ong

It is an irony that in an era of globalization, we are once again revisiting oriental and occidental societies as rival cultural regimes. Recent discourses about "the clash of civilizations" generally pit Western civilization based on Enlightenment values of individualism against non-Western civilizations based on communitarian values for the greater good (Huntington, 1993).[1] In this chapter, I discuss how the traditional anthropological concept of culture may have influenced some of these views, and suggest that our new attention to the anthropology of the state and citizenship will make our understanding of the interplay of liberalism and culture in non-Western countries more complex. The second part of the chapter suggests how our assumptions about Western liberalism have obscured our understanding of Asian liberalism, as represented by Malaysia and Singapore, former colonies of Great Britain.

Anthropological views of culture and politics

Traditional anthropological treatment of culture as *sui generis*, and our focus on cultural relativism can be seen as strongly allied to assumptions that non-Western societies are communitarian in nature, stressing the collective good, as opposed to the emphasis on individualistic values in post-Enlightenment Western cultures. Furthermore, the demarcation of culture as a discrete sphere separable from economic and politic processes, or having overwhelming determination over them, has limited anthropological investigation of the relation between culture and politics. While there has been a strong and lively exploration of the complex interactions between economic processes and cultural change, earlier generations of anthropologists have tended to limit their analysis of politics to indigenous forms in Asian and African "tribal" societies. Joan Vincent attributes this to the "intellectual hegemony of the Oxbridge structural-systems approach to primitive government and small-scale societies" (Vincent, 1990: 227). These classic ethnographies viewed politics as conflicts and the processes for restoring social stability in societies conceived of as encapsulated systems held together by collective goals (Leach, 1954; Gluckman, 1955; Fortes and Evans-Pritchard, 1940; Barth, 1959). [2] This naive view of culture as an organic whole and the notion of cultural relativism have influenced public views of non-Western cultures as enduring communitarian systems radically different from Western ones, long after anthropologists themselves have given up such static notions.

Marxist-inspired anthropologists concerned about colonial and post-colonial struggles against capitalism and the state produced new perspectives on the intertwining of culture and politics. Studies of colonial-induced rebellions have contributed most strongly to an anthropological view of politics internal to agrarian societies and small-scale communities, albeit with a limited view of the overarching state (Worsley, 1957; Swartz, Turner, and Tuden, 1966). At the height of the American involvement in the Vietnam War, Eric Wolf's *Peasant Wars of the Twentieth Century* (1969) stressed how an anthropological grasp of peasant political culture was key to an understanding of the dynamics of large-scale wars engulfing nations and continents. E. P. Thompson's *The Making of the English Working Class* (1963) was also influential in promoting the view of culture as an on-going process produced out of daily action and struggle. Because they concerned themselves with the everyday practices of subordinated groups in opposition to structures of colonialism and capital, anthropologists paid particular attention to the informal, the "interstitial, supplementary, and parallel structures" of coalition, clique, and network (Wolf, 1966a: 2) that are often ignored in more conventional analyses that view politics mainly in terms of the formalized processes of national movements, electoral politics, and state government. [3]

Since the 1970s, anthropologists studying post-colonial formations have increasingly dealt with the articulation between such "peripheral gray areas" and "the commanding heights of sovereign power" (Vincent, 1978: 176). Influenced by the concept of "the invention of tradition" (Hobsbawm and Ranger, 1966), anthropologists began to explore "the politics of culture" in struggles by different factions of a nation to fashion nationalist ideologies and movements (Handler, 1988; see also Fox, 1990; Verdery, 1991). Jim Scott's *Weapons of the Weak* (1985) further refined politics as modes of everyday resistance, and it foreshadowed a trend in studying minority movements that focus on the politics of violence and resistance to state rule (Feldman, 1991; Hale, 1995). Thus anthropologists no longer think of culture as a self-reproducing system but rather as contingent and disparate sets of values that are organized, manipulated, and deployed in a power context. The cultural systems of subordinated groups are viewed as in tension with and in contestation to elite control and state power.

Because we have tended to focus on the political dynamics of culture from below, we have paid very little attention to the ethnography of the state as an institution of government producing society. Sociologists and political scientists have produced an important body of work on the development of the modern states (e.g. Held et al., 1983), but anthropologists can provide insights on the cultural integument of power that interweaves state and society. Our contribution is especially needed for an understanding of the modern state, outside Western Europe and North America, that links cultural transformation with economic development.[4] Taking into account the strategic role of the post-colonial state, recent ethnographies (Ferguson, 1990; Coronil, 1997) have focused on the plans and categories through which governments foster development as a matter for the rational and cultural management of social life. When we consider the state as an agent that intervenes in the social and biological reality of the population, we historicize cultural forms as the effects of particular strategies, techniques, and procedures deeply implicated in the contemporary art of government, and its (re)production of particular kinds of citizen-subjects.

Variations in liberalism and citizenship

Liberalism as political philosophy

On a visit to South-East Asia, Huntington calls Asian democracies like Singapore, Malaysia, and so on "illiberal systems," contrasting them with American democracy. He claims that "free, fair, and competitive elections are only possible if there is some measure of freedom of speech, assembly and press, and if opposition candidates and parties are able to criticize incumbents without fear of retaliation. Democracy is thus not only a means of constituting authority, it is also a means of limiting authority."[5] While Huntington recognizes that Malaysia and Singapore are parliamentary democracies, he is critical of their political culture that puts limits on the capacity of citizens to express their views without fear of state retaliation.

Huntington's concern is part of his overall clash-of-civilizations thesis, which is a global version of the liberalism-communitarian debate about fundamental Western and non-Western cultural differences. In the West, the debate assesses the pros and cons of the eighteenth-century view that citizens' allegiance could be grounded on enlightened self-interest, versus the republican ideal of community grounded on citizens' alliance to pursue common action for the common good (Klymlicka, 1988). The ideals of the unencumbered self (individualism) and of the situated self (communalism) are linked and form the dynamic tension in democratic societies. The liberalism-communitarian debate seeks to weigh how the democratic government should respond to the range of citizens' demands for individual rights *and* for the good of collectivities. Charles Taylor notes that the body of liberal theory dominant in the Anglophone world sees the goal of society as to help citizens realize their life-plans "as much as possible and following some principle of equality" (1995: 186).

But when the debate expands to include Asian nations, the tendency is to lump them under the communitarian camp, since non-Western societies are viewed as giving the highest priority to community life, often at the expense of individual freedom.[6] For Western political theorists, the paradox presented by most Asian democracies is that the growth of market economies has not led to the growth of civil society, in particular the cherished Western ideals of full-fledged individual rights, and the freedom to check state power. Instead, it seems to theorists like Huntington that economic growth has enabled Asian states to strengthen their ability to subordinate individual rights to the collective good. This underdeveloped nature of civil society in Asian countries has led Western observers to conclude that they lack political accountability to individuals and to society. Huntington's "explanation for this paradox – representative democracy and capitalist economy coexisting with an authoritarian state (minus civil society) – lies in enduring Asian values, which have survived Western colonialism and become dominant in the post-colonial formations.

Liberalism as the art of government

But instead of resorting to cultural essentialism, it might be interesting to investigate the symbiosis between economic liberalism and political conservatism as characteristic of a different form of liberalism. After all, the most successful forms of Asian liberal economies – the so-called Asian tigers of Hong Kong, Singapore, and Malaysia – were colonies of Great Britain and inherited many institutions of government, law, and education associated with the Enlightenment values Huntington claims are missing in Asia. I discern that what appears particularly illiberal to Western observers is the fact that the Asian tiger state defines for the citizenry what is the public good. This flies in the face of Western assumptions that liberalism is fundamentally about rights rather than a particular vision of the good society; "the principle of equality or nondiscrimination would be breached if society itself espoused one or another conception of the good life" (Taylor, 1995: 186). Second, Asian tigers have a different conception of political accountability which is not immediately apparent to Western observers focused on the protection of individual rights according to principles of absolute equality. For these middle-range economies, political accountability tends to be measured in terms of the state ability to sustain economic growth for society as a whole.[7]

Thus, if one considers liberalism not as political philosophy, but as an "art of government" (Foucault, 1991), it may be possible to discover that the particular features of Asian political culture are rooted not in some timeless cultural values but in the logic of late-developing liberal economy. It becomes necessary to examine the array of strategies whereby a government attempts to resolve problems of how to govern society as a whole in relation to economic growth. In *The History of Sexuality* (1978), Michel Foucault draws our attention to politics as the government of the biological existence of modern human beings, i.e. bio-power. The new disciplinary force based on the rational management of social and biological life – repetitive exercises, detailed hierarchies, normalizing judgments, and the surveillance of bodies – had made possible the triumph of capitalism (Foucault, 1979). Bio-politics refers to the point when bio-power schemes become part of state strategies of social engineering for economic development.[8] Given the traditional anthropological concern with interstitial relations, strategic practices, and shifting norms of social life, our ethnographic method is ideally suited for capturing the bio-power configurations that link state strategies to the constitution of modern subjects.

Foucault views liberal government as a "pre-eminently economic government in the dual sense of cheap government and government geared to securing the conditions for optimum economic performance. There is a sense in which the liberal rationality of government is necessarily pegged to the optimum performance of the economy at minimum economic *and socio-political* cost" (Burchell, 1996: 26; italics in the original). Nikolas Rose maintains that as "a rationality of rule" liberalism is fundamentally concerned about "a series of problems about the governmentality of individuals, families, markets, and populations" (Rose, 1996: 39). This means that the liberal government necessarily engages in the control of individual body and the social body – by inducing and organizing certain capacities, aptitudes, and daily conduct – to produce rational citizens who will be entrepreneurial and competitive.

An ethnography of the state would focus on the bio-power of regula-

tion, identifying the particular logic underpinning the production, proliferation, and reproduction of cultural values, as well as the kinds of subject that are produced by such strategies of governing. States participating in capitalist development will vary their strategies for managing society, depending to a great degree on when they undertake capitalist development and their competitiveness in the world economy. Thus whereas early-developing countries in the West combine affluent economies with individualistic ethos, late-developing countries which rely on the state to play a major role tend to enforce greater social control over the population. Any consideration of differences in national cultures must take into consideration these different strategies for managing society that vary with the country's location and participation in the global capitalism. As late-developing formations, many Asian market economies become midwife to the middle classes, who must be subsidized, trained, and adapted to conditions often set by global labor and consumer markets. This state-centered strategy results in a higher degree of social regulation in everyday life, and a state control over the definition of public interest, than in many Western democracies.

By ignoring the regulative aspects of liberalism, both Huntington and Asian communitarian theorists can rhetorically dismiss the role of liberal rationality in constituting subjects in Asian societies, pointing instead to the exclusive role of Asian values in shaping a collectivist ethos.[9] By insisting that culture is the basis of social order, Huntington can claim the unbridgeable divisions between the West and the Rest. His evolutionary assumptions about the clash of civilizations suggest that non-Western societies have failed to change despite centuries of intercultural exchanges, including colonialism by Western powers. In addition, by ignoring the vexed relations between political liberalism and economic liberalism, he has not pursued the tantalizing link between economic competition and cultural authoritarianism in Asian countries. Without attention to the particular historical trajectory of post-colonial countries, and their current challenges in producing society and meeting global market forces, one misses the liberal logic that informs so much of the Asian state strategy in defining for their citizens what is the good life (dressed up in cultural terms), and the kind of citizen desirable to economic liberalism.

Citizenship as the product of particular liberalisms

An approach that connects the state's economic strategy to its regulation of society also calls for a more plural notion of citizenship than that of a rational, autonomous subject associated with an ideal vision of Western liberalism. An anthropological approach to the state would be wary of projecting a "strong" concept of the sovereign subject focused on individual rights and equal treatment that underpins Western liberalism (Taylor, 1995: 200). Nevertheless, this view of a universal, autonomous subject fighting for individual rights has informed social sciences' approach to individual action and motivation, regardless of the nature of the local society. For instance, in *Weapons of the Weak,* Jim Scott simply regards Muslim-Malay peasants as political agents struggling to retrieve individual rights, in the context of social dislocations produced by state-directed development in Malaysia (1985).[10] This projection of the ideal Western citizen-subject onto Malay peasants does not take into account the complex ways religion, ethnic politics, and the state shape the individual subject and his sense of a broader set of political struggle and goals *vis-à-vis* the government. Anthropologists might ask how politics in the post-colonial society may have been shaped by local culture as well as by the state, not only through the process of opposition (as individuals and as groups), but also through the processes of government.

Variations in the mix of economic and political liberalism will produce different kinds of subject for whom particular forms of sociality – the kinship network, the religious group, the ethnic community – become morally legitimized or delegitimized by the state, either in its insistence on "universal human rights," or on the primacy of indigenous culture. In many non-Western democracies then, the sovereign subject (which implies the fullest realization of individual rights) may not be the proper measure of citizenship. Instead of a universal conception of citizenship as self-rule, it may be more instructive to focus on citizenship capacity, i.e. the ways citizens in different democratic countries seek to realize particular interests, including resources and citizen dignity, and the kind of political accountability they expect from their government.[11] Whereas Western liberal theory may focus on the citizen's capacity to retrieve individual rights (Taylor, 1995: 200), in Asian tiger countries, economic liberalism translates citizenship capacity into the ability to hold the state accountable in terms of the delivery of material and social goods. The rest of the chapter compares and contrasts state-society relations in Malaysia and Singapore, and sometimes Hong Kong – tiger economies that are highly responsive to globalization and yet have said "no" to Western liberalism. While this rhetorical stance may seem to support the clash-of-civilizations thesis, I argue that these states represent an alternative liberalism whereby there is an implacable link between economic liberalism and cultural communitarianism. They differ in important respects from varieties of Western liberalism in their regulation of particular kinds of sociality based on family and community bonds, and in the production of particular kinds of dependent yet calculative subject who help to make their societies competitive in the global market.

Post-developmental strategy: Governing "the caring society"

The public repudiation of Western rationality and culture has become something of a trend in Asian elite circles. In 1996 a Chinese best-seller called *China Can Say No* expressed a high level of Han chauvinism in criticizing American trade policies. Referring to China's scientific and cultural glories of the past, the book claims that "In the next century ... Chinese thought, and Chinese entrepreneurial abilities will deeply influence the world, becoming the sole force leading human thought" (Song et al., 1996, quoted by Gries, 1997: 181). Furthermore, in a direct challenge to American economic power, the authors assert, "We don't want MFN [the 'most favored nation' treatment], and in the future we won't offer it to you either" (ibid). The intertwining of cultural chauvinist discourses and trade conflicts reflect fundamentally a clash of economies that are represented and experienced in cultural (and even racial) terms. The authors of *China Can Say No* were inspired by a book entitled *The Voice of Asia* (1995), published by prime minister Mahathir Mohamad of Malaysia and politician Shintaro Ishihara of Japan; the book also came out in Japanese, retitled *The Asia that Can Say No*. Ishihara had written *The Japan that Can Say No* (1990), the first Asian book to publicly reject American-imposed trade policies. Mohamad and Ishihara vigorously reject Western "liberal" values (in the narrow sense of political freedom), insisting that Asian cultural values underlie an Asian model of capitalism and maintaining that an Asian renaissance is challenging Western domination of the region. This crescendo of nay-saying Asians reflects the common stance taken by Asian economies toward the Group of Seven (Western industrialized powers and Japan), and the trade barriers represented by NAFTA (the North American Free Trade Association), as well as by the European Union common market. As the rhetoric of cultural difference became inseparable from trade wars, the fundamental question is not irreducible civilizational divisions but rather how the state, seeking optimal growth, uses cultural "expertise to translate society into an object of government" (Barry, Osborne and Rose, 1996: 13).

The liberal rationalities of many post-colonial Asian states have evolved in conjunction with Western ones since the Second World War. They reveal the imprint of the political modernity that came with Western colonialism and the adoption of socialism. Capitalist development and the rise of middle classes in Asia have, however, followed a different trajectory from that experienced by Western countries. Whereas in Europe capitalism emerged from independent merchant and trade guilds, culminating over the centuries in struggles for bourgeois democracy, in the late-developing Asia the state has played a major role in transforming pre-modern agrarian societies, colonial bureaucracies, and lately command party rule into capitalist formations, all compressed within a few generations (Robison and Goodman 1996: 5). In what Barrington Moore calls a "revolution from above" (1966), state-driven transitions to socialist or capitalist development also included the formation of middle classes, whose structural position and loyalty are much more firmly tied to state projects than was the case of the early bourgeoisie in the West.

In Asian liberal economies then, state grooming and regulation of the middle classes are essential to the competitiveness of their economies. Thus one should view with skepticism fears for the future of Hong Kong, now returned to Chinese rule as a "special administrative zone" (SAR). I argue that Western liberalism – the mode of government that promotes economic growth – has taken root in Asia, and that it plays a major role in shaping realities there today. Singapore has been ranked as one of the most competitive economies in the world, while Hong Kong, under a special administrative arrangement relatively autonomous of Beijing, continues to be one of the most liberal economies. My goal is not to diminish political problems in Asian democracies but rather to point to their institutional roots in economic liberalism, and to grasp the particular liberal rationality underlying a mode of government that produces the kind of society and subject that is objectionable yet uncomfortably familiar to Western liberal critics.

The earlier picture of developing Asian countries – South Korea, Taiwan, Singapore – was that of the strong developmentalist state. Following the Latin American prototype, Herbert Feith (1982) argues that the "repressive-developmentalist state" arose in conjunction with state-driven export-oriented industrialization, and the disciplining of the new workers, and the maintenance of the new technical, professional, and bureaucratic elites that manage state apparatuses and interface with transnational corporations (ibid). Asian tiger states like South Korea and Taiwan have become "strong" by creating cohesive political alliances with corporate capital, and have played a role in the formation of a bourgeoisie. Singapore, Malaysia, Thailand, and Indonesia represented varying degrees of the centralized, strong state that engineered the rise of middle classes, and that formed strategic alliances with capital, thus facilitating conditions for profit-maximization. I will not discuss the varied arrangements and relative successes of such industrialization programs in different economies here;[12] but the point is that by taking draconian measures against labor to serve the interests of transnational corporations, these nation-states have become "strong," in both the political ("authoritarian") and economic ("industrializing") senses. Through a carrot-and-stick approach, strict laws against labor and political activism were balanced against overall increases in the standard of living. Scholars of South-East Asia have occupied themselves with determining the balance between development and repression in each nation-state; Malaysia, for instance, has been described as ruled by a "repressive-responsive regime," meaning that authoritarian rule has been leavened by greater multi-ethnic representation in the government (Crouch, 1996: 236–47). But the exclusive focus of political scientists on party politics in determining state strategies overlooks other forms of power that go beyond the electoral and legal systems.

An anthropology of state practices would conceive of the state not simply in terms of grand strategies of political power over legal subjects, but also as a plurality of forms of government that are circulated throughout the body politic (Foucault, 1981). In particular, we need to focus on the micro-mechanisms of power through which the state seeks to produce society, and constitute particular kinds of subject. Our understanding of such everyday state practices can gain precision and clarity if we distinguish between what Foucault calls disciplinary power – the rules and regulations aimed at instilling self-discipline and productivity – and pastoral power – which concerns itself with the biological and the social existence of human beings.[13]

To discover the particular features of Asian liberalism, we need to look at both their state of economic development, and at their regimes for producing and managing particular kinds of society. Going beyond the easy label of repressive states, I argue that Singapore and Malaysia, having attained a certain level of industrial development, are increasingly focusing on regimes of cultural caring and sociality. I call this shift a "post-developmental" state strategy, whereby the state relinquishes much of the control over development to private enterprises and relies more and more on non-repressive measures to regulate society, especially the middle classes.[14] The post-developmental strategy denotes a new kind of relationship whereby the state, through a plurality of forms, seeks to produce the kind of subjects that are attractive to global capital, both as low-skilled and technical workers and as newly affluent consumers. The role of the state has become less that of the vital economic actor than as a guarantor of the social and legal conditions – stability, legitimacy, accountability – for the free play of market forces. What is distinctive (but by no means unique) about Asian liberal forms of "governmentality" (Foucault, 1991: 92) are the ways essentialized cultural terms are deployed to regulate the population, constitute modern subjects, and to culturally authenticate social policies of control.

The post-developmental strategies of Asian tigers are distinctive for dealing with the liberal problem of "too much government" by deploying the cultural logic of collective values in administering the working and professional classes.[15] Labels like "Malaysia, Inc.," "communitarian capitalism," and "the caring society" have come to stand for programs that favor urban interests and that promote the training, consumption, and profit-making activities through which state power helps to build up the credentials, skills, and overall well-being of the middle classes so critical to attracting foreign capital. I discern the moral economy of South-East Asian liberalism whereby the caring state constitute subjects who are both dependent and calculative agents embedded within networks of sociality and national accountability.

The moral economy of the state

Although Singapore and Malaysia have been called authoritarian or re-pressive, they fall far short of the police state.[16] In contrast to the fully authoritarian state, these ruling regimes tie expert knowledge in the social and human sciences to government, thereby translating the practical rationalities of liberalism into strategies and programs that shape ethico-political mentalities of their subjects who are increasingly middle class. More than in the West, the liberal Asian state plays a pedagogical role in educating the public as to the ethico-political meaning of *citizenship*. Ex-pertise in the social and human sciences are deployed to provide "a cer-tain style of reasoning." According to Nikolas Rose, one must consider the ways in which expert language is used as "a set of 'intellectual tech-niques' . . . for rendering reality thinkable and practicable, and constitut-ing domains that are amenable – or not amenable – to reformatory intervention" (1996: 42). In Asian democracies, narratives of cultural au-thenticity not only make certain regulations reasonable and "natural," they also regulate the ways responsible / good subjects accept such au-thoritative norms of ruling. I use the term "moral economy of the state" to describe this social contract whereby the government guarantees eco-nomic and social well-being in return for economic discipline and social conformity on the part of the population (Ong, 1997). Moral codes justi-fying such exchanges do not merely emerge from pre-existing cultural norms, but must be continually invented and organized by the ruling elites, both in the ritual pronouncements about Asian cultural values, and in policy mechanisms that reinforce citizens' discipline and compliance with national goals.[17]

Sociality and dependent subjects

The rise of the "new rich" in Asia requires new forms of civilizing and caring from the regimes that have played a major role in their formation. In the countries of the ASEAN (Association of South-East Asian Nations), the expansion of middle classes requires a government that can train not only the professional skills and expertise desired by multinational corporations, but also the kind of cultural sensibility that is loyal to the state. For instance, Malaysia, in following the example of Japan Inc., puts the government in charge of co-ordinating the public and private sectors. This kind of state-induced partnership with capital is hailed by leaders as "communitarian capitalism," since it is claimed that capitalist development is orchestrated with the goal of benefiting the entire society, and not just a segment of it (Mohamad and Ishihara, 1995a: 11). Pastoral power – or attending to the material and social well-being of the population – is linked to a conception of citizenship as one framed within a communal network of dependency and obligation, endorsed by cultural traditions. The term "caring society" stresses a mutual caring between state and society, and the expectation that even when citizens attain "technological proficiency" and "exemplary work ethic," they will ensure "a high and escalating productivity," and find fulfillment in making the nation attain its goal of becoming a fully industrialized country in the year 2020 (Khoo, 1995: 328).

Relying on cultural notions of sociality rather than on laws, this communitarian capitalism justifies social regulation in terms of religion because "[y]ou cannot legislate the empathy and affection that bind family and close friends. In the years ahead the Asian tradition of stressing these bonds will provide us with guidelines for increasingly complex information societies. The fundamentals of Eastern thought – avoiding unnecessary conflict, eschewing coercive tactics, living within one's means – will sustain us" (Mohamad and Ishihara, 1995a: 10). Islam is invoked to legitimize the call to establish "a fully moral and ethical society whose citizens are strong in religious and spiritual values and imbued with the highest of ethical standards" (Khoo, 1995: 328). Through the concept of a caring society, the government casts itself as a custodian not only of the population's welfare but also of its cultural traditions, thus wedding its goal of attaining economic competitiveness to the political disciplining of its population as a moral community.

In the 1980s the government instituted an Islamization policy, not to transform the state into an Islamic theocracy (as in Iran), but rather to deploy Islamic values as part of a massive social engineering of the Malays.[18] Through the invocation of Islamic traditions of learning, entrepreneurship, and piety, the goal of social programs – Islamic university, Islamic banks, Islamic businesses – was to work as a counter-force against "Malay fatalism" and to train and discipline Muslims "so that they can take the place of the civil mercenaries upon whom the Muslim countries have to depend now" (Mahathir Mohamad, quoted in Khoo, 1995: 174, 172). A new kind of Malay subject – *Melayu Baru* (new Malay) – is promoted who is self-disciplined, entrepreneurial, and devoutly Muslim.[19] The new

Malay is a middle-class subject who is self-reliant, able, and wealth-accu-
mulating, but in a way that is cast as within the precepts of Islam rather
than of capitalism. Authoritative leaders from the prime minister down-
wards proclaim not the contradiction but rather the spiritual fit between a
Malaysian "can-do*ism*" – *Malaysia Boleh* – and Islamic modernity. In
opposing the new Malay subjectivity to its colonial representations – hard-
working rather than "easy-going," profit-seeking rather than interest-
avoiding, knowledgeable rather than ignorant, cosmopolitan rather than
"narrow-minded"[20] – government policies seek to bring Islam in line with
capitalism. The array of programs to inculcate capitalist practices includes
the systematic training of Malay students for college education in Western centers of science and capitalism; encouraging Muslims to save in
special Islamic banks; and to work with ethnic Chinese and foreign businesses. The new Malay subject – receiver of government scholarships,
credit, business licenses, civil service jobs, and innumerable perks associated with being *bumiputera* (indigenous subject) – has been trained to
obtain credentials, to be effective on the job, and also to view their dependency on state largess as within the dictates of benevolent Islam.

Even in religious practice, an attitude seeking wealth and prestige is
presented as in line with Islamic calling. On television, the call to Islamic
prayers, following the invocations that "Allah is Great," are followed by
the proclamations "Let us perform the *sorah*" (Islamic prayer) and "Let
us follow the path of prosperity!" They are accompanied by images of
Muslims at prayer in mosques, followed by pictures of Muslims receiving
certificates at university convocations. While this standard call to prayer
is not new, the commercially infused vocabulary of classic Islam has been
used to good effect to promote the newly credentialized elite. This state
investment in and nurturing of the new Malays reinforce their lack of
political autonomy from official definitions of what is culturally appropriate behavior for Muslims and for Malaysian citizens. The effect rather
is to induce an enlightened Islamic attitude towards capitalism and progress
which will promote Islamic sociality and strengthen the links between
state, economy, and the moral community of Muslims.

This new Islamic identity has not gone unchallenged, of course. A dissident group of Muslims called Darul Arqam has criticized state developmental projects as based on un-Islamic capitalist principles of profit-making
and individual gain. Their own organization sought to exemplify "true"
Islamic sociality by setting up a communally based economy that linked
families and villages. But in an unprecedented move against a non-politi-
cal Muslim group, the government arrested the Darul Arqam leaders and
dispersed their followers. For many upwardly mobile new Malays, the
rituals and words of an official Islamic culture fused with capitalism has
become a meaningful way of being modern citizens. In the government

rhetoric then, there are different levels of cultural differences so that certain activities – "unnecessary conflict, coercive tactics" – are marked as foreign (Western), whereas entrepreneurialism is not so marked, but rather recast as an integrating ingredient in progressive Islamic society.[21]

In neighboring Singapore, experts also invoke Asian ethics to both authenticate and naturalize the authority of the state over individually directed knowledge, values, and behavior. For instance, in a debate with Huntington, political scientist Chan Heng Chee[22] argues that a key feature of Asian political systems is the de-emphasis of individual rights but with a new emphasis on respect for authority, so that opposition to those in power is "not a normal reflex."[23] Frequently, academic experts are employed to cast such state calculation in terms of a culturally distinctive reasoning. Tu Wei Ming is a Harvard professor often invited to Singapore to make universalizing pronouncements about Chinese culture. In a recent visit he defined Confucianism as a Sinicized Asian humanism that is "anthropocosmic," balancing self-transformation with duty consciousness, within a series of concentric circles consisting of "self, family, community, society, nation, world, and cosmos." (Tu, 1995: 20–2, 24). By posing these philosophical questions as pedagogical lessons on what being a Chinese subject is all about, this expert knowledge authenticates governing strategies that normalize submission to state authority as the work of heavenly principles, rather than the product of technologies of calculation reflecting the logic of liberal economics. For instance, an official of the foreign ministry had claimed that Asian religions – Confucianism, Hinduism – have made Singapore a more efficient, caring, and united society than the United States, which in his view is suffering from an "unfettered individual freedom" that leads to "massive social decay" (Mahbubani, 1993). These officially sanctioned views of Chinese culture do produce meaningful effects on subjects who are proud of the achievements of their country and its focus on families, productivity, and security.

Such a liberalism imbued with quasi-religious pastoral power appears to be a strategy borrowed by the new merchant-politicians in Hong Kong. Under China's "one country, two systems" formula, the economic liberalism Hong Kong is now guaranteed by a group of ruling tycoons, largely nominated (not elected) by Beijing. They have suspended labor laws giving workers the right to collective bargaining and curbed the right to public rallies. It appears that under self-Chinese rule, Hong Kong liberalism is based on a revival and elaboration of British colonial labor regulation, but now justified in terms of Chinese culture. When the international media points to actions against trade unions, public assemblies, and the expulsion of illegal immigrant children from the mainland as anti-liberal,[24] they fail to note that these actions are taken in the interests of economic liberalism, to make Hong Kong more competitive, and politically stable, for business interests, and in the process also administratively differentiating itself as a system from the mainland. Pro-consul Tung has linked future economic growth to an unquestioning posture towards authority. He invokes "Chineseness" as respect for power-holders in the family and in the government, "a belief in order and stability," and "an emphasis on obligations to the community rather than the rights of the individual."[25] The program of collective security appears directed primarily at the middle classes dependent upon state employment and services. Tung's minimal pastoral program has made home ownership the top priority of his administration. This housing program – whereby the government hopes to attain 70 percent home ownership in ten years[26] – deals with both problems of economic and social regulation. The high cost of real estate in Hong Kong threatens its future growth as an Asian regional hub for multinational corporations, and economic competitiveness requires the cooling down of the housing market. At the same time, near universal home-ownership is a strategy of social regulation whereby grown children are urged to live and care for aged parents, a mode of governmentality that borrows from Singapore. But by casting these modes of regulation as ways of being Chinese, a view reinforced by Western interpretation of "a quasi-Confucian paternalism,"[27] these programs regulating family support systems and controlling the influx of mainland Chinese are intended to ensure that Hong Kong remains socially stabilized and economically viable in the aftermath of the transition to mainland rule.

These variants of South-East Asian liberalism thus indicate that in the tiger economies, social regulation is perhaps to a greater extent than in the West explicitly spelled out in terms of cultural authenticity, and in identifying the kinds of sociality that stress dependency on state power. But the stress on the caring and the cultural authority of government does not mean that these citizens who seek fulfillment through dependent relations are not also calculating in their assessment of government performance.

Bureaucratic benevolence and calculative subjects

Nikolas Rose observes that "Liberalism inaugurates a continual dissatisfaction with government, a perpetual questioning of whether the desired effects are being produced, of the mistakes of thought or policy that hamper the efficacy of government, a recurrent diagnosis of failure coupled with a recurrent demand to govern better" (Rose, 1996: 47). How can subjects in Asian liberalism engage in continual questioning of the authority of rule when, in most cases, they are electoral democracies frequently ruled by a single dominant party, and when there are various curbs on the freedom of speech? In recent years, Taiwan is pointed to as a robust East Asian democracy where street demonstrations and fist-fights in the legislature have become rather common everyday affairs. The middle classes in the Philippines and Thailand too have overthrown dictatorships, but without bringing about more democratic regimes in power. I claim, however, that in the so-called "authoritarian" states of Malaysia and Singapore, subjects nevertheless do engage in continual assessment of their rulers. The basic assumptions about citizenship capacity are, however, different from that in many Western liberal democracies. In Asian democracies, citizens' dignity and their demands for better government are understood not so much in terms of the degree of democratic representation, or in terms of the retrieval of individual rights,[28] but rather in terms of state efficiency in ensuring overall social security and prosperity.

If, as Rose maintains, in advanced democracies, individuals are expected to "enterprise themselves" – seeking to fulfill themselves by maximizing "their quality of life through acts of choice" (1996: 37) – in Asian liberal societies, the state seeks to enterprise itself as a particular kind of moral economy within which subjects expect to fulfill their national obligations through relations of dependency linking family, neighborhood, and ethnic group, to the nation. As Chan Heng Chee has argued, the legitimacy of the ASEAN state derives from "the ability of the government to deliver the goods," but in return for the loyalty and dependency of the population. The operative term is not "individual rights" but "communitarianism" or the "trust" that is socially constructed between the government and its subjects, and that is continually tested by the aspiring middle classes.

Singapore is a unique city-state of 3 million where Asian economic liberalism has been honed to a science. For these reasons, it is a telling case of Asian liberalism taken to the extreme, a model that is admired though hardly reproducible in larger countries like Vietnam and China. Because of its infamous global image as an authoritarian regime, and the periodic repressive moves, analysts have tended to view Singaporean politics in terms of a negative model of power. But most areas of Singaporean life, in its quotidian aspects, are governed not by repression but by a multiplicity of programs – housing, health, savings, education – that provide such a secure social net that they produce the social cohesiveness and consensus that facilitate national efficiency and competitiveness. State-directed social regulation involves the co-option of selected elements of the corporate and professional elites nominated to parliament, state committees, think tanks. Their technical expertise is used to assist in refining government policy, while their partial integration into the state provides "feedback" channels for monitoring dissension and managing society.[29] But beyond regulating society through a range of welfare and social mechanisms, the government must also be accountable to its citizens for maintaining very high standards of living and continual economic growth.

The structure of accountability in Singapore is determined by the population trusting in the expertise and cultural authority of the political leadership, and the state to deliver in terms of social stability and economic performance. Rather than focusing on individual liberties, the rational Singaporean subject holds the government accountable for universal home-ownership, high-quality education, and unending economic expansion. The country prides itself as a "home-owning democracy" (Chua, 1995: ix–x) and has the highest rate of near-universal provision of public housing anywhere in the world. About 70 percent of dwellers in public sector apartments are owner-occupiers (ibid, 129). The assertiveness of citizen grievances *vis-à-vis* the government provision of "collective welfare" has grown as lower classes demand better quality subsidized housing, and the aspiring middle classes the ability to buy affordable housing. The government now provides subsidies for both sets of demands, as a way to maintain the boast of a Confucianist ethos of honor and benevolence. These social programs are taken to be guided by Confucian ethics expressing "a moral leadership which governs in the interest of the people rather than through self-interest" (Chua, 1995: 193–4).

The Confucian emphasis on education is also reflected in the state support of a fine educational system. The ferocious demands of parents for quality education have made Singapore's primary-school students among the world's most competitive in science and math. Every year, Singaporeans anxiously await measures of their nation's global competitiveness. In 1997 Singapore was ranked by a US-based company as the second most profitable country (after Switzerland), according to operations risk (the general economic environment), political risk, and remittance and repatriation of profits.[30] As the favored Asian destination of foreign capital, Singapore is an excellent case of the fact that the simple discipline of a labor force is no longer the most desirable feature; just as important are the provision of efficient state services and resources to well-trained middle and working classes.

The technologies of security, interwoven through an array of programs into the very fabric of everyday life – subsidized housing, education, compulsory retirement and saving schemes, incentives for child-bearing (ibid, 116) – are so entrenched that perhaps the worst punishment that the government can mete out to an errant subject is not a bout of whipping in jail, but rather throwing him into the whirlwind of bankruptcy. A new strategy of political authorities is to file defamation suits against opposition leaders and government critics (e.g. Seow, 1994). When judged guilty, defendants are punished with multi-million-dollar damages which have effectively bankrupted individuals, or forced them into exile.[31]

Through this strategy, the state exposes intransigent Singaporeans to the unaccustomed privatized management of risks, a condition more commonly found in advanced liberal societies. These defamation suits operate as public lessons reinforcing the authority of the state and the technologies of security to which Singaporean subjects have become habituated. By exposing dissident subjects to the individualized risks of advanced liberalism – depleted social supports, risks of bankruptcies, *de facto* loss of citizenship – the liberal Asian state makes yet another case for "Asian communitarianism."

Similarly, in Malaysia, individual rights to dissent are balanced against the imperatives of the state to deliver on economic and social performances. The prime minister provides a defense of state-engineered liberalism when he says that in Asia, "We believe that strong, stable governments prepared to make decisions which, though often unpopular, are nevertheless in the best interests of the nation, are a prerequisite for economic development. . . . When citizens understand that their right to choose also involves limits and responsibilities, democracy doesn't deteriorate into an excess of freedom" (Mohamad and Ishihara, 1995a: 8). Although the Malaysian regime comes nowhere near providing the kind of collectivized support for the majority of its population as in Singapore, the government is also held accountable in terms of its ability – through the series of affirmative action rights and benefits (the provision of credits, jobs, education, goods, and services) – to promote Malay entrepreneurship. As the country becomes more affluent, the government and high-ranking individuals are resorting more and more to defamation suits as a way to silence political critics who challenge the state strategies that both discipline and shape the social existence of the Malay majority as a population attractive to global capitalism.

The caring society model in South-East Asia is thus not the same as the welfare liberalism one associates with Western societies. Whereas the latter institutionalized claims on the national product of those who could not "fairly compete" – women, urban poor, the unemployed, the sick, and so on – the caring society institutes stability-through-bureaucratic benevolence, thus welcoming global capital in.[32] In other words, while the welfare state developed as a way to deal with class conflict, the post-developmental strategy of middle-range Asian economies seeks to produce technically proficient and socially unified citizens attractive to capital. The precedent for the Asian model of pastoral care may be found in Bismarckian Germany, probably historically the most important example of a state producing a society through caring. The German state not only managed to usher in industrial development but also addressed the "social question" of class relations by producing a social policy of caring (Steinmer, 1993). There is therefore nothing intrinsically unique or unprecedented about the Asian model of pastoral care that seeks to be the guarantor of social and legal conditions – stability, legitimacy, account-ability – through producing citizens with the human, social and cultural capitals that allow them to flourish in a global economy.

This responsiveness and accountability to their subjects, rather than their expressions of cultural authenticity, are what make the "guardianist governments" in Asia appealing to their subjects. Through a varied mix of disciplinary and pastoral schemes, the different regimes seek to pro-duce middle-class subjects who are technically competent and socially cohesive, qualities that make them appealing to international business. In short, while Asian tigers used to govern too much through repressive measures, the shift to post-developmental strategies reveals that the solu-tion to the liberal paradox of maximizing gain and minimizing govern-ment is increasingly to exercise disciplinary and pastoral powers cast in the cultural logics of Asian traditions. The post-developmental state must produce socio-political order and modern technical efficiency in order to compete in the global economy. Finally, given the current financial crisis in South Korea and in South-East Asia, the question whether the exercise of pastoral power cast in the cultural logic of Confucianism or Islam is an enduring solution remains to be seen.

Conclusion

Anthropologists must participate in discussions about late twentieth-cen-tury questions of cultural difference, geopolitical clashes, and global cul-tures. We have moved beyond essentializing and compartmentalized views of culture, with their ill-thought-out notions of communitarianism in so-cieties outside Western Europe and North America. But our avoidance of subjects like citizenship, and the state production of individuals and soci-ety continues to hamper our exploration of the intricate connections be-tween politics, society, and culture. We need to go beyond simple assertions that nations are different because they "have" different cultures, and we should avoid using culture as the starting point of any investigation of social phenomena. Attention to the relations between state and society, in relation to the global economy, will allow the discussion of different forms of liberalism, a perspective that will challenge simple assertions of East-West cultural differences. It will also enable us to focus on the varying kinds of conditions under which different, but equally modern citizens are formed in a range of societies. Anthropology, perhaps more than any other discipline in the Western social sciences, can show that we can no longer afford to ignore the "alternative modernities" (Ong, 1995) pro-duced elsewhere in the world.

Notes

1 Huntington's thesis has been expanded into a book, *The Clash of Civilizations* (1996), which is widely read and invoked by policy-makers in Asia.

2 For an overview of British political anthropology, see Vincent, 1990: 225–83.

3 For examples of such studies, see Banton, 1966; Wolf, 1966b; and Bailey, 1969.

4 A point made by Arturo Escobar, 1995; see also Ong, 1999, chs 8 and 9.

5 *The Straits Times Weekly Overseas Edition*, March 13, 1993, 14. See also John Rawls, *Theory of Justice* (Cambridge, Ma.: Harvard University Press, 1971).

6 For an attempt to defend a particular view of the good communitarian society in Singapore, see Bell, 1993.

7 In fact, this vision of liberalism is not so different from that of current "revisionist" democratic theory that "a mature liberal society doesn't demand very much of its members, as long as it delivers the goods and makes their lives prosperous and secure" (Taylor, 1995: 195).

8 Stephen Collier (1997) makes this important distinction between the micro and the macro economies of bio-power.

9 For a political economic analysis of "Asian values" discourse, see Ong (1997: 171–202).

10 In contrast to his approach in *The Moral Economy of the Peasant* (1976), where peasants are presented as operating in terms of collective interests against the destructive powers of global markets and rapacious states.

11 I follow Taylor (1995: 200) in making this analytical distinction between self-rule and citizenship capacity.

12 For an overview of industrial strategies and state accommodations in Asia, see Deyo, 1987; White, 1988; Appelbaum and Henderson, 1992.

13 For Foucault's concept of disciplining power, see *Discipline and Punish* (1979); and for his notion of pastoral power, see "*Omnes et Singulatim*" (1981).

14 In contrast to other anthropologists (e.g. Escobar, 1995: 217–22), I use "post-developmental" to mean a new stage of state *engagement* (rather than disengagement) with global agencies and capital that also requires a new relationship between state and society.

15 Whereas in Western neo-liberalism, the cultural logic is one of the individual as "expert of the self" and privatized management of skills; see Rose, 1996: 37–64.

16 See Chua, 1995; Crouch, 1996. The charge of authoritarian rule is more accurate for Indonesia, where there is the form of democracy but little substantive content, and political repression is much more frequent and extensive; see for instance Schwarz, 1994.

17 Jim Scott (1976) has argued that Asian peasant communities operated according to a moral economy system; the subordinated groups perceive unequal exchanges with their landlords as collaborative and morally legitimate because they ensure security for all. He assumes that moral economy concepts emerge from the precarious circumstances of peasant livelihood that

foster social values of reciprocity and exchanges that can help avert disaster for individual households and the community as a whole. While I do not contest this view of peasant society, in my formulation of the moral economy of the modern South-East Asian state, I argue that the ideology of morally justified exchanges must be continually produced and organized by the state, regardless of whether there is a pre-existing set of moral values that will support such unequal collaborations between citizens and the state.

18   For an overview of the government's Islamization program, see Khoo, 1995: 163–97.

19   All Malays (also known as *bumiputeras*) are Muslims. Malaysia is a multi-ethnic country with a population of 20 million (Malays, Chinese, Indians, aboriginals). In the aftermath of racial riots in 1969, the Malaysian government introduced the New Economic Policy (NEP), which includes a set of affirmative action measures favoring the Malay majority in the ownership of corporate stocks, government jobs, and employment in the private sector. The extraordinary success of the NEP in engineering the rise of Malay urban workers, middle-class professionals, and a powerful corporate elite has led to a new *National* Economic Policy that seeks to emphasize poverty eradication regardless of ethnicity, but Malay middle and upper middle-classes continue to receive an array of special favors. See Crouch, 1996.

20   See Khoo (1995: 24–41), who enumerates the moral problems of Malay culture as viewed by Mahathir Mohamad.

21   In contrast to the Malay middle classes, the ethnic Chinese, although economically and culturally more independent of the state structure, are politically too weak to pose a significant political challenge to state power. Much of their energy is invested in economic interests and structures that can free them from the disciplining of the state, and by eluding political-cultural control through plotting emigration strategies or participating in transnational business. See Nonini, 1997.

22   He is also the Singapore ambassador to the United States, and thus a major translator of Singaporean political rationalities.

23   *The Straits Times Weekly Overseas Edition*, March 13, 1993, 14.

24   See, for instance, Wang Hui Ling, "Sowing Seeds of Potential Discord," *The New Straits Times,* July 25, 1997, 50.

25   Bruce Gilley, "Hong Kong Handover: Is Hong Kong Having an Identity Crisis?," *The Asian Wall Street Journal* , June 17, 1997.

26   Edward A. Gargan, "A New Leader Outlines his Vision for Hong Kong," *The New York Times*, July 2, 1997, A1.

27   "A New Leader Outlines his Vision for Hong Kong," *The New York Times,* July 2, 1997, A1.

28   Obviously there is always a minority of activist citizens and politicians who seek to expand the meaning of democracy in both countries.

29   Garry Rodan, "Expect Asia's Values to Turn Out Much Like Everyone Else's," *International Herald Tribune,* August 4, 1997, 8.

30   "Singapore Ranked Second Again for Profitability," *The Straits Times*, August 8, 1997, 40.

31   In a defamation suit against an opposition politician, the Prime Minister and

his colleagues won US $5.7 million in damages. The opponent fled the country. See Louis Kraar, "A Blunt Talk with Singapore's Lee Kuan Yew," *Fortune*, July 21, 1997, 32. For a recent case, see "Singapore Leader is Accused of Lying," *The New York Times*, August 20, 1997, A5.
32 Don Nonini urged me to make this clarification.

Bibliography

Appelbaum, Richard, and Jeffrey Henderson, eds. 1992. *States and Development in the Pacific Rim*. Newbury Park, Ca.: Sage.

Bailey, F. G., 1969. *Strategems and Spoils: A Social Anthropology of Politics*. New York: Basil Blackwell.

Banton, Michael, ed. 1966. *The Social Anthropology of Complex Societies*. London: Tavistock.

Barry, Andrew, Thomas Osborne, and Nikolas Rose, 1996. "Introduction," in *Foucault and Political Reason*, ed. Barry, Osborne, and Rose. Chicago: Chicago University Press, 1–18.

Barth, Frederik. 1959. *Political Leadership among the Swat Pathans*. London: London School of Economics Monograph on Social Anthropology, no. 19.

Bell, Daniel, 1993. *Communitarianism and its Critics*. Oxford: Clarendon Press.

Borneman, John, 1993. *Belonging in the Two Berlins*. Cambridge, Mass.: Harvard University Press.

Burchell, Graham, 1996. "Liberal Government and Techniques of the Self," in *Foucault and Political Reason*, ed. A. Barry, T. Osborne, and N. Rose. Chicago: University of Chicago Press, 19–36.

Chua, Beng-huat, 1995. *Communitarian Ideology and Democracy in Singapore*. London: Routledge.

Collier, Stephen J. 1997. "Further Notes on the Genealogy of Development," Department of Anthropology, University of California, unpublished ms.

Coronil, Fernando, 1997. *The Magical State: Nature, Money, and Modernity in Venezuela*. Chicago: University of Chicago Press.

Crouch, Harold, 1996. *Government and Society in Malaysia*. Ithaca: Cornell University Press.

Deyo, Frederic C., ed., 1987. *The Political Economy of New Asian Industrialism*. Ithaca: Cornell University Press.

Escobar, Arturo, 1995. *Encountering Development: The Making and Unmaking of the Third World*. Princeton: Princeton University Press.

Feith, Herbert. 1982. "Repressive-Developmentalist Regimes in Asia," *Alternatives* 7: 491–506.

Feldman, Allen, 1991. *Formations of Violence: The Narrative of the Body and Political Terror in Northern Ireland*. Chicago: University of Chicago Press.

Ferguson, James, 1990. *The Anti-Politics Machine: 'Development,' Depoliticization, and Bureaucratic State Power in Lesotho*. Cambridge: Cambridge University Press.

Fortes, Myer, and E. E. Evans-Pritchard, 1940. *African Political Systems*. London: Oxford University Press.

Foucault, Michel, 1978. *The History of Sexuality,* vol. I, trans. M. Hurley. New York: Pantheon.

——1979. *Discipline and Punish: The Birth of the Prison,* trans. Alan Sheridan. New York: Vintage.

——1981. "*Omnes et Singulatim,*" in *The Tanner Lectures on Human Values,* vol. II, ed. Sterling M. McMurrin. Salt Lake City: University of Utah Press, 225–54.

——1991. "Governmentality," in *The Foucault Effect: Studies in Governmentality,* ed. G. Burchell, C. Gordon, and P. Miller. Chicago: University of Chicago Press, 87–104.

Fox, Richard G., ed., 1990. *Nationalist Ideologies and the Production of National Cultures.* Washington, DC: American Anthropological Association, American Ethnological Society Monograph Series, no. 2.

Gluckman, Max, 1955. *Custom and Conflict in Africa.* Oxford: Basil Blackwell.

Gries, Peter, 1997. Review of *Zhongguo keyi shuo bu, The China Journal* 37 (Jan): 181–2.

Hale, Charles R., 1995. *Resistance and Contradiction: Miskitu Indians and the Nicaraguan State, 1894–1987.* Stanford: Stanford University Press.

Handler, Richard, 1988. *Nationalism and the Politics of Culture in Quebec.* University of Wisconsin Press.

Held, David, et al., eds, 1983. *States and Societies.* New York: New York University Press.

Hindess, Barry, 1996. "Liberalism, Socialism, and Democracy – Variations on a Government Theme," in *Foucault and Political Reason,* ed. A. Barry, T. Osborne, and N. Rose. Chicago: University of Chicago Press, 65–80.

Hobsbawm, Eric, and Terence Ranger, eds, 1966. *The Invention of Culture.* Cambridge: Cambridge University Press.

Huntington, Samuel P., 1993. "The Clash of Civilizations?", *Foreign Affairs* (Summer) 72 (3): 22–49.

——1996. *The Clash of Civilizations and the Remaking of the World Order.* New York: Simon and Schuster.

Ishihara, Shintaro, 1990. *The Japan that Can Say No,* trans. Frank Baldwin. New York: Simon and Schuster.

Khoo Boo Teik, 1995. *Paradoxes of Mahathirism.* Kuala Lumpur: Oxford University Press.

Klymlicka, Will, 1988. "Liberalism and Communitarianism," *Canadian Journal of Philosophy* 18 (2).

Leach, Edmund R., 1954. *Political Systems of Highland Burma.* London: Bell and Sons.

Mahbubani, Kishore, 1993. "The Dangers of Decadence: What the Rest can Teach the West," *Foreign Affairs* 73 (4): 1–15.

Mohamad, Mahathir, and Shintaro Ishihara, 1995a. "Will East Beat West?" *World Press Review* (December): 6–11.

Mohamad, Mahathir, and Shintaro Ishihara, 1995. *The Voice of Asia.* Tokyo: Kondasha Int.

Moore, Barrington, Jr., 1966. *The Social Origins of Dictatorship and Demo-*

cracy. New York: Beacon Press.

Nonini, Donald, 1997. "Shifting Identities, Positioned Imaginaries: Transnational Traversals and Reversals by Malaysian Chinese," *Ungrounded Empires: The Cultural Politics of Modern Chinese Transnationalism*, ed. Aihwa Ong and Don Nonini. New York: Routledge, 203–27.

Ong, Aihwa, 1995. "Anthropology, China, and Modernities: The Geopolitics of Cultural Knowledge," in *The Future of Anthropological Knowledge*, ed. Henrietta Moore. London: Routledge, 60–92.

——1997. "Chinese Modernities: Narratives of Nation and of Capitalism," in *Ungrounded Empires: The Cultural Politics of Modern Chinese Transnationalism*, ed. Aihwa Ong and Don Nonini, New York: Routledge, 171–202.

—— 1999. *Flexible Citizenship: The Cultural Logics of Transnationality*. Durham, NC: Duke University Press.

Robison, Richard, and David S. G. Goodman, 1996. "The New Rich in Asia: Economic Development, Social Status, and Political Consciousness," in *The New Rich in Asia*, ed. Richard Robison and David S. G. Goodman. London: Routledge, 1–16.

Rose, Nikolas, 1996. "Governing 'Advanced' Liberal Democracies," in *Foucault and Political Reason*, ed. A. Barry, T. Osborne, and N. Rose. Chicago: University of Chicago Press, 37–64.

Schwarz, Adam, 1994. *A Nation in Waiting: Indonesia in the 1990s*. St. Leonards, Sydney: Allen and Unwin.

Scott, James, 1976. *The Moral Economy of the Peasant*. New Haven: Yale University Press.

——1985. *Weapons of the Weak*. New Haven: Yale University Press.

Seow, Francis T., 1994. *To Catch a Tartar: A Dissident in Lee Kuan Yew's Prison*. New Haven: Yale's Southeast Asian Studies Monograph 42, Yale Center for International and Areal Studies.

Song Qiang, Zhang Zangzang, Qiao Ben, Gu Qingsheng, and Tang Zhenyu, 1996. *Zhongguo keyi shuo bu* [*The China that Can Say No*]. Beijing: Honghua Gongshang Lianhe Chubanshe.

Steinmer, G., 1993. *Regulating the Social: The Welfare State and Local Politics in Imperial Germany*. Princeton: Princeton University Press.

Swartz, Marc. J., Victor W. Turner, and Arthur Tuden, eds, 1966. *Political Anthropology*. Chicago: Aldine.

Taylor, Charles, 1995. "Cross Purposes: The Liberal-Communitarian Debate," in Charles Taylor, *Philosophical Arguments*. Cambridge, Mass.: Harvard University Press, 181–203.

Thompson, E. P., 1963. *The Making of the English Working Class*. New York: Vintage.

Tu Wei Ming, 1995. "A Confucian Perspective on Human Rights," *The Inaugural Wu The Yao Memorial Lectures, 1995*. Singapore: UNI Press.

Verdery, Katherine, 1991. *National Ideology under Socialism: Identity and Cultural Politics under Ceausescu's Romania*. Berkeley: University of California Press.

Vincent, Joan, 1978. "Political Anthropology," *Annual Review of Anthropology* 7: 175–94.

Vincent, Joan, 1990. *Anthropology and Politics: Visions, Traditions, and Trends.* Tucson: University of Arizona Press.

White, Gordon, ed., 1988. *Developmental States in East Asia.* New York: St. Martin's Press.

Wolf, Eric, 1966a. "Kinship, Friendship, and Patron-Client Relations in Complex Societies," in *The Social Anthropology of Complex Societies,* ed. Michael Banton. London: Tavistock, 1–22.

——1966b. *Peasants.* Engelwood Cliffs, NJ: Prentice-Hall.

——1969. *Peasant Wars of the Twentieth Century.* New York: Basic Books.

Worsley, Peter, 1957. *The Trumpet Shall Sound: A Study of "Cargo" Cults in Melanesia.* London: MacGibbon and Keo.

4 The Economies of Violence and the Violence of Economies

Catherine Lutz and Donald Nonini

Introduction

Anthropology is a discipline made in the century that has been made by war and the threat of war. It has been made in a century also character-ized by radical changes in the forms of political economy that set the context for the lives of the people anthropologists study. Socio-cultural anthropologists have increasingly paid attention to the latter, but rela-tively little mind to the former. War's dangers clearly account for some of this avoidance, especially when ethnography is our method. Even when looking at warfare, however, anthropological theorizing has generally skirted around the important question of what the forms of violence and the forms of political economy have to do with each other.[1] This omission has, among other things, prevented any significant attention being given to the historical, social, and political economic significance of "the end of the Cold War" and other changes in the prevailing modes of warfare. To step into this gap, in this chapter we trace a view of the historic transfor-mations in and contemporary reality of this relationship between violence and political economies. We view violence less as an epiphenomenon of economic process than a narrative and institutional force requiring its own reckoning and its own history. We view political economies as vari-ously built in and through violence rather than, as some do, parallel forms of power, the "economic" and the "military."

Our objects of interest, "violence" and "political economy", require an initial brief exposition. While violence is often taken to be a self-evident entity – in the "classic definition", brutal acts (Nordstrom, 1997) – an-thropological research has shown both its more ineffable nature (e.g. Feldman, 1994) and the practices and cultural discourses it subsumes that sometimes put non-physical violence at its center. Violence has forms both legitimate and non-legitimate (war and terrorism), state-sponsored and individual (capital punishment and murder), physical and symbolic (wife-beating and class humiliations), and anthropology has a long history of close attention to at least some of them.[2]

It is no surprise that anthropological theorizing about violence has fol-lowed the trends of theorizing on other subjects.[3] It took, for example, a sharp focus on child-rearing and the psychocultural as the root of societal violence during the period of psychological anthropology's ascendancy (Montagu, 1978)[4] and gave primacy to environmental pressures during the first burst of enthusiasm for the ecological and adaptationist view of human society (Vayda, 1976). It moved to a more politicized/historicized view in which violence is constituted through inequalities of race, gender, class, and sexuality in the wake of the Vietnam War and racist violence in the 1960s (Wolf, 1973; Ferguson, 1994) and the feminist movement's attention to violence against women (Sanday, 1997). Finally, it turned as well to a concern with violence as performative and discursive with post-structuralism's rise (Feldman, 1994; Malkki, 1995; Daniel, 1996). There has been an unabated interest in archaeological and ethno-historical work on war, focused on ancient civilizations and European colonial expansion (Brumfiel, 1983; Wiener, 1995). Many accounts remain technocentrist, this being the view that new or introduced technologies of war are the key variables explaining the incidence of war and its changing nature (Otterbein, 1985). The propensity for weaponry to take center stage is a feature of American technophilism and runs across the disciplines that study war.[5]

The processes of political economy and their shaping of both inequality and everyday life have been the focus of much study. Anthropologists and scholars in other disciplines have studied the history of "people without history" and their encounters with expanding Euroamerican capitalisms and state systems (Wolf, 1982); they have examined how the study of commodities illuminates both the history and daily character of capital-ism's diverse modes of operation (Appadurai, 1986; Mintz, 1985; Miller, 1997); considered the relationships between gender and capitalist exploi-tation and domination (Di Leonardo, 1991; Ong, 1987 and 1991), and between race relations and capitalism (Du Bois, 1935 [1962]; Robinson, 1983; Marable, 1992); and looked ethnographically and historically at subordinate groups in non-European settings who have experienced na-tional and international capitalist forces (Nash, 1979; Taussig, 1980; Sider, 1986; Rey, 1979; Dupre and Rey, 1978; Meillasoux, 1981).

These studies have focused on encounters between groups oriented around fundamentally different economic, social, and political ways of living. On the one hand, are groups whose lives have been organized by industrial and agroindustrial production based on waged or coerced labor. This production has been achieved by recourse to labor, capital, commodity, and land markets, and by arrays of economic inequality closely tied to racial, gender, and ethno-national asymmetries of power. These groups have most frequently been European in origin. On the other are indigenous groups whose livelihoods have been largely agrarian and non-industrial, and who have resorted to kin-based arrangements (e.g. lineages) and networks as alternatives to labor, capital, and land markets. While gender, age, and local/regional asymmetries do sometimes coincide with differential control over the means of production, such differences are not as large as in the former societies. These groups have resided in Africa, the Americas, most of Asia, Australia, and in Oceania prior to and during the modern era. We are not novel in referring to the arrangements of the former groups as "capitalist" and those of the latter groups as "non-capitalist."

During the last three centuries, these encounters have involved contests over the labor process in systems of production instituted under European regimes of imperialism and colonization. The outcome of these encounters is that all peoples and groups in the world have by the late 1990s come under the ambit and influence of modern capitalist systems of production, exchange, and consumption. Over the last three decades, this encompassment has taken the prevalent form of transnational or multi-national corporations whose operations are worldwide. Nonetheless, non-capitalist forms of economic activity still exist, as among certain tribal groups and others on the margins and in the interstices of the capitalist economy, even if these have become less prevalent or central to subsistence. Most recently, the spatial reorganization of the global economy has led to the emergence of certain "refuse" regions, whose populations, though fully dependent on wage labor and other capitalist markets, are superfluous or "surplus" with respect to the functioning of capitalist economies (Hoogvelt, 1997; Foerstel, 1996; Meillasoux, 1981). Many such unfortunate regions and their populations have been the objects of anthropological attention, and we discuss them – and the violences inflicted on them – below.

Six relations between violences and economies

What are some principal points of connection between violence and the prevailing economic order?[6] Although this chapter as a whole is devoted to this topic, a few preliminary words are in order. First, the rise of modern industrial capitalisms has been coextensive with the emergence of modern administrative states, and both have developed through innovations in administrative rationality associated with new industrial technologies. This has led over the last two centuries to the invention of "industrialized war" under the pressure of rivalries between modern nation-states and their power blocs, culminating in the post-war period of high nuclearism (Giddens, 1985). One implication of this point for theory is that anthropologists need to reconceptualize the implicit theories of history they use. The shift from the 1960s onward away from cultural evolutionist models of the state and economy to studies in the history of capitalism as it impinges on local communities, and emphases on "global/local" interfaces, has been helpful in this regard. It is important to extend this recognition, noting that all local settings in which contemporary ethnography is being carried out are pervaded with the rationalities associated with industrial capitalisms and with modern states; these can never be bracketed out from the field setting, nor, in contrast, should they a priori be universalized. Instead, their operation needs to be the object of ethnographic study, whether in the investigation of frontiers of commodification or of militarization.

A second connection is between the conceptual near-synonymy of certain kinds of capitalist social relations and structural violence. This represents the costs to life and its enjoyment generated by the class, gender, and race inequalities promoted within modern capitalist production (Johnston, O'Loughlin, and Taylor, 1987), especially those with a large complement of physical labor (plantations, mines, factories, etc.). Stated demographically, for example, certain groups and individuals are prone to premature suffering and death due to the injuries and wear-and-tear on their bodies suffered in wage work, and due to underemployment, unemployment, and the lack of adequate food or medical care. Gender and race categories have histories which reflect their use to underwrite the non-random costs of capitalist processes of production. Contemporary anthropological theorizations of "the body" and of race and gender relations need to incorporate structural violence, rather than ignoring it as an externality in their explanations. Ethnographers can investigate the interplay between gender and racial identities and embodiment, on the one hand, and lived-in, spoken-about experiences of physical abuse in relation to work, whether it occurs in public or domestic spaces (Dolan, 1997).

What can be called "retail" or "petty" violence carried out by "blue-collar criminals" in contrast to this "wholesale" violence constitutes a third type of relationship. Carried out or attributed to individuals and groups structurally disadvantaged by their class, race, and ethnic identities in capitalist labor and other markets, this criminality and criminalization has accelerated during the late twentieth century.[7] This is especially the case as neo-liberal programs of economic restructuring have constricted economic opportunities for the majority of populations in both the global North and South. At the same time, the vastly more consequential elite "white-collar crime" has become systematic, particularly since the expansion of speculative or "casino" capitalist forms (Calavita, Tillman, and Pontell, 1997). Ethnographers can go beyond a fascination with "deviant" criminal subcultures to study the processes of criminalization in both retail and wholesale cases. These can then be related to consumerist individualism, the mythologization of wealth, the question of "system trust", and the hypertrophy of speculation and "risk-taking" (Bourgois, 1996).

A fourth connection is in the historical relationship between modern Euro-American expansion across the lands of non-European peoples, the processes of tribalization, colonization, and imperialism, and the infliction of increasingly industrialized warfare against these peoples (Ferguson and Whitehead, 1992). Factories, mines, plantations, land surveys, population censuses, as well as global markets and trade have followed the flag – and the army regiments that held it. Recent work in historical anthropology reminds us that imperialism and colonialism have had an important cultural dimension implicating both the colonizers and the colonized (e.g. Thomas, 1994; Comaroff and Comaroff, 1991). These insights can be applied to colonial warfare (Wiener, 1995).

Fifth is the connection proposed by several economists, who argue that the very internal dynamics of capitalism promotes a "permanent arms economy." Mandel (1975: 178–217),[8] for instance, has argued that a "valorization" crisis arises from an increasing incapacity of capitalism to absorb surplus capital in further cycles of profit extraction. This crisis can be blunted or forestalled when a new sector manufacturing means of destruction is added to those manufacturing means of production and consumer goods. The sector producing weapons and other military commodities "sops up" the surplus capital realized in the other two sectors of the economy, and puts it – and an increasing number of exploitable workers – "to work" on weapons production, thus generating further profits downstream (1975: 293–300). Moreover, one by-product of arms production is state-sponsored (i.e. socially subsidized) technological innovations that can be adopted at discount elsewhere in the economy, as in, for example, computer, radar, and satellite applications (1975: 301). This connection points to a need for ethnographic study of the relationship between business cultures and commitments to nationalism and militarization (e.g. Nash, 1989), and of the politics of scientific innovation.

Finally, the instability and disorientation associated with the most recent stage of economic globalization produces violences. As a result of liberalization in transnational capital flows, of the creation of new institutions for regulating global and regional economies (IMF, WTO, World Bank, NAFTA, APEC, Mercusor, etc.) and of privatization and contraction in state revenues, the capacities of nation-states to control their economies, territories, boundaries, and resident populations have been significantly reduced (although in some cases that capacity was never fully established, as in the Pacific; Thomas, 1994). As consequences, smuggling and flows of illicit capital have accelerated, while "antisystemic movements" (Arrighi, Hopkins, and Wallerstein, 1989) have arisen, and transnational labor migration, much of it across porous borders, has increased in response to global labor markets. Nation-state militaries and police forces have dealt with these pressures by inventing new forms of "flexible" warfare. State armies, multilateral armed forces (e.g. IFOR, the United Nations), private armies, militarized police, and parastatal militias have come to wage a systematic form of "low intensity" warfare, often against stigmatized populations "outside the grids" of global capitalist activity and superfluous to labor, capital, and consumption markets. Since the end of the Cold War, moreover, these conflicts have been exacerbated by a burgeoning and highly profitable transnational small arms trade. Because the connections between this new form of warfare and the global economy have been given little attention, despite the fact that the groups and persons targeted have also often been the objects of anthropological study, we discuss it extensively below.

The implications of investigating these six connections between economies and violence are not merely theoretical, for as our limited comments above on areas needing ethnographic investigation suggest, reflection on these connections requires a fundamental rethinking of the enterprise of ethnography. Conventional views of the method too often presuppose a stability and predictability to events in the field which are belied by what appears as the randomness and capriciousness of violence visited on a field site, when "informants" flee, are tortured, or killed. They presuppose the "givenness" of the modern "host" nation-state to whose officials one applies in order to reside for an extended period of time – but who themselves may be implicated in state violence against those one "studies." They ask for specificity in describing one's field site and context, at a time when such precise description may end up in a government dossier, to be used against one's informants collectively, even if the anthropologist confers individual pseudonyms on them. They require an a priori preference for a modern subject who shows "agency" and uses language (or "discourse") precisely when the victims (and perpetrators, often) of warfare or other forms of organized violence feel themselves to be powerless and unable to speak of what was done to them, or by them. While demanding that meanings (symbols, discursive metaphors, etc.) be elicited from informants, and their interpretations be privileged, they fail to account for what appears to be the meaninglessness at the core of much violence by those who experience it, or the at times compromised positions of those who are their informants and of the ethnographer as citizen of a militarized state.

Innovations in anthropological theory also present special problems for the study of these issues. Post-structuralism usefully draws attention to rigidities in and social contexts of conceptualization of "the economy", "capitalism", and "violence." At the same time, it has discouraged attention to the systematicity of the connections between economies and violences. When issues of representation are fetishized, squeezed out is systematic attention to the cogency of what is being represented and why, or to the material conditions that generate wealth and power. In recent reformations, there is a turn away from theorizations of transformation, yet it is precisely an historical sensibility which is needed to understand how, and why, systematic violence occurs, and what economies have to do with it. While realizing the inadequacies of earlier theorizations (cultural evolutionism, modernization theory, Marxism), we hope in what follows to attempt a more modest sketching out of the theoretical terrain.

Below, we revisit these six possible connections between political economic and violent processes, while we trace historical shifts in the trajectories of both.

Transformations in political-military economies

The history of the connections between capitalist, social, and economic relations and forms of violence can be understood in terms of several major transformations which, given the uneven yet interconnected development of capitalist production systems across the globe, have overlapped and interacted in complex ways. We note four such transformations : (1) the simultaneous emergence of early industrial capitalism and the modern nation-state; (2) the expansion of both Euroamerican capitalist enterprise and forms of imperialist rule to the non-European world up to the end of the Second World War; (3) the post-war consolidation of industrial Fordism in the US, Europe, and Japan, combined with US military hegemony over the "Free World" power bloc of nominally independent new nation-states, marked by the years of high nuclearism; and (4) from the mid-1970s onward, the shift from industrial Fordism to a globalized post-Fordist flexible but disordered capitalism, associated with a neo-liberal hegemony of liberalized markets, free capital flows, and privatization, combined with new methods of "flexible" low intensity conflict strategies. We examine the first two together in the next section.

The state, mass industrial armies, and colonial capitalism

A major historical and social transformation has been the emergence of modern nation-states and the coextensive appearance of forms of industrial and agrarian capitalism. As the study by Anderson (1991) and others show, this transformation has occurred unevenly and at different times in different regions of the world. In Europe and North America, the decline of the absolutist state and rise of the modern nation-state takes place from the late seventeenth century to the mid-nineteenth, during the period of what Marx called capitalist "manufacturing", associated with mercantile trade, the establishment of Caribbean plantation economies and the African slave trade. In Asia, the formation of the modern state and the appearance of extensive industrialization in Japan dates from the Meiji Period (1868–1912). Modern state formation and the emergence of capitalist industrialization in these settings is not coincidental, for there is ample evidence that capitalist industrialization was driven, in various ways, by the elites of modernizing states in these settings.

Giddens (1985) has argued for an inherent connection between capitalist industrialization, the formation of modern nation-states, and the emergence of industrialized warfare. Each exhibits parallel processes of administrative co-ordination, labor regulation, heightened centrality of research and technological innovation, and the extensive use of information retrieval and control systems or surveillance. In the case of the modern nation-state, its warfare has chained the industrial production of vastly destructive weapons to administrative rationalities of co-ordination and control adopted by modern armies in warfare. The effects of slaughter – if not always the sheer number slain – have been greatest in the non-European world, particularly in the "tribal zone" (Ferguson and Whitehead, 1992). Moreover, Euroamerican industrial warfare waged abroad has left its traces on British state formation, as Corrigan and Sayer (1985) have pointed out. They discuss the ways in which the integration of Scots, Irish, and Welsh into the British army in defense of empire confirmed their integration into a modern nation-state under ethnic English hegemony; index the ways in which imperial wars reinforced spokesmen who held that "the appropriate model of factory, farm, office or school discipline was military" (1985: 152); and present evidence of the increased representation and prominence of army and naval officers in the British Parliament during the decades of Victorian imperialism (1985: 153).

In Asia, Oceania, Africa, and Latin America, therefore, the simultaneous emergence of the modern nation-state form and capitalist enterprise took place in the course of a second major transformation, the geographic expansion and consolidation of Euroamerican forms of imperial rule and colonial capitalist enterprise from the mid-nineteenth century to the end of the Second World War. Here we examine briefly one such episode – the coming of European settlement to New Zealand and the Maori Wars of 1845–72.

Settling New Zealand, and the geoeconomics of imperial war European and North American white expansions into the lands of non-European peoples in the nineteenth and twentieth centuries recurrently involved military incursions, whether the justifying ideology was "manifest destiny" or the "civilizing mission." Historians of modern Euroamerican imperialism distinguish between the colonizations of settlement – as in the case of North America, Australia, and New Zealand – and colonizations of rule, as in the case of India, and most of South-East Asia, although most colonizations have been a mixture of the two. In remarking that the objectives of Euroamerican colonists have been land and mineral resources in the case of settlement colonies, and control of labor power and markets in colonies of rule, we are not being economistic in holding that, historically, there have been close connections between modern Euroamerican imperialism and military conflict. As cultural formations, modern imperialisms have been organized around grand racial projects which presume control not only over non-European peoples and material resources, but also over the cultural rhetorics and practices that define the essence of these peoples ("a backward race"), the territories they have occupied ("an empty land"), and their material resources ("things the natives have no use for" such as gold or petroleum) (Said, 1993; Spurr, 1993). "Economic" activities as such are inseparable from the forays of modern imperialisms that have come to define the relative ranking of different human groups, the role of technological innovation, and economic "values" as determined by early modern imperial markets in people, labor, commodities, and land. From the early nineteenth century through the post-war period of independent nation-states, an increasingly industrialized form of warfare conducted against non-European peoples has been evident. We discuss here one such campaign, the protracted New Zealand wars from 1845 to 1872 that pitted the increasingly rationalized forces of Anglo-European (*pakeha*) (i.e. British imperial and white New Zealander) troops against the indigenous ethnic groups of New Zealand subsumed under the name Maori.

Belich (1986) describes aptly what was at stake in the New Zealand wars. During the early nineteenth century, two zones of sovereignty divided the North Island of New Zealand – the zone of indigenous, longstanding settlement by Maori, and the British-controlled zone which was expanding due to the alienation of Maori land to colonists. Both zones were politically autonomous yet ecologically and economically symbiotic, but neither autonomy nor interdependence squared with the British Victorian racial project of empire.

The great threat to the Maori-European symbiosis was less a material conflict than a conflict of aspirations. A situation of parity with, or inferiority to, peoples like the Maori simply did not accord with British expectations. The British were not satisfied with part of the land, part of the economy, or part of the government (Belich, 1986: 304). Yet *pakeha* paid a high price for their racial arrogance, for, as Belich puts it, "with all due respect to British humanitarianism, one reason why New Zealand settlers did not treat the Maoris as their Australian counterparts did the Aborigines was that, when they tried, they got killed" (ibid). By the 1840s, violent encounters had escalated to the point where they not only involved New Zealand settlers, but also, in increasing numbers, both British imperial and other colonial troops seeking to subdue autonomous Maori in the inland North Island of New Zealand.

Over a protracted period of engagements from 1845 to 1872, a total population of 60,000 Maori men, women, and children dispersed over 3.5 million acres fought and defeated regiments of as many as 18,000 British imperial and colonial forces. In any one engagement, British forces not only outnumbered the Maori but also had greater firepower. Over twenty years' battles in New Zealand, they grew increasingly superior. Moreover, the British officer corps, veterans of the Crimean War, were well-trained, and some were brilliant strategists.

Yet for several years, Maori warriors successfully defended their lands, and inflicted heavy casualties on British troops, with as many as 40 percent of British forces killed in some battles. Maori avoided open battle and massed assaults, and instead constructed defensive fortifications on tactically commanding ground. Within these fortifications were underground earthen and timber anti-artillery bunkers, and maze-like trenches dominated by hidden firing positions. British imperial infantry forces, on the other hand, had been well trained in the mid-nineteenth-century European military techniques of set-piece engagements using massed infantry volleys and disciplined charges of the enemy's positions following artillery bombardment. They were confronted with false targets that would draw infantry charges, whose lines of soldiers would be cut down by fire from Maori defenders.

Despite their innovative resistance, however, Maori were finally overwhelmed by the sheer number of British troops assaulting them, and, most critically as the years of warfare wore on, the indigenous horticultural economy could not sustain Maori warriors against British forces with their rationalized mobile logistics of supply, transport, and communications. Henceforth British colonial rule changed from a legalistic claim appended to a coastal commercial center to the actual, hands-on administrative transformation of the hinterlands of New Zealand. Maori capitulation, far from complete in many areas of the North Island, was nonetheless sufficient to allow the process of white settlement inland to proceed, with the eventual establishment of a *pakeha* pastoral capitalism on lands previously occupied by the troublesome indigenes.

Structural violence: capitalism's "normal" effects? Under specific geographic and historical circumstances, structural violence is one of capitalism's "normal" effects, in that injury is done systematically to a large proportion of the population of a society – those who survive through their labor for wages. Although alienation has been seen by most political economists as pivotal to the process of exploitation which defines the capitalist wage-labor relation, here we point instead to the physical wearing-down of the bodies of working women, men, and children which at times occurs "normally" in labor processes, and to the physical injuries, illnesses, and premature deaths imposed on working people which arise due to insufficient wages and working abuse. In *Capital*, Marx for polemical purposes focused on the equilibrium condition in which the laborer is recompensed in wages equivalent to the cost of reproducing her labor power. He of course finessed what is in part a cultural issue – the definition of what it takes to adequately reproduce oneself – with an economistic gloss. Yet it is also quite clear that the history of capitalism has episodically been rife with instances where workers receive less in wages than they need to reproduce their labor power and work under conditions of physical danger and stress; when no longer fit for further work due to injury or illness, they have simply been replaced with other workers. They have been studied ethnographically by Murray (1981); Scheper-Hughes (1992); and Farmer, Connors, and Simmons (1996), among others. Johnston, O'Loughlin, and Taylor (1987: 254) bluntly state the cost of all this when they write that "the major cost of premature death in the world is structural violence."

Death, injury, and illness of this sort occur most frequently where labor-power is overabundant and thus easily replaced, and the work is unskilled, as in the case of agroindustrial and extractive enterprises in the global South. As we argue below, not only do these laborers and their families suffer from structural violence, but they are also the special objects of state terror aimed at protecting new global elites and the cores they reside in. Unlike these elites, they benefit little from industrialization or the consumption of new commodities. Thus, for example, the sugarcane cutters of Bom Jesus in Brazil's rural Nordeste state studied by Scheper-Hughes (1992) live in a constant state of undernourishment, chronic fatigue, and illness. Chronically underemployed due to the seasonal nature of plantation work, Bom Jesus sugarcane cutters tried to "make ends meet" during a period from the late 1960s through the mid-1980s marked by severe inflation, an upward redistribution of income, and falling public health expenditures, while undergoing the terrors of military rule and the rigors of a neo-liberal "structural adjustment" program imposed on Brazil by the World Bank. Working adults engaged in hard labor ate between 1,500 and 1,700 calories per day, while their children ate far less and suffered far more (1992: 157). During these years, infant and child mortality rates increased precipitously. Mothers anxiously watched their children for attacks of "madness from hunger" (*delirio de fome*), while they themselves suffered "nervous sickness" (*nervoso*), due to combined hunger, sickness, fatigue, and anxieties over uncertain incomes and the violence directed against them by state paramilitary death squads. As children fell ill, their mothers engaged in a desperate triage, using scarce emotional and economic resources to assist some to recover, while leaving others to die.

Such conditions of life still mark what passes for "normal" capitalism in many regions of the world. However, most scholars have until recently seen "normal" capitalism instead as large-scale, geographically concentrated industrial enterprise, and proposed a rather different narrative of labor and life centered on it – one generally of worker "embourgeoisment" and increased and widespread prosperity. We now turn to industrial Fordism and its connections to violence.

Post-war industrial Fordism, US military hegemony, and high nuclearism, 1946-73

In the years after the Second World War, the connections between warfare and the rise of the United States to a position of world hegemony were close and inextricable. According to Baran and Sweezy (1966), only two phenomena have prevented monopoly capitalism over the twentieth century from falling into a terminal crisis due to its incapacity to absorb the capital surplus its own systems of exploitation have generated: war and "epoch-making innovations" such as the steam engine, railroads, and automobiles. Both phenomena generated not only new commodities but also new markets and new ways of organizing everyday life, and both were crucial to the new postwar prominence of the United States.[9]

The economic effects of war, Baran and Sweezy argue, occur in two phases – "combat" and "aftermath." In the case of the United States in the Second World War, during the combat phase, civilian demand for goods was forcibly deferred and production redirected toward the production of weapons and supplies for the war effort (Baran and Sweezy, 1966: 223–4). In the process, the manufacture of weapon systems was rationalized through technological innovations and the systematic monitoring of products' effectiveness, providing the prototype for post-war high-tech industrial production (Giddens, 1985: 241–2), and new commodities and technologies invented – for example computers, radar, atomic fission, artificial rubber, penicillin. In the aftermath phase, industrial production was regeared to meet pent-up civilian demand, while much of the wartime industrial infrastructure had to be scrapped – all this being extraordinarily wasteful, but absorbing enormous amounts of surplus capital.

War, of course, did not end with the Second World War. With the advent of the nuclear arms race of the Cold War (and its "hot" phase of the Korean War), Baran's and Sweezy's "epoch-making innovation"[10] – the mass-produced automobile – came into its own. A variety of conditions resulted in the car being added to food, clothing, and shelter as a necessity and central cost of most households. The construction of highways on a massive scale in these years was facilitated in the United States through the use of national security rhetoric which portrayed the highways as key for military transport and evacuation of cities under nuclear attack; the automobile and development interests that would profit from this infrastructural investment otherwise confronted a Congressional interest in minimal non-military spending (Sherry, 1995). During the 1950s and 1960s, the existence of such a growing infrastructure, combined with retooled wartime mass production – now directed toward car manufacturing and deferred civilian demand and the new domesticity in refurbished women's roles – led to ubiquitous automobile use and the suburbanization of a new mass-consuming population. Extensive population and business relocation in turn reorganized the North American landscape, and was responsible in part for the (temporarily) self-sustaining cycles of economic growth in the US economy through the early 1970s. During the same years, in Western Europe and Japan, the reconstruction of infrastructures destroyed by the Second World War, funded by US private and state capital (the Marshall Plan), and under the "protection" of the US nuclear umbrella, created new prosperities elsewhere.

In the United States, the outcome of these post-war transformations was the heyday of industrial Fordism,[11] represented as a stable and affluent social and economic order – one that could serve as the "free world's" model of "success" set against the Cold-War foil of Soviet totalitarianism. Rationalized Taylorist production methods separated management, design, and control from the execution of the labor process, and provided the basis for mass production of commodities. As Mandel (1975) noted, these methods extended to the sector producing means of destruction – to the mass production of nuclear weaponry, missile delivery systems, and "conventional" arms of all kinds. The large numbers of well-paid workers – overwhelmingly white and male – engaged in such production thus served as new mass consumers as well for new post-war markets in standardized consumer goods. A growing and flourishing economy in overall equilibrium was thus created, where at least in theory every citizen wore equally capacious hats as "consumer" and "producer." "Big government" used Keynesian fiscal policies to stimulate specific sectors through government expenditures – notably the nuclear and "conventional" arms industries and their ancillary sectors, which in turn favored the growth of specific regions – the West Coast and the North-East – over others in the US (Markusen et al., 1991). The inter-war programs of the Rooseveltian welfare state expanded to provide broader funding for the education, health care, and Social Security services crucial to upward social mobility – beginning with the massive welfare program of the "GI Bill" which, among other things, privileged males and allowed large numbers of Jewish and other Eastern European males to become "white folks" in the US (Sacks, 1994).

Although we can speak qualifiedly of a generalized prosperity, it is clear that the celebratory romance of the "American Dream" with its Fordist underpinnings driven by the Cold War had serious shortcomings. To start with, although labor unions ceded control over the labor process to "big business" in return for the high wages and benefits of the new industrial order, many did so only when intimidated by the McCarthy anti-communist terror, which broke the back of radical labor unions. Moreover, labor unions were the province, largely, of white males. Women and minorities, especially African-Americans, were selectively excluded from the economy's affluence. Militarization had not only benefited white males, who received veterans benefits and high-paying military industrial jobs in disproportionate numbers, but had deflated the demand for a social welfare state, which was increasingly associated with and then dismissed along with the needs of African-Americans and women and children (Hardin, 1991). After the Second World War, white women, who had been called into the wartime industrial labor force in large numbers, were forcibly – by law, layoffs, and sexist rhetoric – retrenched from the industrial labor force, and relegated to new suburban "homes" or to poorly paid secondary labor markets like part-time and seasonal clerical work. This dependent status further ensconced them in the position of objects of patriarchal "protection." This only began to change with the advent of the women's movements in the 1960s. Minorities, also drawn into wartime employment, were after the war largely banished to other secondary labor markets in rural and urban casualized physical labor, until the changes associated with the Civil Rights movement and affirmative action in the 1960s – changes prompted, in part, by the rhetorical view of the United States as a "land of freedom and opportunity" within the public polemics of the Cold War (Horne, 1986).

Although state-induced heavy industrialization characterized the Soviet Union and officially socialist states of Eastern Europe, in retrospect, the social mobilization and economic wastage brought on by the nuclear and "conventional" arms races of the Cold War critically deformed their economies, beggared their civilian populations, and eventually led to the end of the Cold War, political fragmentation, and the emergence of new forms of "mafia capitalism" throughout the ex-socialist states, about which little is known ethnographically (Czegledy 1998).

In Latin America, Oceania, Asia outside of Japan and China, and Africa, military and political assaults took place on what the US government viewed as "Communist" or "Marxist" revolutionary movements during the first two post-war decades. These movements for independence and decolonization had formed not only in response to the loosened threads of geostrategic control of the colonies brought about by the Second World War, but also to the newly reasserted controls and regulation by Euro-American nation-states and private corporations over Asian, African, and Latin American minerals, energy, foodstuffs, and raw materials, and over those rural populations who produced them. Industrial Fordist economies were nowhere in evidence. Instead, plantations, mines, cash-crop sharecropping, and so on were complex combinations of agroindustrial, tributary, and kinship-based modes of economy, characterized by extraordinarily high levels of exploitation, physical, sexual, and structural violence, and undergirded by racial color lines and gender hierarchies. Colonial and post-colonial conditions of "unequal exchange" (Emmanuel, 1972) pitted rural producers against Euro-American-based oligosonies, marketing boards, and trading cartels. The latter underwrote new post-war North American, European, and Japanese prosperities by delivering industrial inputs at regulated low prices and providing foreign markets for excess manufactured goods.

These colonial arrangements were challenged by radical decolonization movements, many of whom had guerrilla forces, in Vietnam, Malaya, Kenya, and elsewhere. The US Government and its elite allies in these regions employed Manichaean Cold-War rhetorics to demonize these movements and their supporters, and engaged in counter-insurgency campaigns to destroy their civil bases of support and military forces, inspired by an early post-war precursor of American Low Intensity Conflict doctrine, discussed below. For instance, Malaya's rubber plantations and tin mines were the largest dollar-generating colony of the sterling zone (essential to a bankrupt Britain repaying Second World War Lend Lease loans from the US). From 1951 to 1957, a unified state civilian, military, and police command, using British imperial troops and local police, imposed martial law, hunted down, hung, imprisoned, and banished Malayan Communist guerrillas and their civilian supporters, and forcibly relocated 500,000 rural Chinese civilians to "New Villages"[12] under the rubric of "winning the hearts and minds" of the people (Nonini, 1992; Short, 1975).

Thus, in Malaya and elsewhere, a global periphery of new nation-states, now called the "Third World", came into being and was consolidated through unequal exchange, economic and cultural imperialism, and military repression, to secure the prosperity of the Euro-American cores of the "free world." Within the new post-war *pax Americana*, "development" discourse arose to deal with the contradictions of capitalist domination in this periphery, along the lines of the Cold-War inspired chauvinisms of "modernization theory", as in W. W. Rostow's *The Stages of Growth: A Non-Communist Manifesto*, published in 1960 (see Escobar, 1995). From early on, the "development" of the new nation-states included the provision of military, police, and counter-insurgency logistical "assistance" by the US Government and its overseas proxies – a militarization with devastating contemporary consequences, as we show below.

Changing modes of warfare   The twentieth century has most obviously been divided into a pre- and post-nuclear warfare age, but nuclearism's characteristics as a mode of warfare have not always been explicitly recognized. For example, it has allowed (although not required) smaller armies, therefore potentially reversing the effects of the mass mobilizations that nineteenth-century armies effected (such as the extension of civil rights to those segments of the population called on for military work). On the other hand, increasing focus on warfare's technological development requires more engineering and less manufacturing labor, which has contributed to social inequalities of race, class, and gender in advanced industrial states (Markusen et al., 1991).[13]

Most importantly, however, this mode of warfare radically eroded the practical distinction between soldier and civilian, as each was equally a target of the other side's weaponry (a distinction also not in abundant evidence in colonial wars). In this way, the power of the state has been tremendously amplified: the "balance of terror", bolstered by the ideology of the national security state, gave political leaders in both democratic and authoritarian regimes a greater claim on citizen trust. Going beyond the protection rackets of early states (Tilly, 1985), nuclear states were trusted with the future of the race. This trust and other domestic benefits are what Kaldor's understanding of the Cold War places in central view (Kaldor, 1990). Theorizing it as the Imaginary War, she sees it gaining its real militarizing impetus and force from its management of internal social divisions in the countries involved rather than any actual defensive goals it achieved. Despite its importance to planetary life in this century of anthropology, the only truly ethnographic work on nuclear warfare culture has been the innovative work of Krasniewitz (1992) on nuclear protest and of Gusterson (1996) on nuclear weapons designers.

The nuclear age has displayed two other major shifts in the mode of warfare. First has been the rise of what Virilio (1990) calls the visual mode of warfare and what Gray (1997) characterizes as post-modern war. These two theorists draw attention to the new social relations of war required or facilitated by the camera,[14] the computer, and the mass media, technologies that vastly increase the possibilities of "war by information control." In Gray's brilliant analysis, "As a weapon, as a myth, as a metaphor, as a force multiplier, as an edge, as a trope, as a factor, and as an asset, information (and its handmaidens – computers to process it, multimedia to spread it, systems to represent it) has become . . . the single most significant military factor" (1997: 22). The interests of military institutions turn to increased budgets for research and information technologies, as well as to secrecy, threatening democratic social life in the process.

The second shift has been the rise in the North of counter-insurgency strategies that led to the formation of Low Intensity Conflict doctrine in the 1980s in response to the rise of anti-colonial armies in the South. This doctrine is in part the outcome of the "falling rate of military effectiveness" (Schaeffer, 1989: 6) brought about by the nuclear stalemate. The effects of this have been grotesquely evident to the anthropologists working in countries like Guatemala, El Salvador, Vietnam, or Laos (Carmack, 1988, Green, 1994; on community response, see especially Smith-Nonini, 1997; and Starn, 1999). One consequence of this shift (and of the rise of "New Wars", noted below) has been a speed-up in the century-long, global process of civilizing war deaths. That is, by the mid-1990s, only 10 per cent of all war deaths were soldiers' (Sivard, 1996); more children than soldiers, in fact, have died in most recent wars (Nordstrom, 1998). A consequence of this mode of warfare has also been a radical increase in the number of refugees worldwide (Manz, 1988) and what Malkki (1995) terms the deterritorialization of identity.

From militarism to militarization: High nuclearism in Massachusetts We see the effects of the period of high nuclearism on American life in Nash's (1989) ethnography of "the culture of militarism" in Pittsfield, Massachusetts, and the role of the General Electric factory in the local economy and in workers' lives. During her fieldwork, this plant (which employed some three-fourths of the working-age male population of Pittsfield in the 1960s) produced the Bradley Fighting Tank and naval ballistics and guidance systems for Trident and Polaris nuclear missiles. During the thirty years from the Korean War through the 1980s, the GE plant and its Ordnance Division in Pittsfield displayed, at a local scale, many of the changes toward flexibilization we have noted which connect up military operations and economic production. By the 1980s, there was an increased reliance on the production of military weapons rather than consumer goods, the downsizing of employment in and offshoring of consumer goods production, the elimination of jobs through robotization and automation, the establishment of new high-tech work for which many local older workers were untrained (and so were laid off), ties with GE expansion projects in Japan and Europe, the use of contingency workers, and high segmentation of job tasks and differential wages by gender. And, by the 1980s, the GE Corporation had 120 employees in their Washington DC office to lobby Congress and the Pentagon for business.

GE workers and their labor unions in Pittsfield find themselves enmeshed in the "corporate hegemony" of a culture of militarism. Managers in the Ordnance Division occupy prestigious roles in local service agencies and community organizations (school boards, hospital boards, etc.) and organize "Good Neighbor Fund" drives to donate funds to needy local charities. Veterans' groups play a prominent legitimizing public role on holidays such as Memorial Day. GE corporate culture binds militarism into the normal life of GE corporate employees: for example, on General Electric Family Day 1985, over 14,000 GE employees and their families toured the Ordnance Systems facility, while children were allowed to don full battle dress and ride in a miniature Bradley Fighting Tank, and a videotape showed the GE-produced Trident guidance system intercept an enemy missile. Yet workers showed ambivalence on moral grounds toward their arms production work – "liking the work itself but objecting to the end product" – while others engaged in small acts of evasion by such tactics as seeking assignment to work in some other division of the plant than Ordnance. Yet by the mid-1980s, the dominant motif for workers and their labor unions at the GE plant in Pittsfield was job security – not a surprise given the restructuring that GE was then undergoing – and consequently an increasing number flocked to vote for conservative candidates supporting Reagan's military build-up in state and national elections.

Nash's ethnography is centered around the concept of militarism, a concept that has been in wide use in the field of peace and war studies. In doing this, she counters evolutionary assumptions common to research that often "others" militarism to distant (atavistic) times and places. Anthropology has not yet, but should, take up the related concept of militarization which avoids focus on the discrete event of war and draws attention to broader processes of war preparation. Militarization is defined by Geyer as "the contradictory and tense social [material and discursive] process in which civil society organizes itself for the production of *violence*" (Geyer, 1989: 79). The material changes involve alteration in the labor and resources allocated to military purposes, including shaping other institutions around military goals.[15] Levels of material militarization are often indexed by such things as changing military employment as a proportion of all employment or military spending as a percentage of

GNP. Discursive changes include shifts in societal beliefs and values in ways necessary to legitimate the use of organized force, the organization of large standing armies and their leaders, and higher taxes or tribute to pay for them. Militarization is evident in the rise and fall of military imagery in popular culture, in more violent masculinities, or in discourses portraying the world as a place of threat. There is, however, no simple list of universal "military values" whose rise indexes a process of cultural militarization, as cultural forms shape military values and practices and vice versa. For example the American cultural faith in technology supports a relatively high ratio of arms to men in its military, something which might otherwise be thought of as a natural outcome of the state's affluence or of that ratio's superior efficacy as a modality of war.[16]

As Geyer's definition claims, militarization is a tense process, because it can create conflict between elites who might benefit from militarization (for example, when it facilitates expanding international markets) and those elites or non-elites who might not profit, and between women and the men who may more likely be either casualties or beneficiaries, or between classes who bear different costs of war. It is contradictory in two senses: militarization and demilitarization may occur simultaneously as in the rise of "environmentally proactive militaries" (Ross, 1996) or "peacekeeping operations"; similarly, controlled demilitarization in one dimension, say, reducing the number of military officers or their social influence, may accompany increased militarization in another, such as the effectiveness of military violence. An example of the latter is the case of professionalized or "modernized" militaries as in the "Panama model" installed after the US invasion of that country in 1989 (Robinson, 1996: 66). And contradictory processes can be set in motion by militarization: both localism and federalism are energized when military spending is spread across a national landscape, and income inequality is increased by arms imports while at least temporarily decreased by higher levels of military employment (e.g. Sharda, 1988).[17] Anthropology might add this processual concept to its more standard tools such as urbanization, globalization, state formation, and colonialization.

The end of the Cold War: Post-Fordist disorder, neo-liberal projects, and new forms of flexible warfare

In the years 1973–4, the industrial Fordist economies of the US and Europe entered into a period of deep crisis due to forces which had gradually intensified over the previous two decades – inflation, dependence on imported oil, and above all, declining corporate productivity and profitability (Harvey, 1989: 141–6). This crisis led Euroamerican private enterprises to reorganize in fundamental ways with consequences extending far beyond the Euroamerican and Japanese core economies, to engender a new era of "flexibility." Although we would argue that much of what passes for "globalization" is not novel, ubiquitous, or inevitable, nonetheless there have been fundamental economic, geopolitical, and military shifts, and that these are connected in turn to new forms of "flexible warfare."

Since the 1960s new communication and transport technologies (e.g. computers, faxes, satellite communication, ship containerization, cheap air transport, miniaturization) have made it possible for corporations to centralize managerial control while geographically decentralizing operations (Harvey, 1989). "Virtual corporations" headquartered in the US or Hong Kong market commodities under their own names by subcontracting their orders out to assembly plants (which in turn subdivide tasks out to their own subcontractors) in southern China, Thailand, Mexico, or South Korea in a transnational division of labor in production, in order to provide "just-in-time" delivery to customers (Harvey, 1989: 156; *Barrons*, 1998: 43–4). The subsidiaries and subcontractors are located in nation-states previously identified as in the "Third World", but now seen as "newly industrializing countries" (NICs) such as Singapore, Brazil, Argentina, Thailand, Malaysia, and Mexico (Fröbel, Heinrichs, and Kreye, 1980). This peripheral industrialization has generated new economic and political elites in these countries. Meanwhile, the populations of less favored regions, such as sub-Saharan Africa or New Guinea, become progressively smaller players in the global economy, relevant only, if at all, for the minerals, fossil fuels, and natural resources their lands possess.

Central to the changes of flexible capitalism have been shifts in labor markets and corporate controls over the labor process. The new business climate entails "downsizing" workforces, "outsourcing" work to subcontractors and consultants, creating large labor forces of temporary, part-time and seasonal workers[18] who replace previously permanent employees, and "offshoring" production. There has also been an inverse movement of transnational labor migrants from the peripheries to the core's "global cities" (Sassen, 1991), its regional metropolises and rural agroindustrial areas. Often illegal immigrants, they join a new native labor force of persons (in both the cores and newly industrializing peripheries) who work as semi-free industrial laborers – including not only migrants, but also impoverished inner-city minority residents, children, prisoners, and debt-peons, who engage in the most temporary, dangerous, and poorly-paid labor in the sweatshops of the new global economy (Greider, 1997; Harvey, 1989 and 1996). The surveillance and disciplining of these underemployed, semi-free, and dependent working populations has become one of the tasks of new paramilitarized police forces – whether these take the form of the anti-immigrant patrols by the US Immigration and Naturalization

Service along the US Mexico Border region (Dunn, 1996), the "disappearance of street children" in São Paulo, Brazil (Scheper-Hughes, 1992), or the recent rousting, torture, and deportation of illegal Indonesian immigrants in Malaysia by police during the Asian financial crisis of early 1998 (*Far Eastern Economic Review*, 1998).

These new conditions have drastically reduced the numbers of Euroamerican and Japanese workers employed in high-paying work, cut the power of labor unions, and decreased real wages and benefits (Harrison, 1994; Martin and Schumann, 1997). The prior stability of core industrial Fordism, which depended on the existence of a mass consumer population of well-paid male workers to purchase the commodities they produced, has now been destroyed, and as a result the living conditions of many have deteriorated, the more so as state welfare programs have been eliminated (Davis, 1986) . One of the most serious socio-political effects of these changes has been the appearance of new xenophobic nationalist and anti-immigrant right-wing and protofascist movements in the US and Western Europe – these sometimes support forms of new warfare by US and European state militaries against foreign "Others" discussed below.

These changes have at least temporarily increased corporate profits, and have generated huge surpluses of liquid capital. Given neo-liberal projects that have "opened" national markets to transnational investment, this capital now flows instantaneously between sites where it lands in the form of investments, nests for a while, then departs as quickly as it came to other sites offering higher profits. The dynamics of capital flow and accumulation operate largely independently of the "real" economies in which such capital, temporarily, is found. There has been a worldwide hypertrophy of "fictitious" financial capital, as many kinds of speculation have become rampant through the instantaneous transfers of capital and information by bankers, stock brokers, corporate treasurers, mutual and hedge fund traders, bond brokers, currency traders, and by various "operators" over vast distances via fax and computer communication for investment in nationally based stock, bond, real estate, currency, mortgage, commodity, commodity futures, options, indexes, and derivatives markets (Greider, 1997; Henwood, 1997) Furthermore, there are markets in illicit arms, drugs, and, by some accounts (Scheper-Hughes, 1992), adopted children and human organs.

The amount of such fictitious capital thus being cycled and moved around the earth in any one day is vastly greater than the amount of wealth produced by the processes that generate real wealth: in May 1996, each day, US $1.25 trillion was transferred between the world's major banks, to the point that "an amount equal to a year's US gross domestic product . . . turns over in a week, and total world product in about a month" of such transfers (Henwood, 1997). Offshore financial centers that cycle capital tax-free into and out of national markets have come to be vital sites in the new global economy; because of their off-ledger financial role, several have been the target of US military action – Panama, Grenada, Kuwait, Lebanon (Maurer, 1995). The emergence of a global casino economy with speculators in bankers' garb making "clever bets" and "hot deals" with time horizons of a few seconds, minutes, or hours has been devastating to national economies, and has become a source of great instability. Recently, the extraordinary financial crisis afflicting South-East and North-East Asia has arisen from the precipitous withdrawal of Western European, US and Japanese bank loans from corporations in Indonesia, Thailand, and South Korea, followed by rapid currency devaluation brought on by currency speculators (Wade and Veneroso, 1998). It has generated a region-wide depression in investment, employment, and consumption that currently threatens to engulf regional markets outside Asia. In this instance, the crisis has set off scapegoating violence against ethnic Chinese in Indonesia, and against illegal Indonesian labor migrants in Malaysia.

Over the same period since the mid-1970s, several major political changes have seriously weakened the fiscal and governing powers of nation-states. First, national governments everywhere have loosened their controls over currency exchange rates[19] and international capital flows. Meanwhile new international organizations pressing for liberalization in transnational capital flows and trade (e.g. International Monetary Fund) have reinforced these policy changes, while political and economic elites have created multilateral "free trade" zones (e.g. European Union) which make national borders increasingly irrelevant to economic activity (Greider, 1997).

Second, the dominant neo-liberal ideology of the new transnational political and economic elites has been implemented in various neo-liberal projects (Reaganism, Thatcherism, etc.) which have entailed the privatization and minimization of state functions, the reduction of state expenditures in order to balance budgets, discipline domestic labor, and attract global investment capital, and the elimination of Keynesian social programs (Tickell and Peck, 1995; Greider, 1997). According to Reno (1995) and Hoogvelt (1997: 175–6), the structural adjustment programs of the IMF and World Bank central to these projects have critically weakened African "patrimonial states" whose elites previously used state wealth not only to aggrandize their own and their supporters' wealth, but also more crucially to "buy off" their opposition. Post-colonial political divisions in these nation-states tended to develop along the lines of elite ethnic cleavage instituted during the colonial period by imperial strategies of divide and rule. Until the 1980s, post-colonial patrimonial states overcame these divisions between elites through coalitions based on sharing state resources. As structural adjustment programs have shrunken state treasuries, such elite accommodations based on state spoils have been destroyed. Elites of ethnic groups opposed to the state have then sought to develop their own power bases through military means. Ethnic strife, warfare, and terror have then ensued. (That "democracy" rather than civil war emerged in Latin America during a similar parallel period of structural adjustment is no doubt due to the prior presence of military juntas and the terror they inflicted on populations in South and Central America.)

Third, these neo-liberal projects set nation-states in competition to attract investors (and thus employment) by offering the lowest possible wages, most permissive environmental standards, and the most favorable "business climates" in what Brecher and Costello (1994) have aptly called a "race to the bottom." The downward spiral of competition continues on the subnational and local levels, where its effects and connections to violence might be observed ethnographically. Popular discontent, criminalization of large numbers of residents, and scapegoating of vulnerable minorities have been the results. As a source of instability which has generated the violence of new forms of warfare, these projects cannot be underestimated. At the same time, the emphasis on state privatization and subcontracting applies to the state military sector, creating novel solutions, such as proxy armies for hire (Sheppard, 1998). Finally, the power of nation-states has grown weaker as large investors and speculators have supplanted governments' political prerogatives with their own.[20]

Even as the sources of instability increase,[21] post-Fordist globalization has set up a radical reorganization in the geography of world wealth distribution, and therefore in the spatiality of surveillance, policing, and warmaking which, in part, guard this wealth. Hoogvelt (1997: 239–40) refers to a "three-tier structure of concentric circles" of increasing poverty and disparities in wealth. In the inner circle are the economic and political elites of all nation-states, irrespective of location, constituting by generous definition about 20 percent of the world's population. Hoogvelt's second tier or circle includes those laboring groups, 20 to 30 percent of world population, who compete desperately for employment, and suffer high levels of structural violence. The outer circle represents everyone else – populations that are "already effectively excluded from the global system . . . performing neither a productive function, nor presenting a potential consumer market" (p. 240). These populations are those most impoverished and marginalized in the new global scenario. The new differentiation is candidly described even by some of those committed to globalization, such as John Reed, the Chairman of Citicorp Bank, one of the largest banks in the United States, who said in the late 1980s:

> There are five billion people living on earth. Probably 800 million of them live in societies that are bankable and probably 4.2 billion are living within

societies that in some very fundamental way are not bankable. I think it's a great danger as we look out between now and the turn of the century that this distinction between bankable and the unbankable parts of the world could become more aggravated.

(quoted in Hoogvelt, 1997: 83)

Drawing on Hoogvelt's and others' analyses, we propose that increasingly the core of the new global order is a transnational network, the global urban archipelago of wealth, *within a sea of differentiated poverty which constitutes its periphery*. What makes an archipelago is not so much the geographic proximity of its islands (decreasingly important in this age of cheap air transport) but the connections between their elite inhabitants.[22] These connections include their shared identifications with modernity and its values (especially those of cosmopolitan consumption), their electronically mediated identities, and the actual functional ties of trade, investment, and administration linking its islands.[23]

Increasingly, these privileged islands of the archipelago take the form of fortified and garrisoned locales where non-elites visit only to work and are otherwise at risk of police violence – whether within the affluent gated communities or controlled-access buildings of New York, São Paulo, Cape Town, New Delhi, Atlanta, or Singapore (Martin and Schumann, 1997). Under these conditions, policing and surveilling the poor residents of the "waters" surrounding the islands of the archipelago – those who seek by informal means to gain illicit access to its riches – have become increasingly more intricate and spatially specific, yet also more brutal and pervasive (with non-criminals / non-combatants being figured as proportionately fewer and fewer) among the populations targeted. In short, we find increasing evidence for the emergence of urban and peri-urban "free-fire" zones where the poor are concentrated, and where police and military violence creates *cordons sanitaires* which insulate the elites living in the archipelago's islands from the negative effects of globalization. Examples include the Los Angeles Police Department's paramilitary treatment of the residents of South Central Los Angeles during the uprising of summer 1992 (Davis, 1993), and the "waste disposal" solution – murder and disappearance – adopted by Brazil's military police against its poor urban children (Scheper-Hughes, 1992). In the hinterlands, beyond these free-fire zones, the scope and extent of state military and police powers have weakened toward strategies of indifference, leaving the populations of rural areas subject to brigandage, mafia domination, and marauding by private ethnic armies. The exception in rural areas is government counter-insurgency directed strategically against populations whose land contains precious minerals, energy, or natural resources.

The new global disorder has created large numbers of surplus populations – underemployed and unemployed proletarians, displaced tribals, forcibly urbanized ex-peasants, landless rural wage laborers, transnational and domestic labor migrants, refugees, racially stigmatized inner-city minorities, and entire populations of "unbankable" nation-states with little realizable wealth except perhaps the minerals or petroleum under their soils. These populations increasingly have no roles to play in global labor markets (as workers), capital markets (as investors), commodity markets (as consumers), or even in debt markets (as taxpayers paying for bonds). They therefore fall "outside the grids" of the new regimes whose elites promote a vicious neo-liberalism that exalts the market, denigrates the nation-state, and finds no place for these populations in the social order, except as a social control problem. The new economy of violence shows a pattern of weakened nation-states whose militaries and police vacillate between two poles. On the one hand, there is a devastating application of coercion and violence against the populations of the free-fire zones and rural "national" resource regions; on the other there is a systematic indifference toward the needs for protection by vulnerable rural populations subject to predation by militarized non-state actors in refuse regions.

New forms of warfare and economy in the era after the Cold War The much heralded end of the Cold War has meant a relatively small decline in world military expenditures and nuclear and conventional arsenals (Sivard, 1996). The political economic engines that fuel militarization have been little dampened by the loss of the Soviet Union as partner to the Imaginary War. Some things have changed, however, in how warfare is thought and practiced in developed and underdeveloped places. Three stand out.

First is decline in use of the Clausewitzian model of inter-state violence. The ideal typical or only war, in this model, is between states which have territorial boundaries and a monopoly on legitimate organized violence. An absolute winner and loser must come out of each contest (Kaldor and Vashee, 1997). It is not surprising that in a new global system where weakened nation-states no longer have exclusive control over large migrant populations that cross their borders, and where the highly selective state violence described above prevails, that the Clausewitzian model, based on a Weberian concept of the state, should have fallen out of favor. Yet some see this decline, not as the loss of a Cold-War-favored paradigm (where cultures defined as stable, bounded wholes were more manageable images), or as the state's self-flattering account of a world where it is weakened, but as an actuality – "the coming anarchy" (Kaplan, 1994) or the rise of savage warrior cults (Dunlap, 1998). Warfare outside this inter-state model is often characterized in Western media as anarchic, flawed, pre-professional, or primitive. The Clausewitzian model, however, while powerfully shaping perception, has characterized little warfare outside a limited period of European history (Kaldor and Vashee, 1997).

Related manifestations of the decline of this prototype of war include the invention of Low Intensity Conflict doctrine in the 1980s, and even more recent Operations Other than War or Operations Short of War given in US and European military mission statements. Military strategists increasingly construct and plan for engagement in what is construed as simultaneous armed combat and peace-keeping or war deterrence through threat and conflict resolution (for an example, see Franke, 1997).

A second and related change is the emergence of what Kaldor (in Kaldor and Vashee, 1997) calls "New Wars." As a mode of warfare, what distinguishes these wars is their prosecution by paramilitaries without clear lines of command, the use of maximal violence including rape, bombing hospitals and markets, and destruction of historical monuments. In these tactics, "the aim is to sow fear and discord, to instill unbearable memories of what was once home, to desecrate whatever has social meaning" (Kaldor and Vashee, 1997: 16; see also Nordstrom, 1997; Daniel, 1996; Nagengast, 1994). Their frequent aim or effect is destruction of civilian life rather than competition with a well-equipped army in border defense. Using tremendous and growing numbers of small arms rather than larger, highly engineered weapons, they have contributed to a recent decline (after a long period of growth) in the total dollar value of global arms sales, an expectable result when the price of 200,000 standard assault rifles is equivalent to the once more robustly purchased modern jet fighter, and when the favored weapons for counter-insurgency and police work are small arms rather than tanks and planes (Klare, 1997; Pearson, 1994).

Many of these New Wars predate the end of the Cold War, but the latter has contributed to some of the more recent ones, through both the erosion of Cold-War identities (see Borneman, 1998), the new availability of surplus weaponry, and the former Warsaw Pact countries' joining Israel, the US, Argentina, and many other countries which host and often facilitate the sales of their arms merchants. Both during and after the end of the Cold War, the new wars have arisen from the erosion of peripheral states and their legitimacy, due (as noted above) in large part to the structural adjustment programs of the IMF and World Bank and dissolution of patrimonial states. In some cases, such as the Rwandan genocide, "violence is so ubiquitous because authoritarian states deliberately cultivated it, and military intellectuals, emerging from the underbelly of the Cold War, can deploy it so easily and effectively for their own ends. But violence has also generated a logic and momentum of its own, and is intrinsic to new extremist ideologies" (De Waal, 1997: 330–31).

Regardless of these wars' sources, many now believe that the world has become more violent and chaotic: a putative primordial hatred or "tribalism" has erupted with the destruction of the dualistic order of mutually assured destruction. Repeated throughout the mass media, this mythic view, though patently wrong in most anthropological eyes for its failure to understand ethnic identity and the state, also fails to help account for the fact that each new war now has half the average casualties of wars in the 1970s and 1980s, although the ratio of civilians to soldiers killed and the number of refugees has gone up precipitously.

The third change has been to more flexible forms of warfare, in striking parallel to changes in the corporate world. One example is the paramilitaries just mentioned, which are no longer vertically organized but use a web of subcontractors and loose partnerships to pursue their goals of societal destabilization with controlled costs and the ability to respond to rapid changes in the context of the relevant war. New doctrines and organization in the US military show even more striking neo-liberal parallels, which have emerged most strongly since the end of the Cold War. "Flexible warfare" consists in more "flexible response" to perceived military crisis through rapid deployment or "just-in-time" delivery of an army to a site of conflict rather than the large permanent overseas basing of units. It involves leaner and more limber economies of military production. The latter is achieved through downsizing soldier employees and privatizing previously corporate military functions (e.g. employing mercenaries and replacing soldiers with less expensive civilians for non-combat functions).[24] And while neo-liberal business doctrine claims regulation as the market's problematic other, military institutions make ever more heightened claims for their own rationality through postulating an ever more chaotic other – the civilian world outside itself.

Ethnographic work on the social consequences of warfare has grown significantly in the last ten years. This research has dealt with three issues, the first and most important being to reveal the hidden body of new and old wars (Carmack, 1988; Daniel, 1996; Malkki, 1995; Nordstrom, 1997). This work has raised the image of the mutilated body that Scarry (1985) has theorized as the very center of war. These anthropologists have detailed how victims' narratives and communities have been shaped by war's violence. They have spoken against the abstractions of war theories ensconced in the chambers of power, whether those of Pentagon theorists or of academics. This work shows that "a culture of terror . . . deconstruct[s] accepted realities . . . fundamental meaning and knowledge" and so steals the cultural meaning that grounds social action. Meaning-destroying effects are found in the bodily praxis itself: the maiming of eyes, ears, and tongues that is meant to render a people senseless (Nordstrom, 1997). It is also found in the inability of survivors to speak and, through speech, to escape the individuating and dehumanizing memory of the pain they experienced (Daniel, 1996). Torture and terror, if sufficiently extensive and apparently enduring, may even transform collective subjectivities, as in the traumatized populations of Tucuman, Argentina, who voted in the country's free elections for one of the generals responsible for the terror there (Isla, 1998).

Second, this anthropological work struggles with the dilemma that writing against the terror of war entails a contradiction: narrative both helpfully raises the disappeared body to awareness but can also reinforce the terror or engage in a "pornography of violence" (Daniel, 1996; Nordstrom, 1997). The reclamation of community life from, and its reshaping by, a decade of warfare is evoked in Starn's sensitive account of the night patrols Peruvian peasants enacted to expel the Sendero Luminoso from their mountain homes, and he does so in terms that resist re-terrorizing (Starn, 1999).

Finally, here as in other anthropological fields of endeavor, ethnographic work on war deals with the difficulty of tracing links to the secret councils of government or paramilitaries or corporations where wars are also shaped. In their work on the Peruvian 'war of shadows' Brown and Fernandez (1991) attempt to do so, as does Smith-Nonini (1997) in her work on the relationship between low intensity conflict doctrine and the local struggles over health and development in wartime and post-war El Salvador. Gusterson's book (1996), mentioned above, is another notable exception.

The end of the Cold War in 1989–91 corresponds, not coincidentally, with the fiscal crisis of the US government and other states whose coffers were drained by years of war preparation. The consequences have been many, including a vast increase in the relative global military power of the United States, which now spends almost as much on national security as the rest of the world combined, and more than six times its closest rival. Nonetheless, as in other sectors of industrial economies, global military industries have been confronted with a crisis of overproduction, and the response has been major restructuring of defense contractors. This has entailed mergers and downsizing, and some conversion to or acquisition of civilian businesses.[25] General Dynamics, for example, had shed 80,000 employees (of 102,000 total employed in 1989) by 1994, while its stock rose 553 per cent between 1991 and 1993. Major public relations campaigns were launched by some corporations in an effort to retain public support for military spending, Electric Boat, for example, floating arguments for the necessity of a "submarine industrial base." Another response to crisis has been to seek out new markets, fanning proliferation, or to create them, as in the notion of the needed (and expensive) "stewardship" of the partially dismantled nuclear weaponry.

Mann (1988) used the term "spectator-sport militarism" for the rise in many post-war industrial states of a form of celebration of military prow-

ess that requires only enthusiastic spectatorship via the media rather than widespread military training and participation. This process began with the rise of affluence at the end of the Second World War, and the rise of a new social contract which necessitated decline in military participation rates. At issue as well are the media profits at stake with the successful commodification of war and violence. "While it could be said that the old militarism glorified war but often failed to prepare for it, the [new form] intensified the preparation while concealing its purposes and obscuring its consequences" (Gillis, 1989: 7). It does this by disappearing the body of war (Gusterson, 1996) in the mass-mediated spectacularization of military adventurism.[26]

The gendering effects of this process – where the protected individual is culturally coded as female – have not been examined ethnographically, with those who have looked at gender tending to focus on the still highly skewed social practices of military and paramilitary work (Cock, 1994; Enloe, 1993; Gibson, 1994). Both wars and war preparation can be recruited to the purposes of shoring up gendered orders in crisis. Radical shifts that economic restructuring has made in the labor force participation rates of various gender/race/class fractions around the world have remade masculinities in many places. They are now defined less by workplace identities and instead, and increasingly, by male participation in violence, both actual and mass-mediated. This has been accompanied by some popular as well as state-based resistance to military interventionism, as nationalism or beliefs in non-violence converge on the need to avoid casualties, at least to the nation, and with the ascendance of geopolitical rather than ideological or constitutional thinking (i.e. the concern to defend boundaries and national power).

At the same time as the return to volunteer rather than conscripted armies in many industrial countries seems to erect a sharper boundary between things military and things civilian, the boundaries between policing and soldiering (Kraska and Kappeler, 1997) and between the enemy within and without (Dunn, 1996) have eroded, and many countries have seen a rise in paramilitary practices (e.g. Gibson, 1994).

Mozambique: Fatal political economic paradigms at work at
century's end

A New War is what Nordstrom describes in her groundbreaking book, *A Different Kind of War Story* (1997). She draws a painful ethnographic portrait of the long and devastating war in Mozambique, a war shaped initially by the rapacious Portuguese brand of colonialism and by the independence movement (Frelimo) that arose in response in the early 1960s.

Before and after independence in 1975, the white minority regimes in Rhodesia and South Africa, fearful of the successes of that movement, and envisioning its threat to their archipelagos of economic privilege, created and then supplied the army (Renamo) that would militarily oppose the new government until 1992. The guerrilla movement was a mere 1,000 person force at independence, but continued strong support from racist South African regimes and international Cold War ideologues, including the United States, created a force that went on to devastate the country.

What is most striking, however, is the inadequacy of the Clausewitzian "two-army face-off" account to explain the war as experienced by Mozambique's 16 million civilians. Not only were the vast majority of war deaths those of civilians, but the violence against them was wreaked by a host of groups other than army troops. They included bandits, private militias set up to protect businesses or communities, ex-soldiers singly and in organized predatory bands, and civilian collaborators who helped the combatants by collecting their taxes and supplies and by disciplining the population. In addition, the violence was orchestrated and interpreted by foreign advisers and mercenaries, journalists, and black marketeers, and by arms merchants and elite planners. The two armies were themselves a heterogeneous mix of trained soldiers, kidnapped boys in their early teens, commanders who ran cattle-poaching rings on the side, and men who extorted money from civilians for crossing bridges. Nordstrom characterizes this "warscape" in ways that make clear how an "economy of pillage" structured much of the violence, both by design of those who funded Renamo and by the profit-taking designs of individuals and groups.

Finally, this ethnography of war also constructs a new understanding of the nature of both violence and "non-violence." In regard to the latter, Nordstrom centers her account around the resistance to violence. "Nonviolent armies" were organized by charismatic leaders whose medicinal knowledge was used to make them invulnerable to bullets. Individuals intrepidly and consistently faced down the violence through such decisions as staying in place to continue teaching children or planting crops, and ultimately by showing up to vote for a new coalition government in 1994. Ritual means were used to cleanse the terror or "take the war out" of individuals who had been either or both victims and perpetrators of violence. She argues from this that creativity in confronting and defeating violence is a widespread human capacity while that creativity is also culturally variable: the Angolans who have struggled with similar problems at this same time have not been as successful in rooting out the violence.

The "classical view" of violence, which she characterizes as centered on fierce physical attack, does not jibe with her or her informants' accounts of the more complex, deep and disturbing qualities of violence, which are "the destruction of home and humanity, of hope and future, of valued traditions and the integrity of the community" (Nordstrom, 1997: 123). So the man who walked across terrifyingly dangerous parts of the war zone to trade his tiny cache of fish became a monumental figure as his gesture said that normal community life was in fact possible.

The New Wars are fought against civilians, and their economy is one of both international profits[27] and local pillage. In a sense, the New Wars seem also to call on civilians to fight back with attempts to re-establish their own local economies that support family and community life. This is one way to see the efforts of Salvadoran women who provided health care in the face of government attempts to destroy their clinics during the war and reinsert government doctors and win hearts and minds afterwards (Smith-Nonini, 1997), the rural Peruvians whose civil patrols made possible sleeping at night and retaining their crops from guerrilla confiscation (Starn, 1999), and the fish trader in Mozambique.

This ethnographic work demonstrates the poverty of political science and other discourses which have constructed most of the widely circulating accounts of violence, accounts which continue to center around "realist" views of power politics and around the sanitized images of war as contests between contending interests.

Conclusion

The twinning of economies and violences has taken many forms through the last two centuries. Rapid change in those relationships makes the job of understanding any place or process that anthropologists study that much more difficult and needful of a "theory of history" (Wallace, 1978) that includes the immediate present and even projects a future. Although the world's peoples all now live under the shadows of contemporary capitalisms and nation-states, anthropology's emphasis on alterity and its historical focus should keep alive the imagined possibility that alternative modes of organizing daily life have existed in the past, and may exist once again in the future. Anthropology's contemporary role as witness to the struggle for life in what are often capital's "refuse regions" has and can even more be the discipline's moral underpinning and the source of insight into the potential sources for even a modicum of increase in the prospects for justice and peace.

Such anticipatory theorization might begin with closer attention to what an ethnography of the economies of violences and violences of economies might look like, especially as it encounters Malinowski's "imponderabilia" of daily life. An ethnography of the relationship of warfare to economies would have to depart radically from the depiction of ethnography based on either received disciplinary wisdom or even recent innovations in theory and ethnographic writing. Of course, the latter would be deeply impli-cated in the reconceptualization. We believe that an ethnography of violences and economies will have to look much more like fine investiga-tive journalism, for instance, than it does now. During periods of rapid transformation such as the present, we will need to turn more to docu-ments, to ephemera, "gray literature" and census studies in archives and libraries as much as to the field. In this way, we can develop analyses of processes that we are not always able to observe personally. We need to attend carefully, as both journalists and ethnographers of violence have, to the politics and cultural constructions of memory, witnessing, and memorialization of events of violence, when we are fortunate enough to interview the victims or perpetrators of violence.

We will need to conceptualize new ways of thinking about systems, even if as ethnographers, we by temperament prize individual performance, Bourdieuian improvisations, and the post-modern cultivation of subjectivities. For instance, if "globalization" is to be adequately theorized, we will need to go beyond the tedious conundrum of "global" vs. "local", or "global/local" which currently haunts and hobbles our investigations, by seriously thinking about global economic systems, and about other (gen-der, racial, ethno-national) structures of inequality. We will also have to examine our fetishizations of "agency": some people, in some places and times, cannot act as agents in anything more than the nominal sense.

In casting about for some extant form of inquiry to amend and extend our ethnographic work on this subject, we can think of no better candidate than conscientious and careful investigative journalism. However, at present, "journalism" serves as a term of deprecation among anthropologists who judge a certain piece of writing "shallow", "unreflective", or worst of all "untheoretical." Such sweeping judgments are both inept and inapt. It per-haps is ironic that in a book called *Anthropological Theory Today* we should warn against the fetishization of theory, but there you have it, for such an ethnography must above all be driven as much by the nature of what is studied as by claims made on it by bodies of theory whose presuppositions are at variance from the nature of the subject matter we seek to study. This is also true for our disciplinary conventions of ethnography when they serve us poorly. This occurs whenever either theory or tradition demand that fieldsites be stable and recurrently visitable, that the presence of the powers of nation-states frame our ethnography rather than being its object of study, that our skepticism about representation should take precedence over our capacities for critique and systematic analysis, that informants' agency and discourse be privileged a priori even when they have been made passive or speechless by specific acts of violence.

Much remains to be done, if that theory of and for the future, is to come about.

Notes

We would like to thank Marc David for his excellent bibliographic and analytic help and Henrietta Moore for her helpful comments.

1 Archaeologists have devoted much effort in this regard, looking at the role of organized violence in the rise or fall of early civilizations.

2 See Nagengast (1994) and Johnston, O'Loughlin, and Taylor (1987) for two reviews that undermine simple dichotomies of war and peace in their global surveys of the forms that violence takes.

3 Ferguson and Farragher (1988) provide a comprehensive bibliography on the anthropology of war through the late 1980s.

4 This has continued, however, to the present (Sponsel and Gregor, 1994).

5 See Mattelart (1994) for an alternative view of the relationship between information technologies and war.

6 The relationship between socialist economies, "socialist accumulation," and socialist imperialism in the case of the Soviet Union is not dealt with here, and is in need of theoretical exploration elsewhere.

7 This is manifested in the US rate of incarceration: the US, with Russia, shows by far the highest rates among industrialized nations. In the US, drug, property, and public order crimes contributed most to the country's increased imprisonment rate (Mauer, 1995).

8 See also Baran and Sweezy, 1966.

9 High rates of unemployment and underemployment among white women and African-American men and women also contribute to the prevention of crisis.

10 "We call 'epoch-making' those innovations which shake up the entire pattern of the economy and hence create vast investment outlets in addition to the capital which they directly absorb" (Baran and Sweezy, 1966: 219).

11 We use Harvey (1989) and Davis (1986) as principal sources in the following discussion of Fordism.

12 These were a prototype of US military's "strategic hamlet" program in the Vietnam War.

13 While this has been true of many industries over the last half-century, it has occurred at a higher rate in military than in civilian industries. The former defense industries have also thereby garnered much higher rates of profit than commercial firms.

14 The camera obviously predates the Second World War and the twentieth century itself, although the military science of surveillance took on exponentially greater import in the era of nuclear weapons as deterrence theory depends on an unstable mix of knowledge and secrecy for its effects. The camera's impact on collective consciousness of war's violence has been eloquently outlined by Feldman (1994), who focuses on the process of "cultural anaesthesia" through media, media criticism, and other means.

15 US cultural discourses on military work as a calling or form of service make it difficult to see soldiering as an aspect of the division of labor. Compa's

(1984) review of the history of "labor and the military" ignores the labor conditions of soldiering altogether.

16   The material and the discursive can change in apparently contradictory ways. While nineteenth- and early twentieth-century American military spending remained low, for example, political culture tended to glorify war and the martial spirit. A poem popularly taught to schoolchildren proclaimed:

> The calls of the true heart ascend;
> And the brave to the battle-field rally;
> And the boom and the danger impend.
> The blood of the foe streams like water,
> And the fields wear the garment of slaughter.

Contemporary American political culture does not tolerate the same martial spirit while substantial resources are allocated to military "preparedness" (Gillis, 1989: 7).

17   What Lotchin (1984) calls the "entrepreneurial city" – which competes for military spending as it does for interstates, businesses, or conventions – curbs the state. This state-controlling effect is also evident when citizens make more extensive claims on the state after having allowed themselves to be mobilized for a war (Marwick, 1988).

18   The largest employer in the United States, for example, is now Manpower, Inc., which administers temporary workers.

19   This occurred with the ending in 1973 of the post-war Bretton Woods agreement to fix currency exchange rates.

20   One recent illuminating episode was the unsuccessful attempt by the French government to exchange a nickel mine (of which it owned a large share) in its colony of New Caledonia in the Pacific for one of lesser value in order to appease a local independence movement. However, other major shareholders – the US College Retirement Equities Fund and Fidelity Investments – threatened "long-lasting negative effects on foreign investment in France," and the French government abandoned its effort (*New York Times*, 1998).

21   It is precisely because there are so many sources of instability to the post-Fordist period, that we reject Harvey's (1989) argument that flexible capitalism constitutes a "regime of accumulation" with its own "mode of regulation" in anything like the sense of industrial Fordism (Tickell and Peck, 1995).

22   Sklair (1991) refers to them as "the transnational capitalist class."

23   "The global political economy – the social infrastructure of globalization – is dominated by, concentrated in, and organized from a number of . . . 'world cities.' These include New York, London, and Tokyo, the principal financial centers, with Frankfurt, Paris, Los Angeles, Toronto, São Paulo, Sydney, Singapore, and Hong Kong in the second tier. . . . The links between these centers are complex. . . . these links are not simply functional – they are social and political. They are consolidated not only by cross-cutting patterns of investment and trade, by information grids and communications facilities, but also by the political networks of fractions of the ruling classes" (Gill, 1996: 218–19).

24 On the official use of mercenaries in Papua New Guinea, Sierra Leone, and elsewhere, see Sheppard (1998).

25 Those who have studied economic conversion from military to civilian uses, however, have noted the difficulty of changing military industry's corporate culture which is based on secrecy, cost-plus accounting, and a reliance on government specification rather than market vagaries and market research (Markusen and Yudkin, 1992).

26 See Hallin and Gitlin (1993) for an example from the Gulf War that shows the broad cultural values recruited to this kind of spectatorship. It is also instructive to note that coverage of foreign conflict on US television has gone up at the same time as has murder coverage, the latter by 700 percent since 1993, suggesting that use of violence as a general strategy of recruitment to commercial attentiveness (*Media Report to Women*, 1997).

27 This applies to the South African apartheid regime, which tried to destroy Mozambique in order to keep the independence movement from allying with anti-apartheid forces.

Bibliography

Anderson, Benedict, 1991. *Imagined Communities*. 2nd ed. London: Verso.

Appadurai, Arjun, ed., 1986. *The Social Life of Things: Commodities in Cultural Perspective*. Cambridge and New York: Cambridge University Press.

Aretxaga, Begona, 1997. *Shattering Silence: Women, Nationalism, and Political Subjectivity in Northern Ireland*. Princeton: Princeton University Press.

Arrighi, Giovanni, Terence K. Hopkins, and Immanuel Wallerstein, 1989. *Antisystemic Movements*. London: Verso.

Baran, Paul, and Paul Sweezy, 1966. *Monopoly Capital: An Essay on the American Economic and Social Order*. New York: Monthly Review Press.

Barrons, 1998. "Buying Future Big-Caps: Interview with Leah Zell," *Barrons Magazine*, March 23: pp. 42–4.

Belich, James, 1986. *The Victorian Interpretation of Racial Conflict: The Maori, The British, and the New Zealand Wars*. Montreal: McGill-Queen's University Press.

Bluestone, Barry, and Bennett Harrison, 1982. *The Deindustrialization of America: Plant Closings, Community Abandonment, and the Dismantling of Basic Industries*. New York: Basic Books.

Borneman, John, 1998. *Subversions of International Order: Studies in the Political Anthropology of Culture*. Albany: State University of New York Press.

Bourgois, Philippe, 1996. *In Search of Respect: Selling Crack in El Barrio*. Cambridge: Cambridge University Press.

Brecher, Jeremy, and Tim Costello, 1994. *Global Village or Global Pillage: Economic Reconstruction from the Bottom Up*. Boston: South End Press.

Brown, Michael, and E. Fernandez, 1991. *War of Shadows: The Struggle for Utopia in the Peruvian Amazon*. Berkeley: University of California Press.

Brumfiel, Elizabeth, 1983. "Aztec State Making: Ecology, Structure, and the Origin of the State," *American Anthropologist* 61: 457–69.

Calavita, K., Tillman, R, and H. N. Pontell, 1997. "The Savings and Loan Debacle, Financial Crime and the State," *Annual Review of Sociology* 23: 19–38.

Carmack, Robert, ed., 1988. *Harvest of Violence: The Maya Indians and the Guatemalan Crisis*. Norman: University of Oklahoma Press.

Cock, Jacklyn, 1994. "Women and the Military: Implications for Demilitarization in the 1990s in South Africa," *Gender and Society* 8: 152–69.

Comaroff, Jean, and John Comaroff, 1991. *Of Revelation and Revolution: Christianity, Colonialism, and Consciousness in South Africa, Volume One*. Chicago: University of Chicago Press.

Compa, Lance, 1984. "Labor and the Military – A History," in *Economic Conversion: Revitalizing America's Economy*, ed. Suzanne Gordon and Dave McFadden. Cambridge: Ballinger Publishing Co., pp. 33–43.

Corrigan, Philip, and Derek Sayer, 1985. *The Great Arch: English State Formation as Cultural Revolution*. Oxford: Basil Blackwell.

Czegledy, Andre, 1998. "Economic Mafia of the Apogee of Capitalist Enterprise? Reflections on Post-Socialist Entrepreneurship in Hungary." Unpublished paper delivered to the panel "Our Disordered World: Reports from the Front," Annual Joint Meetings of CASCA/AES, Toronto, May 7.

Daniel, E. Valentine, 1996. *Charred Lullabies: Chapters in an Anthropology of Violence*. Princeton: Princeton University Press.

Davis, Mike, 1986. *Prisoners of the American Dream*. London: Verso.

Davis, Mike, 1993. "Uprising and Repression in L.A.: An Interview with Mike Davis by the *Covert Action Information Bulletin*," in *Reading Rodney King/ Reading Urban Uprising*, ed. Robert Gooding-Williams. New York: Routledge, pp. 142–56.

De Waal, Alex, 1997. "Contemporary Warfare in Africa," in *New Wars: Restructuring the Global Military Sector: Vol. 1, New Wars*, ed. Mary Kaldor and B. Vashee. London: Pinter, pp. 287–332.

Di Leonardo, Micaela ed., 1991. *Gender at the Crossroads of Knowledge: Feminist Anthropology in the Postmodern Era*. Berkeley: University of California Press.

Dolan, Catherine, 1997. *Tesco is King: Gender and Labor Dynamics in Horticultural Exporting, Meru District, Kenya*. Ph. D. dissertation, Department of Anthropology, Binghamton University, Binghamton, NY.

Du Bois, W. E. B., 1935 (1962). *Black Reconstruction in America 1860–1880*. New York: Macmillan and Co.

Dunlap, Col. Charles J., 1998: "Technology and the Twenty-first Century Battlefield: Re-complicating Moral Life for the Statesman and the Soldier." Paper presented at the Carnegie Council on Ethics and International Affairs, February 6.

Dunn, Timothy J., 1996. *The Militarization of the U.S.-Mexico Border 1978–1992: Low-Intensity Conflict Doctrine Comes Home*. Austin: University of Texas Press.

Dupré, Georges, and Pierre Philippe Rey, 1978. "Reflections on the Relevance of a Theory of the History of Exchange," in *Relations of Production: Marxist Approaches to Economic Anthropology*, ed. David Seddon. London: Frank Cass, pp. 171–208.

Emmanuel, Arghiri, 1972. *Unequal Exchange: A Study of the Imperialism of Trade.* New York: Monthly Review.

Enloe, Cynthia, 1993. *The Morning After: Sexual Politics at the End of the Cold War.* Berkeley: University of California Press.

Escobar, Arturo, 1995. *Encountering Development: The Making and Unmaking of the Third World.* Princeton, NJ: Princeton University Press.

Far Eastern Economic Review, 1998: "Migration: Deport and deter – Indonesian Illegal Workers get a Harsh Send-off from Malaysia," *Far Eastern Economic Review,* April 23.

Farmer, Paul, Margaret Connors, and Janie Simmons, eds, 1996. *Women, Poverty and AIDS: Sex, Drugs, and Structural Violence.* Monroe, Maine: Common Courage Press.

Feldman, Allen, 1994. "On Cultural Anaesthesia," in *The Senses Still,* ed. Nadia Seremetakis. Boulder: Westview.

Ferguson, R. Brian, 1994. *Yanomamo Warfare.* Santa Fe: School of American Research.

Ferguson, R. Brian, and Leslie E. Farragher, 1988. *The Anthropology of War: A Bibliography.* New York: Occasional Papers of the Harry Frank Guggenheim Foundation.

Ferguson, R. Brian, and Neil L. Whitehead, eds, 1992. *War in the Tribal Zone: Expanding States and Indigenous Warfare.* Sante Fe: School of American Research Press.

Foerstel, Lenora, ed., 1996. *Creating Surplus Populations: The Effects of Military and Corporate Policies on Indigenous Peoples.* Washington, DC: Maisonneuve Press.

Franke, Volker C., 1997. "Warriors for Peace: The Next Generation of U.S. Military Leaders," *Armed Forces and Society* 24: 33–58.

Fröbel, Folker, Jürgen Heinrichs, and Otto Kreye, 1980. *The New International Division of Labor: Structural Unemployment in Industrialized Countries and Industrialization in Developing Countries.* Cambridge, Cambridge University Press.

Geyer, Michael, 1989. "The Militarization of Europe, 1914–1945," in *The Militarization of the Western World,* ed. John Gillis. New Brunswick: Rutgers University Press, pp. 65–102.

Gibson, James W., 1994. *Warrior Dreams: Violence and Manhood in Post-Vietnam America.* New York: Hill and Wang.

Giddens, Anthony, 1985. *The Nation-State and Violence.* Berkeley: University of California, Cambridge, Polity.

Gill, Stephen. 1996. "Globalization, Democratization, and the Politics of Indifference," in *Globalization: Critical Reflections,* ed. J. H. Mittelman. Boulder, CO: Lynne Rienner.

Gillis, John, ed., 1989. *The Militarization of the Western World.* New Brunswick: Rutgers University Press.

Gray, Chris Hables, 1997. *Postmodern War: The New Politics of Conflict.* New York: Guilford Press.

Green, Linda, 1994. "Fear as a Way of Life," *Cultural Anthropology* 9: 227–56.

Greider, William, 1997. *One World, Ready or Not: The Manic Logic of Global*

Capitalism. New York: Simon and Schuster.

Gusterson, Hugh, 1996. *Nuclear Rites: A Weapons Laboratory at the End of the Cold War*. Berkeley: University of California Press.

Haas, Jonathan, 1990. "Warfare and the Evolution of Tribal Polities in the Prehistoric Southwest," in *The Anthropology of War*. ed. J. Haas. Cambridge: Cambridge University Press.

Hallin, Daniel C., and Todd Gitlin, 1993. "Agon and Ritual: the Gulf War as Popular Culture and as Television Drama," *Political Communication* 10: 411–24.

Hardin, Bristow, 1991. *The Militarized Social Democracy and Racism: The Relationship between Militarism, Racism and Social Welfare Policy in the United States*. Dissertation, Department of Sociology, University of California at Santa Cruz.

Harrison, Bennett, 1994. *Lean and Mean: The Changing Landscape of Corporate Power in the Age of Flexibility*. New York: Basic Books.

Harvey, David, 1989. *The Condition of Postmodernity*. Oxford: Basil Blackwell.

Harvey, David, 1996. *Justice, Nature, and the Geography of Difference*. Cambridge, Mass.: Blackwell.

Henwood, Doug, 1997. *Wall Street: How It Works and For Whom*. London: Verso.

Hoogvelt, Ankie, 1997. *Globalization and the Postcolonial World: The New Political Economy of Development*. Baltimore: Johns Hopkins Press.

Horne, Gerald, 1986. *Black and Red: W.E.B. DuBois and the Afro-American Response to the Cold War, 1944–1963*. Albany: State University of New York Press.

Isla, Alejandro, 1998. "Terror, Memory and Responsibility in Argentina," *Critique of Anthropology* 18: 134–56.

Johnston, R. J., J. O'Loughlin, and P. J. Taylor, 1987. "The Geography of Violence and Premature Death: a World-Systems Approach, in *The Quest for Peace. Transcending Collective Violence and War among Societies, Cultures and States*, ed. R. Vayrynen. Beverley Hills: Sage.

Kaldor, Mary, 1990. *The Imaginary War: Understanding the East-West Conflict*. Oxford: Oxford University Press.

Kaldor, Mary, and Basker Vashee, eds, 1997. *Restructuring the Global Military Sector: Vol. 1. New Wars*. London: Pinter.

Kaplan, Robert D., 1994. "The Coming Anarchy: How Scarcity, Crime, Overpopulation, Tribalism, and Disease are Rapidly Destroying the Social Fabric of our Planet," *The Atlantic Monthly* 273 (2): 44–65.

Klare, Michael, 1997. "An Avalanche of Guns: Light Weapons Trafficking and Armed Conflict in the Post-Cold War Era," in Kaldor and Vashee, 1997, pp. 55–77.

Kraska, Peter B., and Victor E. Kappeler, 1997. "Militarizing American Police: the Rise and Normalization of Paramilitary Units," *Social Problems* 44: 1–18.

Krasniewitz, Louise, 1992. *Nuclear Summer: The Clash of Communities at the Seneca Women's Peace Encampment*. Ithaca, NY: Cornell University Press.

Lotchin, Roger, ed., 1984. *The Martial Metropolis: U.S. Cities in War and Peace*. New York: Praeger.

Malkki, Liisa H., 1995. *Purity and Exile: Violence, Memory, and National Cosmology among Hutu Refugees in Tanzania*. Chicago: University of Chicago Press.

Mandel, Ernest, 1975. *Late Capitalism*. London: Verso.

Mann, Michael, 1988. *States, War and Capitalism: Studies in Political Sociology*. Oxford: Basil Blackwell.

Manz, Beatriz, 1988. *Refugees of a Hidden War: The Aftermath of Counterinsurgency in Guatemala*. Albany: SUNY Press.

Marable, Manning, 1992. *The Crisis of Color and Democracy: Essays on Race, Class and Power*. Monroe, ME: Common Courage Press.

Markusen, Ann et al., 1991. *The Rise of the Gunbelt: The Military Remapping of Industrial America*. New York: Oxford University Press.

Markusen, Ann, and Joel Yudken, 1992. *Dismantling the Cold War Economy*. New York: Oxford University Press.

Martin, Hans-Peter, and Harold Schumann, 1997. *The Global Trap: An Attack on Democracy and Prosperity*, trans. P. Camiller. New York: Zed Books.

Marwick, Arthur, ed., 1988. *Total War and Social Change*. New York: St. Martin's Press.

Mattelart, Armand, 1994. *Mapping World Communication: War, Progress, Culture*. Minneapolis: University of Minnesota Press.

Mauer, Marc, 1995. "The International Use of Incarceration," *Prison Journal* 75(1): 113–23.

Maurer, Bill, 1995. "Complex Subjects: Offshore Finance, Complexity Theory, and the Dispersion of the Modern," *Socialist Review* 25(3/4): 113–45.

Media Report to Women, 1997. "TV Network Murder Coverage up 700% since 1993," *Media Report to Women* 25(3): 1–3.

Meillasoux, Claude, 1981. *Maidens, Meal and Money: Capitalism and the Domestic Economy*. Cambridge: Cambridge University Press.

Miller, Daniel, 1997. *Capitalism: An Ethnographic Approach*. Oxford: Berg.

Mintz, Sidney W., 1985. *Sweetness and Power: The Place of Sugar in Modern History*. New York: Viking Press.

Montagu, Ashley, ed., 1978. *Learning Non-Aggression*. Oxford: Oxford University Press.

Murray, Colin, 1981. *Families Divided: The Impact of Migrant Labour in Lesotho*. Cambridge: Cambridge University Press.

Nagengast, C., 1994. "Violence, Terror, and the Crisis of the State," *Annual Review of Anthropology* 23: 109–36.

Nash, June, 1979. *We Eat the Mines and the Mines Eat Us: Dependency and Exploitation in Bolivian Tin Mines*. New York: Columbia University Press.

Nash, June, 1989. *From Tank Town to High Tech: The Clash of Community and Industrial Cycles*. Albany: SUNY Press.

New York Times, 1998. "Compliments of U.S. Investors: New Activism Shakes Europe's Markets," *New York Times*, April 25, pp. B1, B3.

Nonini, Donald M., 1992. *British Colonial Rule and the Resistance of the Malay Peasantry, 1900–1957*. Yale University Southeast Asia Studies Monographs, 38. New Haven: Yale University Southeast Asia Studies.

Nordstrom, Carolyn, 1997. *A Different Kind of War Story*. Philadelphia: University of Pennsylvania Press.

Nordstrom, Carolyn, 1998. "Deadly Myths of Aggression," *Aggressive Behavior* 24: 147–59.

Ong, Aihwa, 1987. *Spirits of Resistance and Capitalist Discipline: Factory Women in Malaysia*. Albany: SUNY Press.

Ong, Aihwa, 1991. "The Gender and Labor Politics of Postmodernity," *Annual Review of Anthropology* 20: 279–309.

Otterbein, Keith, 1985. *The Evolution of War: A Cross-Cultural Study*. 2nd ed. New Haven: HRAF.

Pearson, Frederic S., 1994. *The Global Spread of Arms: Political Economy of International Security*. Boulder: Westview Press.

Reno, William, 1995. *Corruption and State Politics in Sierra Leone*. Cambridge: Cambridge University Press.

Rey, Pierre Philippe, 1979. "Class Contradiction in Lineage Societies," *Critique of Anthropology* 4: 13–14, 41–60.

Robinson, Cedric, 1983. *Black Marxism: The Making of the Black Radical Tradition*. London: Zed Press.

Robinson, William L., 1996. *Promoting Polyarchy: Globalization, US Intervention, and Hegemony*. Cambridge: Cambridge University Press.

Ross, Andrew, 1996. "A Few Good Species'. *Social Text* 46/47(14): 207–15.

Rostow, W.W., 1960. *The Stages of Economic Growth: A Non-Communist Manifesto*. Cambridge: Cambridge University Press.

Sacks, Karen B., 1994. "How Did Jews Become White Folks?," in *Race*, ed. Steven Gregory and Roger Sanjek. New Brunswick, NJ: Rutgers University Press.

Said, Edward W., 1993. *Culture and Imperialism*. New York: Random House.

Sanday, Peggy, 1997. *A Woman Scorned: Acquaintance Rape on Trial*. Berkeley: University of California Press.

Sassen, Saskia, 1991. *The Global City: New York, London, Tokyo*. Princeton, NJ: Princeton University Press.

Scarry, Elaine, 1985. *The Body in Pain*. Oxford: Oxford University Press.

Schaeffer, Robert K., 1989. *War in the World-System*. New York: Greenwood Press.

Scheper-Hughes, Nancy, 1992. *Death without Weeping: The Violence of Everyday Life in Brazil*. Berkeley: University of California Press.

Sharda, Bam Dev, 1988. "Third World Militarization and Income Inequality," *International Journal of Contemporary Sociology* 25: 3–4, 141–54.

Sheppard, Simon, 1998. "Foot Soldiers of the New World Order: The Rise of the Corporate Military," *New Left Review* 228: 128–38.

Sherry, Michael, 1995. *In the Shadow of War: The United States since the 1930s*. New Haven: Yale University Press.

Short, Anthony, 1975. *The Communist Insurrection in Malaya, 1948–1960*. London: F. Muller.

Sider, Gerald M., 1986. *Culture and Class in Anthropology and History: A Newfoundland Illustration*. Cambridge: Cambridge University Press.

Sivard, Ruth, 1996. *World Military and Social Expenditures*. Washington, DC: World Priorities, Inc.

Sklair, Leslie. 1991: *Sociology of the Global System*. Baltimore: Johns Hopkins Press.

Smith-Nonini, Sandra, 1997. " 'Popular' Health and the State: Dialectics of the Peace Process in El Salvador," *Social Science and Medicine* 44(5): 635–45.

Sponsel, Leslie E., and Thomas Gregor, 1994. *The Anthropology of Peace and Non-Violence*. Boulder: L. Rienner.

Spurr, David, 1993. *The Rhetoric of Empire: Colonial Discourses in Journalism, Travel Writing, and Imperial Administration*. Durham, NC: Duke University Press.

Starn, Orin, 1999. *Night Watch: The Politics of Protest in Peru*. Durham, NC: Duke University Press.

Taussig, Michael, 1980. *The Devil and Commodity Fetishism in South America*. Chapel Hill: University of North Carolina Press.

Thomas, Nicholas, 1994. *Colonialism's Culture: Anthropology, Travel and Government*. Princeton: Princeton University Press.

Tickell, Adam, and Jamie A. Peck, 1995. "Social Regulation *after* Fordism: Regulation Theory, Neo-Liberalism and the Global-Local Nexus," *Economy and Society* 24(3): 357–86.

Tilly, Charles, 1985. "War Making and State Making as Organized Crime," in *Bringing the State Back In*, ed. Peter Evans, Dietrich Rueschemeyer, and Theda Skocpol. Cambridge: Cambridge University Press.

Vayda, Andrew, 1976. *War in Ecological Perspective: Persistence, Change and Adaptive Processes in Three Oceanian Societies*. New York: Plenum.

Virilio, Paul, 1990. *War and Cinema: The Logistics of Perception*, trans. P. Camiller. London: Verso.

Wade, Robert, and Frank Veneroso, 1998. "The Asian Crisis: the High Debt Model Versus the Wall Street-Treasury-IMF Complex," *New Left Review* 228: 3–24.

Wallace, Anthony F. C., 1978. *Rockdale: The Growth of an American Village in the Early Industrial Revolution*. New York: Knopf.

Wiener, Margaret J., 1995. *Visible and Invisible Realms: Power, Magic and Colonial Conquest in Bali*. Chicago: University of Chicago Press.

Wolf, Eric, 1973. *Peasant Wars of the Twentieth Century*. New York: Harper Torchbooks.

Wolf, Eric R., 1982. *Europe and the People without History*. Berkeley: University of California Press.

5 Toward an Ethics of the Open Subject: Writing Culture in Good Conscience

Debbora Battaglia

This chapter concerns the interpretative ethics of producing ethnography. As such, it participates in anthropology's brave but ever unfinished project of examining its implication in differentials of power, and its own colonizing impulses (see especially Clifford and Marcus, 1986). To a substantial extent, this self-critique has been fueled by text-driven agendas of cultural studies that take ethnographic writing as always and only a site of pernicious constructions of Otherness. My concern is that such agendas would effectively disconnect anthropology from on-going social engagement. Too, they would lead to writing only of and for oneself, in the certain terms of one's own cultural knowledge. I argue here in the direction of radical rapprochement. On the one hand, ethnography can save cultural studies, as it were, from itself, by shifting the focus of moral inquiry beyond the horizon of narrativity, and beyond familiar subject positions. On the other hand, ethnography must be willing to embrace its own under-recognized capacity to engage and to "own" contingency and ambiguity – its capacity, as a technique of knowledge production, to generate productive uncertainties and disjunctive possibilities for social engagement.

This line of thought finds its motivation in the value Walter Benjamin has described as "convergence with the real" (1978: 177). Anthropologically, getting real means examining the cultural imaginary, as it is revealed and configured in social practice, in order to determine the value of particular relationships to people at particular times and places. Getting real is finding points of comparison and contrast in these contingencies. It is grasping the pragmatism and imagination and feelings people reveal, in their common, and uncommon practices. It is recognizing one's self, or an other's, as anything but given.

The self in contingency

Basically, discourses of contingency flow from the premise that persons, their subjectivities and identities (selves) are shaped by and shape relations to others, under the press of historical and cultural contingency.[1] From this it follows that selves are "not given to us" by natural law (Foucault, 1984: 341), not fixed or unchanging. And certainly they are not ontologically prior to relations of power; any such notion is simply unreal. Rather, selves are from the start an open question: subject to the constraints and manipulations of cultural forces, on the one hand, and on the other hand capable, upon reflection, of breaking with and transforming the situations in which they are formed.[2]

Of course, all of the above can be said without ever mentioning anthropology. But any study of social contingency gains by its encounters with anthropology, and acquires from ethnographic methods specifically what might be termed an ethnographic conscience. This is because doing and writing ethnography demands awareness of the complex uncertainties both of "being there" at the site of difference (as Geertz, 1988, sets out the project) and, too, of "getting there" (as Clifford, 1992, argues by contrast) – wherever "there" is. And it might not be far afield, as we know from ethnographic studies of the practices of science, technology, and artworld culture, of evangelical cults and school class reunions and the "tribes on the Hill" of our own governments. The "field" is necessarily unfamiliar only to one's own subject-positions.

From this approach, any ethically aware social theory of contingency fulfills its potential insofar as it (a) engages cultural difference in subjects' own terms, and (b) undertakes its own on-going self-analysis within sight of the dialogic, inherently contingent enterprise of ethnography. And the obverse is equally true: anthropology succeeds ethically insofar as it recognizes the contingencies – the slippages, ambivalences, aporias, and generally speaking, the ambiguities – which inhere in its own and others' ideas and practices, as being constitutive of, and not merely lapses in, moral orders. In fact, the correspondence of ethnography's productive destabilizations with subjects' self-destabilizing practices has been underexplored. "Writing culture" will find its future only within the fullness of its embrace of such ambiguous productivities.

Essentialisms within

There is no self alone at the start.
                    Paul Ricoeur, *Oneself as Another*

If contingency discourse is, at the start, about the differing of humanity within itself, it cannot but acknowledge its intimate relationship to essentialism, which it calls up as its logical and rhetorical opposite. Thus, I might take the position that the "self" is a representational economy: a reification continually defeated by mutable entanglements with other subjects' histories, experiences, self-representations (see Battaglia, 1995a: 2). Selfhood by this figuration is a chronically unstable project brought situationally – not invariably – to some form of order, shaped to some purpose, consciously or otherwise, in indeterminate social practice.

Meanwhile, however, the "essential self" and notions like it continue to have a compelling force for those who use them. Marilyn Strathern has discussed the "integratory capacity" (1991: 5) of such essentialist concepts – their effect of producing an experience or evoking an image of integration which nonetheless fails to encompass the diversity of possible experiences. This capacity of the language of subjectivity to gloss over and conflate significant differences goes straight to the heart of the larger issue, that similar to the "self", notions such as "identity", "agency", "subject-position", "modernity," "culture", "society", and even "ambiguity" have this kind of integratory capacity for the diverse discourses of contingency. We use these newly reified categories and imagine that we are speaking the same language, which is the language of a post-essentialist movement. But like all rhetorics, this one runs the risk of harboring its own worst enemies – the risk of essentializing, summarizing, programmatizing, and in other respects naturalizing its own terms of reference. This point about the trouble our categories gets us into is important for anthropology, but not only for anthropology.

Take the case of the "subject-position" and the problematic of "identity." A central problematic – some would say "the" central problematic – of any post-essentialist theory and practice concerns how subjects are positioned within culturally patterned and socially constituted differentials of power. This problematic asserts an unwavering value for acknowledging the social, historical, and cultural locatedness of persons.

To some degree, this interest in locatedness is tied to critical interest in the forces of modernity which have a destabilizing effect on subjects. Thus, we read of the subject in modernity who dwells in bifocality; a subject at once global and local, self-assertively different and similar to others in a "saliently transcultural world" and a "world-historical political economy" (Marcus, 1992: 311). Further still, subjects in modernity are "internally differentiated" and typically take "multiple subject positions within a range of discourses and social practices" (Moore, 1994: 54).[3] Marcus likens the interdisciplinary consciousness of this complexity of subject-positions – what he writes of as the consciousness of human diversity – to nothing less momentous than the revolt against realism by aesthetic modernists in art and literature.[4]

By these instances alone it would appear that the "subject-position" has acquired the paradoxical status and stability of a "root metaphor" of contingency discourses. It is acknowledged across disciplinary fields of analysis, applies across the divide of observers and observed, is the elementary structure of reflexivity. One could say that the "subject-position" imparts a kind of "aura" of authenticity to post-essentialist texts.[5]

But are subjects always as attached to their subject-positions so invariably, so unequivocally, as their writers take them to be? Are subject-positions being written as they are lived, and if not, why not? While acknowledging that this is a matter of different analytic levels, there is much to be gained by submitting the notion of subject-position to an "analytic of ambivalence" (to take a phrase from Homi Bhabha, 1994), and in particular, by specifying the value *for subjects* of being locatable at all. With this critical action our point of departure shifts from a given value to a contingent value for locatability, a value emergent in the voices and visions of self of the subjects concerned, and answerable to them. On one level, this action reduces the risk of "writing" persons who do not wish to be written. On another level, but in equally practical terms, it reduces the risk of mistaking the *value* of the subject-position for the *value* of the locatable subject – the subject *in some* position (see also Moore: 1994, 54). Put another way, the presumption of value for situating a subject – including the ethnographer as an interlocutor – must not be allowed to close off the question of who controls ambiguous situations.

I am thinking of the subject we seek to clarify but who herself seeks obscurity. I am thinking of persons striving as a matter of physical or political survival to maintain or achieve the blurred contours of a moving target, unaccountability of narrative agency, relief from an identity displaced, obviated, or shed, under some form of social pressure. I am thinking of cases where ambiguity is an aesthetic or poetic goal, or where it is a subject's only hope of self-preservation against the forces of colonial expansion, the manipulations of late capitalism, a sorcerer's determined program of power, or against others' proprietary interests in subjects' knowledge, or their bodies, or body parts.

From this perspective, the foreign shore of knowledge and experience we seek to engage may be a region of an *undeclared* race, gender, or class; a place of virtual homelands, statuses, selves, where being or staying in the game on one's own terms is its own objective. Departing from this shore, which is precisely not that of an Aristotelian project of *dis*ambiguation, we are moved to seek and to represent the conditions and motivations of non-locatablility. From this perspective, too, self-ambiguation can be appreciated as a supplementary capacity of persons, and not in all cases a problem or definitional lack. I would go so far as to say that until we shape a challenge to the hegemony of the locatable sub-ject-*in*-position, we shall come nowhere near an understanding of the lim-its and explanatory power of "situated knowledges" (Haraway, 1991).

Supplementation and ambiguity

Foucault has remarked that ethics concerns "the kind of relationship you ought to have with yourself, *rapport a soi*" (1984: 352). At one point he called this "a kind of ethics which [is] an aesthetics of existence," rather than one "founded on so-called scientific knowledge of what the self is" (1984: 343)."[6] Such an ethics is not reticent to acknowledge its location in the interstices of ours and others' models of value and social conduct. In fact it uses the privileges of this location to move the issues that con-cern anthropology beyond questions of human existence (as Foucault, too, moved off this notion), toward new horizons of social engagement (see Rabinow, 1994).

Inevitably, such an ethics will run precisely counter to the programs of "objectivist" inquiry (see La Capra, 1985) – programs that require sub-jects and identities to be stable, finite, and bounded. Along these lines, one may perceive oneself to be more or less stable, and even deeply want stability for oneself and for that matter, for one's body politic. But stable states tend to resist unsettling exchanges with the outsiders their self-definition requires – exchanges of the sort that an open subject invites. Too, the notion of the open subject refuses to limit issues of subjectivity to the skin-bound individual, or identity to the boundaries of the body politic. It resists any notion of an ideal or "core" self, authentic and ide-ally unchanging, other than as one "folk model of self" (Spiro, 1993) among others. Correspondingly, it resists writing "society" as if it were such a corporate entity, for the simple reason that it cannot delude itself that reality offers any such condition. Being resolutely anti-reductionist, it follows that the open subject looks askance at any *program* of universalism, including arguments from ethnographic evidence for an "ir-reducible" condition of self-awareness (Cohen, 1994), or for cognitive frameworks as objects of analysis separable from historically emergent moral orders (D'Andrade, 1995).

The problem the open subject finds with fundamentalist programs is less a matter of goals than of ethics: by depersonalizing and despecifying humanity, these programs stand to render "humanity" only in the terms of their own projects. Further – and this is the key – this approach denies human subjects different openings to claim their particular actions as instances of the universal, and to garner a sense of responsibility from their participation in a historically specialized "sense of the universal" (Derrida, 1992: 74).

Identity politics is probably the most obvious site of this kind of moral specialization, where cultural identity presents itself, paradoxically, as "the irreplaceable inscription of the universal in the singular, the unique testimony to the human essence and to what is proper to man" (Derrida, 1992: 73, sexist language noted with unease). Edward Said makes the point for decolonized people's efforts to reclaim a "repressed native essence" in response to histories of slavery, colonialism, and "most important – spiritual dispossession" (1991: 22). Especially in the light of the spiritual, the struggle for identity reveals itself as based in claiming a *distinctive moral order*, rather than in maintaining national, ethnic, or other sorts of mappable boundaries. It is in the terms of such moral claims that we are enjoined to seek (using Clifford Geertz's crucial formulation) "models of and models for" *un rapport a soi*. That is, we must seek such models in the aesthetics of engagement of local and global, particular and collective formations of self that have as much to do with generating an enabling and purposive ambiguity as of creating enduring profiles and structures.[7]

In this spirit, the project I undertake here takes "another shore" (Derrida, 1992: 27) of knowledge and experience as its point of departure. It sets its compass at the start by the point of view of an other, seeking challenges to its own most dedicated perspectives. This is why contingency needs ethnography: to articulate a *discourse of responsibility* as a discourse of reflexive awareness achieved across difference. Foucault asks "Departing from what ground shall I find my identity?" (1994, 230). The ground is the relation to subjects other than oneself, a relation established on their far shores.

Emblematically, the far shores of ethnographic inquiry are the regions of the marginalized, the subaltern, the otherwise authoritatively de-centered human subject. There is nothing that improves upon the ethnographic method for drawing out and drawing into relationship the thoughts and feelings of the invisible and unheard people of these regions, whom anthropology seeks to make visible and heard – to "write" – in its capacity as a counter-hegemonic practice.[8] We might even say that the ethnographic method finds its greater purpose in its struggles against the heavy currents of colonizing narratives and totalizing theories; that it discovers its potential in its ideologically motivated travels to other shores. The interpretative goal in this regard is to shape a discourse that converges with the real by whatever appropriate means available.

But this is the place to note that ethnography's function of supplementing current knowledge in the terms of an other can work for or against an ethics of the open subject. The *Oxford English Dictionary* defines a supplement as something "added to supply deficiencies." Supplementation, as a concept from philosophies of deconstruction (see especially Derrida, 1974), is a process of new knowledge acting upon prior (never total or sufficient) knowledge, and in consequence destabilizing it. Supplementation, then, may be extending or delimiting of knowledge, and a good thing or problematic in either capacity. This *double problematic of the supplement* is the source of some of the best critiques of ethnographic writing (e.g. Clifford, 1988). On the one hand, they place anthropology on alert for the dangers of ethnocentrism – of non-demarcated extensions of its own assumptions into the realm of its subjects: ethnography must guard against finding *itself* – its own notions of what counts – on other shores, *and in good conscience*.

On the other hand, even the best ethnography stands to close off certain paths of inquiry that subjects would regard as essential to the meaning and value of their lives. In short, while an ethics of the open subject cannot, as it were, have a full life without ethnography, it is only compatible with an ethnography that is critically self-aware. This is the sense in which an ethnographic conscience finds its full reach as a "technology of self" (to return to Foucault). Our hope must be that our self-aware and "close readings" (De Man, 1986: 64) of cultural practices and "text-artifacts" (Ricoeur, 1992) will involve us in problematization as a moral aesthetic of engagement.

To proceed along these lines, we must take a few steps backward.

Practicing displacement

The process of supplementation is least problematic – least hegemonic – in forms that are most open to on-the-spot negotiation and corrective supplementation: spoken language, and dialogue specifically, is the model form (see Bakhtin, 1981; and for anthropology, Maranhao, 1990). The significance of dialogue for anthropology is that it models the exchange of knowledge – as Maranhao writes, "dialogue is change rather than repetition" (1990: 11). Being open-ended, dialogue does not foreclose on the promise of an ethics of the open subject. Although dialogue still assumes a dichotomy of sorts, ethnographic dialogues stand as model moments of social exchange in these terms. Their contextualization in the "ethnographic moment", and anthropology's commitment to context, promote a situation in which claims, ideally in the moment of fieldwork, may elicit counter-claims, rather than inscribing fixed domains of knowledge and power.[9]

The ethical situation alters when dialogue is displaced by textuality and the productivity of "writing." Writing, defined broadly as *formalized traces of a materially concrete productivity*, makes an issue of openness. This is because written texts are detachable (see Derrida, 1974) and transferable from their originary contexts of use; are consequently inclined to repetition. Silverstein and Urban (1996) theorize this process of detachment and recontextualization as "entextualization": a process of texts or bits of them traveling from one site of social exchange to another, eliciting corresponding shifts in meanings and values. The concept of entextualization emphasizes discourse as socially situated practice, by way of which knowledge is "reanimated" in different contexts. Thus, in contrast to dialogue, such texts run the risk of closing off the exchange of knowledge; their repetition can make them appear as eternal givens, stable truths across contingencies of time and space (Keane, 1997; Silverstein and Urban, 1996). However, they also assert ambiguity (Kondo, 1990; Robertson, 1998) or open themselves up to different senses being made of them, to the pleasure of coming to familiarity through an experience of the repeatable, to the craft of study, and so on. No matter how thoroughly canonized or firmly inscribed as doxa,[10] writing, in its quality of what Derrida termed "iterability", exceeds its own stubborn materiality (De Man, 1984).

Both dialogues and writing move cultural meanings and values from one site of social action to another, displacing them. On the one hand, inscription freezes the frame. Thus, written or visual ethnographies, as inscriptions of knowledge gained in dialogues on "another shore", carry with them the inherent danger of representing this knowledge as more stable and more bounded than it actually is, more objective than intersubjective. In their materiality, they can interdict the flow of knowledge exchange, at some point or at some level. Of course, the critical literature on ethnography's failures of representation is in no short supply. Meanwhile, the effects of this critique on the theory and practice of anthropology reads as a seismic event. As I mentioned at the start, an ethics of the open subject traces its genealogy to such critiques of representation, particularly in turning away from an ancestry of colonizing discourses that claimed to be representing "whole" cultures and universal truths. But it turns likewise away from the negativity of critiques of ethnography. As apart from early, negative deconstruction, *rapport a soi* requires an affirmative investment in the shaping practices of moral orders. Cast in this light, one of the great gifts to ethical scholarship of writing culture is its activity of self-problematization.

Strathern recognizes the point in her comments that ethnographic representation is exemplary in extending knowledge the only way it is ever extended, as a process of making "partial connections" (Strathern, 1991).

In order to free itself to seek its affirmative goal of *rapport a soi*, anthropology needs, then, to turn from the level of comparative content to the level of comparative process. Comparison on this level is an ethical matter of achieving *a correspondence with the process of one's subjects*, what Edmund Leach once termed "ethnographic congruency." The conventions of doing and writing ethnography should, by this figuration, reflect subjects' sociality as a matter of good form, an injunction that precludes treating persons as inanimate things, or ignoring their historicity (micro- or macro-historical, lineal or recursive). The creative disjunction inheres in the fact that ethnographic congruency is motivated in the first place to plot a convergence with the real.

Certain ethnographically informed writings make the point by taking correspondence to the level of literal form, eliciting an experience of homology in readers. Strathern's *Partial Connections* (1991), which is dedicated to the effect of intermittency in social and cultural practice, is organized into parts of other parts of itself. Its model is Mandelbrot's rendering of "the Cantor dust": the dust of points that remain after a loss of information. The book's structure reproduces the "dust" of remaindered points, Part II ending in the particles of what was Part I, and vice versa, such that the end result is a kind of gap icon. Likewise, Michael Taussig's *Mimesis and Alterity* formally mimes the organization of Walter Benjamin's *One-Way Street* into "dialectic images", which in turn mimes the "dialectic images" of the modernity it observes. Or, to reverse the order as if to show a genealogy, the interrupted culture of modernity finds its homologic supplement in Benjamin's writings, which Taussig extends in form, but with a slip to Adorno's critique of Benjamin, in writing on the "question of the mimetic faculty" and the "magical power of replication" (Taussig, 1993: 2) of authority on the far colonial shores of Cuna Indians. Steven Feld's essay on oral performances of Kaluli of Papua New Guinea (1998) interweaves verbal texts with verbal and gestural asides: "[into the microphones I'd just set up in front of him] . . . [pointing to a corner of the house] . . . [taking the rat's voice **xcxc**. . .]," and so on. The radical effect is to give the reader an experience of entextualization, and to avoid privileging the verbal content of the text.

Ethnography's credibility derives from the fact that, traveling to other shores, it happens there upon its own participatory process, differently situated, and invests its process in this new location as a matter of *ethical correspondence*. That is, alongside subjects, it participates in and may claim responsibility for the "inscription of the universal in the singular"; in this particular human exchange as a "model of and model for" all possible exchanges of knowledge. This action casts ethnographers as "bricoleurs" who, as Lévi-Strauss (1966) said, always introduce something of themselves into their project. Clifford and Marcus (1986) have written the point into anthropological history that ethnographers write themselves as they write others. But on the level of process, this is not necessarily a problem. Standing where "the shadow of the other falls upon the self" (Bhabha, 1994: 59), ethnographic writing is positioned to expose, as a feature of its own hybridizing process, the inescapable ambivalence and ambiguity of subject-positions. It thus subverts any reading of itself as a true representation, or substitute for, the subjects, knowledge, and experiences that its writing displaces. It subverts likewise any labeling of its contents as "original" or "authentic" instances of the social processes with which it seeks affinity in its mission of openness. The "story" of ethnographic supplementation becomes in this light a story of the multiple authors – the multiple subjectivities – which produce it, and are produced in respect of it. This is also the open set of subjects to which it is answerable. The ethnographer offers a method for engaging in supplementation across difference, as a method of "answering to" another as if to oneself.

Given ethnography's concern with "human meanings and values *as they are actively lived and felt*" (Williams, 1977: 132; my emphasis), "writing culture" is thus a business of possibly unparalleled complexity. It succeeds only – though at its best inspirationally – as a discipline of "partial connections" and, I would add, of partial severances. Returning to the aporia of ethnography, its most natural environments are the gaps between social entities and cultural categories, and resoundingly, between textuality and embodied experience – the realm of the "knowing subject", as Foucault (1972) has put it. In placing social practice at the heart of the matter, the project of ethnography will always exceed the realm of "textuality" (verbal texts, images, or things) – while under-reaching experience.[11] This *practical economy of the supplement* is not, then, a matter of addition or subtraction[12] or of any other simple arithmetic of knowledge: the subjectivities involved forbid it being.

Ethnoscapes of displacement

Apart from the practical ethics of doing fieldwork and handling or housing material culture or physical remains, an interpretative ethics draws into relationship politics and poetics in debates about such things as the location of authorship, subjectivity and subjectification, the centrality of the indigenous voice, and so forth. These latter concerns have been to a large extent dominated by writers who come to their commitment by other routes – other technologies of knowledge production – than ethnographic practice. It is to the "ethnoscape", then (to take Appadurai's term, 1991), that one must turn, in order to advance the argument for a less Euro-self-centered *rapport a soi*.

Issues of naming

Recently, the cultural production of names and naming has figured importantly in formulating an ethical discourse for "recentering" subjects, particularly those subjectified by colonial agendas (Chow, 1998). Ethnography can constructively complicate that project. For example, in a major ethnographic study of ambiguity and displacement in the cultural practice of Anakalang (Indonesia), Webb Keane (1997) describes the "ambiguous authority of spoken words" (p. 24) across a range of cultural scenarios of exchange. At one point he discusses the "recursive displacement" of Anakalangese teknonyms, giving as an example the teknonym "Mother of Bani", which he tells us is

> a product of recursive displacement, because it avoids the child's real name (which is Kaledi) and appropriates instead the child's uttered name (Bani). This uttered name in turn involves still another set of displacements, since Kaledi takes his uttered name from another man, his "namesake" (tamu). This older man named Kaledi has a "horse name" (ngara jara), "Valiant Male" (Moni Bani), the abbreviated form of which becomes young Kaledi's uttered name. . . . Thus we arrive at the teknonym "Mother of Bani" through a series of steps away from her "real name" . . . Most horse names involve yet further displacement, since they derive from (and thus allude back to) the owner who takes their name: they permit a man, in effect, to speak of himself as if he were speaking of a horse. (Keane, 1997: 129–30)

Of course, the sense to be made of these displacements lies only with knowledgeable users of the teknonyms. But Anakalang are in relation as well to others outside the local language group. An Indonesian census officer, for example, would hear and record official names, not teknonyms, in the course of which his agenda for national identification would displace entire chains of teknonyms, and the relationships to which they refer. The detachability of names, not only from the physical person but also from a political value, points to the importance of a context- and relationship-sensitive analysis of acts of naming, and of displacement more generally. This analysis would situate naming at all levels of differentiating function; would specify its centering or de-centering effects for subjects on both sides of any conversation of power.

Compare this approach to Spivak's from cultural studies, and from her native India where, she tells us, official names may function not reductively, but as "master words" which "ground" in absolute terms a subject de-centered by colonial agendas (in Chow, 1998: 47). To give one's name in this particular situation would be a self-essentializing action with a pro-tective purpose – an action of circling the wagons (as it were) on identity, creating a shielding self-closure. Yet, self-centering may have value in some situations and de-centering or evasion value in others. The name, that is, is anything but "a sublime object", to cite Žižek's formulation. Its value as an alternative "body" to the physical one (Žižek, 1989) is an open question. For a politics of naming, then, the issue becomes to decide which names have value and significance for whom, situationally.[13] From this point of view we would ask how teknonyms and other de-centering strat-egies operate in Spivak's India, or conversely, what political functions Anakalangese find for their official names. Under what conditions, in other words, does naming open up possibilities for social connection – open relational tropes to the play of signification – and under what conditions does it close off or inhibit social connection and social capacity?

Ironically, the valorization of the name as a re-centering resource for marginalized persons can further marginalize their diverse positions, and overpower their own strategic ambiguation of identity and difference. This would seem on the surface of it unproblematic when the writer is indig-enous to the culture she writes of: her own recaptured centrality – her own name – makes her case. But this nativism needs to be interrogated. Ebron and Tsing (1995) give the example as co-authors who, writing across their ethnic identifications, destabilize these as authoritative formations sufficient for the purpose of claiming any kind of ownership of ethno-graphic knowledge. The question in this light is whom we disown by our choice of analytics and rhetorics, and how we might achieve a more prop-erly nuanced understanding of the practices in which we are implicated.

A supplementary point out of ethnography's comparative project is that names, as well as recovering a position for subjects, have a use in claiming new positions prospectively. Keane (1997), commenting on the ambigu-ity of substitution, writes that "substitute names are not simply negations of the real name but often point toward something else as well. . . . Strat-egies of displacement highlight the fact of avoidance, pointing to some-thing that is suppressed" (p. 130). Too, substitute identities may "point toward" some identity quality they wish to elicit or attract to themselves, revealing not evasive action but its opposite.

I have in mind some observations from Port Moresby, where in 1985 Trobrianders whose most striking identities were as elite Papua New Guinea "nationals", were engaged in actively prospecting *backwards* for identities as authentic Trobriand Islanders of ranked lineage. These men had lived away from the Trobriand Islands most of their adult lives. Their self-fashioning was a *self-exoticizing* or "practical nostalgia" (Battaglia,

1995a), both personally and politically motivated. Critics of colonialism (e.g. Todorov, 1993) have not acknowledged self-exoticization, the circumstances of which may reveal a great deal about identity play. In this case, men who were literally the "writers" of nationalism (one, Charles Lepani, was a co-author of the Constitution of Papua New Guinea, while another, John Noel, had a role to play in setting out the national budget) were now claiming traditional identities in images and objects that tied them to what they termed the "work" of indigenous "custom."

Meanwhile, on another level, they were seeking to acquire identities as men of high matrilineal rank, separating themselves not only from their elite urban identifications but also from their low rank at birth as men of the Bau matrilineage. They did this by sponsoring an urban gardening competition. Challenging the local wisdom that "yams don't grow in Moresby soil", they assembled displays of yams, debated the moral qualities of their growers as interpreted from the yams' appearance, marked their produce and yam shelters with insignia of high rank, and otherwise asserted lineal connections to ancestral entitlements. In short these assertions were indigenous acts of supplementation. They amounted to saying: I am not *purely or only* Bau. They were also acts of strategic ambiguity. The rhetoric of identity was kept alive as an open issue because inscriptions of "authentic" identity were deferred and displaced from particular persons to other persons and material objects – to multiple sites of social action (Battaglia, 1995a). In short, these examples suggest that extensions and limitations of self are products of the social relational gaps, ambiguities, and aporias of moral orders, as certainly as of rules and norms.

Ambiguities of closure

While less fluid than the open-ended slippages of teknonyms or prospective rhetorics of identity, public rituals and other cultural performances may be no less active sites of cultural ambivalence and ambiguity. These performances in some sense occupy a "third space" of displacement, being at once embodied inscriptions – bodies writing culture – and ephemeral artifacts (Battaglia, 1990). Accordingly, the representational ethics of performance ethnography has its work cut out for it, since it begs the question of whether its work is formally, anyway, at cross purposes with its subjects' goals. For example, can it justify seeking to converge with a reality that is denied by local actors, or to transcribe and extend a performance valued locally as an act of resolution and closure?

While on Sabarl, I asked to hear a particular myth. The correct person to tell it was someone who had inherited the myth through the lineage – someone "close to the body" of its ancestral origin. Yet when the time came to perform the narrative, this teller prefaced his performance by saying *Tahamtohon ega*, "We are only rehearsing/trying it out." Thinking that the "real" performance would follow, I took this as a cue to turn off my tape recorder. But the "real" performance never did take place. As other performances on other occasions were prefaced by the same phrase, I came to understand that there was only, for Sabarl, and where cultural performances were concerned, the "trying out." No one claimed to reproduce the ancestral word exactly: it is the work of the living to aspire, not to succeed in our efforts to represent.

In "acting like" ancestors, as Keane tells us also for Anakalang, persons foster a "tension between identity and disjunction, like that between inside and outside the frame" of ritual action." (Keane, 1997: 26).

This kind of tension is for Sabarl most apparent – in their mortuary rituals. On the one hand, people "act like" their ancestors by engaging in ritual action; on the other hand, Sabarl also regularly leave out significant elements of the ritual, revealing their human imperfections – their difference from ancestors. On one occasion, someone pointed out to me that the "most important part" of a burial, where a pot is placed in the grave so that the dead can cook in the other world, was inadvertently "left out." But this inadvertent omission was not just accepted as a law of nature; it was cause for comment. Indeed, Sabarl ran a critical discourse on all of their ritual practices, for example: an oracle's efforts produced an unreadable message; or someone failed to burn enough coconut husks to draw off witches during the funeral. Over time, I have come to view such slippages as an essential element of ritual practice. Through them, the difference between disembodied (ancestral) and embodied (mortal) practice could become apparent, and be entered into on-going social life as information for living.

Insofar as slippages are engaged by those involved, and not merely dismissed as accidental, they have the consequence of dislodging the certainty of a given cultural order. Whether advertently or not, they expose the human element in any claim to an essential value for "authentic custom" (Sabarl say *paga suwot*), and mitigate any responsibility people might take for making such a claim. I would go so far as to say that without such slippages, the actual project of using ritual to effect connections and disconnections among the living would be compromised. For Sabarl, rituals renewed a debt of form – the "custom" that the ancestors ceded to descendants, at the moment they were displaced as exchanges among the living. They raised that indebtedness as an on-going, debatable issue by producing *something to answer to*. Ethnography does this also, but with a difference, when it takes its ancestral method to far shores, and turning this method to positive purpose, produces something for its ancestors to answer to.[14] In other words, the difference is that Sabarl were answering to the living as if (in the name of) answering to the ancestors; meanwhile, ethnography was answering first to subjects, involving its ancestors with a view to holding them to account, as much as honoring their practices. The ethical correspondence is, then, on the level of process, namely, that contemporary practice loads a moment of self-conscious displacement with the power to transform its enterprise, and otherwise come into line with lived realities. In the end, neither cultural performances nor ethnography can be thought of as a finished "work" *in any fixed sense.*

Ironically, both lapses of custom and commemorative acts are for Sabarl instances of forgetting. Sabarl stated that the overarching purpose of the entire sequence of mortuary rituals was to "forget" the dead (cf. Foucault, 1977). Whereas lapses of memory raised issues of indebtedness, extending that discourse, social acts of willed forgetting were for settling debts that objectified relationships to the dead, and those formed in respect of the dead. The object was to "finish" these relationships – to arrest displacement – and "clear" space for new relational histories to form. These acts of clearance took the form of symbolic "openings" of survivors' eyes, mouths, ears, and genitals – an act of correspondence to the dead, who as an ancestor was figured as all-"open" to knowledge and relationships (on social forgetting, see Battaglia, 1993). It occurred to me while on Sabarl to ask if there were any "stories of" mortuary rituals from ancestral times. I was told, paraphrasing the response, "We don't need stories, because we do it all the time." Narratives were compensatory substitutes for bodily experienced and inscribed correspondences.

As we see by the ritual openings and closures of Sabarl, a value for openness need not negate a value for closure. The delimiting supplement is not invariably problematic: Sabarl say that they seek to "finish" their relationships to the dead in their commemorative rituals, seek in that context to arrest displacement. An ethics of the open subject sets itself against *problematic closure*, not against closure *per se.*

The point about cultural performances is that even when they are given the status of official culture, the identities and differences they inscribe have the material quality of disappearing ink. This quality ensures that the values it captures will be released from the performative context to futures undetermined by it: performances are formal invitations to recombinant significance. It could almost be said that their formalization ensures that other objects will be found to carry the values they inscribe into contingency.[15] Whether as an action of confronting contingency with the ideological force and face of official culture (e.g., as in rituals of state), or as an action of taking official texts to the negotiating table of practical use or popular cultural "play" (e.g., theatrical cross-dressing; see Robertson, 1998), the porous boundaries of performative texts problematize as certainly as they reiterate social identities and relationships.

The felt place of displacement

The contingent relation of closure to openness finds a homologue in the relation of emplacement to displacement. Ethnographically, the latter notions appear in dialectical relationship as tropes of "dwelling" and "traveling" – of "being there" and "getting there."

"Dwelling", from Martin Heidegger (1977),[16] signals a phenomenological orientation toward sites of social practice, in which place is taken to be "the most fundamental form of embodied experience – the site of a powerful fusion of self, space and time" (Feld and Basso, 1996: 9). This discourse is oriented to embodied experience, and to embodiments more than to representations of cultural orders. As Feld states: "Experiential layerings from one's birthplace to other places lived and traveled actively map place into identity, conjoining temporal motion and spatial projection, reinscribing past in present, creating biography as itinerary" (Feld, 1996: 113).

Ethnographies in this cast are compelling to the extent that they avert the most damning critique of experiential models, namely, that their rhetoric "appeal[s] to experience as *uncontestable* evidence and as an originary point of explanation – as a foundation on which analysis is based" thus "naturalizing difference" (Scott, 1991: 777; emphasis mine). "Being there" as ethnographer is, then, taken as crucial to, but not an essential entitlement of, the project of "writing" persons in their social, historical, and cultural locatedness. Likewise, the experience of the people being studied is acknowledged to be always to some extent inaccessible – even to indigenous ethnographers.

In his interpretations of illness and healing practices of Yolmo Sherpa of Nepal, Robert Desjarlais (1992) details how Yolmo bodies code knowledge, morality, and gender in spatial formations: "inside/outside, right/left, high/low (themselves rooted in the structuring structures of the house)" (p. 186). These cardinalities of the body become lived maps for Yolmo seeking protection against evil forces in rites that demarcate the body's "geography" – "giving imaginative form" to the sense that "body and house are more bound than open" (p. 190) and accordingly closed to penetration by the forces of evil. In other rituals, the body's maladies as the *active traces* of evil-doing, are displaced from body interiors to exteriors, and from high (dominant) to low (subordinate) positions of power by reference to the same cardinalities. Thus, for example, a shaman embodying in his trance state the "heartmind" of a protective spiritual tiger, bites a patron's neck and sucks out the tainted blood of her affliction; as described by the patron, he "sucks away the pain-distress. . . . By biting, he picks up the pain" (p. 193).

Within the "kinetics of healing" the stress on displacement actually recenters the patron – the "ritual processes mirror[ing] the displacements, movements, and postures engaged in the everyday life of the flesh" (p. 194) – "writing" them, I would say, to different purpose. Desjarlais continues: "The rites do not influence some 'I' or ego detached from the flesh. They work directly with the body through gestures, smells, and sensations" (p. 196). Thus the ritual *prescriptions* effect the cure, in dialogue with the "active imagination" (he cites Nietzsche) of the patron. For actors, then, the value for opening and displacement does not contradict the value for bodily closure and a bounded emplacement. Indeed, healing occurs as the relation *between* the two kinds of enactment.

An observation of the fine and fine-grained ethnographies oriented to the "senses of place" and the place of the senses is that almost by definition the relationality of the persons involved is conveyed in terms of its function for particular bodies. Bodies travel, illnesses travel through the body, and so on, in relation to other bodies and forces, but the vehicle of social relationships is almost beside the point of subjects' existential and micro-historical embodiments. This approach has the advantage of recalling displacement from exclusive engagements in the realm of the political, foregrounding instead the kinaesthetics of moral orders (e.g. Feld, 1996; Basso, 1996; Weiner, 1991) in more or less delimited localities – among the Yolmo, the Kaluli, the Navaho, the Foi, and so forth. Not surprisingly, these ethnographies may be unsympathetic, even hostile, to post-modernism's themes of interference, rupture, and the arbitrary fragmentation of subjects.

Broadly speaking, the larger-scale issues of experienced disruption, interruption, and interference are the preferred space of the trope of "travel" (for a position statement, see Clifford, 1992; for recent discussion, see Kaplan, 1996). In its emphasis on political displacements, this discourse abides in the borderlands of social practices and entities – the geopolitical space between homelands and strange lands (for comment see Clifford and Dhareshwar, 1989; Clifford, 1994; Bammer, 1994; Kaplan, 1996) – and may even take positional ambiguity as its stated point of departure. Fred Myers (1994), for example, situates his ethnographic account of Pintupi (Aboriginal Australian) artists in New York gallery spaces, where the artists are shown as agents of their own enterprising displacement into the artworld, and co-authors of its terms of identification and difference. Here, ritualized performances and other forms of art travel in the form of exhibitions, inscribe relational values, especially to "place" and the lived geography as embodiment of ancestral histories, and articulate valued social relationships (including those with the anthropologist) within and between local and global value systems. Myers shows Pintupi self-practice in its dimension of a moral aesthetic; artists make ethical decisions regarding the presentation of their sacred rituals, in their own terms. Thus, the discourse of displacement converges with the realm of aesthetic judgments, which are revealed in their contingency as inscriptions of complex power relations, as well as of coherent moral orders.

Taking as a classic location of the dialectic of dwelling and travel the literature of diaspora, Brian Axel (1998) explores the issues of ethnography's relationship to diaspora studies in his ethnography of Sikh displacement and identity. In his work of exposing the "othering" practices of torture within India's borders, Axel gives the case of Sikh home pages on the Internet which disseminate photographs of dismembered Sikh bodies in response to a history of political torture. Located in on-going dialogues at sites around the world where Sikhs have migrated, these images are constitutive, Axel argues, of the collective Sikh subject, which directs itself to the imaginary homeland of Khalistan. He continues:

> Indeed, the sight of the ... radically non-totalized ... body in bits and pieces provides the opportunity to repeatedly elaborate a fantasy of a time before contemporary violence and before a history of movement and mobility which scattered the members of a Sikh nation – a fantasy of the total body politic for which the idea of the homeland has become the icon.
>
> (*Axel, 1998: 24*)

The idea of Khalistan, an "unrealized territory" which has had at no time a corresponding political domain, could not be inscribed within a methodology of a bounded or ahistorical anthropology. Yet, Axel shows, even the displacement-oriented discourse of diaspora has a history of participating in the objectification and "othering" of subjects. Once disengaged from assimilationist programs and from the Jews, diaspora studies in particular, in its status of defining the post-colonial other for academic, governmental, and other organizational labors, has sometimes produced diaspora as a "pathologized subject." This subject is a monstrous abstraction – "the diaspora" as a totality. Axel continues: "Diaspora studies, thus, makes possible the production of certain forms of knowledge that inscribe abstract qualities of originary difference, of 'the homeland,' onto the sensuous bodies of 'its' people" (p. 8). Within this process, "the production of humanity relies upon the repeated production of the monstrous, of inhumanity" such that "violence locates the limits of the knowable" (p. 25).

The displacement of their dismemberment onto a larger operation of re-membering their Khalistan "homeland" shows some Sikhs slipping free of the corporealizations (and free too of brutally delimited masculine bodies) that diaspora studies then proceeds to recall to the service of its own ideals and programs. That this movement, as Axel notes, is allowed by the original ambivalence of a Sikh desire to dwell within their own dismemberment, shows the sort of correspondence that we must not avoid confronting: here, of ambivalence which opens the subject to a problematic despecification. William Connolly writes that "the modern ideal of the unambiguous agent is one of the costs we pay for the demand that there be an ethical life without paradox" (1991: 80). An ethnographic conscience makes it possible to ask whether the cost to subjects is unacceptably high; whether we can continue doing business as usual in our academic and other sites of knowledge production, in good conscience.

Contemporary ethnography, to the extent that it recognizes its own contingency – its own genealogy – writes in correspondence to its ancestors without seeking to replicate their projects; indeed, it takes its contingency as a mandate to overwrite hegemonic or essentializing legacies. This action entails answering to living subjects, whose processes it seeks to represent as a matter of ethnographic congruency. But it would appear that rather than seeking correspondence with the functions that subjects ascribe to their own actions – for example, essentializing an identity for subjects who essentialize theirs, or ascribing a gender or an "aura" to our texts and embodiments in respect of theirs – the goal must be to achieve a negative relation. That is, in order not to be politically at odds with its subjects, anthropological writing must resist supplementation (in dialogue or writing) which participates in or identifies with the inhibitors of social connection across difference. In this commitment, which again, is a commitment to resisting its own programmatic heritage and inclinations, anthropology will place itself in a position to answer as a dynamic process not only to its co-producers, but as well to its future readers. In phenomenological terms, an ethnographically aware ethics of the open subject is "protensive" in orientation, extending a self-consciousness of its present actions into the future.

The double problematic of the supplement

> I will critically analyze, or "deconstruct," only that which I love and only that in which I am deeply implicated.
>
> Donna Haraway, '*Deanimations*'

We have just seen how extending and delimiting supplementation can be a good thing. But supplementation has a double capacity: it can *problematically* delimit and *problematically* extend knowledge.

Problematic delimitations

Derrida (confessing to being arbitrary) recognizes three forms of problematic delimitation, which I find useful in the context of this discussion.
One form we have already encountered as the limit of "problematic closure" which, as Derrida (1993) defines it, "assigns a domain, a territory,
or a field to an inquiry, a research, or a knowledge" (p. 40). A second
form is the limit of the "anthropological border" which, taken as a human capacity distinct from the territories of animals, "designates the spacing edge that, in history, and in a way that is not natural, but artificial and
conventional . . . separates two . . . linguistic and cultural spaces" (pp.
40–1). A third form is the limit of conceptual demarcation, whereby two
opposing, "essential" categories – emblematically here, Self and Other –
are purified of "all contamination, of all participatory sharing" (p. 41).[17]
   Spectres of irresponsible delimitation, when they take the shore of an
other as their point of reference, do not allow us to escape the injunction
(along the lines of the physician's ethical code) to *first do no moral harm*.
We must first, and perhaps ultimately, take responsibility for any act that
socially diminishes or "kills" the connective potential of another, as if of
oneself. This injunction returns us to the premise of the relational nature
of the self, even in societies that practice and culturally elaborate an ideology of individualism. For accepting that persons are locations of relations, any limitation of another's sociality moves them in the direction of
social disconnection and death. Heidegger's statement that "I am responsible for the other insofar as he is mortal" (Heidegger, 1971: 107) suggests the horizon. Taking mortality as socially constructed, and the moment
of death as culturally relative, the point is to accept responsibility for the
social life of an other, as a social person. Physiological demise is not in
this light everywhere and always the highest priority.
   I once experienced a painful return to Sabarl Island. During the month
I was away a baby had been born who was now near death. Though
healthy at birth, the baby was being starved because the father had rejected it. The village was outraged, the father ostracized by the neighbors
who had to endure the infant's feeble cries – in totally benign circumstances, one of the most "heart-piercing" sounds to Sabarl ears. The
mother, on threat of more beatings than she had already endured, was
not permitted to feed the infant. Her mother, furious, berated her son-in-
law publicly, but husband and wife remained together. The day after I
returned to the village the child died, and was buried without ceremony.
Why did no one from its matrilineage adopt the infant? Or take it to the
Catholic mission nearby? Sabarl ascribe agency to infants while they are
still in the womb. Conception beliefs hold that the child's body is an arti-

fact of father's and mother's bloods – in other words, an embodiment of their relationship (Conklin, 1995). Yet the moral outrage of the child's abandonment was overridden by the father's deauthorization of its social future: the child had been declared socially dead at birth. No one would ever talk to me about this death, which shamed the entire village and which even now haunts me. Durkheim is over my shoulder referring this case to a larger "universe of moral discourse", of which most Sabarl were, too, actively a part. My grief is/was to do with the fact that the death closed off contingencies that might have played out the child's life in terms other than those envisioned.

The ambivalent values which are revealed in this sad, and for Sabarl, deviant narrative, reveal the "structures of feeling" (Williams, 1977) which culture brings to bear on ethical negotiations of its own limits of tolerance. Writ large as conventional practice, the scale of the problem demands a different kind of attention, entails new aporias.[18] What anyway is clear is that, when the question of life and death becomes not what limits individual autonomy and agency, but rather what limits social futures, all bets on a universal code of ethics are off. But far from prompting us to relinquish the search for the universal in a particular that we can stand by, we must be moved to recommit more fiercely to this quest.[19]

We cannot afford, then, as I have tried to indicate by ethnographic example, to idealize others. An ethics of the open subject moves "beyond idealism", as Chow (1998) has argued (see also Narayan, 1997, for a stridently anti-anthropology discussion), and is agreeable to supplementing benevolent readings as much as malignant ones. By countering any tendency to idealize, that is, to "relate to alterity through mythification; to imagine 'the other' as essentially different, good . . . and beyond the contradictions that constitute our own historical place" (1998: xx), we admit the contradictions, too, of the ethnographic process which moves in correspondence with it – not as a negative injunction, but as a moral imperative to move beyond.

Problematic extensions

In dialectical tension with problematic delimitations, a discourse can extend problematically when its intent is hegemonic, or when it resists self-critique in the face of evidence that its effects are hegemonic. A solution that suggests itself is to "up-value" under-represented knowledge, placing all knowledge on morally equal footing. A characteristic of economistic discourses, this program of cultural relativism problematically treats knowledge as commensurable units, as if it were information moving within a closed system. Within this cybernetic consciousness, knowledge is lost or gained, rather than open-endedly transformed. Also, this consciousness offers no resistance to idealization at the hands of those who would see knowledge preserved, or to demonization by those who would discard it: it opens itself to stereotype. Cultural relativism, then, cannot be a solution in the terms of an ethics of the open subject. Rather, as Donna Haraway makes the point for scientific knowledge, we must take an approach to knowledge as "located and heterogeneous practice, which might (or might not) be 'global' and 'universal' in specific ways *rooted in ongoing articulatory activities that are always potentially open to critical scrutiny from disparate perspectives*" (Haraway, 1996: 7; emphasis mine).

I have taken the position that the most tenacious threat to an ethnographic, relational *rapport a soi* is the figure of the given, natural, or universal Self. This danger is distilled in what Haraway has termed "corporealization." Defining corporealization as an act of "corporeal fetishism", Haraway gives the example of the maps of "gene fetishists" who " 'forget' that the gene and gene maps are ways of enclosing the commons of the body – corporealizing – in specific ways which, among other things, often put commodity fetishism into the program of biology" (p. 18). A result is that "human beings, in all their social, historical, and moral complexity" are equated, metaphorically, with their genes (Nelkin and Lindee in Haraway,1996: 17). Metaphor, from this perspective, shows its proprietary side. A "close reading" of corporealizations reveals their nature as cultural: "deeply contingent, physical, semiotic, tropic, historical, interactional" (p. 18). Thus, corporealization both problematically extends totalizing metaphors of person, and problematically delimits our understanding of science as culture (a form of "problematic closure") and of the levels of relationality which constitute personhood by designating the "spacing edge" of the skin-bound individual as the natural boundary of the total person.

Two striking corporealizations, the figures of the autonomous, Ego-based self, and its near relative, the proprietary self[20] have recently been "reanimated" in the spectre of human cloning (Battaglia, 1995b). Following successful experiments in twinning human embryos (in 1993) and cloning an adult sheep (in 1997), fierce ethical debate erupted across the popular and scientific mediascapes as well as in official spaces for evolving national-level policy on genetic research. Cloned frogs have since opened the issues again, though to an inured press and public. To date, the concerns of bio-ethicists, journalists, and the general public have tended to focus on a small set of issues: the commodification of human bodies and body parts, the displacement of reproductive agency to sites of control beyond oneself, the moral limits of the use of new reproductive technologies generally speaking (Battaglia, 1995b). This set of issues points to widespread awareness of the scale and rapidity of social change – an awareness inseparable from the media's attraction to cloning.

Arguably, the originary site of popular and expert resistance to cloning is the notion of an individual identity. Cloning defies the categorical differences that form the foundations of self-recognition. The exclusivity of Self *vis-à-vis* Other and Subject *vis-à-vis* Object is challenged by the idea of the clone. An other self, and as well an acting, agentive artifact, the human clone is a monstrous embodiment of slippage, revealing the capacity of the knowing subject to exceed the limits of knowledge – of humanity as we know it. In line with other triangulating categories (e.g., bisexual identity) this idea would have little purchase on the cultural imagination were it not for the fact that the crisis of self-recognition is already with us. In their highly mediated everyday lives, people are already experiencing themselves as in some sense prefabricated replicants or copies of models produced off-site of themselves.

Hence the "auratization" of the value of individuality; its entrenchment as an ideology of individualism. By their responses in talk shows, press editorials, and the like, it would seem that Euro-Americans seek a stable, perdurable, and invariably identifiable sense of self in negative correspondence with times of media-enhanced and expedited social transformation. One result is a socially impelled (as distinct from a psychologistic) will to self-laminate – a will to fix and define the boundaries of self. Issues of individuality become acute at historical moments of social dividuality – for example, when human diversity, cultural hybridity, public image "spin management", and geopolitical displacement show the detachability of people's own texts, images, and bodies from their original context. The florescence of interest in new reproductive technologies and "genetic" families give this action its current focus and compelling features (Strathern, 1992). In our "brave new world" where new technologies render the products of human reproduction a kind of "standing reserve" for future use, where resources are "enframed" as useful only for consumption (Heidegger, 1977b; 17), persons in their complexity and historicity are inevitably devalued. In short, the discourse of cloning cannot be understood apart from conditions of post-modernity, and apart from the dark side of supplementation.

Along these same lines, the romantic rhetorics of individuality, for example in popular science-fiction films of the replication "genre", tend to feature the hyper-potentiation of individual characters' capacities for good or evil, usually cast in moral terms (*The Boys from Brazil*, 1978; *Blade Runner*, 1982; or *Multiplicity*, 1996). Replication functions in these films ironically to produce beings "more human than human" (to quote a character from *Blade Runner*), a prophecy they fulfill by showing powerfully heightened affect – usually compassion or malice. It is their renegade affect which in turn resists the replicant's *raison d'être*, namely, its "use value" for powerful agents of capital production: although its personhood inheres in these relations of power, its particular character comes to distinguish it from a droning humanity.

Agency and disagency

Although cloning may exhibit the dangers of the contingency of agency and selfhood, doubts about the nature and location of agency are central to any ethics of contingency. In a Sabarl Island mortuary ritual, an agent acting on behalf of maternal ancestors breathes the magical words he has inherited from his mother's brother into a construction of ceremonial axes, called "the corpse." The words urge the "corpse" to "reproduce" stone blades, which are an item of wealth in this region of Melanesia. The expert leaves the "corpse" alone, giving it privacy. The hope is that more axe blades will materialize – *but no one considers this inevitable* (Battaglia, 1990). So far as anyone can remember, at least one new axe blade is found beside the "corpse" construction after the expert has left its side. But the possibility of disappointment always exists. Where in time or in space would the problem be located if more axe blades failed to materialize? Whose agency would be at issue, whose "will" exercised or defeated? Whose neglect? The expert's? The ancestors'? The "corpse" or its constructors? Or might it be the host of the mortuary ritual, or his lineage, or their enemies? Agency, like persons, is always an open subject. Indeed, an important effect of the ritual was its foregrounding of agentive ambiguity, its assertion of ambiguity as an essential element of (re)productive life. One could say that the ritual was *for* acknowledging the tension between intention and outcome, the imaginary and the material, as a productive ambiguity of everyday life.

In the mundane activities of Trobriand gardening, the subjectivity of yams elicits the same point – seemingly intact for its radical displacement from the Homeland to the gardens of Port Moresby, as I observed in 1985 and 1986.

Yams, it was held, were subjects. They could smell and feel and move about of their own agency. Yams would also shrivel or grow in response to the moods and knowledge of their gardeners, whose "self-discipline" (as I often heard it called) they accordingly elicited. Yams, then, the "children of the garden", as much grew their gardeners as the other way around: the "child" was "father" to the man – for a further difference to be noted is that the gardener who mattered in political competition was male. But here the gender discourse reveals its ambiguity. Competitive gardening was a "man's game" alternative to the more famous "game" of kula ceremonial trading expeditions. Women, whose competitive interests were focused on mortuary exchange and internal trade, figured in this masculinist discourse primarily as "warriors" against weeds. Thus, father and child co-produced one another as allowed not passively, but by the aggressive efforts of women to clear space for it. The yam as a "text artifact" embodied a covertly bilineal program of familial relations (Trobrianders are matrilineal), in which the nurturant capacities of men and the aggressive capacities of women were co-ordinated to productive purpose (Battaglia, 1995a).[21]

For Trobriand gardeners, the agency of yams, and the deep satisfaction of engaging with them, to some extent counteracted the depersonalizing effects of the "cash economy" of Port Moresby. But post-colonial conditions likewise opened Trobriand subjects to complexifications of agency – a point I would wish to explore at some length.

I revisit, then, a moment of ethnographic "first contact".[22] It is 1985. I am aboard an Air Niugini flight from Melbourne to Port Moresby, planning to do urban fieldwork. My hope is to work among migrants from a region of Milne Bay Province, where I have previously lived. I am impatient to start, and I ask a cabin attendant if any Milne Bay people are on this flight (cosmopolitan Papua New Guineans sometimes play at guessing "ethnic" identities through physical features, though in this case the attendant knows most of her passengers from previous flights). She scans the rows and directs me to a man in a gray business suit. The man is John Noel, a high official of the National Planning and Budget office for Papua New Guinea, and a Trobriand Islander. He and I chat; mainly I ask him questions about cultural life in Port Moresby. Then, unexpectedly, he raises a point of ethnography: Do I think that Malinowski was correct about the system of rank in the Trobriand Islands and the position of chiefs in Trobriand society? Trying to recall what Malinowski wrote on the subject, I pause, then tell him that, in all truth, I have only the vaguest idea. The plane is approaching Jackson's Airport when Noel turns to me and says that he is sponsoring a "big event" in Port Moresby, the First Annual Trobriand Yam Festival – "many VIPs" will be attending. Would I like to be "the anthropologist"? He hands me his business card.

There are any number of things to be said about this exchange, but I recount it here by way of raising the ghost of Malinowski, and with it certain issues of agency. Specifically, I am concerned to show how the notion of agency is employed in social discourse; how agency is invoked or ascribed, concealed or obfuscated, more or less strategically. In this light, agency is useful to people not so much for controlling or determining a site of authorship or authority, as for ambiguating authorship or authority. Indeed, ambiguation analysis is necessary for nuanced consideration of how agency is attached or detached in social practice, how it is owned or disowned, to whom or to what agency is referred, and what motivates agency to go around, come around, and otherwise slip around.

To approach agency thus as an element in ambiguating social relationships – to take agency as a vehicle or site for problematizing sociality – is very different from a program to situate, fix, attribute, or reveal the "real" or "true" agency or agents of, say, an ideological schema. For one thing an approach to agency that recognizes indigenous programs of ambiguation, will tend away from issues of intentionality and free will (see key discussions in Keane, 1997; Ortner, 1984). Likewise, such an approach will tend toward openings of discursive space in which social relationships – and more particularly here relations of power – may emerge in their mutability, and their displaceability. *Disagency*, then, might be the better term.

I return, then, to Malinowski's ghost – though by way of a notion from classical rhetoric. Theorists of rhetoric have used the term *prosopopeia* in reference to the "[summoning] up an absent, dead, or ghostly personage by ... an act of naming" (Norris, 1988: xix–xx). Logically, this rhetorical action is ambiguous: on the one hand, it evokes a presence; on the other it functions as a reminder of "the distance that separates [that presence]" (Norris, 1988: xix–xx) from the phenomenally present-day. In other words John Noel, summoning Malinowski's ghost, simultaneously dislodged it from one time and place and relocated it to the space of our conversation. However, for me to mention this technique without cultural and historical qualification is to make merely a point of style, whereas effectively Noel's act of recovery was resoundingly political. On one level, he had challenged a hegemonic order: he had recovered the scribe-idol, the anthropologist, in the shadow of which Trobriand culture continued to figure itself, and to be figured by a Western audience – an audience included as "VIPs" in the plans for the First Annual Trobriand Yam Festival. Likewise, Noel had confronted the singularity of Malinowski's authority – a singularity which had effectively erased Trobriand agency; he had disturbed that authority's nest in a colonial past, and in the process distanced himself from a fixed hierarchical order by representing that order as a product of Malinowski's ethnography.

No notion of hierarchy can survive such a moment intact. The act of authorial slippage Noel committed made any kind of essentialist notion of inherited rank appear nonsensical. Of course as one might suspect, this relocation was politically motivated – Malinowski's ghost did not appear out of nowhere. John Noel was an elite Papua New Guinea "national", some twenty years a resident of Port Moresby. He was not by birth a member of a chiefly subclan, but its opposite: a Bau man, a member of the Bau subclan described by Malinowski [himself] as the "pariahs" of the Trobriands, possessors of the most lethal forms of sorcery, nobility's opposite – the basest subclan of the social order. Noel, however, was planning to claim connection to a ranked chiefly subclan, M'labwema, and by arguing that subclan's supremacy over others was planning to contest the order Malinowski had represented. This claim to nobility would be stated officially on the occasion of the yam festival awards ceremony in the form of a display of the insignia of chiefly rank. Thus, one way to interpret his invitation to me was as a kind of prefiguration of his own act of reauthorship in which "the anthropologist" could now be conscripted: prospectively, protensively, Noel had complicated his own project of self-fashioning by throwing anthropological agency back into the stream of political discourse (Battaglia, 1995a) – but this time, wearing a tracking collar that he, the host, had attached. As "Trobriander", then, the object of Malinowski's anthropology had both reclaimed initiative and made a claim to his own subject status. The inscribed, within the category "Trobriander", had reinvented the tool of both a former inscription and a former erasure.

In overview, it might be said that Malinowski's colonizing ethnography not only denied Trobriand subjects their own discourse of agency, but likewise denied them a capacity for the practical ambiguation of agency – and denied ambiguation itself any positive value for its users. Elaine Chang talks about the political capacity of ambiguation in terms of a "politics of equivocation" – a politics of "negotiating paradoxical or contradictory imperatives that orients itself . . . by a map of a world which is defineable only in *relational* terms" (in Bammer, 1994: 253). Within this political realm operate shifting authorities, unofficial discourses of power, ambivalent or anochronistic self-identifications – all elements of a working poetic of ambiguity. Beyond inhabiting this realm, John Noel was reinventing it in the harvest months of 1985.

Of course, in discussing agency as discourse I am privileging agency's metonymic dimension – agentive transformations, displacements, disconnections or ruptures, and so forth – over metaphoric or mimetic acts of agency and the question of what figurative forms might encode, represent, or more generally "mean." My purpose in doing so is to focus attention on "agency play", that is, I foreground discourse in order that agency play might derive an unaccustomed place of privilege from the centrality accorded it by indigenous models. Also, I highlight agency play in order that the Aristotelian project of meaning's disambiguation – the project to which so much of meaning-centered anthropology is heir – might be interrogated and more accurately situated within the politics of culture.

In the context of urban Trobriand practice, ambiguation took, for the most part, two forms. One entailed the (apparent) concealment of agency; the other its (apparent) revelation. In the case of concealment, agency was masked, but to paradoxical effect: a site of agency, asserted as an absence, was thereby identified. I have called this phenomenon *invisible foregrounding* (for more detailed discussion see Battaglia, 1997b). For example, a stone axe blade, an important item of wealth, is promised as a prize of the festival. However, it fails to be produced by John Noel on the occasion of the awards ceremony. This is taken as a significant absence. No one doubts that Noel possesses the axe blade, or has access to one. Rather, people assume that it has been concealed or withdrawn, with the consequence that the axe blade moves to the fore in people's speculative thinking. Taken as an ambiguated space or place – an absent presence – the axe blade does not simply occupy the logical space or place of a product of discourse. Rather it makes apparent Noel's attempt to assert that space or place – in a word, to control it, to control the relationships wealth elicits, to control wealth's agency. The story of the axe blade is the story of its non-appearance.

An understanding of Noel's withholding "gesture" – the "gathering of a bearing" as Heidegger describes it (1971: 18) – requires, minimally, that we understand how the appearance of a stone axe blade might have been interpreted at this point in the yam festival narrative. The theme of sorcery had been raised by the death of a chief, Pulitala, who had recently visited Port Moresby in order to observe the proceedings. Noel, as a Bau man associated with sorcery and as host of the yam festival, was a prime suspect. By not producing an axe blade he in effect disassociated himself from the discourse of sorcery – disowned his agency, self-marginalized – and also asserted control over whatever space the axe blade occupied in the cultural imaginary.

One can observe the obverse of invisible foregrounding in the case of Malinowski's ghost. Here, the (putatively) absent figure of colonial authority was brought out of obscurity into a position of felt dissonance. This new position or "third space" exposed the power relations articulated by the ghost, showing these in the light of new historical circumstances; it likewise illuminated the irony of our shared identities as cosmopolitans *vis-à-vis* the ghost and his Trobriand "Others". But more generally, and in common with acts of making something significant by absence, agency play here demanded acknowledgment of persons' capacities to abandon as well as to take up positions of power. Its process was a "model of and for" disowning as much as owning social and historical positions, and showed among other things the capacity of actors to exceed their cultural mandates.

These examples indicate the capacity of agency to travel, and they prevent us from attaching agency exclusively to an autonomous individual's intentions; and in no uncertain terms detach agency from social determinacy. I would go so far as to say that to represent agency as individually or constantly situated would be a breach of ethics.

Arguably the most sustained ethnographic analysis of agency and disagency is Keane's for the Anakalangese. Keane (1997) examines the "quandry of agency as Anakalangese publicly construct it" (p. 16) and the "hazards to which agency is prone" (p. 28) on occasions of ceremonial exchange and formal oral performances. He highlights in these contexts the ambiguity of objects which "can be damaged, lost, diverted away from their rightful recipients, their value debated, their meanings confused" (p. 22) and the "ambiguous authorship of the spoken word" (p. 24) which imputes to actors an authority it simultaneously problematizes. Keane's analysis inhabits the "fracture lines" of Anakalangese social structure that ritual encounters make apparent, "such as those between wealth and rank, solidarity and domination, artistic performance and coercive force, commodity and ancestral valuable, textual tradition and verbal power" (p. 27). He finds in these "lines of tension" (p. 28) the sites of a profound, and sometimes tactical, "ambiguity about agency" (p. 25) – collective and individual. Along the lines I discussed earlier in the context of Sabarl saying that they are "only rehearsing" or their "leaving things out" of ritual performances, this ambiguity is embodied in Anakalangese descriptions of their ritualized actions as "mere 'shadows,' [or] incomplete remnants of the more powerful capacities of their ancestors" (p. 23). Keane goes on to make the important assertion that "the difficulty of representation seems to localize the more diffuse uncertainties of politics and even the contingencies of life in general" (p. 23).

The point is of no little import here, since it returns us to the cultural complexities of taking responsibility for claiming one's actions as what Derrida terms an "advanced point of exemplarity" (1992: 24) – of taking responsibility for one's efforts to delimit moral contingencies. Sabarl and Anakalang live the ambiguous question of whether giving voice to ancestral truths confers authority or voices a challenge grounded in their own insufficiency to the task. It is a question that raises itself anew at each successive scene of formalized encounter. But we might allow it a further displacement, a further slippage, into the question of whether giving voice delimits or extends knowledge problematically in ethnographic practice.

Conclusion

> I will even venture to say that ethics, politics, and even responsibility . . . will only ever have begun with the experience and experiment of the aporia. When the path is clear and given, when a certain knowledge opens up the way in advance, the decision is already made, it might as well be said that there is none to make; irresponsibly, *and in good conscience*, one simply applies or implements a program. Perhaps, and this would be the objection, one never escapes the program.
>
> Derrida, *The Other Heading (emphasis mine)*

Anthropology sets its sights by another shore, sending its ethnographic methods traveling, displacing its own cultural assumptions, and its own colonial history. This process finds its positive value, and its risks, in its interpretative function of supplementation: the knowledge it gains both extends and delimits previous knowledge, in useful and problematic ways for all concerned. Supplementation, then, makes a difference beyond narrativity both to anthropology and to the subjects of its inquiry. However, supplementation occurs not within closed mechanical or cybernetic systems, but in social discourse. Subjects, and not impersonal forces or bits of information, are invested in the process, which in turn constitutes their subjectivities. This discourse of anthropology is inseparable from differentials of power. Accordingly, self-extension and self-limitation may have the effect of "overwriting", overpowering, arrogantly or "in good conscience" substituting for others' knowledge and experiences; self-extension and self-limitation may be hegemonic in their effects if not in their intent. Or, alternatively, they may counter hegemony: to the extent that the ethnographic method acknowledges its responsibility to others as its originary responsibility, its displacements will open up dialogue, and delineate the different subject-positions involved, or the absences thereof. Far from a disembodied philosophical discourse, ethnography is powerful and valid precisely because it replays, finds its process replayed correspondingly in, social practices of displacement on other shores of knowledge and experience.

The main argument of this chapter is that a tenacious hold on a notion of an essentialist or natural self is the greatest ethical threat to a project of convergence with the real motivated by *un rapport a soi*. This project requires that we embrace the ambiguities of social practices of far shores, and compare and contrast them with our own. The result could be a new social attitude and better relations within studies of culture, in correspondence with the kinds of relationship we seek within our own disciplinary practice.

Notes

This essay owes an enormous debt of gratitude to the frank, generous, and insightful comments of Brian Axel, Mario Biaggioli, Joan Cocks, Henrietta Moore, and Karen Remmler; and to Paul Staiti, especially.

1 Anthony Giddens's writing on the "contingent subject" and the structuration of identity has been particularly contagious to anthropology (see especially Giddens, 1991); so have the insights of Foucault and Bourdieu, whose approach to the subject as constructed by and within external forces of sociality finds a counter-voice in the notion of the transformative subject, as articulated with force by De Lauretis (1986).

2   From social theory, see especially Giddens on the self in modernity as a "re-flexive project" according to which "we are what we make ourselves" (1991: 75) *as individuals*; also, for a succinct summary of the "contingent," socially constructed self in the context of narratives of social naturalism in political culture, see Somers, 1995. Katherine Ewing's important thoughts (1997) on shifting contexts of selfhood should also be noted here.

3   Moore's powerful insight is worth quoting more fully. "Individuals," she writes, "are multiply constituted subjects, and they can, and do, take up multiple subject positions within a range of discourses and social practices. Some of these subject positions will be contradictory and will conflict with each other. Thus, the subject in post-structuralist thinking is composed of, or exists as, a set of multiple and contradictory positionings and subjectivities. What holds these multiple subjectivities together so that they constitute agents in the world are such things as the subjective experience of identity, the physical fact of being an embodied subject and the historical continuity of the subject where past subject positions tend to over-determine present subject positions. The notion of the subject as the site of multiple and potentially contradictory subjectivities is a very useful one" (1994: 54).

4   Certainly we do not have to look far for rhetorics of similarity and difference which, "vertiginous" and "manifesto-like" (Marcus, 1992: 310), display this revolutionary quality. Marcus quotes Charles Bright and Michael Geyer that "the problem of world history appears in a new light. At its core is no longer the evolution and evolution of world systems, but the tense, ongoing interaction of forces promoting global integration and forces recreating local autonomy. ... At the center of this study is the question of who, or what, controls and defines the identity of individuals, social groups, nations and cultures" (1992: 309–10).

5   As Walter Benjamin described it, the concept carries a sense of being above and beyond the social particulars of its production and application, enduring, and uniquely valuable.

6   For me, the phrase recalls one of Nietzsche's that we must attend to the "rich ambiguity of existence" in our studies of the courses of human history (for an inspiring discussion of contingency from political theory, see Connolly, 1991; I have taken these words of Nietzsche's from p. 80). Here, I take this conjunction as suggestive on another level also. For an ethics of contingency – a properly ethnographic ethics of the open subject – unfolds in ambiguity, that is, in what Walter Benjamin referred to as the "law of the dialectic at a stand-still" (as quoted by Bhabha, 1994: 18, where the topic of cultural ambiguity receives sustained attention). Also, I am indebted to Karen Remmler's observation that the "now time" of the standstill is a location to recognize (*erkennen*) the potential for change trapped in the past, which is a political or moral intent of memory, assuming self-awareness. An interesting further point is how this standstill has an afterlife that becomes embedded in cultural artifacts, texts, and remembrance (personal communication) – a point that would be well worth pursuing ethnographically. From the ethnography of ambiguity, I would note Herzfeld, 1987 on the "embarrassments of ambiguity" of Greek social and cultural discourse (p. 104) – for example between official

and daily usage of language, classical and folk models of Greek culture.

7 Clifford Geertz's "Thinking as a moral act" (1968) calls fieldwork specifically to account in critical terms. For a noteworthy discussion of this and other points of anthropological complicity, see Marcus, 1997.

8 As Raymond Williams discusses the concept, hegemony exists as "a lived system [a process] of meanings and values – constitutive and constituting – which as they are experienced as practices appear as reciprocally confirming. [This includes] practices and expectations, over the whole of living: our sense and assignments of energy, our shaping perceptions of ourselves and our world" (1977: 110).

9 For anthropological debate in the context of gender issues see Strathern (1988), who argues that engendering work is a matter of practicing claims to power (see also Butler, 1990), rather than participating in domains of power (see Josephides, 1985).

10 Bourdieu represents doxa within a framework of cultural determinism in which, as put succinctly by Dirks, Eley, and Ortner (1994), the limits of one's subjective desires are isomorphic with the limits of objective possibility. They go on to state that Bourdieu's sense of the constructed and limited subject establishes the limits of subjectivity itself; underplays the transformative potential of human agency (1994: 13).

11 Derrida acknowledges the dimension of embodied experience in his early definition of discourse as "the present, living, conscious representation of a text within the experience of the person who writes or reads it" (1974: 101). Urban's emphasis on culture's *localization* in "concrete, publicly accessible signs, the most important of which are actually occurring instances of discourse" (1991) contributes the "difference that makes a difference" to this definition. Local knowledge is not merely represented, then, but is constituted in the actions of social persons (see Geertz, 1980).

12 I found it interesting that an explicit rendering of selfhood in these terms is offered in fiction by Kundera (1993: 100).

13 See also Tsing (1993) on the shifting sense of what constitutes a "center" of power and significance and what constitutes a "periphery" from different subject-positions.

14 See Raymond Williams on Adorno's use of correspondence as displaced connection, as distinguished from resemblances and analogies (1977: 104).

15 On performative frameworks, see Goffman, 1974; Turner, 1986; Schechner, 1985.

16 Julian Thomas writes cogently on "dwelling," which is about a lack of distance between people and things, a lack of casual curiosity, an engagement which is neither conceptualized nor articulated, and which arises through using the world rather than through scrutiny. So it is impossible to begin to look at traces of past human presence without seeing them from the first as bound up with human social action and subjectivity. The structures which we excavate have not simply been affected by discontinuous human actions, they are both the outcome and the site of generation of human projects, and are meaningless if divorced from the structure of dwelling.

17 I would note that Derrida designates the anthropological border as a "na-

tional, state-controlled border" (1993: 41), whereas I see a broader application for the term.

18   Scheper-Hughes (1992) makes the point for the lives foreclosed on by Amazonian mothers who, living in post-colonial poverty, conventionally choose to nurture only children who will "survive", as this is culturally defined. In this case, the external agency of late capitalism opens the field of inquiry further, as we seek to interrogate those responsible for constricting the possibilities of social futures for infants and no less for all their kin.

19   See discussion of Heidegger on death in Derrida (1993: 39).

20   Writing in 1890, William James defined the "self" – what he termed the "empirical me" – as the "sum total of all that [a man] *can* call his, not only his body and his psychic powers, but his clothes and his house, his wife and children, his ancestors and friends, his reputation and works, his lands and houses, and yacht and bank-account. *All these things give him the same emotions*" (1983: 279; emphasis mine).

21   The Derridean notion of women as a negative difference to men is strained by this example, though not the position that differing is essentially gendered.

22   Portions of this discussion have appeared in the *American Anthropologist* (Battaglia, 1997a).

Bibliography

Appadurai, A., 1991. "Global Ethnoscapes: Notes and Queries for a Transnational Anthropology," in *Recapturing Anthropology: Working in the Present*, ed. R. Fox. Santa Fe: School of American Research, 199–210.

Austin, L., [1955] 1975. *How to Do Things with Words*. Cambridge: Harvard University Press.

Axel, B. [n.d.] (1998). "The Tortured Body." Unpublished paper.

Bakhtin, M., 1981. *The Dialogic Imagination*. Austin: University of Texas Press.

Bammer, A., ed., 1994. *Displacements: Cultural Identities in Question*. Bloomington: Indiana University Press.

Basso, K., 1996. "Wisdom Sits in Places: Notes on a Western Apache Landscape. In *Senses of Place*, ed. S. Feld and K. Basso. Santa Fe: School of American Research Press, 53–90.

Battaglia, D., 1990. *On the Bones of the Serpent: Person, Memory and Mortality in Sabarl Island Society*. Chicago: University of Chicago Press.

Battaglia, D., 1993. "At Play in the Fields (and Borders) of the Imaginary: Melanesian Transformations of Forgetting." *Cultural Anthropology*, 8(4): 430–42.

Battaglia, D., 1995a. "On Practical Nostalgia: Self-prospecting among Urban Trobrianders," in *Rhetorics of Self-Making*, ed. D. Battaglia. Berkeley: University of California Press.

Battaglia, D., 1995b. "Fear of Selfing the American Cultural Imaginary or 'You are never alone with a clone.'" *American Anthropologist* 97: 672–8.

Battaglia, D., 1997a. "Ambiguating Agency: The Case of Malinowski's Ghost." *American Anthropologist* 99: 506–10.

Battaglia, D., 1997b. "Displacing the Visual: Of Trobriand Axe-blades and Ambiguity." in *Rethinking Visual Anthropology*, ed. M. Banks and H. Morphy. New Haven: Yale University Press, 203–15.

Benjamin, W., [1978] 1979. *One-Way Street and Other Writings*, trans. E. Jephcott and S. Kingsley. London: Harcourt Brace.

Bhabha, H., 1994. *The Location of Culture*. London: Routledge.

Bourdieu, P., [1972] 1977: *Outline of a Theory of Practice*, trans. R. Nice. Cambridge: Cambridge University Press.

Butler, J., 1990. *Gender Trouble: Feminism and the Subversion of Identity*. New York: Routledge.

Chang, E., 1994. "A Not-so-new Spelling of my Name: Notes toward (and against) a Politics of Equivocation," in *Displacements: Cultural Identities in Question*, ed. A. Bammer. Bloomington: Indiana University Press.

Chow, R., 1998. *Ethics after Idealism: Theory-Culture-Ethnicity-Reading*. Bloomington: Indiana University Press.

Clifford, J., 1988. *The Predicament of Culture: Twentieth-century Ethnography, Literature, Art*. Cambridge: Harvard University Press.

Clifford, J., 1992. "Traveling Cultures," in *Cultural Studies*, ed. L. Grossberg, C. Nelson, and P. Treichler. New York: Routledge Press, 96–116.

Clifford, J., 1994. "Diasporas." *Cultural Anthropology* 9: 302–38.

Clifford, J., and Dhareshwar, V., eds, 1989. "Traveling Theories, Traveling Theorists." *Inscriptions* 5 [special issue].

Clifford, J., and Marcus, G., eds, 1986. *Writing Culture*. Berkeley: University of California Press.

Cohen, A., 1994. *Self Consciousness: An Alternative Anthropology of Identity*. London: Routledge.

Conklin, B., 1995. "Thus are our Bodies, thus was our Custom: Mortuary Cannibalism in an Amazonian Society." *American Ethnologist* 22: 75–101.

Connolly, W., 1991. *Identity/Difference: Democratic Negotiations of Political Paradox*. Ithaca: Cornell University Press.

D'Andrade, R., 1995. "Moral Models in Anthropology." *Current Anthropology* 36: 399–408.

De Lauretis, T., ed., 1986. *Feminist Studies/Critical Studies*. London: Macmillan.

De Man, P., 1984. "Phenomenality and Materiality in Kant," in *Hermeneutics: Questions and Prospects*, ed. Gary Shapiro and Alan Sica. Amherst: Universitiy of Massachusetts Press, 121–44.

De Man, P., 1986. *The Resistance to Theory*. Minneapolis: University of Minnesota Press.

Derrida, J., 1974. *Of Grammatology*. Baltimore: Johns Hopkins University Press.

Derrida, J., 1987. *The Post Card: From Socrates to Freud and Beyond*, trans. Alan Bass. Chicago: University of Chicago Press.

Derrida, J., [1991] 1992. *The Other Heading: Reflections on Today's Europe*. Bloomington: Indiana University Press.

Derrida, J., 1993. *Aporias*, trans. Thomas Dutoit. Stanford: Stanford University Press.

Desjarlais, R., 1992. *Body and Emotions: The Aesthetics of Illness and Healing in the Nepal Himalayas*. Philadelphia: University of Pennsylvania Press.

Dirks, N., Eley, G., and Ortner, S., eds, [1992] 1994. *Culture/Power/History: A Reader in Contemporary Social Theory*. Princeton: Princeton University Press.

Ebron, P., and Tsing, A., 1995. "In Dialogue? Reading across Minority Discourses," in *Women Writing Culture*, ed. R. Behar and D. Gordon. Berkeley: University of California Press, 390–411.

Ewing, K., 1997. *Arguing Sainthood: Modernity, Psychoanalysis, and Islam*. Durham, NC: Duke University Press.

Feld, S., 1996. "Waterfalls of Song: An Acoustemology of Place Resounding in Bosavi, Papua New Guinea, in *Senses of Place*, ed. S. Feld and K. Basso. Santa Fe: School of American Research Press, 91–136.

Feld, S., 1998. "They Repeatedly Lick their own Things." *Critical Inquiry* 24: 445–72.

Feld, S., and Basso, K., eds, 1996. *Senses of Place*. Santa Fe: School of American Research Press.

Foucault, M., [1969] 1972. *The Archaeology of Knowledge and the Discourse on Language*, trans. A. M. Sheridan Smith. New York: Pantheon.

Foucault, M., 1977. *Language, Counter-Memory, Practice: Selected Essays and Interviews*, ed. D. Bouchard, trans. D. Bouchard and S. Simon. Ithaca: Cornell University Press.

Foucault, M., 1984. "On the Genealogy of Ethics: An Overview of Work in Progress," in *The Foucault Reader*, ed. P. Rabinow. New York: Pantheon Books, 340–72.

Foucault, M., 1994. *Ethics, Subjectivity and Truth*, ed. P. Rabinow and R. Hurley. New York: The New Press.

Geertz, C., 1968. "Thinking as a Moral Act: Ethical Dimensions of Anthropological Fieldwork in the New States." *Antioch Review* 28: 139–58.

Geertz, C., 1980. *Negara: The Theatre State in Nineteenth-century Bali*. Princeton: Princeton University Press.

Geertz, C., 1988. *Works and Lives: The Anthropologist as Author*. Stanford: Stanford University Press.

Giddens, A., 1991. *Modernity and Self-Identity: Self and Society in the Late Modern Age*. Cambridge: Polity and Stanford: Stanford University Press.

Goffman, E., 1974. *Frame Analysis*. New York: Harper and Row.

Haraway, D., 1991. *Simians, Cyborgs, and Women: The Reinvention of Nature*. New York: Routledge.

Haraway, D., 1996. "Deanimations: Maps and Portraits of Life Itself." Paper presented in the session "Animation and Cessation," American Anthropological Association Annual Meetings, San Francisco.

Heidegger, M., 1971. *On the Way to Language*, trans. Peter D. Hertz. New York: Harper.

Heidegger, M., 1977a. "Building Dwelling Thinking," in *Martin Heidegger: Basic Writings*, ed. D. F. Krell. London: Routledge and Kegan Paul, 319–40.

Heidegger, M., 1977b. *The Question Concerning Technology*, trans. W. Lovitt. New York: Harper and Row.

Herzfeld, M., 1987. *Anthropology through the Looking-Glass: Critical Ethnography in the Margins of Europe*. Cambridge: Cambridge University Press.

James, W., [1890] 1983. *The Principles of Psychology*. Cambridge: Harvard University Press.

Josephides, L., 1985. *The Production of Inequality: Gender and Exchange among the Kewa*. London: Tavistock Press.

Kaplan, C., 1996. *Questions of Travel: Postmodern Discourses of Displacement*. Durham, NC: Duke University Press.

Keane, W., 1997. *Signs of Recognition: Powers and Hazards of Representation in an Indonesian Society*. Berkeley: University of California Press.

Kondo, D., 1990. *Crafting Selves: Power, Gender, and Discourses of Identity in a Japanese Workplace*. Chicago: University of Chicago Press.

Kundera, M., [1991] 1993. *Immortality*, trans. Peter Kussi. New York: HarperCollins.

La Capra, D., 1985. "Rhetoric and History." *History and Criticism*, Ithaca, NY: Cornell University Press, 15–44.

Lévi-Strauss, C., 1966. *The Savage Mind*. Chicago: University of Chicago Press.

Marcus, G., 1992. "Past, Present and Emergent Identities: Requirements for Ethnographies of Late Twentieth-century Modernity Worldwide," in *Modernity and Identity*, ed. S. Lash and J. Friedman. Oxford: Blackwell.

Marcus, G., 1997. "The Uses of Complicity in the Changing Mise-en-scene of Anthropological Fieldwork." *Representations* 59: 85–108.

Maranhao, T., ed., 1990. *The Interpretation of Dialogue*. Chicago: University of Chicago Press.

Moore, H., 1994. *A Passion for Difference*. Bloomington: Indiana University Press.

Myers, F., 1994. "Culture-making: Performing Aboriginality at the Asia Society." *American Ethnologist* 21: 679–99.

Narayan, U., 1997. *Dislocating Cultures: Identities, Traditions, and Third-World Feminism*. New York: Routledge.

Norris, C., 1988. *Paul De Man: Deconstruction and the Critique of Aesthetic Ideology*. New York: Routledge.

Ortner, S., 1984. "Theory in Anthropology since the Sixties." *Comparative Studies in Society and History* 26: 126–66.

Rabinow, P., 1994. "Introduction: The History of Systems of Thought," in M. Foucault, *Ethics, Subjectivity and Truth*, ed. P. Rabinow and R. Hurley. New York: The New Press.

Ricoeur, P., 1992. *Oneself as Another*, trans. K. Blamey. Chicago: University of Chicago Press.

Robertson, J., 1998. *Takarazuka: Sexual Politics and Popular Culture in Modern Japan*. Berkeley: University of California Press.

Said, E., 1991. "The Politics of Knowledge." *Raritan* 11: 17–31.

Schechner, R., 1985. *Between Theatre and Anthropology*. Philadelphia: University of Pennsylvania Press.

Scheper-Hughes, N., 1992. *Death without Weeping: The Violence of Everyday Life in Brazil*. Berkeley: University of California Press.

Scott, J., 1991. "The Evidence of Experience." *Critical Inquiry* 17: 773–97.

Silverstein, M., and Urban, G., 1996. "The Natural History of Discourse," in *Natural Histories of Discourse*, ed. M. Silverstein and G. Urban. Chicago: University of Chicago Press, 1–20.

Somers, M., 1995. "Narrating and Naturalizing Civil Society and Citizenship Theory: The Place of Political Culture and the Public Sphere." *Sociological*

Theory 13: 229–74.

Spiro, M., 1993. "Is the Western Conception of the Self 'Peculiar' within the Context of World Cultures?" *Ethos* 21: 107–53.

Strathern, M., 1988. *The Gender of the Gift.* Berkeley: University of California Press.

Strathern, M., 1991. *Partial Connections.* Savage: Rowman and Littlefield.

Strathern, M., 1992. *Reproducing the Future: Anthropology, Kinship and the New Reproductive Technologies.* Manchester: Manchester University Press.

Taussig, M., 1993. *Mimesis and Alterity.* New York: Routledge.

Thomas, J., 1996. *Time, Culture and Identity: An Interpretive Archaeology.* New York: Routledge.

Todorov, T., 1993. *On Human Diversity: Nationalism, Racism, and Exoticism in French Thought.* Cambridge: Harvard University Press.

Tsing, A. L., 1993. *In The Realm of the Diamond Queen: Marginality in an Out-of-the-way Place.* Princeton: Princeton University Press.

Turner, V., 1986. *The Anthropology of Performance.* New York: PAJ Publications.

Urban, G., 1991. *A Discourse-Centred Approach to Culture: Native South American Myths and Rituals.* Austin: University of Texas Press.

Wagner, R., 1995. "If you have the Advertisement you don't need the Product," in *Rhetorics of Self-Making*, ed. D. Battaglia. Berkeley: University of California Press.

Weiner, J., 1991. *The Empty Place: Poetry, Space, and Being among the Foi of Papua New Guinea.* Bloomington: Indiana University Press.

Williams, R., 1977. *Marxism and Literature.* Oxford: Oxford University Press.

Žižek, S., 1989. *The Sublime Object of Ideology.* London: Verso.

Whatever Happened to Women and Men? Gender and other Crises in Anthropology

6

Henrietta L. Moore

The 1970s were great years: Mick Jagger and the Rolling Stones, flared trousers, low-fat margarine, Charlie's Angels and a wine that went by the name of Bull's Blood. A decade when women were women and men were men. The 1970s were great years for anthropology because back then was the only time we've ever been sure in our minds that we knew what sex and gender were. Like all good things, this certainty has since come to an end. This chapter is about certainty and uncertainty, and about the instability of particular kinds of conceptual project.

What is gender?

It was in the 1970s that the distinction between sex and gender was established in the social sciences and subsequently took hold in all the academic disciplines in the humanities, with the exception of philosophy. The proposition that gender was to be understood as the cultural elaboration of the meaning and significance of the natural facts of biological differences between women and men came to assume an almost unquestioned orthodoxy (Moore, 1988). The only rearguard action that continued to be fought was with our cousins the biological anthropologists, among whom even the most liberal would only go so far as to say that while sex might not determine all of gender, it certainly determined a part of it. Social anthropology took the lead in arguing that sex could not determine gender, and provided evidence in terms of divergent cultural elaborations and examples of third genders and other forms of transsexualism. The work produced in the 1970s was fairly uniformly referred to as the anthropology of women, and was primarily concerned with documenting women's lives ethnographically and seeking explanations for the position of women in society, their universal subordination. It was only in the 1980s that the critical focus of the field shifted sufficiently for it to be renamed as the anthropology of gender: the study of gender relations as a structuring principle in all human societies; the study of women and men in their relations with each other. In both decades, gender was the object of study and sex remained remarkably under-theorized (Moore, 1988). This was not surprising since the latter's relegation to the category of the natural removed it from the purview of an anthropology concerned with matters social and cultural. The easy overlap between the categories of sex and gender and those of nature and culture made complete sense not only in terms of the influence of structuralist thought on the analysis of gender in anthropology, but also in terms of the salience of the nature/culture divide for the definition of disciplinary parameters, and in regard to the importance of this distinction for theories of the relationship between the body and representation and consciousness.

However, despite all the theorizing about gender, there was a curious, but unacknowledged problem about what exactly gender was. On the one hand, gender and gender relations were concerned with the sexual division of labour, with the roles, tasks and social statuses of women and men in social life broadly understood. On the other, gender was about cosmological beliefs and symbolic principles and valuations. It was not difficult to establish that the two were not always concordant. Societies where women were apparently clearly subordinate in domestic, economic and political life could also be those where symbolic principles and cosmological beliefs valued powerful aspects of femininity. Likewise, societies where symbolic systems created hierarchical and relatively fixed relations between the male and the female might also be those where women carried influence and power in day-to-day contexts. The social and the symbolic while never completely divergent resisted any easy theory of reflection and could certainly not be said to determine each other. Some of the best anthropological work during this period was concerned with investigating the refracted relationship of these different aspects of gender, but the continuing influence of Marxist and neo-Marxist frames of reference meant that the issue was most often treated as a problem about ideology rather than one about how to theorize the intractable relation between the social and the symbolic. This was to have interesting consequences. In any event, in the 1970s we were not seemingly worried about the apparent ubiquity of gender, that everything seemed to be about gender, that we were using one term to refer, as one scholar nicely put it, to everything 'from the description of the gods to the terms for a carpenter's joining' (Belo, 1949: 14, cited in Errington, 1990).[1]

What is sex?

Tracing a chronology involves creating a narrative history, but there is always more than one way to tell a story, and stories often tell us more about the present than they do about the past. With this in mind, I want to describe what happened next in the great sex/gender story. If the 1970s and 1980s had established that gender existed, the late 1980s suggested that sex did not. Within the narrow confines of anthropology itself, Collier and Yanagisako (1987) reopened the formerly neglected question of sex by asking what it means to say that gender is the cultural elaboration of the natural facts of sexual difference. Their contention was that this model is predicated on a Western assumption that sex differences are about reproduction, and that this assumption also underpins anthropological work on kinship, thus leading them to the conclusion that anthropological theories of kinship are simultaneously Western folk theories of biological reproduction (p. 31). In this, of course, they were simply continuing an old line of argument that anthropologists are weighed down by their own cultural baggage when analysing data and constructing analytical categories and models. Their overall argument was that there is no reason to assume that the biological difference in the roles of women and men in sexual reproduction will necessarily lie at the core of differing cultural conceptions of gender (p. 32). They subsequently suggested that the study of gender should be disassociated completely from the concept of sex because of the latter's culturally specific meanings, thus apparently abolishing sex altogether.

Shelley Errington took issue with Collier and Yanagisako on this point and introduced a distinction between three terms: sex (lower case), Sex (upper case) and gender. Her contention was that we should distinguish between biologically sexed bodies – sex – and a particular construction of human bodies prevalent in Euro-America – Sex – which influences the way anthropologists understand the sex/gender distinction (Errington, 1990: 19–31). Gender as a term would be reserved for 'what different cultures make of sex (lower case)' (p. 27). Errington argued that Collier and Yanagisako had confused Sex with sex, and thus her analysis – far from making sex disappear – appeared temporarily to double it, but this too was an illusion.

The analyses by Collier and Yanagisako and by Errington marked one of the points of entry of neo-Foucauldian thinking into anthropology. Both sets of argument rested on the idea that sex, and not just gender, was socially constructed, or rather that some aspect of sex was so constructed because the problem of what to do about the residual category of sex (lower case) remained, namely the inconvenient fact that people have bodies that are present in a differentiated binary form. However, once we allow for a distinction between sexed bodies – sex (lower case), the cultural construction of those sexed bodies – Sex (upper case) and gender – the cultural construction of sex (lower case), we might ask what is gender that Sex (upper case) – the cultural construction of sexed bodies – is not? To put it more simply: what is the difference between 'a socially con-structed sex' and 'a social construction of sex'? There are answers one can give to this question. We could say that Sex (upper case) is the cultural construction of sexed bodies, while gender is about the sexual division of labour, cosmological beliefs and symbolic valuations. This would be fine except that these two domains of human social life are not readily separa-ble from each other, and there is therefore considerable confusion about where the boundary should lie between sex and gender. One possible way to handle this confusion is just to get rid of Errington's intermediate cat-egory Sex (upper case), and go back to talking about the relationship between sex and gender, that is between sexed bodies and cultural repre-sentations.

In such discussions as these, sex appears and disappears; it is different from gender and it is not different from gender. Women are no longer just women, and men are no longer just men. But then do not forget that this debate is taking place in the late 1980s and early 1990s, and this is the era of Michael Jackson, Boy George, Prince and Madonna: neither sex nor gender are stable any more!

The idea that sex itself might be ambiguous, that the natural facts of sexed bodies might be comprehensible and persuasive only as cultural constructions raises the interesting question of whether sex classification is enough to determine gender categorization. Anthropology's early work on third genders and transsexuals had always suggested that it is not, but in the 1980s and early 1990s the impact of praxis theory in anthropology gave particular emphasis to the idea that gender assignments and catego-ries are not fixed, but have in some sense to be constructed in practice, to be performed.[2] This theoretical framework took something from Turn-er's earlier work on performance and symbols, but it was reinvigorated by ideas from well outside the discipline.

In effect, gender became reconceptualized not as something you were, but as something you did. What encouraged 'a man to do what a man's gotta do' was discourse. A version of radical social constructivism was distilled from Austin's speech-act theory, Foucauldian analysis and a rag-bag of ill-digested ideas about post-modernism and deconstruction. The result was a provocative rethinking of the relationship between sex and gender: where formerly gender had been conceived as the cultural elaboration of a sex that preceded it, now gender became the discursive origin of sex. Sex became understood as the product of a regulatory discourse on gender in which the surfaces of bodies are differentially marked and charged with signification.

Gender trouble?

The inversion of the relationship between sex and gender had been suggested by a number of theorists before Judith Butler published her famous book *Gender Trouble* (1990), but when this inversion is referred to in the contemporary literature Butler is most often cited as its point of origin. Butler's argument once again raises the instability of the analytic categories sex and gender: 'If the immutable character of sex is contested, perhaps this construct called 'sex' is as culturally constructed as gender; indeed, perhaps it was always already gender, with the consequence that the distinction between sex and gender turns out to be no distinction at all' (Butler, 1990: 7). Butler's point is that gender is the effect of a set of regulatory practices that seek to render gender identity uniform through the imposition of a compulsory heterosexuality (Butler, 1990: 31). In this way gender is seen as central to a process of becoming, of acquiring an identity, of structuring one's subjectivity, and can no longer be thought of as a structure of fixed relations. This process of becoming explains Butler's emphasis on performance, on what she calls gender performativity: 'If there is something right in De Beauvoir's claim that one is not born but rather becomes a woman, it follows that woman itself is a term in process, a becoming, a constructing that cannot rightfully be said to originate or to end. As an ongoing discursive practice, it is open to intervention and resignification' (Butler, 1990: 33).

However, it is not only that the regulatory practices that construct the categories woman and man are open to resignification – as well as the gender identities feminine and masculine – but that they can never be complete. Thus, gender performativity as a theory is not only concerned with how one enacts a gender within a specific set of regulatory practices, but is particularly focused on the disjunction between the exclusive categories of the sex/gender system and the actuality of ambiguity and multiplicity in the way gender is enacted and subjectivities are formed. Butler argues that the 'disciplinary production of gender effects a false stabilization of gender in the interests of the heterosexual construction and regulation of sexuality within the reproductive domain' (Butler, 1990: 135). This false stabilization conceals the discontinuities within heterosexual, bisexual, gay and lesbian practices and identities: 'where gender does not necessarily follow from sex, and desire, or sexuality generally, does not seem to follow from gender' (Butler, 1990: 135–6).

The categories of gender through which Western sex/gender systems naturalize sex difference are always ideal constructions, and no individuals will ever find an exact correspondence between their experience of their body and their gender and these ideal constructions. The theory of performativity thus offers the possibility of reworking gender, of shifting its meanings through the repetition of performance, of challenging and possibly subverting the normative constructions of the sex/gender system. The fascination of the possibility of resistance accounts for much of the contemporary appeal of this theory, and as such the theory of gender performativity suffers from the same general problem that afflicts all theories of resistance in the social sciences. More seriously, as Rosalind Morris has pointed out (Morris, 1995: 571), ambiguity as a concept has been elevated far above its explanatory potential – just like the concept of resistance in fact – and is held in many analyses to function as a kind of originary moment. A number of contemporary accounts of gender in anthropology suffer from this problem, where ambiguity is now the very grounds for sex and gender difference, a kind of pre-discursive, pre-ontological condition (Morris, 1995: 570). The idea that ambiguity is the basis of gender difference – in so far as it has a basis – has found ready acceptance in much recent ethnography which seeks to demonstrate that sexed bodies, sexual practices and gender identities do not necessarily go together. Recent work in Brazil, Thailand, Samoa and the Philippines, much of which has been greatly influenced by gay and lesbian anthropology (Weston, 1993a), all provide good examples (e.g. Johnson, 1997; Cornwall, 1994; Jackson, 1996; Parker, 1991; Kulick, 1998; Mageo, 1992).

Does gender exist?

The theory of gender performativity as developed outside anthropology has close links with a body of work on sexuality and sexual practice that is generally referred to as queer theory (cf. Graham, 1998). If the 1980s and early 1990s abolished sex, as the millennium approaches the race is on to abolish gender. If feminists and anthropologists had already raised the question of the indeterminate boundary between sex and gender, asking what was the difference between a socially constructed sex and a social construction of sex, developments in more recent feminist theory and queer theory have suggested that there is no need for a concept of gender at all. There are a number of strands to these arguments.

The first of these draws on the reconceptualization of gender as process rather than as category, the focus on the 'doing' of gender rather than the 'being' of it developed in performative theory and elsewhere. Queer theory emphasizes that gender is not the issue, but rather the way you live your sexuality, the way you enact a sexual identity. The result is a focus on sexual practice and sexuality, albeit one that draws on radical constructivist and neo-Foucauldian approaches to sexed identities by emphasizing their discursive construction. The fulcrum of much queer theory is sexual difference understood as sexual variety or different sexual practices (Abelove et al., 1993; Rubin, 1994; De Lauretis, 1991). This work emphasizes that genitals, sexual practice, sexual identities and sexual desire do not necessarily fit together in any conventional sense or rather that conventions can and should be subverted. Queer theory thus provides a problematic status for sex and for gender.

Sex appears to be coterminous with sexuality understood as sexual practices and sexual identities, and since what is in focus is the subversion of any necessity for the effects of the physically sexed body, some aspect of sex is conveniently pushed out of sight. The same aspect of sex that was lost in previous theoretical formulations: the fact that people have bodies that are present in a differentiated binary form. Queer theory also manages, however, to wish away gender since it has inherited the lessons of recent feminist theory where sex and gender can no longer be properly distinguished. The result is either that sex is 'always already gender' or alternatively a rather specious argument is advanced where queer theory gets to do sex understood as sexuality and feminism gets to do gender understood as the social roles of women and men. All this might be less confusing if feminist theorists had not already claimed that they were doing sex understood as gender. The issue, of course, is not really a theoretical one, but rather a kind of territorial war waged over the sexed body (Butler, 1994).

The origins of this dispute lie, as ever, in kinship metaphorically understood, by which I mean in intimacy and shared substance. Butler's original emphasis on the potentially disruptive effects of gender performativity, on its capacity for subversion and resistance, drew on theories of drag and camp to bolster the notions of both performance and resistance on which her theory depends. In fact, *Gender Trouble* ends on quite a clarion note, with the suggestion that the parodic repetition of gender can be used to subvert instutionalized gender identities (Butler, 1990: 146–7). The interpretation of drag and camp as mimetic forms of gender identity that serve only to reveal the imitative nature of the institutionalized heterosexual identities they seek to subvert provided performance theory with the crucial examples of gender performance and instability it needed.[3] This was particularly the case since Butler's theory of sex as the effect of the regulatory discourses on gender depended on an assumption that such discourses work by seeking to impose a compulsory heterosexuality. Thus in the great hall of mirrors in which we are now confined, feminist theory and queer theory – at least in some of their manifestations – are parodic repetitions of each other.

Anthropological work on sexuality and on gay and lesbian identities has a slightly different position. It certainly draws on feminist and gay and lesbian theory developed outside the discipline, but it has resolutely refused to confuse sex, sexuality and gender (Weston, 1993a; 1993b; 1998). In fact, it is in the gaps between these terms that anthropologists work to demonstrate that dominant Western assumptions about the interrelations between these terms are sometimes inappropriate for studying sex/gender systems cross-culturally – hence the continuing importance of, for example, work on Thailand, where we are being asked to consider systems that contain three sexes and four sexualities (Morris, 1994; Jackson, 1996). Anthropology's saving grace here is its commitment to empiricism (see chapter 1 above). This allows it to document the perceptions and practices of individuals and the relationship of those perceptions and practices to dominant and subdominant views about sex, gender and sexuality.[4] The relentless process of contextualization that is the basis of anthropological methodology and interpretation works against any tendency to privilege parody over convention. Although it could be argued that anthropological accounts, if anything, still have a tendency to privilege culture as against human agency and therefore downplay the potentially subversive effects of individualized practices (Weston, 1993a; Graham, 1998).

Butler has certainly been criticized on the grounds that the theory she puts forward in *Gender Trouble* proposes a view of agency that is far too voluntaristic. This is a pervasive misreading, but one so prevalent that Butler was forced to address it directly in *Bodies that Matter* (1993); not only to counter her critics (e.g. Copjec, 1994), but also her supporters who regularly read her work as supporting voluntaristic and philosophically essentialist accounts of agency and subjectivity. Butler perhaps opens herself to misreadings of this kind because she does emphasize parody and hyperbole, as if parody would free us all from the regulatory norms of gender, and as if we could choose when and how we engage in hyperbole (Walker, 1995: 72), the sort of approach that says 'I'm coming out of the closet today with my new gender identity on'.

The available anthropological data actually suggests that most people do not find their gender identities particularly fluid or open to choice, and this applies as much to those people who are seemingly resisting gender norms as it does to those who are apparently accepting them. In terms of anthropological analysis, this point needs some theoretical and critical elaboration because of the problematic relationship that academic and popular theories of gender, sex and sexuality have to anthropological work itself.

This is a relationship that has a history. In the 1970s anthropology was very largely responsible for providing the data on which the theory of the distinction between sex and gender could be based, as discussed above. Anthropology has continued to play a pivotal role in providing evidence of third genders, transsexualism and transgendering (Weston, 1993a). This evidence has not always come from 'other cultures': gay and lesbian anthropology has often been based on work in Europe and the Americas (e.g. Herdt, 1992). But anthropologists do not and cannot police the boundaries of their own knowledge, and so it is unsurprising to find that people around the world wanting to build and live alternative sexualities, identities and genders are aware of anthropological data and theory in the specific form in which it has entered the domain of popular culture. Even if people are not aware of the anthropological data directly, they are aware of the theories, practices and consumption items that make up gay and lesbian culture, and these cultures have long made use of a form of anthropology. In other words, anthropology – often unwittingly – has a long history of providing the evidence for the exotic and the alternative (see chapter 1 above).

In studying contemporary gender and sexuality, anthropologists are increasingly aware of the impact on so-called traditional sex/gender systems of the media, international tourism, music and dance forms, club culture and a whole range of other influences. New forms of sexuality and of gender identity are taking shape, and it might be easier to characterize this as a process of 'Westernisation' or 'trade in exports' were it not for the fact that so-called Western gay and lesbian culture and other forms of popular culture have long depended on influences from non-Western sources. Anthropologists, particularly those who are part of gay and lesbian culture themselves, are thus in an interesting position when studying alternative genders and sexualities and engaging in a process of 'us' and 'them' comparison (cf. Kulick and Wilson, 1995; Newton, 1993). It is important to recall here that anthropological comparison necessarily revolves around a fictive version of Euro-American culture, and thus this problem exists for all anthropologists regardless of their specific cultural backgrounds. The point then is that the study of gender and sexuality is as much about 'the study of ourselves through the detour of the other' as any other aspect of anthropology, except that it is even more obvious that the boundary between self and other is an unstable one in some respects. We should be critically aware that the writing of contemporary ethnography on sex, gender and sexuality is just as much about performing gender as are the cultural practices and perceptions that such ethnography seeks to describe (Morris, 1995: 574).

Bodies and the art of identity

One curious fact of the Western or Euro-American discourse on sexuality is its link to the production of identity and subjectivity. The degree to which, and the form in which, this link works in other contexts is I think a matter for empirical study. However, what becomes apparent not only within feminist and queer theory, but also in terms of certain forms of popular culture around the world, is a strange paradox. The paradox is the way in which ambiguity and fluidity in sexuality and gender are used to form the basis for identity politics: what is shifting provides the grounds for what is fixed. This paradox is instructive for what it reveals about some of the more problematic assumptions of gender performativity. Performative theory argues that it is possible to destabilize the regulatory discourses on sex and gender through repetition and the mimicking of gender categorizations, as well as through alternative practices that bring into question the interlinkages between bodies, desires, sexual practices and identities on which the sex/gender system depends. What becomes absolutely crucial in this theory, but usually remains remarkably under-theorized, is the use and the management of the body as a mechanism for the construction and management of identity. This has the extraordinary effect of collapsing the form of identity and the form of the body. This privileging of the body at the very moment when sexualities and identities are said to be fluid and ambiguous begs various questions.

Many contemporary cultures, including Euro-American culture, are obsessed with body modification. I would like to turn to a brief consideration of body performance art and body modification because they do furnish us with an example of a set of discursive practices concerned with bodies and identities, and one which apparently raises the issue of voluntaristic choice in an alarming fashion. Body modification and body performance art are also examples of a particular kind of relationship between anthropology and popular culture.

Fakir Musafar is the founder of the 'Modern Primitive Society' and is widely regarded as the guru of 'body-piercers, waist-cinchers and lobe-stretchers all over the world. Early in life, Musafar succumbed to a fascination with distorting his own body, only to realise as he matured and researched, that he was tapping into an ancient tradition shared by numerous cultures' (Mullen, 1997: 20). A recent discussion of Musafar's body practices, and those of a number of others, made reference to the practices of the Maoris, the Eskimos, the Kraimbit of Papua New Guinea, the Ndebele, the sadhus of Hindu tradition and Native Americans as sources of inspiration. Not all performers are concerned, of course, with exotic data and theory. Sebastian Vittorini, the Wasp Boy, acknowledges Musafar as an initial inspiration, but claims that he is just a masochist experimenting with his body, and that he likes to have an audience. However, other practitioners do use bowdlerized – and sometimes racialized – bits of anthropology as the rationale for their own and others' practices and experiences. Alex Binnie, one of London's top tattoo artists, explains:

> Traditional societies have used all types of body modification as part of the rites of passage. It's a transitional point in their lives, and it's important that they remember the lessons they're learning. One way of making that stick is to permanently inscribe it on their bodies. . . . If you think getting a tattoo is painful, you should look at what Aboriginal scarring is like, or look at circumcision rites in Africa. What we do is light-weight.
>
> (*Mullen, 1997: 21–2*)

The appeal to anthropology and to traditional cultures is partly a fascination with the exotic, partly a desire for authenticity and origins, and possibly part of a larger search for ritual. Ron Athey is a former Pentecostal preacher turned queer body artist. 'He speaks in tongues, whilst dressed as Miss Velma – the white-haired evangelist of his Californian childhood – he pierces his scalp with fourteen-inch lumbar needles to form a crown of thorns, and crucifies himself with meat hooks through his arms' (Palmer, 1996: 8). However, not all artists are making direct appeals to religious symbolism, even though the audience may take a different view. The Italian artist Franko B explicitly distances himself from Christian symbolism: 'I don't want to be a cheap Jesus'. However, his latest performance at the Institute of Contemporary Arts in London in 1996 involved standing naked while he bled profusely from stigmata-like wounds on his elbows. The pools of blood on the floor, the outstretched arms and the beatific pose all invoked Christian religious imagery (Palmer, 1996: 8). Franko B's other performances have involved cutting words – such as 'protect me' – into his flesh, and his current project entails opening up a vein in his arm, inserting a valve to control the bleeding, and then letting blood flow out around his white-painted, foetally crouched body. When you think you can take no more, his assistants hang him upside down by his ankles and more blood pours out (Mullen, 1997: 29).

Commentators on such performances often interpret them, as do some artists, as attempts to transcend the body. Such interpretations are perhaps inspired by the religious and spiritual images and rationalizations with which some performances are redolent. However, not all performers appeal directly to the spiritual: Franko B says 'My main thing is to try to make the unbearable bearable' (Palmer, 1996: 8). But what is the unbearable? Perhaps it is just his terrifying performance art, and it is the audience who are dealing with the unbearable. A kind of parody on Oscar

Wilde's famous comment on a less than succesful evening: 'great show, pity about the audience'. Or perhaps the unbearable is something in Franko himself. 'I was brought up to be ashamed of my body. I use blood, urine and shit as a metaphor because this is what I am'. The literalization of the body as self is a rather dramatic example of collapsing the form of identity into the form of the body.

Working up identities, creating difference is certainly a theme in the explanations not only of body performance artists, but also in those of body modifiers. Kate is into body decoration and tattooing: 'It's not that I'm insecure about my body. It's just a way of making you like certain bits of yourself better. And anyway, skin's very boring. If we all got naked and shaved all our hair off we'd all look alike. This is one way of ensuring that you're completely different' (Mullen, 1997: 26).

If body art and body modification is about anything it would seem to be about the stabilization of personal identity rather than its destabilization: perhaps the point is that it is both. But the degree to which it is genuinely subversive seems to me to be very questionable. The horrific is not necessarily subversive: Mary Shelley's *Frankenstein* was actually a great morality tale. It may also be true in relation to bodies, sexualities and genders that setting out to be subversive is not enough to effect subversion, and may have the opposite effect. The body, despite the fact that it is a physical entity, is not enough on which to build a personal or social identity. It is not and could never be completely stable as an origin point for an identity. Body performance art makes this very clear as each return to the body forces a further search for the perfected body, the one that most evidently provides the grounds for a chosen identity. This accounts, perhaps, for the need not only to modify the body, but also to technologize it. The anxiety is that a kind of obsoletion threatens the natural body in this period of late capitalism. Steve Hayworth, a body-modifier and amateur surgeon from California, has successfully implanted a metal plate in a man's head, into which can be screwed a variety of accessories, functional and decorative (Mullen, 1997: 29).

All forms of technology are, of course, prosthetic and, this accounts, in part, for their symbolic role in the construction and mediation of identity, particularly gender identity. Stelarc is a body performance artist who extends his body with technological additions: 'Death, he claims, is an outmoded evolutionary strategy. If the body can be redesigned in a modular fashion, then technically there would be no reason for death. The body need no longer be repaired, but could simply have parts replaced. The body must become immortal to adapt' (Palmer, 1996: 9). The goal would appear to be one of perfecting the body to sustain self-identity through time, to outmanoeuvre death and conserve identity. As more traditional ways of grounding identity slip away, some would appear to cling more tenaciously to the body as the one remaining source of a self-authorized existence. But this body cannot be the natural body; it must be one more stable, more perfected, and that means one more consciously fashioned.

The issue here is one about representation, and the relationship of the body not just to language, but to forms of representation that both exceed and cannot be reduced to words. Orlan is a body performance artist who has had at least nine plastic surgery operations. These operations are carried out under local anaesthetic, while Orlan chats to her audience and reads aloud from the writings of Julia Kristeva and Eugénie Lemoine-Luccioni. These performances are beamed live by satellite to galleries around the world, and some are available on the Internet and on CD-ROM. Orlan has recently released a CD-ROM called *This is my body...This is my software*. 'I have given my body to art', she declares. 'After my death, I won't give it to science therefore, but to a museum. There, mummified, it will be the centrepiece of an interactive video installation' (Palmer, 1996: 9). Orlan, like Stelarc, intends to stay with us, her dead body representing her in communication with the living through interactive video technology. There have been many ways of course to seek for immortality and for life after death, but Orlan's work is particularly revealing of the relationship between the body and self-identity, and thus between the body and representation. Orlan's body is a representation, it is a work of art. This literalization is revealed by the fact that Orlan uses bits of her flesh in 3D artworks and has stated her intention to do so until there is nothing left of her (Mullen, 1997: 31). How this is to be reconciled with being mummified for posterity remains unclear! However, Madonna is reported to have decorated her apartment with 'a small perspex box containing a Shylockian morsel of flesh freshly liposuctioned from Orlan's artistic posterior' (Palmer, 1996: 7).

Orlan's work reminds us, if we needed reminding, that the body cannot take any form without being subjected to representation. The human body is never just a natural body, but always has imaginary and symbolic dimensions. This symbolized body is necessary not only for a sense of self, but for relations with oneself and with others. It is symbolism that brings us into being, and hence the necessity for bodies to be brought into relation with representation and with language. This is not just another way of saying that bodies are socially constructed, but is rather to say that the very experience of embodiment entails a confrontation with the imaginary and the symbolic. One way to demonstrate this is to consider the question of transsexualism – now often referred to by the preferred term transgendering – which provides another example of an effort to transform identity through the modification of the body. The important point here is that there is a great difference between thinking of an individual as a subject and thinking of them as a patient.[5] The confusion in the case of transsexuals can be expressed as imagining that someone is seeking an anatomical change when what they are really after is a different embodiment. This is another way of saying that the confusion is between a naturally sexed body and lived sexual difference (Shepherdson, 1994: 171). There is a paradox here, since the frequent claim by those seeking sex change operations, that they are individuals 'trapped in the wrong body' and should have the right to choose what is right for them, can imply a step beyond the real of embodiment to a fantasy body that would be completely under the subject's control, fully socially constructed (p. 172).

Catherine Millot in her book *Horsexe* discusses the clinical problem of how to decide which individuals would benefit from surgery and which would not (see Shepherdson, 1994). She distinguishes between a group who are oriented towards sexual difference, that is towards identification with 'a man' or 'a woman', with all the ambiguity, uncertainty and symbolic mobility this implies, and a second group who are oriented towards a fantasy of 'otherness' that amounts to the elimination of sexual difference because it is a fantasy of replacement, the acquisition of a sex that would not be uncertain. Those who belong to the latter group seek to eliminate the symbolic ambiguity that accompanies sexual difference, and to replace it with the certainty of a perfected body. They are not so much demanding to occupy the position of the 'other sex' as a position outside sex, a perfection attributed to the other and then sought for oneself (Shepherdson, 1994: 175–7). This perfection is, of course, a sex that is complete, that lacks nothing. Such perfection is well expressed by one client:

> Genetic women cannot claim to possess the courage, compassion and breadth of vision acquired during the transsexual experience. Free from the burdens of menstruation and procreation, transsexuals are clearly superior to genetic women. The future is theirs: in the year 2000, when the world is exhausting its energies on the task of feeding six billion souls, procreation will no longer be held to be an asset.
>
> (cited in *Shepherdson, 1994: 177*)

Once again, as the millennium approaches, the race would appear to be on to abolish gender, an abolition prefigured as taking place through the replacement of the 'natural' woman.

It seems clear that however we are to understand transsexualism, transsexuals are not necessarily examples, as has been argued, of the ultimate freedom, the very embodiment of the malleability of gender. The discussion above helps to make some sense of one of Orlan's most famous statements where she characterizes herself as a 'woman-to-woman transsexual'.

This comment may have been tongue-in-cheek, but it is extremely reveal-ing (Stone, 1996: 47). Plastic surgery is about the refiguration of the face and body. Orlan chooses the images towards which this refiguration is directed from Old Master paintings. She is adding images of women to herself, while simultaneously becoming the flesh made image. Just as the male transsexual may be seeking not to become a woman, but to become *The Woman*, the perfected sex that is complete and thus denies sexual difference, Orlan may be seeking something of the same completion (Adams, 1996: 58). There is clearly an element of this in any desire to be surgically altered, but it does raise the question of whether body perform-ance artists, and others who perform operations on their bodies and iden-tities, are really subverting sexual difference and gender, or just becoming locked into a deadly embrace with them.

Sexual difference and the art of love

It has been suggested that body performance art and body modification are just extreme forms of a culture's obsession with how to ground iden-tity and enter into relations with oneself and with others. A way of trying to control the symbolic and the forms of symbolic exchange in a world where most intersubjective relations are mediated as much by the exchange of goods as words. These forms of body modification and transformation make the body into a product, a commodity, but one over which the subject has a degree of control. Shakespeare's long rumination on this theme was *The Merchant of Venice*. The body comes in not necessarily when words fail, but when they get hard to control as Leader argues (Leader, 1997). It is interesting in this regard to recall the debt that the theory of gender performativity has to Austin's work on speech acts. What defines a speech act is that it does something by saying something, a situ-ation is created out of words, something is effected. All speech is in fact a form of doing, but what is interesting about explicit performatives is the way they often tie the identity of the individual to the act of speaking. This is particularly true of pledges, promises, vows and the like. How-ever, words may not be enough: as Shylock found out, there may be a need to ground promises in the forfeits of the flesh (see Leader, 1997).[6]

When is a man's word good enough and when does it have to be sup-ported by a pound of flesh? Gender performativity is about acts of doing, many of which may not be linguistic; but proponents of the theory some-times forget that an individual's relation to gender, sexuality, sex and the body is through the symbolic. They thus forget something, that Judith Butler does not, that gender performativity is not all in the realm of con-sciousness. Butler is explicit about the impact of psychoanalytic theory on her own thinking. The very notion of the unconscious introduces the idea that a subject is never at one with their consciousness, that subjectivity does not coincide with consciousness. Gender performativity could thus never be just a matter of conscious wishes and desires. To parody Marx, we may construct ourselves, but not under conditions of our own making. What we do not control is our relation to the symbolic, to language.

It is language that brings women and men into relation with each other. This relation is both social and symbolic, but proponents of gender performativity and of other forms of radical social constructionism and voluntarism often seem to discuss sexuality, sex and gender as if they were wholly in the domain of the individual, as if they were not intersubjective, not in fact relational. Sexual relations have a fascinating connection to speech acts, and especially to those that are about promises and pledges: 'I promise never to leave you' (Leader, 1997: 1). Such promises can be problematic since promising love, as Leader has pointed out, can often mean that its end is in sight (Leader, 1997: 8). The fact that commitment is a problem reveals how important language is in mediating the relationship between being female and being male.

Getting married is a problem for lots of people. In the film *Four Weddings and a Funeral* much is made of the anxiety of getting married. Charles, played by Hugh Grant, is perennially late for everyone else's weddings and as a best man he is more of a liability than a facilitator. He manages to turn up on time for his own wedding, but then fails to go through with it because he's fallen in love with a beautiful woman called Carrie. *Four Weddings and a Funeral* is about the problem of the relation between the sexes, and this problem is revealed to us through a problem about speech (Leader, 1997: 69–73). In the opening sequence of the film, only two words are spoken – both refer to sexual acts – and their repetition signals a problem about a relation to the world. This sense of not being quite at one with the world is part of the character played by Hugh Grant. When he sits down beside an elderly gentleman at the wedding feast and says 'My name's Charles', the old man replies 'Don't be ridiculous, Charles died twenty years ago'. 'It must be a different Charles', replies Grant. The old man is furious with exasperation: 'Are you telling me I don't know my own brother?!' Charles's mishaps continue and they are almost all about problems of naming, misapprehensions and misunderstandings.

It is Gareth, the jovial, larger than life figure with the dreadful waistcoats, who reveals the mediating role of language in establishing relations between the sexes. During one of the weddings, he opines that he has now discovered the reason why couples get married: 'They run out of conversation. They can't think of a single thing to say to each other. . . . Then the chap thinks of a way out of the deadlock and they have something to talk about for the rest of their lives'. Charles's problems with language are indicative of the fact that he cannot establish proper relationships with the opposite sex. When Charles pursues Carrie and confronts her on the embankment, he tries to tell her 'in the words of David Cassidy' that he loves her and is then unable to finish the sentence. When it comes to making a commitment, he cannot use his own words. His inability to establish a relationship is reflected in the dumbness of his brother who has to intervene on Charles's wedding day to say, in sign language, that he thinks the groom loves somebody else. Charles cannot speak for himself. When Charles finally commits himself to Carrie, he says: 'Will you agree not to marry me?' Even after she says 'Yes', he hedges his bets: 'and is not agreeing to marry me something you think you could do for the rest of your life?' (Leader, 1997: 70).

Relations between members of the opposite sex are problematic for almost all the characters in the film: Fiona who loves Charles, but he does not know it; duck-face whom Charles abandons at the altar; Carrie with her endless list of boyfriends; the aristocrat whose only secure object of love is his labrador and so on. These relations are explicitly contrasted with bonds between men, not only Charles's love for his brother, but also the hidden marriage of Gareth and Matthew that accounts for the purpose of the funeral in the film (Leader, 1997: 72). As Charles reveals when he notes that the group of friends had never realized that 'two of us were to all intents and purposes married'. Love relations between men are signalled in a whole variety of contexts throughout the film, but never made explicit until the funeral scene. After the funeral Charles has a further revelation: 'There is such a thing as a perfect match. If we can't be like Gareth and Matthew, then maybe we should just let it go. Some of us are not going to get married'. It is love between men that represents the perfect match, and it is for this reason that love relations between members of the opposite sex are so fraught, if not impossible. What has to be given up for these love relations to work is the idea of the perfect match, the complete relation of likeness embodied in the relation between men. What has to be acknowledged is sexual difference and the role of the symbolic, of language, in mediating that relation. There is nothing natural – in the biologically reductionist way we usually understand that word – about sex or sexual relations or sexuality or gender.

Conclusion

Voluntaristic interpretations of gender performativity work on the assumption that if sex is made up then it can be unmade (Copjec, 1994). In other words, they reduce sexual difference to a construct of historically variable discursive practices, and reject the idea that there is anything constant about sexual difference. This rejection is an absolute one because the terms of the sex/gender debate in all its various forms revolve around the question of nature versus culture, essentialism versus construction, substance versus signification. A number of writers, who are often referred to as sexual difference theorists, reject the terms of these polarities and point out that it was Freud who eschewed the limitations of these alternatives, arguing that neither anatomy nor convention could account for the existence of sex (Copjec, 1994). Lacan went further and argued that our sexed being is not a biological phenomenon because to come into being it has to pass through language, that is to take up a position in relation to representation. Sexual difference in this sense is produced in language, in the realm of the symbolic. Feminist critics who are wary of psychoanalysis have challenged this view claiming that it removes gender from actual social relations and posits sexual difference as something foundational, outside history and impervious to change. The same critics have also pointed out that psychoanalytic theory privileges sexual difference over other important axes of difference crucial for the construction of identity, such as race, ethnicity, class, sexual orientation and so on.

This disagreement is, of course, just another version of the set of binary polarities that underpin the sex/gender debate. But the main intellectual issue is how to reconcile theories that prefer unconscious desire to wilful choice, the unchanging structures of linguistic difference to discursive playfulness, the register of the symbolic to that of the social? The answer is not to give up on the sex/gender debate, not to try to define absolutely the boundary between sex and gender or that between sexuality and gender or between sex and sexuality. The boundary between sex and gender may be unstable, but that does not mean that they can be collapsed into each other. We may be able to enter into multiple constructions of gender and sexuality; we may be able to play with our gender identities and our sexual practices and resist dominant social constructions, but we should not confuse the instability of sexual signifiers with the imminent disappearance of women and men themselves, as we know them physically, symbolically and socially. Bodies are the site where subjects are morphologically and socially constructed, they mark the intersection of the social and the symbolic; each subject's relation with his or her body is both material and imaginary. Sexed bodies cannot be comprehended either by arguing that all of sex is socially constructed or by arguing that there is a part of sex that remains outside social construction. Sex, gender and sexuality are the product of a set of interactions with material and symbolic conditions mediated through language and representation. We need to bring into connection and manage as a complex relation a radical materialism and a radical social constructionism. This is what the sex/gender debate allows us to do. In a sense we need to manage the sex/gender debate as we live our lives, that is as a complex relation between a radical materialism and a radical social constructionism. The sex/gender debate is particularly fraught because we do use our embodied selves as a point of reference even in the most abstract theoretical discussions, and there are in fact very good reasons why this should be the case. A parody perhaps on Diderot's comment that 'There is always a little bit of testicle at the bottom of our most sublime ideals'.

Notes

1 Mary Hawkesworth (1997) has questioned whether one concept can really be used to encompass such a vast terrain, and discusses critical debates about the utility of gender as an analytic category.
2 The importance of practice theory in the field of gender studies continues; see, for example, Connell (1997), who develops a notion of 'body-reflexive practice'. Recent theories of gender that stress performance often also emphasize embodiment, and thus draw on an amalgam of phenomenology and practice theory.
3 See also Newton, 1979; Garber, 1992.
4 This is as true of the anthropologists, of course, as it is of those who are the subjects of anthropological enquiry, see Lewin, 1991; Kulick and Wilson, 1995.
5 I base my discussion here on Charles Shepherdson's analysis (1994), and I am grateful to him for his insights in this area.
6 I base my comments about promises on Darian Leader's (1997) brilliant analysis, and draw directly on his analysis of the film *Four Weddings and a Funeral* to develop my own arguments. His insights have profoundly influenced my own thinking in this section.

Bibliography

Abelove, H., M. Barale, and D, Halperin, eds, 1993. *The Lesbian and Gay Studies Reader*. London: Routledge.
Adams, P., 1996. 'Operation Orlan', in *Orlan*, ed. S. Wilson, M. Onfray, A.-R. Stone, S. François, and P. Adams. London: Blackdog Publishing.
Belo, J., 1949. *Bali: Rangda and Barong*. Monographs of the American Ethnological Society no. 16. Seattle: University of Washington Press.
Butler, J., 1990. *Gender Trouble: Feminism and the Subversion of Identity*. London and New York: Routledge.
Butler, J., 1994. 'Against Proper Objects', *Differences* 6(2–3): 1–26.
Connell, R., 1997. 'New Directions in Gender Theory, Masculinity Research, and Gender Politics', *Ethnos* 61(3–4): 157–76.
Copjec, J., 1994. *Supposing the Subject*. London: Verso.

Cornwall, A., 1994. 'Gendered Identities and Gender Ambiguity among Travestis in Salvador, Brazil', in *Dislocating Masculinities: Comparative Ethnographies.* ed. A. Cornwall and N. Lindisfarne. London: Routledge.

De Lauretis, T., 1991. 'Queer Theory: Lesbian and Gay Sexualities: An Introduction', *Differences* 3(2): iii–xviii.

Errington, S., 1990. 'Recasting Sex, Gender and Power: A Theoretical and Regional Overview', in *Power and Difference: Gender in Island Southeast Asia*, ed. J. Atkinson and S. Errington. Stanford: Stanford University Press.

Garber, M., 1992. *Vested Interests: Cross Dressing and Cultural Anxiety.* London: Routledge.

Graham, M., 1998. 'Follow the Yellow Brick Road: An Anthropological Outing in Queer Space', *Ethnos* 63(1): 102–32.

Hawkesworth, M., 1997. 'Confounding Gender', *Signs* 22(3): 649–85.

Herdt, G., ed., 1992. *Gay Culture in America: Essays from the Field.* Boston: Beacon Press.

Jackson, P., 1996. 'Kathoey><Gay><Man: The Historical Emergence of Gay Male Identity in Thailand', in *Sites of Desire/Economies of Pleasure: Sexualities in Asia and the Pacific*, ed. L. Manderson and M. Jolly. Chicago: Chicago University Press.

Johnson, M., 1997. *Beauty and Power: Transgendering and Cultural Transformation in the Southern Philippines.* Oxford: Berg.

Kulick, D., 1998. *Travesti: Sex, Gender and Culture among Brazilian Transgendered Prostitutes.* Chicago: Chicago University Press.

Kulick, D., and M. Wilson, eds, 1995. *Taboo: Sex, Identity and Erotic Subjectivity in Anthropological Fieldwork.* London: Routledge.

Leader, D. 1997. *Promises Lovers Make When It Gets Late.* London: Faber and Faber.

Lewin, E., 1993. 'Writing Lesbian and Gay Culture: What the Natives have to Say for Themselves', *American Ethnologist* 18(4): 786–91.

Mageo, J., 1992. 'Male Transvestism and Cultural Change in Samoa', *American Ethnologist* 19(3): 443–59.

Millot, C., 1990. *Horsexe: Essay on Transexuality.* New York: Autonomedia.

Moore, H. L., 1988. *Feminism and Anthropology.* Cambridge: Polity Press.

Morris, R., 1994. 'Three Sexes and Four Sexualities: Redressing the Discourses on Sex and Gender in Contemporary Thailand', *Positions* 2(1): 15–43.

Morris, R., 1995. 'All Made up: Performance Theory and the New Anthropology of Sex and Gender', *Annual Review of Anthropology* 24: 567–92.

Mullen, L., 1997. 'The Cutting Edge', *Time Out* 10–17 December: 20–31.

Newton, E., 1979. *Mother Camp: Female Impersonators in America.* Chicago: Chicago University Press.

Newton, E., 1993. 'My Informant's Best Dress: The Erotic Equation in Fieldwork', *Cultural Anthropology* 8(1): 3–23.

Palmer, J., 1996. 'Extremes of Consciousness', *Artists Newsletter* August: 7–9.

Parker, R., 1991. *Bodies, Pleasures and Passions: Sexual Culture in Contemporary Brazil.* Boston: Beacon Press.

Rubin, G., 1994. 'Sexual Traffic', *Differences* 6(2–3): 62–99.

Shepherdson, C., 1994. 'The *Role* of Gender and the *Imperative* of Sex', in *Sup-*

posing the Subject, ed. J Copjec. London: Verso.

Stone, A-R., 1996. 'Speaking of the Medium: Marshall McLuhan Interviews', in *Orlan*, ed. S. Wilson, M. Onfray, A-R. Stone, S. François, and P. Adams. London: Blackdog Publishing.

Turner, V., 1967. *The Forest of Symbols: Aspects of Ndembu Ritual*. Ithaca, NY: Cornell University Press.

Turner, V., 1969. *The Ritual Process*. Harmondsworth: Penguin.

Walker, L., 1995. 'More than Just Skin Deep: Fem(me)inity and the Subversion of Identity', *Gender, Place and Culture* 2(1): 71–6.

Weston, K., 1993a. 'Lesbian/Gay Studies in the House of Anthropology', *Annual Review of Anthropology* 22: 339–67.

Weston, K., 1993b. 'Do Clothes Make the Woman?: Gender, Performance Theory and Lesbian Eroticism', *Genders* 17(2): 1–21.

Weston, K., 1998. *Long Slow Burn: Sexuality and Social Science*. London: Routledge.

Yanagisako, S., and J. Collier, 1987. 'Toward a Unified Analysis of Gender and Kinship', in *Gender and Kinship: Essays Toward a Unified Analysis,* ed. J. Collier and S. Yanagisako. Stanford: Stanford University Press.

7   The Body's Career in Anthropology

Thomas J. Csordas

The body has always been with us in cultural and social anthropology, but it has not always been a problem. Ethnographic accounts have never hesitated to document bodily practices associated with lip plugs, neck lengthening, penis sheaths, clothing, scarification, circumcision, tattoos, and costumes, or to document the ritual highlighting of body parts, processes, and fluids. The body has especially impinged on the ethnographic consciousness in regions such as New Guinea and Amazonia where such practices and rituals are particularly striking. What makes it relevant to talk about the body's "career" in anthropology is that its theoretical status has gradually evolved in what can roughly be outlined as four stages. Beginning as an implicit, taken-for-granted background feature of social life, since the 1970s the body has become an explicit topic of ethnographic concern, thence a problem to be accounted for with respect to its cultural and historical mutability, and finally an opportunity for rethinking various aspects of culture and self. This conception of the changing status of the body in anthropology guides the exposition that follows.

Early reflections on the body

While acknowledging that the body was traditionally implicit in anthropological writing, it is also well worth recognizing that from the present standpoint, a rereading of older sources is likely to offer a surprising richness of insights on bodiliness in the history of the discipline. I will mention only a few examples to point to what a more extended enterprise might uncover.

Paul Radin explicitly discusses indigenous philosophy of the body in a chapter on "The Ego and Human Personality" (1927/1957). In what we would today call an attempt to formulate an ethno-psychology of the person, he emphasized the Maori distinction between material (substance) and immaterial (form) aspects of the body as the resting place of various components of the person including an eternal element, a ghost shadow, and a tripartite ego with a dynamic life principle symbolized by a material object, a life-essence or personality, and a physiological aspect or breath. In its anatomical aspect the Maori body was associated with psychical rather than physiological functions. Radin was impressed by the Maoris' conception of relation between the physiological and the vital essence in a temporal body, as well as their analysis of the body into form, substance, and resting place for the several elements of the person. He also saw this ethno-psychology as recognizing a kind of "multiple personality" in which the various elements could "become dissociated temporarily from the body and enter into relation with the dissociated elements of other individuals" in a way that is "utterly different from anything that a Western European can possibly imagine" (1927/1957: 264). Yet this multiple personality "happens to be in consonance with the very latest results of psychological and psychiatric research," and is a result of "primitive man's . . . realism and his refusal to assume fictitious and artificial unities" (1927/1957: 264). After going on to discuss the person among the Oglala Dakota and the Batak, he concludes that these ethno-theories display an "inability to express the psychical in terms of the body" but must project it onto the external world:

> The Ego, in other words, cannot contain within itself both subject and object, although the object is definitely conditioned by and exists within the perceiving self. Thus we have an Ego consisting of subject-object, with the object only intelligible in terms of the external world and of other Egos. This does not in any sense, of course, interfere with the essential dualism of primitive thought but it does imply a tie between Ego and the phenomenal world foreign to that which we assume. And this connection is very important, for it takes the form of an attraction, a compulsion. Nature cannot resist man, and man cannot resist nature.
>
> (*Radin, 1927/1957: 273–4*)

Although Radin's conclusions may not be acceptable to current ethnological sensibility, in this passage we see an early instance of concern with the body offering the occasion for reflection on the relation between subject and object, a topic which has recently come to the fore in anthropological discussions of embodiment (Csordas, 1990).[1]

Robert Lowie, in a chapter on "Individual Variability" in religious experience, dealt with issues relevant to embodiment under the heading of "sensory types" (1924/1952: 224–31). His data for this discussion were instances of visionary or revelatory imagery. He was not, however, primarily interested in the content or interpretation of these visions, or with the distinction between imagery experienced in the waking and dreaming states, or again with the manner in which experience and meaning were subsequently shaped through narration in conventional form, though he touched on all these topics. Instead, and noting the absence of studies in this area by anthropologists, he was concerned with what we might refer to today as embodied imagery (Csordas, 1994b; 1999), or the manner in which imagination is concretely engaged with the various sensory modalities. Drawing primarily on Crow material supplemented by evidence from other North American tribes and from the southern African Bushmen (San), he suggested that the cross-cultural data conformed with then-current psychological findings that visual imagery predominates in frequency over imagery in other sensory modalities, though certain individuals might show a propensity toward auditory or even motor, tactile, and kinesthetic imagery. Of considerable interest was Lowie's observation that a mixed type of image compounding several modalities was also quite frequent. These included mixed auditory and visual images,[2] as when an animal appeared to bequeath a sacred song to an individual, and the rarer experience that included feeling an animal or object enter and inhabit one's body. He cited further evidence of kinesthetic and visceral imagery in the "Bushman presentiments" constituted by a distinctive tapping or other sensation in various parts of the body that could be interpreted according to a traditional set of meanings.

Another early reflection on embodiment appears in Maurice Leenhardt's classic ethnography of New Caledonia, *Do Kamo: Person and Myth in a Melanesian World* (1947/1979). Leenhardt reports a conversation between himself and an elderly indigenous philosopher about the impact of European civilization on the cosmocentric world of the Canaques in which he suggested that the Europeans had introduced the notion of "spirit" to indigenous thought. His interlocutor said, on the contrary, we have "always acted in accord with the spirit. What you've brought us is the body." For Leenhardt this is a startling pronouncement – startling because it upends a stereotype that presumes the body lies on the side of nature and spirit on the side of culture, that the body lies on the side of the primitive and spirit on the side of the civilized. Leenhardt interprets the elderly philosopher's remark as follows:

[The body] had no existence of its own, nor specific name to distinguish it. It was only a support. But henceforth the circumscription of the physical being is completed, making possible its objectification. The idea of a human body becomes explicit. This discovery leads forthwith to a discrimination between the body and the mythic world

(Leenhardt, 1947: 164)

This passage vividly suggests that the very possibility of individuation, the creation of the individual that we understand (following Louis Dumont and others) as the core of the ideological structure of Western culture, has as its condition of possibility a particular mode of inhabiting the world as a bodily being. It suggests that prior to European dominance the body was for the Canaques neither a subject of experience nor an object of discourse. In Leenhardt's view this had profound implications for the nature of the person in Canaque culture, and by extension it challenges the generalizability of conventional Euro-American understandings of a person articulated in phrases like having a body, being a body, made up of body and mind, or being a mind in a body.

Some of the earliest sustained treatments of the body in its cultural and social dimensions were Robert Hertz's (1909/1960) study of the symbolic pre-eminence of the right hand and Marcel Mauss's (1934/1950) justly famous article on techniques of the body. Mauss's work is almost universally cited as a precursor of the contemporary interest in the body, and is hardly in need of uncovering in the sense I have just invoked. This work anticipates the notions of practice and habitus later elaborated by Pierre Bourdieu (1977 and 1984), though the notion of habitus had already passingly been used with a similar sense by Max Weber (1934/1963: 158) in discussing religions of ethical salvation. Interesting historically is the relation between this article and Mauss's fragmentary but influential discussion of the person, appearing only four years later (1938/1950). In that article he suggested that all humans have a sense of spiritual and corporal individuality, and saw the person as associated with the distinction between the world of thought and the material world as promulgated by Descartes and Spinoza. In this light it is of relevance that Mauss himself had already reproduced this duality by elaborating his concept of *la notion du personne* quite independently from that of *les techniques du corps*. In the present theoretical disposition, intent on collapsing dualities such that corporal practice is profoundly implicated in the development of persons and person perception, these two articles by Mauss should ideally be read as a pair.

Anthropology of the body

In later decades attention to the body largely took the form of studies of gesture, non-verbal communication, kinesics, and proxemics (Hall, 1959 and 1969; Birdwhistell, 1970; Hinde, 1972; Benthall and Polhemus, 1975). In these studies interest in the body in its own right was subordinated to interest in communication as a cultural process, with the body serving as the means or medium of communication. In other words, rather than beginning with a concern for bodiliness *per se*, these analyses took language as their model, using a linguistic analogy to study various types of languages of the body. Perhaps for this reason, they are rarely cited in the literature on the body and embodiment that has appeared in abundance since the late 1980s, though an important exception is the collection edited by Moerman and Nomura (1990). Nevertheless, they are worth returning to both for their own contributions and insofar as they set the stage for the first explicit formulations of an "anthropology of the body", beginning with the powerful influence of Mary Douglas (1966 and 1973) and the volume edited by John Blacking (1977).

Two books by Douglas define the threshold of a true anthropology of the body. In *Purity and Danger* (1966) she made her famous argument that the dietary rules in the biblical book of Leviticus summarized the categories of Israelite culture, and made the general claim that social system controls induce consonance between social and physiological levels of experience. In *Natural Symbols* (1973) Douglas made her equally famous argument that the bodily state of trance in different societies corresponds to the state of social organization characterized in terms of the "grid" of cultural classifications and the "group" control over the ego as an individual actor. Building on Mauss, she rejected the work of Hall (1959) on non-verbal communication and that of Lévi-Strauss (1964, 1966 and 1968) which used features of bodily practice such as eating, cooking, and mobility to build an analysis of mythical thought, on the grounds that they lacked hypotheses to account for variation across cultures. In presenting such a hypothesis, she committed herself to understanding the body as a "medium of expression" and in terms of bodily "techniques of expression." She argued that a drive to achieve consonance across levels of experience requires the use of the body to be "coordinated with other media" so as to produce distinct bodily styles, and that "controls exerted from the social system place limits on the use of the body as medium" (1973: 95). For Douglas, the body is molded by or expressive of social force: "The physical body is a microcosm of society, facing the centre of power, contracting and expanding its claims in direct accordance with the increase and relax of social pressures" (1973: 101); "The physical body can have universal meaning only as a system which responds to the social system, expressing it as a system" (1973: 112).

In the end, Douglas's legacy to the anthropology of the body is encapsulated in her conception of "two bodies", the physical and the social. Yet there is a telling ambiguity in her formulation. On the one hand it is

possible to understand the two as the physiological (the natural) and social (or cultural) aspects of the human body *per se*. On the other hand one
can understand the distinction as referring to relation between the individual's body (the corporal) and society's body (the corporate) understood in a Durkheimian or metaphorical sense akin to that of the Church
as "mystical body of Christ." Her own statement that "The two bodies
are the self and society" (1973: 112) appear to favor the latter interpretation, though the accompanying notion that the two may be either merged
or far apart does little to clarify the distinction.

In his introduction Blacking (1977) offers a programmatic outline for
an anthropology of the body that is both more concerned with the body
per se and its contribution to social processes than with the manner in
which it reflects or expresses those processes, and which is more explicitly
concerned with the relation between the biological and the cultural. Its
"chief concern is with the cultural processes and products that are
externalizations and extensions of the body in varying contexts of social
interaction", and it rejects the distinction between biological and cultural
anthropology on the grounds that culture has shaped the physical body,
while features of culture such as language are biologically based (1977:
2). Blacking sketches four premises for the anthropology of the body. The
first makes Douglas's metaphor of society as corporate body literal, stat-
ing that society is a system of active forces that is "not merely *like* a single
organism: it is a biological phenomenon, a product of the evolutionary
process" (1977: 8). Second was a version of the psychic unity principle, in
that all humans possess a common repertoire of somatic states, altered
states of consciousness, and properties of cognitive function (1977: 10).
Third was that non-verbal communication is fundamental, and should be
understood as the meeting point of the micro-analysis of human movement by proxemics and kinesics and the macro-analysis of group adaptation processes by demography and population genetics (1977: 13). The
final premise was that the mind cannot be separated from the body (1977:
18), which Blacking understood as relevant to a liberatory potential in
anthropology of the body in contributing to de-alienation and "ownership of our senses."

Once the body emerged from theoretical anonymity to become a recognized topic in its own right, its omnipresence in social life led to a multi-
plication of ways to organize its study. Following Douglas's inspiration
to recognize "two bodies", Nancy Scheper-Hughes and Margaret Lock
(1987) suggest we instead consider "three bodies." First is the individual
body, referring to the lived experience of the body as self. Second is the
social body, constituted by representational uses of the body as a symbol
of nature, society, and culture. Third is the body politic, which has to do
with the regulation and control of bodies. John O'Neill (1985) ups the

ante to "five bodies." For O'Neill, the world's body refers to the human tendency to anthropomorphize the cosmos. The social body refers to the common analogy of social institutions to bodily organs as well as the use of bodily processes such as ingestion of food to define social categories. The body politic refers to models of city or country as the body writ large, forming the basis of phrases such as "head" of state or "members" of the body politic. The consumer body refers to the creation and commercialization of bodily needs such as for sex, cigarettes, labor-saving devices, or cars, a process in which doubt is created about the self in order to sell grace, spontaneity, vivaciousness, confidence, and so on. The medical body refers to the process of medicalization in which an increasing number of body processes are subject to medical control and technology.

The body as a theoretical problem

I mentioned at the outset that it was not long between the emergence of the body as a topic and the transformation of the body into a problem. This aspect of the body's career in anthropology is deeply bound up with the career of anthropology in interdisciplinary studies. Scholars from virtually every branch of the human sciences have been influenced by reformulations of basic understandings of the body through the work of Michel Foucault on the discursive formations that have constituted body and population-transforming institutions such as the hospital (1973) and the prison (1977), as well as the very nature of sexuality (1978, 1985 and 1986); the work of Pierre Bourdieu (1977, 1984 and 1990) on practice and habitus; and the work of Maurice Merleau-Ponty (1962, 1964 and 1968) on perception and embodiment. Equally, scholarly understandings of the body have been transformed by feminist works including Luce Irigaray's (1985a, 1985b, and 1993) extended critique of psychoanalysis, Judith Butler's (1990, 1993) analysis of gender in terms of performativity, and Donna Haraway's (1991, 1997) studies of the encounter between gendered bodies and technology (see also the literature cited in the appendix, pp. 187–92 below).

Although it is a simplification to formularize the scope and nature of the theoretical sea-change effected through such works, two aspects stand out. First, though work such as Blacking's called into question the distinction between mind and body, and between biological and cultural anthropology, subsequent work has gone even farther in calling into question the degree to which biological nature can be considered a stable substrate of human existence. Second, though Douglas encouraged us to think in terms of two bodies corresponding to self and society, subsequent work has gone beyond her tendency to treat the body-self as a passive lump of clay or *tabula rasa* upon which society imposes its codes, toward understanding it as a source of agency and intentionality, taking up and inhabiting the world through processes of intersubjective engagement. This radical shift has made the body a central problem, and one of some urgency, across a range of disciplines. Thus Emily Martin, whose own work on gender, science, and technology (1987 and 1994) has contributed significantly to the body's move to center stage in social theory, has posed the question of the "end of the body" as we have known it (1992), and clinician and scholar Eric Cassell (1992), though recognizing the enduring facts of bodily structure and function, has referred to "the body of the future" in clinical practice. There has been a chorus of statements to the effect that the body can no longer be considered as a fact of nature, but is instead "an entirely problematic notion" (Vernant, 1989: 20), that "the body has a history" insofar as it behaves in new ways at particular historical moments (Bynum, 1989: 171), that the body should be understood not as a constant amidst flux but as an epitome of that flux (Frank, 1991: 40), and that "the universalized natural body is the gold standard of hegemonic social discourse" (Haraway, 1990: 146).

By some analyses, the context for this contemporary transformation of bodiliness is global "consumer culture." In this milieu, the sociologist Michael Featherstone has identified the importance of the multiplicity of images that stimulate needs and desires, and the corresponding changes in material arrangements of social space (in Featherstone, Hepworth and Turner, 1991: 192). Fixed "life cycle" categories have become blurred into a more fluid "life course" in which one's look and feel may conflict with one's biological and chronological age (Featherstone et al., 1991). The body/self in this culture of narcissism has become primarily a performing self of appearance, display, and impression management (Featherstone et al., 1991: 187), as the goals of bodily self-care have changed from spiritual salvation, to enhanced health, and finally to a marketable self (1991: 170; cf. Foucault, 1986; Bordo, 1993: 85). As Susan Bordo has observed, techniques of body care are not directed primarily toward weight loss, but toward formation of body boundaries to protect against the eruption of the "bulge," and serve the purposes of social mobility more than the affirmation of social position (1993: 90, 95). The asceticism of inner body discipline is no longer incompatible with outer body hedonism, but has become a means toward it, and one not only exercises to look good, but wants to look good while exercising (1993: 171, 182). This stands in sharp contrast not only to early historical periods, but to other societies such as that of Fiji in which the cultivation of bodies is not intended as an enhancement of a performing self, but is regarded as a responsibility toward the community (Becker, 1995).

On the theme of the "obsolescence of the body", Donna Haraway argues forcefully that "Neither our personal bodies nor our social bodies may be seen as natural, in the sense of existing outside the self-creating process called human labour" (1991: 10). She elaborates her position with analyses of the ideological roles of primatology and immunology in contemporary science. In particular, Haraway understands the concept of the "immune system" as an icon of symbolic and material systematic "difference" in late capitalism. The result is the transformation of the body into a cybernetic or cyborg body – not one that we have chosen, but one that Haraway embraces with a call for a cyborg ethics and politics. For the contemporary cyborg not to become a cog in a post-modern mechanistic universe, "politically engaged attacks on various empiricisms, reductionisms, or other versions of scientific authority" (1991: 194) are required. This position requires a commitment not to relativism but to recognition of *location*, accepting the interpretative consequences of being grounded in a particular standpoint – the consequences of relatedness, partial grasp of any situation, and imperfect communication. This situatedness extends to the domain of biology itself, as is evident in the feminist theory that eliminates "passivity" as an intrinsic characteristic of the female body, and reworks the distinction between sex and gender (Haraway, 1991: 197–8; Fausto-Sterling, 1992), as well as the decoupling of female sexual pleasure with the act of conception (Jacobus, Keller, and Shuttleworth, 1990). With biology no longer a monolithic objectivity, the body is transformed from object to agent (Haraway, 1991: 198; see also Frank, 1991: 48).

The contemporary cultural transformation of the body can be conceived not only in terms of revising biological essentialism and collapsing conceptual dualities, but also in discerning an ambiguity in the boundaries of corporeality itself. Arthur and Marilouise Kroker have suggested that in contemporary civilization the human body can no longer be considered a bounded entity, due to the destabilizing impact of social processes of commodification, fragmentation, and the semiotic barrage of images of body parts (1987: 20). Haraway points to the problematizing of boundaries between animal and human, between animal/human and machine, and between the physical and non-physical (1991: 151–4). Michel Feher, in his introduction to the influential *Fragments for a History of the Human Body*, construes the boundary between subhuman animal or automaton (machine) at one end of a continuum whose opposite pole is defined by deity (1989: 11). Exploring these cultural boundaries can be incredibly rewarding and remarkably problematic given the circumstances of corporeal flux and bodily transformation sketched above. This is especially the case when the question goes beyond the distinction between natural and supernatural bodies, or between natural corporeality and divine incorporeality, to the question posed by Feher of the kind of body with which members of a culture endow themselves in order to come into relation with the kind of deity they posit to themselves (1989: 13).

Embodiment and culture

This radical rethinking has also created an opportunity for a rethinking of culture and self from the standpoint of the body and embodiment. If the body was often a background feature in traditional ethnographies, so it has often remained implicit in anthropological theories of culture, which historically have been cast in terms such as symbols, meanings, knowledge, practices, customs, or traits. The problematizing of the body and its movement to center stage in social theory has also led to the emergence of studies that do not claim to be about the body *per se*, but instead suggest that culture and self can be understood from the standpoint of embodiment as an existential condition in which the body is the subjective source or intersubjective ground of experience.

This development can be seen taking place concretely in the work of a variety of anthropologists. For example, in the early 1970s Strathern and Strathern (1971) produced a conventional monograph on body decoration in Mount Hagen, New Guinea. Both authors went on to develop their thought in light of a reformulated understanding of embodiment (A. Strathern, 1996) and its gendered nature (M. Strathern, 1988 and 1992). Terence Turner (1980) published an influential essay on body decoration among the Brazilian Kayapo, and since then has moved from this conception of the "social skin" to a more thorough development of the place of "bodiliness" among the Kayapo and more generally in anthropological thinking. James Fernandez, following his powerful treatment of metaphor and body symbolism in the Bwiti religion among the Fang in Gabon (1982), later turned his attention to the place of the body in Bwiti explicitly with respect to developing theorizations of embodiment (Fernandez, 1990). In my own work on ritual healing and the cultural constitution of self among Catholic Charismatics in contemporary North America, I elaborated an earlier argument cast in terms of rhetoric (Csordas, 1983) with an argument made from the standpoint of embodiment (Csordas, 1990).

The theoretical crux of these new syntheses is a critique of tenacious conceptual dualities such as those between mind and body, subject and object, sex and gender, body and embodiment (Haraway, 1991; Jackson, 1989; Frank, 1991; Ots, 1991; Csordas, 1990; Leder, 1990). Among these, the distinction between *body* and *embodiment* is initially most critical to this theoretical move. The central issue is the manner in which the body is an existential condition of life – of course we have bodies, but there are multiple modes of embodiment, and it is the modulations of embodiment that are critical for the understanding of culture. What is salient in this distinction is precisely analogous to what for some might be a more familiar distinction between text and textuality. Recall Barthes' distinction between the work as a material object that occupies space in a bookstore or on a library shelf, and the text as an indeterminate methodological field that exists caught up within a discourse and that is experienced as activity and production (1986: 57–68). If for Barthes' notions of work and text we substitute text and textuality, we can then usefully juxtapose the parallel figures of the body and embodiment. The body, then, is a biological, material entity and embodiment is an indeterminate methodological field defined by perceptual experience and by mode of presence and engagement in the world.

This parallel between textuality and embodiment is by no means fortuitous or coincidental. In the 1970s the interpretative turn, the linguistic turn, the move to cultures defined as systems of symbols, were in full swing. One of the most powerful elements of this movement was understanding the nature of culture via the metaphor of the text as borrowed from Paul Ricoeur and disseminated into anthropology by the persuasive and eloquent voice of Clifford Geertz. This notion of culture as a system of symbols that could be read as a text gave way to a stronger view that what we recognize as culture is in fact an artifact of ethnographic practice, that is, the product of the genre conventions that produce texts called ethnographies. Along with the broad appeal of structuralism and then post-structuralism these developments had the profound consequence of making the methods of literary criticism available and relevant to anthropology, and of stimulating a wave of interdisciplinary thinking in at least two ways. It became possible to conceive ethnology, the comparative study of cultures, and comparative literature as cognate disciplines; and it offered a channel of communication between historians who worked through texts and anthropologists who worked through the metaphor of the text.

Over the past decade or so it has perhaps become less common to use terms like signs and symbols than terms like discourse and representation, but if anything the general trend toward semiotics broadly conceived has become even more prominent and productive in the human sciences. In fact, textuality has become a hungry metaphor, swallowing all of culture to the point where it became possible and even convincing to hear the deconstructionist motto that there is nothing outside the text. It has come to the point where the text metaphor has virtually (indeed, in the sense of virtual reality) gobbled up the body itself, as evidenced in phrases like "the body as text", "the inscription of culture on the body", or "reading the body." It may well even be that for many contemporary scholars the text metaphor has ceased to be a metaphor at all, and is taken quite literally.

Having made this assertion about the hungry metaphor, I hasten to acknowledge that notions like textuality, discourse, and representation have made it possible to launch the reflexive critique of ethnography that has been so productive and influential in the 1990s. However, at the height of this move to text and structure in anthropology through the 1970s and 1980s, the notion of "experience" virtually dropped out of theorizing about culture, and indeed might be said to have been purged from theoretical discourse. The radical epistemological move was that representation does not denote experience, but constitutes it. This move closes the gap between language and experience, and thereby eliminates a dualism, but does so not by transcending the dualism but by *reducing* experience to language, or discourse, or representation. It allows for a powerful critique of specific representations, but does so by insulating representation as a mode of knowledge from epistemological critique. That is, it makes difficult the posing of questions about the limits of representation, or whether there is anything beyond or outside representation, implying that to ask "representation of what" is fallaciously essentialist.

There is an alternative from the phenomenological tradition that does not reduce experience to language, and which is captured by Heidegger's dictum that language can *disclose* experience. When this tack is chosen, the key theoretical term that comes to take its place *alongside* representation is *being- in-the-world*. I emphasize the word "alongside" because my argument is not that representation should be replaced or overturned as a methodological figure, but that it will in the long run benefit from a dialogical partner that requires us to keep in mind the possibilities that representation may be understood to constitute experience and reality a text, or to disclose their embodied immediacy.

Among the phenomenological thinkers who have in some respect highlighted embodiment (e.g. Martin Heidegger, Helmut Plessner, Gabriel Marcel, Herbert Pflugge, and Max Scheler), it is doubtless Maurice Merleau-Ponty (1962 and 1964) who has had the most influence on recent work. He defined phenomenology as a science of beginnings, and so insisted that the starting point for philosophical, historical, and cultural analysis of how we are in the world be perception. For Merleau-Ponty perception is basic bodily experience, where the body is not an object but a subject, and where embodiment is the condition for us to have any objects – that is, to objectify reality – in the first place. His work suggests that culture does not reside only in objects and representations, but also in the bodily processes of perception by which those representations come into being. These creative processes are closely bound up with intentionality, which throughout his work Merleau-Ponty describes with phrases like a tending toward the world, a taking up of the world, a sense of intentional threads that trace the connections between ourselves and our worlds, an image of perception as tracing an intentional arc through the world – all phrases meant to convey a sense of existential meaning beyond representational meaning. My suggestion is that this phenomenological tradition offers us being-in-the-world as a dialogical partner for representation. In brief, the equation is that semiotics gives us textuality in order to understand representation, phenomenology gives us embodiment in order to understand being-in-the-world.

This understanding in turn requires that, when we once again focus on the body *per se*, we recognize that it can be construed *both* as a source of representations *and* as a ground of being-in-the-world. Again, we are much more familiar with the former: the body as source of representations à la Mary Douglas, or as the product of representation à la Foucault. Meanwhile, if we focus on embodiment *per se*, it is not in its own right but as an avenue of approach to culture and self, just as we can use textuality as an approach to the study of culture and self. Thus to work in a "paradigm of embodiment" (Csordas, 1990) is not to study anything new or different, but to address familiar topics – healing, emotion, gender, or power – from a different standpoint. Embodiment is about neither behavior nor essence *per se*, but about experience and subjectivity, and understanding these is a function of interpreting action in different modes and expression in different idioms. There is not a special kind of datum or a special method for eliciting such data, but a methodological attitude that demands attention to bodiliness even in purely verbal data such as written text or oral interview.

Embodiment and methodology

The preceding discussion raises the further issue of the mode in which a scholar engages the data – whether it is sufficient to attend to the body and embodiment or whether one must in addition attend with the body, now understood as a tool for research. Is there a sense in which bodily experience can or should be raised to the consciously reflective level of method? The historian Morris Berman poses the issue like this: "History gets written with the mind holding the pen. What would it look like, what would it read like, if it got written with the *body* holding the pen?" (1989: 110). Berman advocates a "visceral history" that not only takes into account that history is made and experienced with the body, but requires the experiential engagement of the historian in the matter of history. A twinge in the gut as an indicator of inner accuracy of interpretation, or the experience of anger as a grounding for writing a history of anger, are examples he cites of bringing bodiliness into method. In ethnography, this agenda has been approached in remarkably similar ways by Paul Stoller

(1989) and Michael Jackson (1989), who quite independently of one another have proposed a marriage between Merleau-Ponty's existential analysis and Dewey's radical empiricism. Jackson's analyses of initiation ritual and bodily metaphors illustrates the theme "that ideas have to be tested against the *whole* of our experience – sense perceptions as well as moral values, scientific aims as well as communal goals" (1989: 14). Stoller's discussions of the social dialogue carried on through the taste of sauces prepared with food and of the constitution of lived space among Songhay merchants offer examples of how ethnography can "enter the sensual world of evocation" (1989: 153).

Explicit recognition of this methodological issue can contribute directly to the contemporary struggle to clarify ethnographic practice. The critique of ethnography associated with post-modernism in anthropology is an effort to locate cultural sensibility not in the representation of reality but in an evocation of reality, not in the representational relation between signifier and signified but in the dialogical relation between ethnographer and indigenes as interlocutors (Clifford and Marcus, 1986; Marcus and Fischer, 1986; Tyler, 1990). This effort is made under the sign of the *reflexive*, both in the sense that the author figures into the text in a self-conscious way and in the sense that the text includes a dialogue with the voice of the indigene. This change of ethnographic practice remains thoroughly textual in orientation, and thus constitutes a restructuring of representation rather than offering an alternative to the primacy of representation. In contrast, we could say that the work invoking being-in-the-world cited above moves forward under the sign of the *reflective*. Here pre-reflective gut feeling and sensory engagement are raised to the level of methodological self-consciousness by insertion of a phenomenological sense of embodiment into the ethnographic enterprise. This was implicitly the strategy of the volume edited by Behar and Gordon (1995), which answered the critique of ethnography from an explicitly gendered standpoint by Clifford and Marcus (1986). In a more explicit sense, the reflexive and reflective can be understood as complementary contributions from textuality and embodiment to the reformulation of ethnographic practice.

Another context in which these issues are relevant is *vis-à-vis* the cognitive approach to ethnography in which culture is described as a form of knowledge, specifically what one needs to know to live within a society (Goodenough, 1957). This approach has grown increasingly sophisticated, describing knowledge in the more elaborate representational terms of schemas, cultural models, or parallel processing networks (Holland and Quinn, 1987; D'Andrade and Strauss, 1992). Despite its sophistication, this is inherently an understanding limited to what we might call "culture from the neck up." Other authors have introduced the notion that the cognitive categories on which cultural knowledge is based are themselves grounded in the body (Johnson, 1987; Lakoff, 1987), and this has led to an understanding of culture as the body in the mind. This is surely an advance, but it allows the body to remain merely a source, the objective raw material of representations rather than the seat of subjectivity and ground for intersubjectivity. A case in point is the treatment of metaphors, which in the recent cognitive work are abstracted from their bodily origins and transported to the representational structures of mind. From the standpoint of embodiment such metaphors remain as phenomena of intelligent and intelligible bodies that animate lived experience (Jackson, 1989; Kirmayer, 1989 and 1992; Fernandez, 1990; Low, 1994; Jenkins and Valiente, 1994). In this respect, to recognize a methodological balance between representation and being-in-the-world would be to move away from the cognitive understanding of "culture from the neck up" that remains implicit in Johnson's notion of the "body in the mind" toward recognition of an equally compelling "mind in the body."

There is indeed evidence that, whereas the predominant conceptual distinction around which anthropological theory has revolved in recent decades has been that between the material and the ideal, the foregrounding of the body has increasingly highlighted the theoretical importance of the relation between representation and being-in-the-world. This is the tenor of the effort of the philosopher Elizabeth Grosz (1994) to understand subjectivity by refiguring bodies simultaneously "from the inside out" and "from the outside in." It is the core of Nicholas Crossley's juxtaposition of Foucault and Merleau-Ponty as advocates respectively of the "inscribed" and "lived" bodies in theory. It appears as well in the distinction between "word" and "world" made by Appadurai (1996) in discussing bodily practices associated with global structures of consumption, and is formulated in a variety of ways by contributors to the volume I have edited on embodiment and experience (Csordas, 1994b). In the work of William Hanks (1990) on the Maya in Yucatan it is framed as the relation between language and lived space. Specifically, Hanks weaves back and forth between analysis of deixis and indexicality in Maya linguistic practice and analysis of embodiment drawing on phenomenological notions such as body schema and corporeal field. Finally, in my own work on the Charismatic Renewal movement (Csordas, 1994a and 1997), it is evident in the alternating application of phenomenology and semiotics, the notions of embodiment and textuality, and the concepts of performance and practice, to phenomena such as revelatory imagery, affliction by evil spirits, ritual language, habitus, and being overcome by divine power.

In sum, the body's career in anthropology has been on an upswing. From an early anonymity as a taken-for-granted background feature of social life, it emerged first as an explicit topic of anthropological research, then as a problem as its cultural and historical instability as a natural object became increasingly evident. Later, embodiment presented itself as an opportunity for reformulating previous interpretations and rethinking fundamental concepts of culture and self. Through the 1990s the problem posed by the body of the relation between representation and being-in-the-world has been an increasingly prominent site at which anthropologists have become engaged in the wider interdisciplinary discourse of the human sciences. On a wide variety of fronts, the body continues to advance.

Appendix: The body's vitae

If the body has a career in anthropology,[3] it must have a curriculum vitae as well, which I present here in the form of a brief bibliographic essay. Margaret Lock's (1993a) excellent review article on the body in anthropology and related disciplines appeared up to date at its appearance, but has been rapidly superseded by a plethora of works that appeared during the 1990s.[4] My intent is both to selectively update Lock's review and to outline fields of inquiry that appear to be coalescing into a more or less coherent intellectual enterprise; I aim to identify exemplary works rather than to be comprehensive. Note also that for the most part, works mentioned above in the body of the text are not necessarily repeated here.

That this is a thoroughly interdisciplinary enterprise must be acknowledged with a nod to those works from cognate disciplines that have most strongly influenced or are most likely to engage anthropologists. In history we begin with the account by Norbert Elias (1939/1978) of the centrality of bodily practices to the development of what we recognize today as "civilization" in the Western world. Historical transformations in sexuality have been treated by Catherine Gallagher and Thomas Laqueur (1987), Laqueur (1990), and Russett (1989), and in gendered religious experience in the Middle Ages by Carolyn Walker Bynum (1987, 1991 and 1995a; see also 1995b, her review article on the body's importance for historians) and Rudolph Bell (1985). The history of the senses appears in forms such as the work by Martin Jay (1993) on vision (see also Levin, 1993 and 1997) and Alain Corbin (1986) on odor in French thought, and the more general survey by Ackerman (1990). Other significant work includes that by Dorinda Outram (1989) on the transformation of the body in the period of the French Revolution, and by Nadia Seremetakis (1993 and 1994) on the body, gender, and the senses. Also of note is a book series on the body in culture, history, and religion published by the State University of New York under the editorship of Howard Eilberg-Schwartz, and interdisciplinary collections edited by Sheets-Johnstone (1992),

O'Donovan-Anderson (1996), Schatzki and Natter (1996), and Weiss (1999).

Reading on contemporary philosophy of the body, much of which centers on critiques of Cartesianism and elaborates a phenomenological approach, can well begin with the collection edited by Stuart Spicker (1970). Critical works are those by R. M. Zaner (1981), Drew Leder (1990), David Michael Levin (1985), Eric Blondel (1991), and Edward Casey (1993 and 1997), and the explicitly feminist works of Iris Young (1990), Susan Bordo (1993), and Elizabeth Grosz (1991 and 1994). Work on literature and the body includes a collection edited by Elaine Scarry (1988), one combining anthropological and literary studies by Catherine Burroughs and Jeffrey Ehrenreich (1993), one combining anthropology and folklore edited by Katharine Young (1995), and a monograph by Paul Smith on gender and sexuality in Spanish and Spanish American literature (1989). A wealth of work in interdisciplinary women's studies and feminist theory includes recent edited volumes by Susan Suleiman (1985), Jaggar and Bordo (1989), Jacobus, Keller, and Shuttleworth (1990), Epstein and Straub (1991), Foster, Siegel and Berry (1996), Conboy, Medina, and Stanbury (1997), and Lancaster and Di Leonardo (1997). Also of note are works by Kathy Davis (1995) and Anne Balsamo (1996) on cosmetic surgery and other transformations of the female body. Work in the cultural studies of science and technology has highlighted the profound impacts on bodily experience of computers, virtual reality, and cyberspace (Benedikt, 1994; Featherstone and Burrows, 1995; Stone, 1995; Aronowitz, Martinson, and Menser, 1996), as well as biotechnology, prosthesis, and the emergence of the cyborg as a new kind of human (Crary and Kwinter, 1992; Brahm and Driscoll, 1995; Gray, 1995; Treichler, Cartwright, and Penley, 1998; Brodwin, 1999), and the relation among modernism, technology, and the body (Armstrong, 1998). Recent works in religious studies have also taken direct account of the body (Feher, Naddaf, and Tazi, 1989; Bynum, Harrell, and Richman, 1987; Law, 1995; Coakley, 1997; McGuire, 1990; Sullivan, 1990).

In sociology, much more attention has been paid to the body by British than by other European or North American scholars. At the center of this group, associated with the journals *Theory, Culture, and Society* and the more recent *Body and Society*, is Bryan Turner (1984 and 1992), whose theoretical stance synthesizes the approaches of Foucault and Weber. Works from this school attempt to place the body more squarely at the center of social theory (Featherstone, Hepworth, and Turner, 1991; Shilling, 1993), as well as treating the body with respect to consumer culture (Falk, 1994), gender (Tseëlon, 1995), cyberspace (Featherstone and Burrows, 1995), space (Thrift, 1996), and religion (Mellor and Shilling, 1997). In neurology and psychology, first mention must go to the works of Oliver

Sacks (e.g. 1985 and 1990), as well as recent works on synesthesia by Richard Cytowic (1989 and 1993) and on body image by Thomas Cash and Thomas Pruzinsky (1990). Literature oriented toward the body in a more clinical, psychotherapeutic vein is rapidly increasing in volume, but exemplary starting points are the existential and phenomenological works of Eugene Gendlin (1962 and 1986) and the work of Don Johnson (1983, 1992 and 1997), as well as the journal *Somatics*.

For anthropology of the body strictly speaking, the body is the principal topic or object of analysis. Central questions revolve around the cultural and symbolic elaboration of body parts, processes, and products, or around dimensions of bodily experience in relation to certain practices or institutions. Recently of note are a theme issue of the journal *Cultural Anthropology* (1995) and an edited volume by Lundin and Akesson (1996). With respect to global understandings of bodily experience in specific cultural settings, important new ethnographic monographs have appeared by Elisa Sobo (1993) on the body in Jamaica, by Anne Becker (1995) on the body in Fiji, and by Maureen Trudelle Schwarz (1997) on the Navajo body. With respect to work focusing on particular bodily processes, exemplary work has appeared in the collection of essays on menstruation by Thomas Buckley and Alma Gottlieb (1988), and the comparative study of menopause in Japan and North America by Margaret Lock (1993b). Paul Farmer (1988) offers an account of blood and milk as bodily fluids with moral/symbolic value in Haiti. Bruce Knauft (1989) and Andrew Strathern (1996) treat the symbolism of bodily subtances and processes in Melanesia. Anthony Synnott (1993) deals with body parts including the face and hair, the gendered nature of the body, and especially with cultural elaborations of sensory experience.

Synnott's work stands at the threshold between anthropology of the body proper and the somewhat distinct enterprise termed anthropology of the senses. Part of the inspiration of this field can be traced to Walter Ong's (1967/1991) analysis of cultural and historical differences in elaboration of the sensorium, and dovetails with the interdisciplinary work mentioned above that highlights the dominance of the visual in Euro-American civilization. It is generally concerned with the differential elaboration of the sensorium across cultures and the nature of cultural knowledge as sensory knowledge. The most comprehensive general statements are by Constance Classen (1993) and the volume edited by David Howes (1991). Important works have appeared highlighting cultural elaborations of aroma (Classen, Howes, and Synnott, 1994), taste (Stoller, 1989), and sound (Feld, 1990), and the role of the senses in doing ethnography has been considered by Stoller (1997). A more critical approach to the senses in culture is that by Michael Taussig (1992 and 1993), whose work is strongly influenced by Walter Benjamin.

The anthropology of space has to do with the way humans inhabit space and alter space into human dimensions, and thus deals with geography, landscape, environment, architecture, and the social distribution of bodies in relation to one another. Although again we must recognize the importance of more philosophical works (e.g. Merleau-Ponty, 1962; Bollnow, 1963), in anthropology we can begin with the seminal work of Edward Hall (1969) in developing a proxemics that treated perception of space, behavior in space, and language about space. Two distinctions can be invoked to begin to organize thinking about this area from the standpoint of studies of the body and embodiment. First is that between cognitive or structural orientations and those concerned with lived space and experience in and of space. As a preliminary example, compare the analysis of space in a Bororo village by Lévi-Strauss (1963) aimed at the issue of dual organization in social structure, and the analysis of the Kabyle house by Pierre Bourdieu (1977) aimed at elaborating the habitus as a structure of bodily dispositions. Other examples in contrast are the recent special issue of the journal *Ethos* (Danziger, 1998) that focuses on linguistic representations of space, and the special issue of *Cultural Anthropology* (Ferguson and Gupta, 1992) that focuses on the relation of space to politics and identity. A second dimension of contrast is that between architectural space or the "built environment" (Lawrence and Low, 1990) elaborated in works such as Setha Low's (1995 and 1996) on plazas in Central American cities and by the papers on housing collected in Low and Chambers (1989), and geographical space as elaborated in Richard Werbner's (1977) studies of the spatial distribution of religious cults or by Nigel Thrift's (1996) studies of the contemporary distribution of knowledge and technologies. Finally, the experience of space as a dimension of habitation is to be distinguished from the experience of place as a specific terrain or site. Emphasis on place in the latter sense is evident in the collection edited by Steven Feld and Keith Basso (1996) and the work of Howard Stein on psychogeography (1987). An example of the applicability of a variety of these approaches to a single culture is the literature on the Navajo, in which can be found the explicitly cognitive and highly formal work of Pinxten, van Dooren, and Harvey (1983), the approach to lived space through cosmology, philosophy, and art in the work of Trudy Griffin-Peirce (1992), and the focus on specific sites within Navajoland and the narratives associated with them by Klara Kelley and Harris Francis (1994).

An anthropology of bodies in space should be complemented by an anthropology of bodies in motion. The only concerted elaboration of this analytic angle is in the relatively small field of the anthropology of dance, which is concerned with dance in ritual and non-ritual settings, and more broadly with the cultural patterning of movement. These studies can be traced at least as far back as the comparative studies of sacred dance by W. O. E. Oesterley (1923) and of possession dance in Haitian Voudoun by Maya Deren (1953). However, they have taken their contemporary form in the works of dance anthropologists such as Judith Lynne Hanna (1979/1987 and 1988) and Joann Kealiinohomoku (1972 and 1976). Exemplary studies from an ethnographic standpoint are those by Cynthia Novack (1990) on contact improvisation in contemporary American dance, and Sally Ann Ness (1992) on *sinulog* ritual dance in the Philippines. Also relevant are the phenomenological study of the body in modern dance by Sondra Fraleigh (1987), and the studies of modern choreographers and dance troupes by Susan Foster (1986) and Mary Lynn Smith (1996).

It might be presumed that the entire field of medical anthropology could be cited as relevant to the body and embodiment, but here my strategy will be to mention works in this and related fields in which bodiliness is most overtly problematized. What these works have in common at their best is a sensibility for the body as existential ground of culture, such that their arguments are rarely focused on disease *per se* but on what it can teach us about broader issues of self, emotion, religion, meaning, transformation, social interaction, institutional control of experience, the human interface with medical technology. Central to the development of this body of work is Arthur Kleinman's movement from concern with the somatization of emotional distress in his work on depression and neurasthenia in China (1980 and 1986) toward a general theory of human suffering (1995; Kleinman, Das, and Lock, 1997). The prominent theoretical position of narrative in this work is highlighted by Byron Good's (1994) approach to the critical phenomenology of illness experience and the problem of rationality in medicine. The body as experiencing agent appears in narratives of patients presented by physicians, exemplified by Arthur Kleinman (1988) and Howard Brody (1987), and first-person narratives of disability by Robert Murphy (1987) and Lucy Grealy (1994). The theme of embodiment as the ground for both symbol and symptom is examined in a special issue of the *International Journal of Psychology* (Devisch and Gailly, 1985). Prominent among studies of pain are the volume edited by Good, Brodwin, Good, and Kleinman (1992), and the work of Joseph Kotarba (1982), Richard Hilbert (1984), and Jean Jackson (1994) on chronic pain in particular. Important work highlighting bodily experience in religious healing has been done by Janice Boddy (1989), Marina Roseman (1991), Carol Laderman (1991), Robert Desjarlais (1992), and Rene Devisch (1993). Also worthy of note are studies in the United States by Gelya Frank's (1986) synthesis and experience of wholeness of a congenital amputee with undeveloped limbs; studies in Italy by Deborah Gordon (1990) of urban cancer patients and by Mariella Pandolfi (1990 and 1991) of psychotherapy patients in a mountain village; and studies in

China by Thomas Ots (1990, 1991 and 1994) of contemporary Chinese medicine and healing cults, and by Scott Davis (1996) in his attempt to reconcile structure and experience in the constitution of the classical medical system. The social and epistemological status of the body in contemporary medicine is treated by Leder (1992) and Young (1998), while David Armstrong (1983) carries Foucault's project of the discursive construction of the body by medicine into the setting of twentieth-century Britain. A particular focus on women's bodies through the life course and in the face of reproductive and other biomedical technologies is found in Martin (1987) and the collection edited by Faye Ginsburg and Rayna Rapp (1995).

Finally, an emergent anthropology of violence links concerns with health and politics. Widely influential across disciplines is the work of Elaine Scarry (1987) on the profound consequences of pain inflicted by violence and torture. The work of Janis Jenkins (1991, 1996 and 1998; Jenkins and Valiente, 1994) on the embodied experience of Salvadoran women refugees highlights both this intimate connection between politics and health, as well as that between domestic and political violence. Allen Feldman (1991 and 1997) and Begona Aretxaga (1995 and 1997) have written on the body, narrative, and gender in the violence of Northern Ireland. E. Valentine Daniel (1994 and 1996) has written on the bodily consequence of political violence in Sri Lanka, and Lindsay French (1994) on the experience of amputated Cambodian victims of land mines. The role of the body in political resistance is highlighted by Jean Comaroff (1985) writing on the Tshidi of South Africa, and Michael Taussig (1987) writing on shamanistic healing in Columbia. Important edited collections have appeared on institutionalized violence (Riches, 1986), on nations afflicted with civil war and internal violence (Nordstrom and Martin, 1992; Suarez-Orozco, 1990; Warren, 1993), and on the experience of suffering in political violence (Green, 1998); a statement on the ethnography of political violence and trauma has been contributed by Arthur Kleinman (1995). Exemplary works on violence against children is that by Barbara Miller (1981) on neglect of girls in India, Nancy Scheper-Hughes (1992) on poverty and neglect in Brazil, and Marcelo Suarez-Orozco (1987) on the treatment of children in Argentina's "dirty war." Collections on violence against and neglect of children have been edited by Jill Korbin (1981) and Nancy Scheper-Hughes (1987). A cross-cultural survey and analysis of domestic violence against women has been done by Jacquelyn Campbell (1985), and exemplary work on both domestic violence and rape includes selections in Zinn, Hondagneu-Sotelu, and Messner (1997), a special issue of the journal *Oceania* on domestic violence (Counts, 1990), and an article on the embodiment of rape trauma in the United States by Kathy Winkler (with Kate Wininger, 1994).

Notes

1   In a later discussion of the soul, Radin seeks the origin of body-soul dualism in the reasoning of of shamans and priests. These specialists not only thereby distinguished their thought from the monism of ordinary people, but elaborated a basis for their authority in arguing that due to their power, for them body and soul were interchangeable, whereas for ordinary people they were distinct and separable elements, with the body as merely perishable and unempowered shell (1937/1957: 273–5).

2   Commenting on an example demonstrating the possibility that an auditory image might take precedence over and stimulate a visual, Lowie offered a revealing personal reflection: "Those who, like the present writer, are subject to auditory hallucinations, both in presomnic and full waking condition, will appreciate the convincing character of such experiences" (1924/1952: 228).

3   The title of this essay was, I must say, assigned by Professor Moore, editor of the present volume.

4   To give a sense of the dramatic recent increase in titles relevant to the body and embodiment, in my biannual graduate seminar of spring 1998 on the body in discourse and experience, the earliest publication date of the nine books we read was 1994.

Bibliography

Ackerman, Diane, 1990. *A Natural History of the Senses*. New York: Random House.

Appadurai, Arjun, 1996. *Modernity at Large: Cultural Dimensions of Globalization*. Minneapolis: University of Minnesota Press.

Aretxaga, Begona, 1995. "Dirty Protest: Symbolic Overdetermination and Gender in Northern Ireland Ethnic Violence." *Ethos* 21: 123–39.

Aretxaga, Begona, 1997. *Shattering Silence: Women, Nationalism, and Political Subjectivity in Northern Ireland*. Princeton: Princeton University Press.

Armstrong, David, 1983. *Political Anatomy of the Body: Medical Knowledge in Britain in the Twentieth Century*. New York: Cambridge University Press.

Armstrong, Tim, 1998. *Modernism, Technology, and the Body: A Cultural History*. Cambridge: Cambridge University Press.

Aronowitz, Stanley, Barbara Martinson, and Michael Menser, eds, 1996. *Technoscience and Cyberculture*. New York: Routledge.

Balsamo, Anne Marie, 1996. *Technologies of the Gendered Body: Reading Cyborg Women*. Durham, NC: Duke University Press.

Barthes, Roland, 1986. *The Rustle of Language*, trans. R. Howard, New York: Hill and Wang.

Becker, Anne E., 1994. "Nurturing and Negligence: Working on Others' Bodies in Fiji," in *Embodiment and Experience*, ed. Thomas J. Csordas. Cambridge: Cambridge University Press, pp. 100–15.

Becker, Anne E., 1995. *Body, Self, and Society: The View from Fiji*. Philadelphia:

University of Pennsylvania Press.

Behar, Ruth, and Deborah A. Gordon, eds, 1995. *Women Writing Culture*. Berkeley: University of California Press.

Bell, Rudolph, 1985. *Holy Anorexia*. Chicago: University of Chicago Press.

Benedikt, Michael, ed., 1994. *Cyberspace: First Steps*. Cambridge, MA: MIT Press.

Benthall, Jonathan, and Ted Polhemus, eds, 1975. *The Body as a Medium of Expression*. New York: E.P. Dutton & Co.

Berman, Morris, 1989. *Coming to Our Senses: Body and Spirit in the Hidden History of the West*. New York: Simon and Schuster.

Birdwhistell, Ray L., 1970. *Kinesics and Context: Essays on Body Motion Communication*. Philadelphia: University of Pennsyvania Press.

Blacking, John, ed., 1977. *The Anthropology of the Body*. London: Academic Press.

Blondel, Eric, 1991. Nietzsche: *The Body and Culture: Philosophy as a Philological Genealogy*, trans. Seán Hand. Stanford: Stanford University Press.

Boddy, Janice, 1989. *Wombs and Alien Spirits: Women, Men, and the Zar Cult in Northern Sudan*. Madison: University of Wisconsin Press.

Bollnow, O. F., 1963. *Mensch und Raum*. Stuttgart.

Bordo, Susan, 1993. *Unbearable Weight: Feminism, Western Culture, and the Body*. Berkeley: University of California Press.

Bourdieu, Pierre, 1977. *Outline of a Theory of Practice*, trans. Richard Nice. London: Cambridge University Press.

Bourdieu, Pierre, 1984. *Distinction*, trans. Richard Nice. Cambridge, MA: Harvard University Press.

Bourdieu, Pierre, 1990. *The Logic of Practice*, trans. Richard Nice. Stanford, Stanford University Press.

Brahm, Gabriel Jr., and Mark Driscoll, eds, 1995. *Prosthetic Territories: Politics and Hypertechnologies*. Boulder, CO: Westview Press.

Brodwin, Paul, ed., 1999 *Biotechnology, Culture, and the Body*. Bloomington: Indiana University Press.

Brody, Howard, 1987. *Stories of Sickness*. New Haven, CT: Yale University Press.

Buckley, Thomas, and Alma Gottlieb, eds, 1988. Blood Magic: *The Anthropology of Menstruation*. Berkeley: University of California Press.

Burroughs, Catherine B., and Jeffrey David Ehrenreich, eds, 1993. *Reading the Social Body*. Iowa City: University of Iowa Press.

Butler, Judith, 1990. *Gender Trouble: Feminism and the Subversion of Identity*. London and New York: Routledge.

Butler, Judith, 1993. *Bodies that Matter: On the Discursive Limits of "Sex."* London and New York: Routledge.

Butler, Judith, 1997. *Excitable Speech*. New York: Routledge.

Bynum, Caroline Walker, 1987. *Holy Feast and Holy Fast: The Religious Significance of Food to Medieval Women*. Berkeley: University of California Press.

Bynum, Caroline Walker, 1989. The Female Body and Religious Practice in the Later Middle Ages, in *Fragments for a History of the Human Body,* Part One, ed. Michel Feher. New York: Zone, pp. 160–219.

Bynum, Caroline Walker, 1991. *Fragmentation and Redemption: Essays on Gender and the Human Body in Medieval Religion*. New York: Zone.

Bynum, Caroline Walker, 1995a. *The Resurrection of the Body in Western Christianity, 200–1336*. New York: Columbia University Press.

Bynum, Carolyn Walker, 1995b. "Why All the Fuss about the Body?: A Medievalist's Perspective," *Critical Inquiry* 22: 1–33.

Bynum, Caroline Walker, Stevan Harrell, and Paula Richman, eds, 1986. *Gender and Religion: On the Complexity of Symbols*. Boston: Beacon Press.

Campbell, Jacquelyn, 1985. "Beating of Wives: A Cross-Cultural Perspective," *Victimology* 10: 174–85.

Casey, Edward S., 1993. *Getting Back into Place: Toward a Renewed Understanding of the Place-World*. Bloomington: Indiana University Press.

Casey, Edward S., 1997. *The Fate of Place: A Philosophical History*. Berkeley: University of California Press.

Cash, Thomas F., and Thomas Pruzinsky, eds, 1990. *Body Images: Development, Deviance, and Change*. New York: Guilford Press.

Cassell, Eric J., 1992. "The Body of the Future," in Drew Leder, ed. *The Body in Medical Thought and Practice*. Dordrecht: Kluwer Academic Publishers, pp. 233–50.

Classen, Constance, 1993. *Worlds of Sense: Exploring the Senses in History and Across Cultures*. New York: Routledge.

Classen, Constance, David Howes, and Anthony Synnott, 1994. *Aroma: The Cultural History of Smell*. London: Routledge.

Clifford, James, and George E. Marcus, eds, 1986. *Writing Culture: The Poetics and Politics of Ethnography*. Berkeley: University of California Press.

Coakley, Sarah, ed., 1997. *Religion and the Body*. Cambridge: Cambridge University Press.

Comaroff, Jean, 1985. *Body of Power, Spirit of Resistance: The Culture and History of a South African People*. Chicago: University of Chicago Press.

Conboy, Katie, Nadia Medina, and Sarah Stanbury, eds, 1997. *Writing on the Body: Female Embodiment and Feminist Theory*. New York: Columbia University Press.

Corbin, Alain, 1986. *The Foul and the Fragrant: Odor and the French Social Imagination*. Cambridge, MA: Harvard University Press.

Counts, Dorothy, ed., 1990. *Domestic Violence in Oceania*. Special issue of *Oceania* 13(3).

Crary, Jonathan, and Sanford Kwinter, eds, 1992. *Incorporations*. New York: Zone Books.

Crossley, Nicholas, 1996. "Body-Subject/Body-Power: Agency, Inscription, and Control in Foucault and Merleau-Ponty," *Body and Society* 2: 99–116.

Csordas, Thomas J., 1983. "The Rhetoric of Transformation in Ritual Healing," *Culture, Medicine, and Psychiatry* 7: 333–75.

Csordas, Thomas J., 1990. "Embodiment as a Paradigm for Anthropology," *Ethos* 18: 5–47 [1988 Stirling Award Essay].

Csordas, Thomas J., 1994a. *The Sacred Self: A Cultural Phenomenology of Charismatic Healing*. Berkeley: University of California Press.

Csordas, Thomas J., ed., 1994b. *Embodiment and Experience: The Existential Ground of Culture and Self*. Cambridge: Cambridge University Press.

Csordas, Thomas J., 1997. *Language, Charisma, and Creativity: The Ritual Life of a Religious Movement*. Berkeley: University of California Press.

Csordas, Thomas J., 1999. "Notes for a Cybernetics of the Holy," in *Essays in Honor of Roy A. Rappaport*, ed. Michael Lambek and Ellen Messer. Ann Arbor: University of Michigan Press.

Cytowic, Richard E., 1989. *Synesthesia: A Union of the Senses*. New York: Springer-Verlag.

Cytowic, Richard E., 1993. *The Man who Tasted Shapes*. New York: Putnam.

D'Andrade, Roy, and Claudia Strauss, eds, 1992. *Human Motives and Cultural Models*. Cambridge: Cambridge University Press.

Daniel, E. Valentine, 1994. "The Individual in Terror," in *Embodiment and Experience: The Existential Ground of Culture and Self*, ed. Thomas J. Csordas. Cambridge: Cambridge University Press, 229–47.

Daniel, E. Valentine, 1996. *Charred Lullabies: Chapters in an Anthropology of Violence*. Princeton, NJ: Princeton University Press.

Danziger, Eve, ed., 1998. Language, space, and culture. Theme issue of *Ethos* 26(1).

Davis, Kathy, 1995. *Reshaping the Female Body: The Dilemma of Cosmetic Surgery*. New York: Routledge.

Davis, Scott, 1996. "The Cosmobiological Balance of the Emotional and Spiritual Worlds: Phenomenological Structuralism in Traditional Chinese Medical Thought," *Culture, Medicine, and Psychiatry* 20: 83–123.

Delvecchio Good, Mary-Jo, Paul E. Brodwin, Byron J. Good, and Arthur Kleinman, eds, 1992. *Pain as Human Experience: An Anthropological Perspective*. Berkeley: University of California Press.

Deren, Maya, 1953. *Divine Horsemen: The Living Gods of Haiti*. New York: McPherson & Co.

Desjarlais, Robert, 1992. *Body and Emotion: The Aesthetics of Illness and Healing in the Nepal Himalayas*. Philadelphia: University of Pennsylvania Press.

Devisch, Rene, 1993. *Weaving the Threads of Life: The Khita Gyn-eco-logical Healing Cult among the Yaka*. Chicago: University of Chicago Press.

Devisch, Rene, and Antoine Gailly, eds, 1985. *Symbol and Symptom in Bodily Space-Time*. Special issue of the *International Journal of Psychology* 20: 389–663.

Douglas, Mary, 1966. *Purity and Danger*. London: Routledge and Kegan Paul.

Douglas, Mary, 1973. *Natural Symbols*. New York: Vintage.

Elias, Norbert, 1939/1978. *The Civilizing Process*. Oxford: Oxford University Press.

Epstein, Julia, and Kristina Straub, eds, 1991. *Body Guards: The Cultural Politics of Gender Ambiguity*. New York: Routledge.

Falk, Pasi, 1994. *The Consuming Body*. London: Sage.

Farmer, Paul, 1988. "Bad Blood, Spoiled Milk: Bodily Fluids as Moral Barometers in Rural Haiti," *American Ethnologist* 15: 62–83.

Fausto-Sterling, Anne, 1992. *Myths of Gender: Biological Theories about Women and Men*. Rev. edn. New York: Basic Books.

Featherstone, Mike, and Roger Burrows, eds, 1995, *Cyberspace/Cyberbodies/Cyberpunk*. London: Sage.

Featherstone, Mike, Mike Hepworth, and Bryan S. Turner, eds, 1991. *The Body:*

Social Process and Cultural Theory. London: Sage.

Feher, Michel, with Ramona Naddaf and Nadia Tazi, eds, 1989. *Fragments for a History of the Human Body.* 3 vols. New York: Zone Books.

Feld, Steven, 1990. *Sound and Sentiment: Birds, Weeping, Poetics, and Song in Kaluli Expression.* 2nd edn. Philadelphia: University of Pennsylvania Press.

Feld, Steven, and Keith H. Basso, eds, 1996. *Senses of Place.* Santa Fe, NM: School of American Research Press.

Feldman, Allen, 1991. *Formations of Violence: The Narrative of the Body and Political Terror in Northern Ireland.* Chicago: University of Chicago Press.

Feldman, Allen, 1997. "Violence and Vision: The Prosthetics and Aesthetics of Terror," *Public Culture* 10: 24–60.

Ferguson, James, and Akhil Gupta, eds, 1992. *Space, Identity, and the Politics of Difference.* Theme issue of *Cultural Anthropology* Vol 7(1).

Fernandez, James, 1982. *Bwiti: An Ethnography of the Religious Imagination in Africa.* Princeton: Princeton University Press.

Fernandez, James, 1990. "The Body in Bwiti: Variations on a Theme by Richard Werbner," *Journal of Religion in Africa* 20: 92–111.

Foster, Susan Leigh, 1986. *Reading Dancing: Bodies and Subjects in Contemporary American Dance.* Berkeley: University of California Press.

Foster, Thomas, Carol Siegel, and Ellen E. Berry, eds, 1996. *Bodies of Writing, Bodies in Performance.* Genders 23. New York: New York University Press.

Foucault, Michel, 1973. *The Birth of the Clinic: An Archaeology of Medical Perception,* trans. A. M. Sheridan Smith. New York: Vintage.

Foucault, Michel, 1977. *Discipline and Punish: The Birth of the Prison,* trans. Alan Sheridan. New York: Vintage.

Foucault, Michel, 1978. *The History of Sexuality: An Introduction,* trans. Robert Hurley. New York: Vintage.

Foucault, Michel, 1985. *The Use of Pleasure,* trans. Robert Hurley. New York: Vintage.

Foucault, Michel, 1986. *The Care of the Self,* trans. Robert Hurley. New York: Vintage.

Fraleigh, Sondra Horton, 1987. *Dance and the Lived Body: A Descriptive Aesthetics.* Pittsburgh: University of Pittsburgh Press.

Frank, Arthur, 1991. "For a Sociology of the Body: An Analytical Review," in *The Body: Social Process and Cultural Theory,* ed. Mike Featherstone, Mike Hepworth, and Bryan S. Turner. London: Sage Publications, pp. 36–102.

Frank, Gelya, 1986. "On Embodiment: A Case Study of Congenital Limb Deficiency in American Culture," *Culture, Medicine, and Psychiatry* 10: 189–219.

French, Lindsay, 1994. "The Political Economy of Injury and Compassion: Amputees on the Thai-Cambodia Border," in *Embodiment and Experience: The Existential Ground of Culture and Self,* ed. Thomas J. Csordas. Cambridge: Cambridge University Press, pp. 69–99.

Gallagher, Catherine, and Thomas Laqueur, eds, 1987. *The Making of the Modern Body: Sexuality and Society in the Nineteenth Century.* Berkeley: University of California Press.

Gendlin, Eugene T., 1962. *Experiencing and the Creation of Meaning: A Philosophical and Psychological Approach to the Subjective.* New York: Free Press of Glencoe.

Gendlin, Eugene T., 1986. *Let your Body Interpret your Dreams*. Wilmette, IL: Chiron Publications.

Ginsburg, Faye, and Rayna Rapp, eds, 1995. *Conceiving the New World Order: The Global Politics of Reproduction*. Berkeley: University of California Press.

Good, Byron, 1994. *Medicine, Rationality, and Experience: An Anthropological Perspective*. Cambridge: Cambridge University Press.

Good, Mary-Jo, Paul Brodwin, Byron Good, and Arthur Kleinman, eds, 1992. *Pain as Human Experience: An Anthropological Perspective*. Berkeley: University of California Press.

Goodenough, Ward, 1957. "Cultural Anthropology and Linguistics," in *Report of the Seventh Annual Round Table Meeting in Linguistics and Language Study: Monograph Series on Language and Linguistics*, No. 9, ed. P. Garvin. Washington, DC: Georgetown University, 141–66.

Gordon, Deborah, 1990. "Embodying Illness, Embodying Cancer," *Culture, Medicine, and Psychiatry* 14: 275–97.

Gray, Chris Hables, ed., 1995. *The Cyborg Handbook*. New York: Routledge.

Grealy, Lucy, 1994. *Autobiography of a Face*. Boston: Houghton Mifflin.

Green, Linda, ed., 1998. *The Embodiment of Violence*, Theme issue of *Medical Anthropology Quarterly*. 12(1).

Griffin-Pierce, Trudy, 1992. *Earth is my Mother, Sky is my Father: Space, Time, and Astronomy in Navajo Sandpainting*. Albuquerque, NM: University of New Mexico Press.

Grosz, Elizabeth, ed., 1991. *Feminism and the Body*. Special issue of *Hypatia* 6.

Grosz, Elizabeth, 1994. *Volatile Bodies: Toward a Corporeal Feminism*. Bloomington, IN: Indiana University Press.

Hall, Edward T., 1959. *The Silent Language*. New York: Anchor Press/Doubleday.

Hall, Edward T., 1969. *The Hidden Dimension*. New York: Anchor Books.

Hanks, William F., 1990. *Referential Practice: Language and Lived Space among the Maya*. Chicago: University of Chicago Press.

Hanna, Judith Lynne, 1979/1987. To Dance is Human: A Theory of Nonverbal Communication. Chicago: University of Chicago Press.

Hanna, Judith Lynne, 1988. *Dance, Sex, and Gender: Signs of Identity, Dominance, Defiance, and Desire*. Chicago: University of Chicago Press.

Haraway, Donna, 1990. "Investment Strategies for the Evolving Portfolio of Primate Females," in *Body/Politics: Women and the Discourses of Science*, ed. Mary Jacobus, Evelyn Fox Keller, and Sally Shuttleworth. New York: Routledge, pp. 139–62.

Haraway, Donna, 1991. *Simians, Cyborgs, and Women: The Reinvention of Nature*. New York: Routledge.

Haraway, Donna, 1997. *Modest_Witness@second_millennium. FemaleMan©_ meets_oncomouse™: Feminism and Technoscience*. New York: Routledge.

Hertz, Robert, 1909/1960. *Death and the Right Hand*, trans. R. Needham and C. Needham. Aberdeen: Aberdeen University Press.

Hilbert, Richard, 1984. "The Acultural Dimensions of Chronic Pain: Flawed Reality Construction and the Problem of Meaning," *Social Problems* 31: 365–78.

Hinde, R. A., ed., 1972. *Non-Verbal Communication*. Cambridge: Cambridge

University Press.

Holland, Dorothy, and Naomi Quinn, eds, 1987. *Cultural Models in Language and Thought*. Cambridge: Cambridge University Press.

Howes, David, ed., 1991. *The Varieties of Sensory Experience: A Sourcebook in the Anthropology of the Senses*. Toronto: University of Toronto Press.

Irigaray, Luce, 1985a. *Speeculum of the Other Woman*, trans. Gillian C. Gill. Ithaca, NY: Cornell University Press.

Irigaray, Luce, 1993. *An Ethics of Sexual Difference*, trans. Carolyn Burke and Gillian C. Gill. Ithaca, NY: Cornell University Press.

Jackson, Jean, 1994. "Chronic Pain and the Tension between Body as Subject and Object," in *Embodiment and Experience: The Existential Ground of Culture and Self*, ed. Thomas J. Csordas. Cambridge: Cambridge University Press, 201–28.

Jackson, Michael, 1989. *Paths toward a Clearing: Radical Empiricism and Ethnographic Inquiry*. Bloomington: Indiana University Press.

Jacobus, Mary, Evelyn Fox Keller, and Sally Shuttleworth, eds, 1990. *Body/Politics: Women and the Discourses of Science*. New York: Routledge.

Jaggar, Alison M., and Susan R. Bordo, eds, 1989. *Gender/Body/Knowledge: Feminist Reconstructions of Being and Knowing*. New Brunswick, NJ: Rutgers University Press.

Jay, Martin, 1993. *Downcast Eyes: The Denigration of Vision in Twentieth-century French Thought*. Berkeley: University of California Press.

Jenkins, Janis H., 1991. "The State Construction of Affect: Political Ethos and Mental Health among Salvadoran Refugees," *Culture, Medicine, and Psychiatry* 15: 139–65.

Jenkins, Janis H., 1996. "Women's Experience of Trauma and Political Violence," in *Gender and Health: An International Perspective*, ed. Carolyn Sargent and Carolyn Brettell. Upper Saddle River, NJ: Prentice-Hall.

Jenkins, Janis H., 1998. "The Medical Anthropology of Political Violence: A Cultural and Feminist Agenda," *Medical Anthropology Quarterly* 12: 122–31.

Jenkins, Janis H., and Martha Valiente, 1994. "Bodily Transactions of the Passions: *El Calor* among Salvadoran Women Refugees," in *Embodiment and Experience: The Existential Ground of Culture and Self*, ed. Thomas J. Csordas. Cambridge: Cambridge University Press, 163–82.

Johnson, Don, 1983. *Body*. Boston: Beacon Press.

Johnson, Don Hanlon, 1992. *Body: Recovering our Sensual Wisdom*. Berkeley: North Atlantic Books.

Johnson, Don Hanlon, ed., 1997. *Groundworks: Narratives of Embodiment*. Berkeley: North Atlantic Books.

Johnson, Mark, 1987. *The Body in the Mind: The Bodily Basis of Meaning, Imagination, and Reason*. Chicago: University of Chicago Press.

Kealiinohomoku, Joann, 1972. "Dance Culture as a Microcosm of Holistic Culture,"*Cord Research Annual* VI: 99–106.

Kealiinohomoku, Joann, 1976. *Theories and Methods for an Anthropological Study of Dance*. Ph.D. dissertation in anthropology, University of Indiana.

Kealiinohomoku, Joann, 1981. "Dance as a Rite of Transformation," in *Discourse in Ethnomusicology II: A Tribute to Alan P. Merriam*, ed. Caroline Card. Bloomington: Indiana University Ethnomusicology Publications, pp.

131–52.

Kelley, Klara Bonsack, and Harris Francis, 1994. *Navajo Sacred Places.* Bloomington, IN: Indiana University Press.

Kirmayer, Laurence J., 1989. "Mind and Body as Metaphors," in *Biomedicine Examined,* ed. M. Lock and D. Gordon. Dordrecht: Kluwer Academic Publishers, 57–94.

Kirmayer, Laurence J., 1992. "The Body's Insistence on Meaning: Metaphor as Presentation and Representation in Illness Experience," *Medical Anthropology Quarterly,* 6: 323–46.

Kleinman, Arthur, 1980. *Patients and Healers in the Context of Culture.* Berkeley: University of California Press.

Kleinman, Arthur, 1986. *Social Origins of Distress and Disease: Neurasthenia, Depression, and Pain in Modern China.* New Haven: Yale University Press.

Kleinman, Arthur, 1988. *The Illness Narratives: Suffering, Healing, and the Human Condition.* New York: Basic Books.

Kleinman, Arthur, 1995. *Writing at the Margin: Discourse between Anthropology and Medicine.* Berkeley: University of California Press.

Kleinman, Arthur, Veena Das, and Margaret Lock, eds, 1997. *Social Suffering.* Berkeley: University of California Press.

Knauft, Bruce, 1989. "Bodily Images in Melanesia: Cultural Substances and Natural Metaphors," in *Fragments for a History of the Human Body,* ed. Michel Feher et al. New York: Zone Books, vol. 3, 198–278.

Korbin, Jill E., ed., 1981. *Child Abuse and Neglect: Cross-Cultural Perspectives.* Berkeley: University of California Press.

Kotarba, Joseph, 1982. Chronic Pain: *Its Social Dimensions.* Beverly Hills: Sage Publications.

Kroker, Arthur, and Marilouise Kroker, 1987. *Body Invaders: Panic Sex in America.* New York: St. Martin's Press.

Laderman, Carol, 1991. *Taming the Winds of Desire.* Berkeley: University of California Press.

Lakoff, George, 1987. *Women, Fire, and Dangerous Things: What Categories Reveal about the Mind.* Chicago: University of Chicago Press.

Lancaster, Roger N., and Micaela di Leonardo, eds, 1997. *The Gender/Sexuality Reader.* New York: Routledge.

Laqueur, Thomas, 1990. *Making Sex: Body and Gender from the Greeks to Freud.* Cambridge, MA: Harvard University Press.

Law, Jane Marie, ed., 1995. *Religious Reflections on the Human Body.* Bloomington: Indiana University Press.

Lawrence, Denise L., and Setha M. Low, 1990. "The Built Environment and Spatial Form," *Annual Review of Anthropology* 19: 453–505.

Leder, Drew, 1990. *The Absent Body.* Chicago: University of Chicago Press.

Leder, Drew, ed., 1992. *The Body in Medical Thought and Practice.* Dordrecht: Kluwer Academic Publishers.

Leenhardt, Maurice, 1947/1979. *Do Kamo: Person and Myth in a Melanesian World,* trans. Basia Miller Gulati. Chicago: University of Chicago Press.

Levin, David Michael, 1985. *The Body's Recollection of Being: Phenomenological*

Psychology and the Deconstruction of Nihilism. London: Routledge.

Levin, David Michael, ed., 1993. *Modernity and the Hegemony of Vision*. Berkeley: University of California Press.

Levin, David Michael, ed., 1997. *Sites of Vision: The Discursive Construction of Sight in the History of Philosophy*. Cambridge, MA: MIT Press.

Lévi-Strauss, Claude, 1963. *Structural Anthropology*. Garden City, NY: Doubleday.

Lévi-Strauss, Claude, 1964. *Le cru et le cuit*. Paris: Plon.

Lévi-Strauss, Claude, 1966. *Du miel au cendres*. Paris: Plon.

Lévi-Strauss, Claude, 1968. *L'Origine des manières de table*. Paris: Plon.

Lock, Margaret, 1993a. "Cultivating the Body: Anthropology and Epistemologies of Bodily Practice and Knowledge," *Annual Review of Anthropology* 22: 133–55.

Lock, Margaret, 1993b. *Encounters with Aging: Mythologies of Menopause in Japan and North America*. Berkeley: University of California Press.

Low, Setha M., 1994. "Embodied Metaphors: Nerves as Lived Experience," in *Embodiment and Experience*, ed. Thomas J. Csordas. Cambridge: Cambridge University Press, 1139–62.

Low, Setha M., 1995. "Indigenous Architecture and the Spanish American Plaza in Mesoamerica and the Caribbean," *American Anthropologist* 97: 748–62.

Low, Setha M., 1996. "Spatializing Culture: The Social Production and Social Construction of Public Space in Costa Rica," *American Ethnologist* 23: 861–79.

Low, Setha M., and Erve Chambers, eds, 1989. *Housing, Culture, and Design: a Comparative Perspective*. Philadelphia: University of Pennsylvania Press.

Lowie, Robert H., 1924/1952. *Primitive Religion*. New York: Grosset and Dunlap.

Lundin, Susanne, and Lynn Akesson, eds, 1996. *Bodytime: On the Interaction of Body, Identity, and Society*. Lund, Sweden: Lund University Press.

Marcus, George, and Michael Fischer, 1986. *Anthropology as Cultural Critique: An Experimental Moment in the Human Sciences*. Chicago: University of Chicago Press.

McGuire, Meredith B., 1990. "Religion and the Body: Rematerializing the Human Body in the Social Sciences of Religion," *Journal for the Scientific Study of Religion* 29: 283–96.

Martin, Emily, 1987. *The Woman in the Body: A Cultural Analysis of Reproduction*. Boston: Beacon Press.

Martin, Emily, 1992. "The End of the Body?" *American Ethnologist* 19: 121–40.

Martin, Emily, 1994. *Flexible Bodies: The Role of Immunity in American Culture from the Days of Polio to the Age of AIDS*. Boston: Beacon Press.

Mauss, Marcel, 1934/1950. *Les techniques du corps: Sociologie et anthropologie*. Paris: Presses Universitares de France.

Mauss, Marcel, 1938/1950. *Une categorie de L'espirit humain: La Notion du personne, celle du "Moi"*. *Sociologie et anthropologie*. Paris: Presses Universitares de France.

Mellor, Philip A., and Chris Shilling, 1997. *Re-forming the Body: Religion, Community, and Modernity*. London: Sage.

Merleau-Ponty, Maurice, 1962. *Phenomenology of Perception*. trans. James Edie.

Evanston, IL: Northwestern University Press.

Merleau-Ponty, Maurice, 1964. *The Primacy of Perception*, ed. James Edie. Evanston, IL: Northwestern University Press.

Merleau-Ponty, Maurice, 1968. "The Intertwining – The Chiasm," in Maurice Merleau-Ponty, *The Visible and the Invisible*, ed. Claude Lefort and trans. Alphonso Lingis. Evanston, IL: Northwestern University Press, 130–55.

Miller, Barbara, 1981. *The Endangered Sex: Neglect of Female Children in Rural North India*. Ithaca: Cornell University Press.

Moerman, Michael, and Masaichi Nomura, eds, 1990. *Culture Embodied*. Osaka, Japan: National Museum of Ethnology.

Murphy, Robert F., 1987. *The Body Silent*. New York: Henry Holt & Co.

Ness, Sally Anne, 1992. *Body, Movement, and Culture: Kinesthetic and Visual Symbolism in a Philippine Community*. Philadelphia: University of Pennsylvania Press.

Nordstrom, Carolyn and JoAnn Martin, eds, 1992. *Pathways to Domination, Resistance, and Terror*. Berkeley: University of California Press.

Novack, Cynthia J., 1990. *Sharing the Dance: Contact Improvisation and American Culture*. Madison, WI: University of Wisconsin Press.

O'Donovan-Anderson, Michael, ed., 1996. *The Incorporated Self: Interdisciplinary Perspectives on Embodiment*. Lanham, MD: Rowman & Littlefield.

Oesterley, W. O. E., 1923. *The Sacred Dance; A Study in Comparative Folklore*. Cambridge: Cambridge University Press.

O'Neill, John, 1985. *Five Bodies: The Shape of Modern Society*. Ithaca, NY: Cornell University Press.

Ong, Walter, 1991. "The Shifting Sensorium," in *The Varieties of Sensory Experience: A Sourcebook in the Anthropology of the Senses*, ed. David Howes. Toronto: University of Toronto Press, pp. 25–30.

Ots, Thomas, 1990. "The Angry Liver, The Anxious Heart and the Melancholy Spleen: The Phenomenology of Perceptions in Chinese Culture," *Culture, Medicine, and Psychiatry* 14: 21–58.

Ots, Thomas, 1991. "Phenomenology of the Body: The Subject-Object Problem in *Psychosomatic Medicine and Role of Traditional Medical Systems," in Anthropologies of Medicine: A Colloquium of West European and North American Perspectives*, ed. Beatrix Pflederer and Gilles Bibeau. Special issue of *Curare*. Wiesbade: Wieweg, 43–58.

Ots, Thomas, 1994. "The Silenced Body – The Expressive *Leib*: On the Dialectic of Mind and Life in Chinese Cathartic Healing," in *Embodiment and Experience: The Existential Ground of Culture and Self*, ed. Thomas J. Csordas. Cambridge and New York: Cambridge University Press, pp. 116–36.

Outram, Dorinda, 1989. *The Body and the French Revolution: Sex, Class, and Political Culture*. New Haven: Yale University Press.

Pandolfi, Mariela, 1990. "Boundaries Inside the Body: Women's Suffering in Southern Peasant Italy," *Culture, Medicine, and Psychiatry* 14: 255–74.

Pandolfi, Mariela, 1991. "Memory within the Body: Women's Narrative and Identity in a Southern Italian Village," in *Anthropologies of Medicine: A Colloquium of West European and North American Perspectives*, ed. Beatrix Pflederer and Gilles Bibeau. Special issue of *Curare*. Wiesbade: Wieweg.

Pinxten, Rik, Ingrid van Dooren, and Frank Harvey, 1983. *Anthropology of Space: Explorations into the Natural Philosophy and Semantics of the Navajo*. Philadelphia: University of Pennsylvania Press.

Radin, Paul, 1927/1957. *Primitive Man as Philosopher*. New York: Dover Publications.

Radin, Paul, 1937/1957. *Primitive Religion*. New York: Dover Publications.

Riches, David, ed., 1986. *The Anthropology of Violence*. New York: Blackwell.

Roseman, Marina, 1991. *Healing Sounds from the Malaysian Rainforest: Temiar Music and Medicine*. Berkeley: University of California Press.

Russett, Cynthia Eagle, 1989. *Sexual Science: The Victorian Construction of Womanhood*. Cambridge: Harvard University Press.

Sacks, Oliver W., 1985. *The Man who Mistook his Wife for a Hat and Other Clinical Tales*. New York: Summit Books.

Sacks, Oliver W., 1990. *A Leg to Stand on*. New York: HarperPerennial.

Scarry, Elaine, 1987. *The Body in Pain: The Making and Unmaking of the World*. New York: Oxford University Press.

Scarry, Elaine, ed., 1988. *Literature and the Body: Essays on Populations and Persons*. Baltimore: Johns Hopkins University Press.

Schatzki, Theodore R., and Wolfgang Natter, eds, 1996. *The Social and Political Body*. New York: Guilford Press.

Scheper-Hughes, Nancy, ed., 1987. *Child Survival: Anthropological Perspectives on the Treatment and Maltreatment of Children*. Dordrecht: D. Reidel.

Scheper-Hughes, Nancy, 1992 *Death without Weeping: The Violence of Everyday Life in Brazil*. Berkeley: University of California Press.

Scheper-Hughes, Nancy, and Margaret Lock, 1987. "The Mindful Body: A Prolegomenon to Future Work in Medical Anthropology," *Medical Anthropology Quarterly* 1: 6–41.

Schwarz, Maureen Trudelle, 1997. *Molded in the Image of Changing Woman: Navajo Views on the Human Body and Personhood*. Tucson: University of Arizona Press.

Seremetakis, C. Nadia, ed., 1993. *Ritual, Power, and the Body: Historical Perspectives on the Representation of Greek Women*. New York: Pella Publishing.

Seremetakis, C. Nadia, ed., 1994. *The Senses Still: Perception and Memory as Material Culture in Modernity*. Boulder, CO: Westview Press.

Sheets-Johnstone, Maxine, ed., 1992. *Giving the Body its Due*. Albany: State University of New York Press.

Shilling, Chris, 1993. *The Body and Social Theory*. London: Sage.

Smith, Mary Lynn, 1996. *Presence and Copresence: Embodiment of Self and Other in American Contemporary Concert Dance*. Ph.D dissertation, Program in American Studies, Cleveland: Case Western Reserve University.

Smith, Paul Julian, 1989: *The Body Hispanic: Gender and Sexuality in Spanish and Spanish American Literature*. Oxford: Clarendon Press.

Sobo, Elisa Janine, 1993. *One Blood: The Jamaican Body*. Albany: SUNY Press.

Spicker, Stuart F., ed. 1970. *The Philosophy of the Body: Rejections of Cartesian Dualism*. New York: Quadrangle/The New York Times Book Co.

Stein, Howard, 1987. *Developmental Time, Cultural Space*. Norman: University of Oklahoma Press.

Stoller, Paul, 1989. *The Taste of Ethnographic Things: The Senses in Anthropology*. Philadelphia: University of Pennsylvania Press.

Stoller, Paul, 1997. *Sensuous Scholarship*. Philadelphia: University of Pennsylvania Press.

Stone, Allucquere Roseanne, 1995. *The War of Desire and Technology at the Close of the Mechanical Age*. Cambridge, Mass.: MIT Press.

Strathern, Andrew J., 1996. *Body Thoughts*. Ann Arbor: University of Michigan Press.

Strathern, Andrew, and Marilyn Strathern, 1971. *Self-Decoration in Mount Hagen*. London: Backworth.

Strathern, Marilyn, 1988. *The Gender of the Gift: Problems with Women and Problems with Society in Melanesia*. Berkeley: University of California Press.

Strathern, Marilyn, 1992. *Reproducing the Future: Esssays on Anthropology, Kinship, and the New Reproductive Technologies*. New York: Routledge.

Suarez-Orozco, Marcelo, 1987. "The Treatment of Children in the 'Dirty War': Ideology, State Terrorism, and the Abuse of Children in Argentina," in *Child Survival*, ed. Nancy Scheper-Hughes. Dordrecht: D. Reidel, pp. 227–46.

Suarez-Orozco, Marcelo, 1990. "Speaking of the Unspeakable: Toward a Psychosocial Understanding of Responses to Terror," *Ethos* 18: 353–74.

Suleiman, Susan Rubin, ed., 1985. *The Female Body in Western Culture: Contemporary Perspectives*. Cambridge, MA: Harvard University Press.

Sullivan, Lawrence E., 1990. "Body Works: Knowledge of the Body in the Study of Religion," *History of Religions* 30: 86–99.

Synnott, Anthony, 1993. *The Body Social: Symbolism, Self, and Society*. London: Routledge.

Taussig, Michael, 1987. *Shamanism, Colonialism, and the Wildman: A Study in Terrorism and Healing*. Chicago: University of Chicago Press.

Taussig, Michael, 1992. "Tactility and Distraction," in Michael Taussig, *The Nervous System*. New York: Routledge, 141–8.

Taussig, Michael, 1993. *Mimesis and Alterity: A Particular History of the Senses*. London: Routledge.

Thrift, Nigel, 1996. *Spatial Formations*. London: Sage.

Treichler, Paula A., Lisa Cartwright, and Constance Penley, eds, 1998. *The Visible Woman: Imaging Technologies, Gender, and Science*. New York: New York University Press.

Tseëlon, Efrat, 1995. *The Masque of Femininity: The Presentation of Women in Everyday Life*. London: Sage.

Turner, Bryan S., 1984. *The Body and Society*. Oxford: Basil Blackwell.

Turner, Bryan S., 1992. *Regulating Bodies: Essays in Medical Sociology*. London: Routledge.

Turner, Terence, 1980. "The Social Skin," in *Not Work Alone*, ed. J. Cherfas and R. Lewin. London: Temple Smith, pp. 112–40.

Turner, Terence, 1995. "Social Body and Embodied Subject: Bodiliness, Subjectivity, and Sociality among the Kayapo," *Cultural Anthropology* 10: 143–70.

Tyler, Stephen, 1990. *The Unspeakable: Discourse, Dialogue, and Rhetoric in the Postmodern World*. Madison: University of Wisconsin Press.

Vernant, Jean-Pierre, 1989. "Dim Body, Dazzling Body" in *Fragments for a History of the Human Body, Part One*, ed. Michel Feher. New York: Zone, pp. 18–47.

Warren, K. B., ed., 1993. *The Violence Within: Cultural and Political Opposition in Divided Nations*. Boulder: Westview Press.

Weber, Max, 1963. *The Sociology of Religion*, trans. Ephraim Fischoff. Boston: Beacon Press.

Weiss, Gail and Honi Fern Haber, eds, 1999. *Perspectives on Embodiment: The Intersections of Nature and Culture*. New York: Routledge.

Werbner, R. P., 1977. *Regional Cults*. London: Academic Press.

Winkler, Cathy (with Kate Wininger), 1994. "Rape Trauma: Contexts of Meaning," in *Embodiment and Experience: The Existential Ground of Culture and Self*, ed. Thomas J. Csordas. Cambridge: Cambridge University Press, pp. 248–68.

Young, Iris Marion, 1990. *Throwing like a Girl and Other Essays in Feminist Philosophy and Social Theory*. Bloomington: Indiana University Press.

Young, Katharine, ed., 1995. *Bodylore*. Knoxville: University of Tennessee Press.

Young, Katharine, 1997. *Presence in the Flesh: The Body in Medicine*. Cambridge, Mass.: Harvard University Press.

Zaner, Richard M., 1981. *The Context of Self: A Phenomenological Inquiry using Medicine as a Clue*. Athens: Ohio University Press.

Zinn, Maxine Baca, Pierette Hondagneu-Sotelo, and Michael A. Messner, eds, 1997. *Through the Prism of Difference: Readings on Sex and Gender*. Boston: Allyn and Bacon.

8 Human Cognition and Cultural Evolution

Pascal Boyer

Experimental evidence and models from cognitive psychology, linguistics, neuro-science and evolutionary biology converge on a precise, empirically testable account of human cognitive capacities, with consequences in many central domains of cultural anthropology. Here I emphasize empirical aspects of the program, showing how cognitive capacities make certain types of concepts more likely than others to be acquired and transmitted in human groups. Cognitive science is most helpful in describing and explaining "ideational culture", that is, the set of mental representations entertained by members of a particular group that makes that group different from others. Traditionally, anthropologists have tended to see the mind as a receptacle for cultural representations. Cognitive processes were seen as technicalities, certainly interesting in their own right, but with little effect on the contents and transmission of cultural concepts. This assumption was never too plausible (Bloch, 1985) and it is now just untenable.

Obviously, there is no space here to give a survey of cognitive science in the last twenty years or so.[1] So I concentrate here on two domains, both of crucial interest to cultural anthropology, for which there are already significant results. The first one is that of the connections between conceptual development (how children acquire concepts) and cultural transmission. The second one is that of the connections between biological evolution and cultural recurrence.

Intuitive ontology and conceptual development

Cognitive development is directly relevant to cultural anthropology, for obvious reasons. If members of a group entertain mental representations that members of other groups do not have it is certainly in great part because they were brought up in that group. It is therefore crucial to understand how a developing mind gradually acquires and builds its conceptual repertoire.

Humans acquire vastly more information from the natural and social environments than any other species. A traditional explanation is that humans have general "learning capacities" that are (1) quantitatively far greater than in other species and (2) not "prejudiced", that is, not predisposed to particular conceptual structures. However, studies of conceptual development suggest that human infants can acquire a lot of concepts and maintain flexibility precisely because of a rich set of prior categories and principles. From the first stages of infant cognition, we can observe that children focus their attention on particular cues in their environment and produce specific inferences on the basis of these cues.

Of special interest to anthropology are distinctions between types of things that can be found in the world, as well as principles that guide inferences about these different kinds of things (Boyer, 1998). There is now massive evidence that children build a sophisticated conceptual repertoire on the basis of *domain-specific principles* (see Hirschfeld and Gelman, 1994 for a survey). That is, the way they use similarity between objects to build categories and the way they notice certain recurrent features rather than others differ according to the ontological domains objects belong to: ARTEFACTS are treated differently from ANIMALS or PERSONS. From an early age, children have concepts of these large ontological "domains", based on complex perceptual cues. Domain-specific principles deliver intuitive explanations for observed states and expectations about future states of affairs.

There is evidence for the presence and salience of categories like HUMAN, ARTEFACT, ANIMAL from infancy. Obviously, human infants can, like most animals, distinguish con-specifics from other types of beings on the basis of complex perceptual cues (Morton and Johnson, 1991) that trigger particular forms of interaction (Meltzoff, 1994). But less obvious ontological distinctions appear very early, like a distinction between living and non-living things grounded in an early sensitivity to the perceptual difference between self- and non-self-generated movement in physical objects (Massey and Gelman, 1988; Premack, 1990; Premack and James-Premack, 1995). Mandler and her colleagues have demonstrated the existence of a variety of ontological categories such as ANIMAL and ARTEFACT in children of eighteen months (Mandler, Bauer, and McDonough, 1991). To say that ontological categories use perception does not mean that they are entirely driven by perception. Indeed, ontological identification often overrides superficial similarity (Soja, Carey, and Spelke, 1992: 102). For instance, children assume that inner, invisible features of animals extend to close natural kinds. If for instance monkeys are said to have a particular organ, then four-year-olds assume that a dog or a cat probably have it too. However, they would not extend this assumption to a statue of a monkey, despite the surface similarity, or even to a mechanical monkey that moves (Massey and Gelman, 1988).

For developmental psychologists, ontological categories are not just conceptual "boxes" for objects intuitively assumed to have some common features. They are *theoretical* entities (Gopnik and Meltzoff, 1997) in the sense that children go far beyond direct experience and make assumptions about underlying processes that apply to each domain. These assumptions are called "skeletal principles" (Gelman, 1990), "modes of construal" (Keil, 1994), or "foundational theories" (Wellmann and Gelman, 1992) that correspond to each domain. Consider for instance our "intuitive physics" for solid objects: a series of tacit expectations about how solid objects collide rather than go through one another, about the fact that their trajectories are continuous, about changes in trajectories caused by collisions, about the likely trajectories of unsupported objects, and so on. Some of these principles are found in infancy, long before children can handle objects in ways that would support the principles in question (Spelke, 1990 and 1994). Another domain of intuitive principles is that of intuitive psychology or "theory of mind", that is, the set of tacit assumptions whereby observable behaviour is interpreted as caused by unobservable thoughts and intentions (Whiten, 1991). Children from the age of three assume that thoughts and intentions are immaterial. They also assume that actual states of affairs cause perceptions that cause beliefs that cause intentions (see for instance Wellmann, 1990; Perner, 1991; Gopnik and Wellmann, 1994). Another domain of specialized principles is that of biological processes. Specific principles include the assumption that members of a living kind have some internal similarity beyond their common external features and sometimes in conflict with observable features (Keil, 1986; Gelman and Markman, 1987). Also, living things are construed as belonging to a set of taxonomic classes (jointly exhaustive of the domain, and mutually exclusive) such that taxonomic proximity predicts non-obvious resemblance (Atran, 1990). Other domains are also structured by specific principles, as discussed below.

Concept acquisition and conceptual development, then, are not informed by uniform, general "learning" principles that would apply to all domains of experience. Rather, what emerges from the evidence is a multiplicity of acquisition mechanisms, each of which is focused on particular aspects of the experienced world and is structured by domain-specific principles. For instance, children parse sentences by applying to the linguistic input a series of recursive rules that have no other domain of application (Pinker, 1984). When they learn to count, they apply to number-concepts principles that are never used in other domains (Gallistel and Gelman, 1992).[2] Children's concepts of animal kinds are "essentialistic", that is, based on the assumption that some inner quality, common to all members of a kind, cause the observable features detected. This assumption is not readily applied to artifacts or natural substances. In each domain, specific expectations appear very early. They orient attention towards certain classes of cues in the environment and constrain inferences about them. Principles and categories constitute an *intuitive ontology* that is tacitly and automatically activated and produces expectations about courses of events.

There is no evidence for major cultural differences in categorical distinctions or inferential engines. Take intuitive biology: there are, to be sure, cultural differences in the way biological phenomena are explained. However, the major features of biological essentialism, as described here, are stable across cultures. That is, in all cultures we find structurally similar taxonomic ranks for living kinds (Atran, 1990). Moreover, at the level of genera (concepts like DOG, GIRAFFE, OAK, TULIP) people assume that an inner structure is common to all members of a kind. This allows inferences such as expecting them to contain similar parts, to have similar behaviour, to have the same susceptibility to illnesses (see the various studies in Atran and Medin, 1998 for cross-cultural illustrations). In the domain of intuitive psychological inferences ("theory of mind"), there is a similar pattern. Explicit cultural theories of the person consist in an enrichment, never a revision of the intuitive principles described above. Developmentally, too, one finds unexpected cultural similarity. For instance, three-year-olds have difficulties entertaining both the representation that *p* (e.g. "there's a marble in the box") and the representation that someone else's representation is *not p* (e.g. "Ann thinks that 'there's no marble in the box'"). However, normal four-year-olds have no difficulty with this "false-belief task" (Wimmer and Perner, 1983). Now this developmental shift occurs in the same way at the same age for American and Pygmy children (Avis and Harris, 1991). There is not much cross-cultural evidence for the concepts and inferences of intuitive physics, but their very early development makes further cultural differences difficult to imagine. More generally, cultural differences in developmental schedule remain within a narrow envelope and lead to the same end-point, as S. Walker showed in a detailed study of American and Nigerian children's intuitive principles (Walker, 1985 and 1992).

Most of these principles are developed before middle childhood and do not seem to change much with development after this age. The categories and principles described here are found in a similar form at the end-point of cognitive development. Obviously, intuitive categories and principles are then completed with a wealth of information inferred from direct experience and cultural transmission. As discussed below, however, processes of cultural transmission cannot be understood without this intuitive background.

Cultural representations as enrichment of intuitive ontology

Intuitive ontology is involved in cultural transmission because it provides a background that allows children and adults to understand cultural input, that is, to make inferences on the basis of that input that produce new concepts. In this way, intuitive ontology imposes some constraints on the range of concepts likely to be "culturally successful", because it makes some concepts much easier than others to acquire, store and communicate. Here I can only give a few illustrations of this process (see Boyer, 1998 for a more detailed survey).

In many domains, cultural input, consisting of people's utterances, gestures, but also artifacts and other aspects of the environment contributes to an *enrichment* of the categories and inferential principles of intuitive ontology. This means that culturally provided information is attended to because prior principles specify that the domain exists and constrain the type of information relevant to that domain. A simple illustration is the domain of NUMBER. Obviously, labels for numbers and counting systems are culturally specific. Now children have no difficulty acquiring numbers as abstract properties of collections, or acquiring names for numbers as an ordered set that obeys particular constraints. This requires that children assume a set of prior principles, namely: (1) one-to-one correspondence (between objects enumerated and names for numbers); (2) stable ordering of labels; (3) item indifference; (4) order indifference for the items counted; and (5) cardinality (see footnote 2) (Gallistel and Gelman, 1992). Easy acquisition stems from the fact that intuitions about number are present already in infancy. Experiments by K. Wynn demonstrated that infants are sensitive to the pure "numerosity" of displays. "Impossible" changes in the number of items displayed (e.g. $1 + 1 = 1$, $2 - 1 = 2$) surprise infants in dishabituation experiments (Wynn, 1992). Prior numerosity principles specify a number of conceptual slots for number-names and these names are provided by cultural input. The extension of the list and the combinatorial principles can vary from one place to another, but they are always consistent with these prior principles (Crump, 1990). A counting system that does not obey the principles listed above would be much more difficult to acquire and store, which may explain cultural recurrence in this domain.

In other domains, cultural input is enlisted to enrich a causal framework that is postulated but not specified by intuitive ontology. For instance, in most cultural environments, one finds a wealth of detailed representations of living kinds, of their relations, their behaviour, structural aspects, and so on. These are not acquired in the context of institutional schooling, but as part and parcel of everyday cultural skills and notions. Most of this knowledge is continuous with early-developed intuitive principles (Atran and Medin, 1998). First, identification of an object as an ANIMAL or HUMAN triggers inferences about agency. For instance, pre-schoolers assume that movement is externally generated for artifacts and internally generated for animals, even when both kinds of items are unfamiliar (Gelman, Gottfried, and Coley, 1994). Second, some principles are selectively applied to living things, in particular "essentialist" assumptions. A living organism is tacitly construed as possessing an unobservable, species-specific essence that causes its appearance and some aspects of behaviour. That a tiger has stripes and is carnivorous is not attributed to external factors but to the fact that all tigers possess some inner, undefined quality that causes these external features. Naturally, these principles are not the end-point of the development of biological notions. Cultural input widens the scope of early biological understandings (it is not obvious for a three-year-old that plants are alive and share common biological principles with animals). Also, it specifies causal processes that were postulated but not specified by intuitive principles. Children for instance assume that growth consists of law-like, internally generated changes (Rosengren, Gelman, Kalish, and McCormick, 1991) but culturally specified information may provide richer causal contexts to explain growth. In the same way, four-year-olds are prepared to assume that different properties appear as a result of inheritance, contagion, and accidents (Springer and Keil, 1989) although the particulars of which properties are transmitted in what way is specified by cultural input (Springer and Keil, 1991). Cultural representations also extend to theoretical constructions about what makes living things live. Consider for instance speculative notions about "life", "vitality", "elan vital", and other such culturally specific concepts (see Karim, 1981 for instance). These are all enrichments of the intuitive understanding that all members of living species share an inner causal essence, an understanding that does not specify what that essence is or how it causes its effects. To sum up, this is a case in which cultural input triggers representations that dovetail with prior intuitive principles.

Enrichment of intuitive categories and expectations also extends to the social domain, to cultural notions of agents and social groups. Let me first consider cultural variations in explanations of behaviour. These cultural representations comprise a range of cultural notions about the "self" or the "person", about the link between consciousness and various organs or bodily properties, about personality and dispositions, and so on, which can take very different forms in different social groups (Heelas and Lock, 1981). A Western emphasis on stable individual *dispositions* can be contrasted with explanations centered on social position or interaction that are found in many other places (Hsu, 1981; Shweder, 1982: 113ff). Such differences do not necessarily stem from globally different "world-views." As Morris and Peng have shown, Chinese and American subjects tend to perceive social interaction but not physical motion in different ways (Morris and Peng, 1994). More generally, theories of the person and of likely causes of behavior enrich but do not modify tacit principles of intuitive "theory of mind." These principles postulate for instance that states of affairs cause perceptions that cause beliefs that trigger intentions, and that the causal chain does not normally go in the other direction. Whatever cultural notions of personhood are explicitly developed, they invariably take for granted (and make use of) this implicit construal of how minds work.

Kinship categories provide another example of the process whereby culturally specific input can be acquired, inasmuch as there are intuitive principles to generate relevant inferences on the basis of that input. Experimental studies show that inferences activated by the term "family" are very different from the usual implications of collection-inclusion (Markman, 1973). Hirschfeld used this and other evidence to show that the child's ontology includes some non-trivial expectations about human co-resident collections ("families") as distinct from other kinds of category. The child's intuitive expectations about some aspects of kinship categories can be inferred from patterns of error in children's usage, or rather from the errors children do not make: for instance about generation and gender (Hirschfeld, 1989). In other words, children in different cultures start with an intuitive understanding of co-resident groups. This postulates that members of such groups share an underlying "nature" that does not extend to members of other groups. This understanding may of course be inaccurate given the local kinship system but it provides a skeleton that is then completed by culturally specific notions of what genealogical links correspond to what label.

In other domains of social categories, local cultural concepts seem to use "essentialist" intuitive principles similar to those applied to living kinds. Membership of many social categories is understood as the effect of a causal essence (Boyer, 1990; Rothbart and Taylor, 1990). That is, in the local ideology one is a shaman, a diviner, a blacksmith, not because of external social factors but because one possesses some inner, inherited and undefined quality that is found only among members of that group or caste (Boyer, 1994b). Racial categories too seem to be based on such essentialistic assumptions. Their reference is not biologically fixed and their extension depends on external historical variables. Where racial categories are routinely used and govern attitudes, people generally represent them in terms of possession of inner qualities that produce the external appearance. Contrary to received wisdom, even young children do not build racial categories as mere labels for pre-existing perceptual differences between people, as Hirschfeld demonstrated with controlled studies of French and American children's race-concepts (Hirschfeld, 1988 and 1993). Indeed, young children make the assumption that some non-obvious underlying features are involved in race-concepts *before* they acquire perceptual stereotypes for each group, not as a result of such acquisition (Hirschfeld, 1996).

In these various domains, we now have: (1) direct experimental evidence for intuitive categories and principles that appear early and extend into adult intuitive ontology; and (2) some anthropological evidence for the fact that cultural concepts are based on those principles. Concepts of "life" or the "person" or "number" may be different from one place to another, yet they are all equally easy to acquire for developing minds. This may be connected to the fact that they are all based on specific principles (described above) that seem to emerge in all developing minds in similar form the world over. In these domains, then, the fact that there are universal principles in intuitive ontology does not result in "cultural universals" but in limits on the range of variation. Cultural representations seem "transmittable" inasmuch as they confirm or enrich intuitive principles.

Cultural representations beyond intuitive ontology

In other domains, cultural representations seem much more diverse than this "enrichment" scenario would suggest. This is true of etiquette, of rules of hierarchy, of concepts of political order, and so on. Rather than list all these different domains and examine their possible connections with intuitive understandings, I will focus on one limiting-case for which we have some experimental evidence, that of religious representations. Despite obvious cultural diversity, recurrent patterns show that religious concepts are constrained by a small number of principles that are not specifically religious (Bloch, 1985; Lawson and McCauley, 1990; Bloch, 1992; Whitehouse, 1992; Boyer, 1994b). This is true in particular of religious *ontologies*, that is, culturally specific assumptions about the existence and causal powers of unobservable entities.

The ontological assumptions found in most religious systems, in otherwise diverse environments, generally constitute direct *violations* of intuitive expectations (Boyer, 1994a). For instance, spirits and ghosts are commonly represented as intentional agents whose physical properties go against the ordinary physical qualities of embodied agents. They go through physical obstacles, move instantaneously, and so on. Gods, too, have such counter-intuitive physical qualities, as well as non-standard biological features; they are immortal, they feed on the smell of sacrificed foods, and so on. Also, religious systems the world over include assumptions about particular artifacts, for instance statues that are endowed with intentional psychological processes, that can perceive states of affairs, form beliefs, or have intentions. Anthropologists are sometimes tempted to say that these religious assumptions are perfectly intuitive to the people who hold them, but this is not based on any experimental evidence, is directly contradicted by everyday life in the cultures concerned, and in any case would make it very mysterious that the people concerned find their religious concepts of any interest.

Such local concepts violate expectations of "intuitive physics" or "naive biology", or "theory of mind." This does not mean that they are perceived as unfamiliar, even less that they are construed as unreal. On the contrary, it is precisely insofar as a certain situation violates intuitive principles *and* is taken as real that it may become particularly salient. It is the conjunction of these two assumptions that gives such representations their *attention-grabbing* potential. In this sense, religious ontologies are constrained by intuitive expectations because they are salient only against the background of assumptions violated.

Counter-intuitive elements do not exhaust the representation of religious entities and agencies. For instance, ghosts are construed as physically counter-intuitive. At the same time, however, people routinely produce a large number of inferences about what the ghosts or spirits *know* or *want*, which are based on an extension of "theory of mind"-expectations to the spirits. Indeed, most inferences people produce about religious agencies are straightforward consequences of activating those intuitive principles that are *not* violated in the representation of those supernatural entities. These background assumptions are generally tacit and provide the inferential potential without which cultural representations are very unlikely to be transmitted.

Religious ontological concepts combine both salient, explicit assumptions that violate intuitive expectations and tacit assumptions that use all other intuitive principles. Now intuitive expectations apply to a limited number of broad ontological categories, for example ANIMAL, PERSON, ARTIFACT, NATURAL SUBSTANCE, and provide only a limited number of expectations. For instance intuitive ontology produces the expectation that some structural features in members of a living kind are caused by an internal "essence" but it says nothing about what causes the other observable features. In the same way, our intuitive physical principles produce the expectation that a force applied to an object will change its speed, but it is very vague about the way mass interacts with the force applied. In other words, intuitive ontology is a very *limited* system of expectations. If religious concepts include violations of intuitive ontology, there is only a limited number of expectations that can be violated. So we should expect that religious ontologies, despite surface variations, are based on a limited number of recurrent assumptions.

Indeed, we find that the limited "catalogue" of ontologies predicted by such combinations accounts for most of the conceptual assumptions actually found in religious categories: agents with counter-intuitive physical properties (e.g. spirits); agents with counter-intuitive biological properties (e.g. immortal gods, or gods who procreate in non-standard ways, or feed on smells and shadows); agents with counter-intuitive psychological properties (e.g. zombies or possessed people); animals with counter-intuitive biological properties (e.g. metamorphosed into other animals); artifacts with intentional properties (e.g. statues that listen, masks that talk). These concepts are culturally recurrent; that is, they are found in many more cultures than an unconstrained variation would predict. However, none of them is universal.

Together with cultural recurrence, this explanation of religious concepts is supported by experimental evidence. The attention-grabbing quality of counter-intuitive assumptions should have some direct consequences on recall and recognition. A systematic study of transmission by J. Barrett showed that subjects transmit counter-intuitive elements better than either standard, non-counter-intuitive descriptions or descriptions that are strange without being counter-intuitive (Barrett, 1996). Using similar material, Boyer showed that both violations of expectations (e.g. objects that have no shadow or suddenly disappear, people with extraordinary cognitive powers) and transfers of expectations to an inappropriate category (e.g. artifacts with psychological processes or biological properties) result in enhanced recall (Boyer, forthcoming). Also, these experiments show that *particular* types of counter-intuitive representations, rather than just any odd concepts, seem better recalled. Replication studies in Gabon and Nepal show that similar effects are achieved in literate and non-literate contexts, using both culturally familiar and unfamiliar material (Boyer, forthcoming).

The evidence also demonstrates the influence of intuitive expectations on the way people reason about religious agents. People's inferences are governed, not by the culturally specific, explicit "theory" but by a background of "default" intuitive expectations. A dramatic illustration of this phenomenon can be found in the study of concepts of God by Barrett and Keil (1996). Participants were first asked to produce explicit descriptions of the special properties of God. These generally center on counter-intuitive claims for extraordinary cognitive powers. God can perceive everything at once, focus his attention on multiple events simultaneously, and so on. The subjects were then tested on their recall of simple stories involving God in various scenarios where these capacities are relevant. In general, subjects tended to distort or add to the stories in ways that were directly influenced by their tacit, intuitive principles of psychology (Barrett and Keil, 1996). For instance, they recalled (wrongly) that in the story God attended to some problem *and then* turned his attention to another, or that God *could not perceive* some event because of some obstacle, although such information was not in the original stories. Barrett and Keil coined the term "theological correctness" ("TC" for short) to denote this tendency for subjects explicitly to entertain a description of supernatural agents that they do not actually use in representing these agents or predicting their behaviour.[3] In other words, people can readily activate and express the "official version" of the God concept, that is compatible with doctrine (and generally quotes directly from official teachings). But they also use an "implicit" concept, of which they are not aware. This implicit concept is the one that makes some inferences and predictions appear more "natural" than others to the people concerned.

Input, support and predispositions

So far, I have described cultural concepts that are acquired effortlessly and constitute either an enrichment of intuitive expectations or else a predictable combination of limited violation and tacit confirmation of expectations. This would suggest that human minds are predisposed, by virtue of early developed intuitive understandings, to acquire a specific range of cultural concepts. This argument is supported, conversely, by the special difficulties encountered in the transmission of cultural concepts that go beyond intuitive ontology. The most salient illustration is scientific understandings that often challenge or displace intuitive expectations. For instance, to be properly understood, scientific physics requires that we suspend ordinary intuitions about force and velocity. One principle of Newtonian mechanics is that the force applied to an object changes its acceleration. Now this is particularly difficult to acquire for human beings, whose intuitive physics has no clear notion of acceleration and assumes that force changes the "speed" of objects. In the same way, acquiring evolutionary biology requires that we discard the notion that each species corresponds to a particular essence found in all members of the species. Finally, learning mathematics requires that we treat a fraction like ⅓ as a number, not as an operation between numbers, a point that leaves most learners puzzled because intuitive arithmetic knows only integers.

In all these domains, acquisition is effortful. The problem is not specific to science, however, and emerges in many domains of cultural knowledge based on assumptions that are different from those of intuitive ontology. Long before science appeared, disciplines like systematic theology or metaphysics required this suspension of intuitive expectations. This, it must be emphasized, is different from the case of direct and limited violations of intuitive expectations, like the religious assumptions described above, which are extremely easy to acquire and remember.

In all these domains, then, cultural transmission requires dedicated institutions with specialized personnel and systematic training extending over many years. Also, transmission in these domains is boosted by literacy that allows external representation of cultural concepts (Goody, 1977; Donald, 1991 and 1993; Lloyd, 1991). It is remarkable, however, how scholarly concepts never quite dislodge intuitive expectations despite systematic and prolonged tuition. The fact that even well-trained specialists still have "wrong", non-scientific intuitions can be observed in physics (McCloskey, 1983), biology (Atran, 1996), statistics (Tversky and Kahnemann, 1982; Gigerenzer, 1991; Koehler, 1996) and logic (Wason and Johnson-Laird, 1972; Wason, 1983).

These three features (acquisition is always effortful; literacy is very often required; intuitive expectations remain) would suggest that cultural concepts in such contexts do not so much replace intuitive ontology as augment it with an explicit component. In particular, such concepts are generally included in *meta-representational* beliefs (Sperber, 1991). That is, they are not entertained merely as representations that "*p*", but as representations that "*p* is true", "*p* is guaranteed by Scripture", "p is confirmed by experiments", and other such validating contexts. This would explain why such concepts can sometimes become objects of belief even when their contents are not fully represented (Sperber, 1996).

To recapitulate: we have surveyed different domains where intuitive ontology seems to impose constraints on cultural concepts. In some domains, like number systems or theories of the person, the cultural input can be easily understood because it provides some conceptual enrichment of intuitive principles. A representation that diverges from these principles is unlikely to become culturally successful. For instance, a theory of the person that diverges from intuitive "theory of mind" assumptions is perfectly conceivable but unlikely to spread.[4] In other domains, cultural input is attended to because it provides attention-grabbing violations of intuitive expectations. But, as I said above, this means that only a limited repertoire of such concepts are easily acquired, because not many possible representations constitute violations of intuitive expectations. Again, we can easily conceive of other possible descriptions of religious agents, but these are unlikely to become culturally successful.[5] In a third kind of situation, cultural input neither enriches nor violates intuitive expectations in a straightforward way. Concepts that realize neither of these conditions are transmitted through explicit meta-representation in effortful conditions.

These cognitive differences cut cross common anthropological categories. Some aspects of the kinship system or religious beliefs in a group may enrich intuitive expectations, while other aspects are salient and counter-intuitive, and yet other concepts in these domains are learned through scholarly traditions. Intuitive ontology is a fragmented system of domain-specific expectations. It is therefore not surprising that cultural acquisition is not amenable to an overarching transmission theory. It consists of piecemeal inferences the structure of which depends on whether intuitive expectations are activated, which ones, and what connection can be established between them and the cultural input available.

From culture to predispositions: evolutionary psychology

Some features of early domain-specific understandings are particularly important for an understanding of the connections between evolved predispositions and conceptual capacities:

1 Experimental evidence suggests that the developing mind is a series of dedicated, small-scale, automatic machines specialized in very limited inferential tasks (see above).

2 Development is based on prior principles that guide inferences long before relevant experience could be accumulated. This is the case for "intuitive physics", but also for language recognition for instance. Two-hour-old infants have some expectations about phonological aspects of their mother's tongue (Mehler et al., 1988).

3 Intuitive ontology is often wrong. The principles are not always optimal, given the experiential input. For instance, the intonation contours infants notice and recognize are not always the best linguistic cues for language identification. Also, children and adults wrongly assume that a living species has an essence, that the velocity of a moving body is proportional to the force applied to it, and so on.

4 Intuitive ontology displays no salient cultural differences. Despite otherwise vastly different cultural environments, people seem to use categories and inference engines that are substantially similar.

Now all four features correspond to what a Darwinian view of cognitive evolution would predict (Cosmides and Tooby, 1987):

1 Evolution by natural selection would probably rule out the development of unprejudiced inductive brains. These would be overwhelmed with true but irrelevant generalizations about their environment and consequently very slow to notice relevant connections. Also, evolution goes by small increments and would therefore result in an accumulation of small capacities than in the sudden emergence of vast, flexible ones.

2 For the same reasons, selection for prior preferences and selective attention to particular cues in the environment is more plausible than putative selection for an unbiased cognitive system. Inter-specific comparisons show that organisms that extract more information from their environments also have more complex predispositions. This follows from straightforward computational reasons. In order to extract information, an organism must not only attend to particular cues, but also activate principles that guide inferences from these cues. To "learn" that scents can guide him to a prey, a wolf must first attend to scents rather than the shapes of trees around him and also assume that scents indicate a prey's past location rather than its future direction. The massive increase in the capacity to acquire and use external information in a flexible way, which is a feature of the modern human species (Donald, 1991; Mithen, 1996), probably goes together with an increase in the number and sophistication of prior principles (Rozin, 1976; Tooby and Cosmides, 1992).

3 Sub-optimal systems – "kludges" that do a specific job by modifying previous adaptations – are the hallmark of evolutionary history and can be found in all sorts of functional adaptations.

4 Being very complex adaptations, cognitive systems are the outcome of gradual changes over a very large number of generations, so that they are probably pan-specific.

These considerations provide the starting point for the program of *evolutionary psychology*, an attempt to put together what we know about the mind and what we know or surmise about evolution in an integrated picture of the foundations of culture (Tooby and Cosmides, 1992). In this framework the mind is described as a "Swiss-army knife" composed of specialized *cognitive adaptations* (see Barkow, Cosmides, and Tooby, 1992 for a survey). These systems were of direct adaptive value in the natural and social environment in which humans evolved. They may be adaptively neutral or even maladaptive in modern environments. Their emergence, in substantially similar form, in all normally developing humans, would result from specific genetic material. To say that cognitive capacities are evolved properties of the mind is not the same as saying that they are "innate" in the sense of being present at birth or present as such in the genome. All it means is that these capacities unfold in the course of development in normal subjects as a result of encountering a large class of normal environments, in the same way as growing adult teeth is a result of this encounter.

A variety of cognitive capacities can be linked to specialized algorithms for adaptive problems. For instance, Cosmides and Tooby have shown how performance on abstract logical tasks (like understanding that, given the proposition "if p then q", then "non-q" implies "non-p" but "non-p" says nothing about "q") improves dramatically if the formulation of the rule suggests some "social contract", that is, establishes that reception of a benefit implies payment of a cost (e.g. "if you are allowed to drink beer then you are over eighteen"). The effect obtains regardless of the familiarity of the rules or of the problems considered. So performance on such tasks seems to activate not a general mental logic or heuristics for the confirmation or refutation of conditionals, but an evolved capacity for the detection of cheaters in social exchange (Cosmides, 1989; Cosmides and Tooby, 1992). To take another example, Symons has shown how the main features of human sexuality could be conceived as the outcome of evolution (Symons, 1979). Further, Buss's extensive cross-cultural studies of mate-choice and sexual strategies have demonstrated the cross-cultural validity of predictions derived from a Darwinian evaluation of the costs (reproductive potential expended, parental care invested) and the genetic benefits involved. In particular, these studies show how predicted sex differences in terms of the attractiveness of potential mates transcend cultural differences in their expression (Buss, 1989). Parental care and investment is another domain where Darwinian predictions illuminate cultural recurrence. For instance, Mann showed that a variety of beliefs that result in selective infanticide are based on unconscious computation of the viability of infants (Mann, 1992). Indeed, parental investment may be tuned to these Darwinian parameters in a way that contradicts cultural values. Cronk for instance showed that preferential investment in boys or girls is sensitive to changing external parameters, while "official" cultural values do not change (Cronk, 1991b). Even homicide can be shown to be influenced by such adaptive mechanisms; degree of genetic relatedness is a better predictor of who kills whom with what accomplices than other social variables (Daly and Wilson, 1988). A variety of other domains of culture can be illuminated by this Darwinian approach (see Barkow et al., 1992 for a collection of such models).

An important aspect of these cognitive predispositions is their context-sensitivity and autonomy from social transmission. People spontaneously activate certain cognitive-behavioural recipes, when the relevant cues are found in their environment; this does not require instruction or "learning". Fiske made a similar argument as regards cognitive models of social organization (Fiske, 1992). For Fiske, social relations make use of four different cognitive models, all of which can be found in all cultures: "communal sharing" (a group is construed as an individual), "authority ranking" (all individuals belong to one of a set of ordered categories), "equality matching" (all individuals are identical in rights and duties), and "market pricing" (individuals get whatever others are prepared to give in exchange). What differs from one culture to another are the domains to which each of these models is applied. In some places relations with gods are a matter of authority ranking and in others those relations are construed in terms of a market. In some places relations with all kin will be conceived of as communal sharing, while equality matching pervades kin relations in other places. Which of these models is applied to what domain is inferred from cues in the social environment; the principles of each model, however, need not be socially transmitted (see an extensive illustration in Fiske, 1991).

Cognitive predispositions of this type have a direct influence on the recurrence of particular cultural representations, because they favor the recurrence of cultural representations that provide some a posteriori explanation for choices that were made on the basis of evolved preferences. For instance, modes of food-sharing are generally influenced by variance in resources. The more unpredictable a source of food (e.g. game as opposed to fruit), the more people engage in unconditional reciprocity (one shares with the whole group). However, people do not necessarily represent this in terms of survival; they may see sharing as the consequence of purely local notions of honesty, reciprocity, honor, and so on. In a similar way, sexual selection results in different values for males and females because of their differential investment in reproduction.[6] Human females are predicted to prefer partners who signal a disposition to engage in long-term parental investment and the ability (e.g. skills, wealth, intelligence) to gather and use resources, simply because whatever genes cause such preferences would have spread quickly in the gene-pool. Human males are predicted to prefer partners who display obvious, unfakeable signs of health and fertility. Now there are impressive cross-cultural differences in the concepts used to express sexual strategies, to do with local notions of beauty, morality, prestige, taboo, purity, and so on. Yet these concepts generally converge on the choices warranted by sexual selection (see extensive cross-cultural illustrations in Buss, 1989).

Like other biologically-inspired frameworks, evolutionary psychology is sometimes criticized for providing "just-so" stories that connect a general cultural trait with an *ad hoc* historical scenario that would make precisely such a trait useful (see for instance Gopnik and Meltzoff, 1997). However, a central assumption of evolutionary psychology is that identifying a specific problem in the ancestral environment is not sufficient to assume that human minds must have some specific solution for it. Two further conditions are required: (1) we must have independent evidence that a corresponding capacity does exist in modern humans; and (2) this must be evidence for complex functional design.[7] For instance, Mann's arguments about twin-infanticide was backed by arguments about its evolutionary advantages and by the recurrence of particular cultural beliefs about twins (e.g. one of the twins "wants to die"). But the crucial point here is that people do have cognitive mechanisms that allow them to assess the viability of infants from particular cues (e.g the way they eat, breathe, cry). This can be easily tested in the laboratory. The argument as a whole stands or falls on this evidence. If there was no such capacity, then we would be left with cultural practices that just happen to converge with survival interests. This is not sufficient to claim that the practices are an outcome of evolution. In the same way, arguments for a special capacity to detect cheaters in social exchange stands or falls on evidence for specialized inferential capacities. The idea is not just that it would have been advantageous to detect cheaters and that people can actually detect them. The crucial point is that there is a *specific* capacity to detect them that is not used in other (structurally similar) logical problems, a point that is still debated (Sperber, Cara, and Girotto, 1995). This is a typical example of the current status of evolutionary psychological arguments. Although the general assumptions are backed by considerable evolutionary and computational arguments, each particular hypothesis will need additional empirical evidence.

The resulting picture: Culture as cognitive epidemics

Cognitive findings and evolutionary hypotheses converge in suggesting a naturalistic explanatory program in the study of culture, based on five major points: (1) that cultural evolution consists in the differential selection of variants; (2) that selection operates on occurrences of mental representations in individuals; (3) that "cultural" representations have no special cognitive characteristics; (4) that transmission works through inferential processes whereby people add to fragmentary cultural input; and (5) that claims about cultural transmission can and should be based on independent evidence.

1 The notion that culture evolves through selection is not altogether new in cultural anthropology and could be found, at least implicitly, in some classical authors (see Ingold, 1986 for a survey). Its modern formulation stems from Campbell's intuition that the Darwinian notions of blind

variation and selective retention can apply beyond genetics to any situation of transmission (Campbell, 1970). The central idea is this: many variants of cultural concepts and behaviors are constantly created; we may idealize and assume that such variation is random; what makes it the case that cultures do not evolve randomly is that some variants are better suited for transmission than others. As Durham put it, "culture evolves through the *differential* transmission of ideas, values and beliefs in a population" 1991: 156; my emphasis).

In the 1980s evolutionary biologists and behavioural ecologists developed general selectionist models of cultural transmission: "cultural transmission models" (Cavalli-Sforza and Feldman, 1981) "gene-culture co-evolution" (Lumsden and Wilson, 1981) "dual inheritance theory" (Boyd and Richerson, 1985), and "co-evolution theory" (Durham, 1991). These are based on mathematical descriptions of the diffusion of "traits", inspired by population genetics. It soon became obvious that applying these models to actual cultural phenomena would be rather difficult. Cultural anthropology provides very few numerical descriptions of cultural traits in a population that are precise enough to serve as input to such models (though Aunger, 1992 and Cronk, 1991a show that it can be done). However, co-evolution models demonstrated that selective models, by opposition to "generative" explanations, are sufficient to explain trends in transmission (Boyer, 1994b). Generative accounts postulate mechanisms that would produce the representations observed. Selective accounts by contrast do not say anything about the origins of particular representations but make claims about their relative "fitness" in cultural transmission. An example of this contrast is the explanation of recurrence in religious representations. Concepts of souls and spirits are found virtually everywhere in similar forms. Intellectualist authors like Tylor explained this as a result of a universal urge to explain and predict experience and universal mental experiences. This is a generative explanation in the sense that the mechanisms postulated are supposedly involved in the emergence of such representations wherever they occur. By contrast, a selective account might state that beliefs about ghosts and souls, whatever their origins, are easier to acquire, or easier to store in memory, or more easily communicated than other possible religious concepts. The aggregation of many cycles of acquisition over generations would ensure that they gradually "crowd out" other concepts. What is studied here are not the historical circumstances that led to entertaining a particular belief but the probability that an occurrence of that belief will result in further occurrences.

2 The object of the selective process consists in *occurrences of mental representations*. The group-wide concepts often used in cultural anthropology (e.g. "American Baptist ideology", "Masai age-class system", "Tai-

wanese ancestor-cult") are a convenient short-hand for the aggregation of many individual phenomena but the locus of explanation remains in the individual. To explain cultural change or stability, for instance, we need to explain the likelihood of change or the likelihood of stability in individuals.

3 We do not need to posit anything special about "cultural" representations that would make them functionally different from other types of mental representation. Any individual mind entertains a huge number of mental representations. Most of these are idiosyncratic. A few seem to be represented in virtually identical form by all members of a community (e.g. syntactic rules for a language). A few again seem to be present in *roughly* similar forms among members of a particular group, a class, a village, a generation. These are the representations we call "cultural." The term denotes only a *similarity* observed between mental representations entertained by different people.

4 Cultural input underdetermines cultural concepts, because cultural acquisition consists of *inferential* processes. Human communication almost never produces a "copy" of someone's representations in someone else's brain. When mental representations occur as a result of communication, they are the outcome of inferences on the basis of cultural input (gestures, utterances, etc.). Tomasello, Kruger, and Ratner 1993) demonstrated that even a constrained domain like tool-making requires sophisticated perspective-taking capacities whereby a cultural "learner" has to represent not just the gestures observed, but also the intentions of a cultural elder and their perspective on those gestures. In most domains of culture it is simply not possible for developing subjects to consider cues provided by cultural elders and to produce relevant inferences about them without representing those elders' communicative intentions. It follows that what matters in explaining the occurrence of similar representations in different people is not so much the properties of "memes" as the properties of memes in interaction with the properties of inferential processes activated about them (Sperber, 1991). In this sense, cultural transmission is much more similar to viral infection than to genetic inheritance. Exposure to cultural "viruses" may lead to changes in the cognitive system that lead to that system exposing other systems to a (roughly) similar condition (Sperber, 1985).

5 If a model of cultural evolution said only that some representations are more "fit" than others, and that this explains their recurrence, it would not be very informative. It would state only that what stays more or less unchanged after cycles of transmission must have more "staying power" than what does not stay (Durham, 1991: 194). So the selectionist assumption is of interest only if we can establish an *independent* measure of cultural fitness that can be demonstrated experimentally, independently of our observations about cultural recurrence.

New methods for old problems

How will cognitive science affect anthropology? The question is not so much whether a cognitive study of cultural representations will take place; this much is certain. The question is whether (and how) this will take place in the context of cultural or social anthropology programs as defined so far. This is not just a question of academic politics, but also raises important issues of method.

A first problem is that a study of cognitive factors in cultural evolution requires a *theoretically motivated data-base* for cultural comparison that is just not available yet. Despite its official goals and interests, anthropology is not in practice a comparative discipline. That is, there is no agreed description format that would make it possible to compare the spread of cultural representations in various places. Past attempts in this direction were flawed for symmetrical reasons: either because there was no theoretical basis for comparison or because the theory itself was unsatisfactory. The gigantic *Human Relations Area Files* data-base is an illustration of the first problem. The a-theoretical collection of facts reported by many ethnographers with incompatible theoretical outlooks is very difficult to use. Compare with the *Notes and Queries*-inspired monographs, the Bishop Museum monographs in Polynesia, or the Africanist monographs of the British structural-functionalist school. These were all coherent attempts at integration that could be used for comparative purposes. They then lost favour because anthropologists realized the limits of the underlying theory.

A second factor to take into account is that the requirement of *independent, non-anthropological evidence* conflicts with a pervasive attitude in anthropological theorizing, following which only anthropological data are directly relevant to anthropological claims. For instance, Lévi-Strauss and other structuralist authors made claims about the organization of diffusion of mythical concepts that implied strong psychological claims.[8] But they never bothered to seek direct psychological evidence for the postulated mechanisms. In the cognitive framework described here this move is just not possible. Making claims about what cultural input is more salient, or more memorable, or more likely to generate inferences, is saying something that is directly testable. Only this external evidence provides reasons to accept them.

Third, even in the description of cultural phenomena proper, a cognitive framework will require evidence produced by *experimental techniques*. As discussed above, people's concepts and conceptual processes are not exhausted by what is accessible to people themselves. In other words, what people believe is not (just) what they believe they believe. As I showed in various domains of cultural representations, tacit principles inform people's inferences and lead them to specific expectations. Most of these principles are not accessible to consciousness. In some cases (see the example of "Theological Correctness" above) the concepts actually used contradict what people believe they believe. This latter example shows that cognitive science is a more radical enterprise than classical sociological models. The latter stated (and sometimes showed) that we do not necessarily know why we have certain beliefs; cognitive science shows that it is seldom known what those beliefs are.

The cognitive study of culture does not address, let alone solve all the classical problems of anthropology. This is because anthropology as traditionally conceived brings together phenomena that belong to different causal systems and therefore require different causal hypotheses. What cognitive models propose is a naturalistic, empirically based description of some aspects of cultural representations, in an explanatory format that is directly connected to evidence about neural functioning as well as the evolutionary history of the species.

Notes

1   A very useful overview is the general series edited by D. N. Osherson (Gleitman and Liberman, 1995; Kosslyn and Osherson, 1995; Smith and Osherson, 1995; Osherson, 1998). Progress in knowledge of brain function has come from dramatic advances in (at least) six domains: (1) *Biochemistry*: a much better understanding of neuro-transmitters, of connectivity, of synaptic growth and decay; (2) *Imagery*: finer-grained functional descriptions of various neural structures and of connections between brain areas are provided by various imagery techniques (PET scans, evoked potentials, fMRI, etc.); (3) *Simulation*, especially through the development of artificial neural networks that model learning and categorization; (4) *Experimental protocols*, that for instance reveal infants' concepts or give us a better grasp of implicit memory and implicit learning; (5) *Study of cognitive pathology*: the neuro-psychology of amnesia, dysphasia, and aphasia as well as attention deficits and other pathological disruptions of cognitive functioning (schizophrenia and autism among others) now gives precious indications concerning normal operation; (6) *Study of cognitive development*: new evidence and models have changed our view of the developing mind, for instance in the domains of language and categorization.

2   For instance, counting obeys a "principle of cardinality." When you count objects, the number-name associated with the *last* object enumerated also denotes the overall quantity of objects ("one, two, *three* . . . there are *three* objects"). This never applies to other kinds of predicates ("green, red, *blue* . . . these are *blue* objects" is not a mistake children make).

3   Neither the "TC" concept nor the actual inferences produced by subjects show any difference correlated with the subjects' particular faith, denomina-

tion or even general attitude towards religion. Atheists, Hindus, and Christians of various denominations have similar performance.

4 Imagine, for instance, the simple theory that if people want x and know they cannot have x unless they do y, this does not usually result in their intention to do y. Or imagine the theory that people's beliefs are influenced by states of affairs, not by their own perception of those states of affairs. We know no human society where such notions would be the foundation of a theory of the person. This does not mean that no human being has ever entertained such theories but simply that they would not be easily acquired by other people.

5 For instance, consider the following notions: that there is an omnipotent God, but only on Wednesdays; that there are gods that watch us and perceive everything we do, but forget it instantly; that there is a God that knows all future events but has no memory of what happened in the past; that a statue of a goddess will hear and understand your prayers but only if you are very far from the statue when you say them. Again, there may well be people in all sorts of cultural settings who speculate along these lines. The point is that, all else being equal, it is very unlikely that such representations will spread, except in the special conditions afforded by literate transmission.

6 The central point of sexual selection is that, in all species, differential cost of reproduction results in different strategies for mate-choice. Each sex favors traits in the other that would minimize the risk of reproductive cost without benefit. As a result, such traits are more likely to spread in the gene-pool.

7 For instance, the idea that the human ability to handle color information is an adaptation is made more plausible by the fact that the specialized structures found in the visual cortex are too complex to have emerged as a simple result of increased crotical size.

8 For instance, it was asserted that binary oppositions and analogies (a:b::c:d) structured the conceptual representation of myths, a claim that could be easily verified by controlled studies of memory for stories. Experimental studies in this domain showed many interesting phenomena but never revealed such cognitive tools.

Bibliography

Atran, S., 1990. *Cognitive Foundations of Natural History. Towards an Anthropology of Science*. Cambridge: Cambridge University Press.

Atran, S., 1996. "Modes of Thinking about Living Kinds: Science, Symbolism and Common Sense," in *Modes of Thought: Explorations in Culture and Cognition*, ed. D. Olson and N. Terrance. New York: Cambridge University Press.

Atran, S., and D. Medin, eds, 1998. *Folkbiology*. Cambridge, Mass.: MIT Press.

Aunger, R., 1992. "The Nutritional Consequences of Rejecting Food in the Ituri Forest of Zaire," *Human Ecology* 30: 1–29.

Avis, M., and P. Harris, P. 1991. "Belief-Desire Reasoning among Baka Children: Evidence for a Universal Conception of Mind," *Child Development* 62, 460–7.

Barkow, J., L. Cosmides, and J. Tooby, eds, 1992. *The Adapted Mind: Evolutionary Psychology and the Generation of Culture.* New York: Oxford University Press.

Barrett, J. L., 1996. *Anthropomorphism, Intentional Agents, and Conceptualizing God.* PhD dissertation, Ithaca, NY: Cornell University.

Barrett, J. L., and F. C. Keil, 1996. "Conceptualizing a Non-natural Entity: Anthropomorphism in God Concepts," *Cognitive Psychology*: 31, 219–47.

Bloch, M., 1985. "From Cognition to Ideology," in *Power and Knowledge. Anthropological and Sociological Approaches*, ed. R. Fardon. Edinburgh: Scottish Academic Press.

Bloch, M., 1992. *Prey into Hunter. The Politics of Religious Experience.* Cambridge: Cambridge University Press.

Boyd, R., and P. Richerson, 1985. *Culture and the Evolutionary Process.* Chicago: Chicago University Press.

Boyer, P., 1990. *Tradition as Truth and Communication: A Cognitive Description of Traditional Discourse.* Cambridge: Cambridge Universiy Press.

Boyer, P., 1994a. "Cognitive Constraints on Cultural Representations: Natural Ontologies and Religious Ideas," in *Mapping the Mind: Domain-Specificity in Culture and Cognition*, ed. L. A. Hirschfeld and S. Gelman. New York: Cambridge University Press.

Boyer, P., 1994b. *The Naturalness of Religious Ideas: A Cognitive Theory of Religion.* Berkeley and Los Angeles: University of California Press.

Boyer, P., 1998. "Cognitive Tracks of Cultural Inheritance: How Evolved Intuitive Ontology Governs Cultural Transmission," *American Anthropologist*, 100.

Boyer, P., (forthcoming). "Cognitive Templates for Religious Concepts. Cross-Cultural Evidence for Recall of Counter-Intuitive Representations."

Buss, D., 1989. "Sex Differences in Human Mate Preferences: Evolutionary Hypotheses Tested in 37 Cultures," *Behavioral and Brain Sciences* 12: 1–49.

Campbell, D. T., 1970. "Natural Selection as an Epistemological Model," in *A Handbook of Method in Cultural Anthropology*, ed. N. Naroll and R. Cohen. Garden City, NY: Chapman and Hall.

Cavalli-Sforza, L. L., and M. W. Feldman, 1981. *Cultural Transmission and Evolution: A Quantitative Approach.* Princeton, NJ: Princeton University Press.

Cosmides, L., 1989. "The Logic of Social Exchange: Has Natural Selection Shaped How Humans Reason? Studies with the Wason Selection Task," *Cognition*, 31: 187–276.

Cosmides, L., and J. Tooby, 1987. From Evolution to Behavior: Evolutionary Psychology as the Missing Link," in *The Latest on the Best: Essays on Evolution and Optimality*, ed, J. Dupré. Cambridge, Mass.: MIT Press.

Cronk, L., 1991a. "Preferential Parental Investment in Daughters over Sons," *Human Nature* 2: 387–417.

Cronk, L., 1991b. "Intention vs. Behavior in Parental Sex Preferences among the Mukogodo of Kenya," *Journal of Biosocial Science* 23: 229–40

Crump, T., 1990. *The Anthropology of Numbers*. Cambridge: Cambridge University Press.

Daly, M., and M. Wilson 1988. *Homicide*. New York: Aldine.

Dawkins, R., 1976. *The Selfish Gene*. New York: Oxford University Press.

Donald, M, 1991. *Origins of the Modern Mind*. Cambridge, Mass: Harvard University Press.

Donald, M., 1993. "Precis of Origins of the Modern Mind: Three Stages in the Evolution of Culture and Cognition," *Behavioral and Brain Sciences* 16, 737–91.

Durham, 1991. *Coevolution: Genes, Cultures and Human Diversity*. Stanford: Stanford University Press.

Fiske, A. P., 1991. *Structures of Social Life: The Four Elementary Forms of Human Relations*. New York: Free Press.

Fiske, A. P., 1992. "The Four Elementary Forms of Sociality: Framework for a Unified Theory of Social Relations," *Psychological Review* 99: 689–723.

Gallistel, C. R., and R. Gelman 1992. "Preverbal and Verbal Counting and Computation," *Cognition* 44: 79–106.

Gelman, R., 1990. "First Principles Organize Attention and Learning about Relevant Data: Number and the Animate-Inanimate Distinction as examples," *Cognitive Science* 14: 79–106.

Gelman, S., and E. Markman, 1987. "Young Children's Inductions from Natural Kinds: The Role of Categories and Appearances," *Child Development* 58: 32–41.

Gelman, S. A., G. M. Gottfried, and J. Coley, 1994. "Essentialist Beliefs in Children: The Acquisition of Concepts and Theories," in *Mapping the Mind: Domain-Specificity in Cognition and Culture*, ed. L. A. Hirschfeld and S. A. Gelman. Cambridge: Cambridge University Press.

Gigerenzer, G., 1991. "How to Make Cognitive Illusions Disappear: Beyond 'Heuristics and Biases'," *European Review of Social Psychology* 2: 83–115.

Gleitman, L. R., and M. Liberman, eds, 1995. *An Invitation to Cognitive*

Science, vol. 1: *Language*. Cambridge, Mass: MIT Press.

Goody, J. R., 1977. *The Domestication of the Savage Mind*. Cambridge: Cambridge University Press.

Gopnik, A., and A. N. Meltzoff, 1997. *Words, Thoughts and Theories*. Cambridge, Mass.: MIT Press.

Gopnik, A., and H. Wellmann, 1994. "The Theory Theory," in *Mapping the Mind: Domain-Specificity in Cognition and Culture*, ed. L. A. Hirschfeld and S. A. Gelman. New York: Cambridge University Press.

Heelas, P., and A. Lock, 1981. *Indigenous Psychologies. The Anthropology of the Self*. New York: Academic Press.

Hirschfeld, L. A., 1988. "On Acquiring Social Categories. Cognitive Development and Anthropological Wisdom," *Man* 23: 611–38.

Hirschfeld, L. A., 1989. "Rethinking the Acquisition of Kinship Terms," *International Journal of Behavioral Development* 12: 541–68.

Hirschfeld, L. A., 1993. "Discovering Social Difference: The Role of Appearance in the Development of Racial Awareness," *Cognitive Psychology* 25: 317–50.

Hirschfeld, L. A., 1996. *Race in the Making: Cognition, Culture and the Child's Construction of Human Kinds*. Cambridge, Mass: MIT Press.

Hirschfeld, L. A., and S. A. Gelman, eds, 1994. *Mapping the Mind: Domain-Specificity in Culture and Cognition*. New York: Cambridge University Press.

Hsu, F. L. K., 1981. "The Self in Cross-Cultural Perspective," in *Culture and Self*, ed. F. L. K. Hsu. London: Tavistock.

Ingold, T., 1986. *Evolution and Social Life*. Cambridge: Cambridge University Press.

Karim, W. J., 1981. *Ma'Betisek Concepts of Living Things*. London: Athlone Press.

Keil, F., 1994. "The Birth and Nurturance of Concepts by Domains: The Origins of Concepts of Living Things," in *Mapping the Mind: Domain-Specificity in Cognition and Culture*, ed. L. A. Hirschfeld and S. A. Gelman. ed. F. L. K. Hsu. New York: Cambridge University Press.

Keil, F. C., 1986. "The Acquisition of Natural Kind and Artefact Terms," in *Conceptual Change*, ed. A. W. D. Marrar. Norwood, NJ: Ablex.

Koehler, J. J., 1996. "The Base Rate Fallacy Reconsidered: Descriptive, Normative and Methodological Challenges." *Behavioral and Brain Sciences* 19: 1–53.

Kosslyn, S. M., and D. N. Osherson, eds, 1995. *An Invitation to Cognitive Science*, vol. 2: *Visual Cognition*. Cambridge, Mass.: MIT Press.

Lawson, E. T., and R. McCauley, 1990. *Rethinking Religion: Connecting Culture and Cognition*. Cambridge: Cambridge University Press.

Lloyd, G. E. R., 1991. *Methods and Problems in Greek Science: Selected Papers*. Cambridge: Cambridge University Press.

Lumsden, C. J., and E. O. Wilson, 1981. *Genes, Minds and Culture*. Cambridge, Mass.: Harvard University Press.

Mandler, J., Bauer, P., and L. McDonough, 1991. "Separating the Sheep from the Goats: Differentiating Global Categories,"*Cognitive Psychology* 23: 263–98.

Mann, J., 1992. "Nurturance or Negligence: Maternal Psychology and Behavioral Preference among Pre-term Twins," in *The Adapted Mind: Evolutionary Psychology and the Generation of Culture*, ed. J. Barkow, L. Cosmides, and J. Tooby. New York: Oxford University Press.

Markman, E., 1973. "The Facilitation of Part-Whole Comparison by Use of the Collective Noun 'Family'," *Child Development* 44: 837–40.

Massey, C., and R. Gelman, 1988. "Preschoolers' Ability to Decide whether Pictured Unfamiliar Objects can Move Themselves," *Developmental Psychology* 24: 307–17.

McCloskey, M., 1983. "Naive Theories of Motion," in *Mental Models*, ed. D. Gentner, and A. L. Stevens. Hillsdale, NJ: Lawrence Erlbaum.

Mehler, J., P. Jusczyk, G. Lambertz, N. Halsted, J. Bertoncini, and C. Amiel-Tison, 1988. "A precursor of Language Acquisition in young infants," *Cognition* 29: 143–78.

Meltzoff, A., 1994. "Imitation, Memory, and the Representation of Persons," *Infant Behavior and Development* 17: 83–99.

Mithen, S., 1996. *The Prehistory of the Mind*. London: Thames and Hudson.

Morris, M., and K. Peng, 1994. "Culture and Cause: American and Chinese Attributions for Social and Physical Events," *Journal of Personality and Social Psychology* 67: 949–71.

Morton, J., and M. Johnson, 1991. "CONSPEC and CONLERN: A Two-process Theory of Infant Face-Recognition," *Psychological Review* 98: 164–81.

Osherson, D. N., ed. 1998. *An Invitation to Cognitive Science*, vol. 4: *Methods, Models and Conceptual Issues*. Cambridge, Mass.: MIT Press.

Perner, J., 1991. *Understanding the Representational Mind*. Cambridge, Mass.: MIT Press.

Pinker, S., 1984. *Language Learnability and Language Development*. Cambridge, Mass.: Harvard University Press.

Premack, D., 1990. "The Infant's Theory of Self-Propelled Objects." *Cognition* 36: 1–16.

Premack, D., and A. James-Premack, 1995. "Intention as Psychological Cause," in *Causal Cognition. A Multidisciplinary Debate*, ed. D. Sperber, D. Premack, and A. James-Premack. Oxford: Clarendon Press.

Rosengren, K. S., S. Gelman, C. W. Kalish, and M. McCormick, 1991. "As Time Goes By: Children's Early Understanding of Growth in Animals," *Child Development* 62: 1302–20.

Rothbart, M., and M. Taylor, 1990. "Category Labels and Social Reality: Do We View Social Categories as Natural Kinds?" in *Language and Social Cognition*, ed. K. F. G. Semin. London: Sage.

Rozin, P., 1976. "The Evolution of Intelligence and Access to the Cognitive Unconscious," in *Progress in Psychobiology and Physiological Psychology* , ed. J. M. Sprague and A. N. Epstein. New York: Academic Press.

Shweder, R. A., 1982. "Does the Concept of the Person Vary Cross-Culturally?" in *Cultural Conceptions of Mental Health and Therapy*, ed. A. J. Marsella and G. White. Boston, Mass.: Reidel.

Smith, E. E., and D. N. Osherson, eds, 1995. *An Invitation to Cognitive Science*, vol. 3: *Thinking*. Cambridge, Mass.: MIT Press.

Soja, N. N., S. Carey, and E. S. Spelke, 1992. "Perception, Ontology and Word-meaning," *Cognition* 45: 101–7.

Spelke, E. S. 1990. "Principles of Object Perception," *Cognitive Science* 14: 29–56.

Spelke, E. 1994. "Initial Knowledge: Six Suggestions," *Cognition* 50: 431–45.

Sperber, D., 1985. "Anthropology and Psychology: Towards an Epidemiology of Representations," *Man* 20: 73–89.

Sperber, D., 1991. "The Epidemiology of Beliefs," in *Psychological Studies of Widespread Beliefs*, ed. C. Fraser. Oxford: Oxford University Press.

Sperber, D., 1996. *Explaining Culture: A Naturalistic Approach*. Oxford: Blackwell.

Sperber, D., F. Cara, and V. Girotto, 1995. "Relevance Theory Explains the Selection Task." *Cognition* 57: 31–95.

Springer, K., and F. C. Keil, 1989. "On the Development of Specifically Biological Beliefs: The Case of Inheritance," *Child Development*, 60: 637–48.

Springer, K., and F. C. Keil, 1991. "Early Differentiation of Causal Mechanisms appropriate to Biological and Non-biological Kinds." *Child Development* 62: 767–81.

Symons, D., 1979. *The Evolution of Human Sexuality*. New York: Oxford University Press.

Tomasello, M., A. C. Kruger, and H. H. Ratner, 1993. Cultural Learning," *Behavioral and Brain Sciences* 16: 495–510.

Tooby, J., and L. Cosmides, 1992. "The Psychological Foundations of Culture," in *The Adapted Mind: Evolutionary Psychology and the Generation of Culture*, ed. J. Barkow, L. Cosmides, and J. Tooby. New York: Oxford University Press.

Tversky, A., and D. Kahnemann, 1982. "Evidential Impact of Base Rates," in *Judgments under Uncertainty: Heuristics and Biases* , ed. D. Kahnemann, P. Slovic, and A. Tversky. Cambridge: Cambridge University Press.

Walker, S. J., 1985. *Atimodemo: Semantic Conceptual Development among the Yoruba.* Unpublished PhD dissertation, Ithaca, NY: Cornell University.

Walker, S., 1992. "Developmental Changes in the Representation of Word-meaning: Cross-Cultural Findings," *British Journal of Developmental Psychology* 10: 285–99.

Wason, P. C., 1983. "Realism and Rationality in the Selection Task," in *Thinking and Reasoning: Psychological Approaches,* ed. J. S. B. T. Evans. London: Routledge, Chapman and Hall.

Wason, P. C., and P. N. Johnson-Laird, 1972. *The Psychology of Reasoning: Structure and Content.* London: Batsford.

Wellmann, H., 1990. *The Child's Theory of Mind.* Cambridge, Mass.: MIT Press.

Wellmann, H., and S. A. Gelman, 1992. "Cognitive Development: Foundational Theories of Core Domains," *Annual Review of Psychology* 43: 337–75.

Whitehouse, H., 1992. "Memorable Religions: Transmission, Codification and Change in Divergent Melanesian Contexts," *Man* 27: 777–97.

Whiten, A., ed. 1991. *Natural Theories of Mind: The Evolution, Development and Simulation of Everyday Mind-Reading.* Oxford: Blackwell.

Wimmer, H., and J. Perner, 1983. "Beliefs about Beliefs: Representation and Constraining Function of Wrong Beliefs in Young Children's Understanding of Deception," *Cognition* 13: 103–28.

Wynn, K., 1992. "Evidence Against Empiricist Accounts of the Origins of Numerical Knowledge," *Mind and Language* 7: 315–32.

Psychoanalysis and Anthropology:
On the Temporality of Analysis

James Weiner

Psychoanalysis and anthropology were both products of the late nine-teenth century, and they were allied right from the start: first, by the fact that neither ethnological and psychological science of that time distanced itself from biology, and second, as Foucault noted at the end of *The Order of Things* (1970), in the way they placed *alterity* not at the fringes or borders of Western life and consciousness but at the core of Western culture's own self-constitution and self-theorization. The recognition of what Foucault called the essential doubleness, or what we could call, following Lacan, the 'otherness of one's self' is how both anthropology and psychoanalysis begin, why they continue to address each other and it is what impels me to comment on their relationship in this chapter.

There have been many forms in which psychoanalytic principles and techniques have entered anthropology in a more ostensive way than this broad convergence on the problem of the constitution self that I inspect below. There was the Culture and Personality School of North American cultural anthropology, largely a legacy of the combination of super-organicism and psychologism of Boasian anthropology. The Culture and Personality approach, associated notably with the figures of Melford Spiro and George and Louise Spindler, is still a vital component of a broader psychological anthropology, and the volume entitled *Personality and the Cultural Construction of Society* (Jordan and Swartz, eds, 1990) attests to the strength and vitality of its contribution to cultural anthropology. The volume edited by Schwartz, White and Lutz, *New Directions in Psychological Anthropology* (1992) also importantly weds cognitivism to current psychological anthropology. Both volumes, however, stress the adaptive and integrational mechanisms of enculturation and socialization at the expense of what I focus on here as the displacing effects of language and other communicative media.

For myself, the other important contribution to the fusion of psychoanalysis and anthropology came by way of George Devereux, and in particular his book *From Anxiety to Method in the Behavioral Sciences* (1967). Anticipating our own contemporary concern with the production of alterity, Devereux states simply that 'it is both psychologically and logically necessary to contrive behavioral science experiments in which the observer and the observed differ *in* kind as much as the physicist differs from the object he studies' (1967: 25). But according to Devereux, this commitment to objectivism only serves to mask 'the way the subjective projections of the anthropologist influence his understanding and the way, likewise, they interact with the unconscious projections of his informants' (in Heald and Deluz, eds, 1994: 12). The volume entitled *Anthropology and Psychoanalysis* (Heald and Deluz, eds, 1994), which is European rather than North American in origin, thus characterizes a contemporary psychoanalytic anthropology with the unique characteristic of a social science whose methodology is a large part of its own subject matter.

Let me then continue this account of the parallel paths of anthropology and psychoanalysis by considering a seeming paradox of psychoanalysis: that although we are used to thinking of it as a technique for the alleviation of an individual's psychic pathologies, its success as psychiatric technique has been at best hard to judge and at worst non-existent. On the other hand, psychoanalysis has secured its most effective role in Western thought in non-clinical fields – in social science, humanities, and in particular literary and art criticism, where it addresses itself to social and cultural instead of (or as well as) individual psychic processes. There it is a central theoretical foundation, along with, for example, Marxism, hermeneutics and structuralism, and like those other theoretical orientations, is in no way opposed to or in conflict with the conventional empirical methodologies of the social sciences.

This paradox has been generated by a long-standing commitment to the post-war neo-Freudian revision within psychoanalysis, particularly in its relation to the social sciences. This revision drew a sharp boundary between the self and its socio-cultural milieu. The Freudian origin of this contrast is located most visibly in *The Interpretation of Dreams*, in which Ricoeur noted Freud's argument that 'dreams make use of [cultural] symbols; they do not elaborate them' (Ricoeur, 1970: 100). This is the antinomy between what Ricoeur termed the genetic and the analytic meaning of a symbol (see also Weiner, 1995 and 1997). The genetic meaning of symbols is their common, supra-individual collective content. The analytic meaning Freud meant to be the private, specific associations given to them by particular subjects (see Juillerat, 1997: 48). Ricoeur noted that for the purposes of charting the history of the patient's own associations, the analysis of what anthropologists would call 'cultural meaning', the genetic meanings, must constitute a subordinate and auxiliary method for Freud (Freud, *SE* 5: 360; Ricoeur, ibid: 102). This antinomy would be confirmed, though in reverse, by the Culture and Personality school which accepted the pre-givenness of the individual as the locus of both culture and personality, defined as a set of behaviours (Spiro, 1951; D'Andrade, 1990). The task of expanding outward the intra-psychic topography outlined by Freud, using it to model the collective register of culture, would henceforth be the abiding challenge of any subsequent psychoanalytic social science and psychoanalytic anthropology in particular.

This neo-Freudian psychoanalytical anthropology can be subject to critique from at least two directions. First, it generates a paradox concerning the self and culture: in this view the individual is the unit of analysis and also the locus of behaviour; the discreteness and coherence of the self is taken for granted; and the externality, contingency and artificiality of social and cultural life emerges as a consequence of this assumption. Second, it introduces an analogous scission between the self and the vehicles through which the self is manifested and made visible. This position sees the foundation of the self as pre-lingual and pre-symbolic, while the collective representations are both symbolic and analysable as a modality of language.

In this chapter, I wish to expand on these two critical assumptions – of a unitary self, and of the compartmentalization of language. Marilyn Strathern, for example, begins her analysis of the Melanesian person with critique of the Western theory of the self:

> The center is where the twentieth-century Western imagination puts the self, the personality, the ego. For the 'person' in this latter day Western view is an agent, a subject, the author of thought and action, and thus 'at the center' of relationships.
>
> (M. Strathern, 1988: 269)

Strathern wishes to substitute for this Western theory – that the self is ontologically and developmentally prior to the relations in which it ultimately finds itself thrown in life – a more properly Melanesian one: that the person is distributively and excentrically constituted, a sum of its relations with others without necessarily centring or cohering itself within them. In Melanesia, 'social relations are the objects of people's dealings with one another' (ibid: 172), and hence the objects that visibly and characteristically move between people in Melanesian social life are efficacious insofar as they personify relationships themselves. Thus, people use these ceremonial objects of various kinds (such as pearl shells, pigs, masks) to make certain aspects of relationality visible and manipulable. 'Persons or things may be transferred as "standing for" (in our terms) parts of persons' (ibid: 178).

It is this critique of the Western theory of the individual that I feel is behind the renaissance of psychoanalysis in late twentiethth-century theorizing, even though social theorists and philosophers such as George H. Mead were aware of the implications a long time ago. Mead articulated a 'Strathernian' theory of the self in the early part of this century. In his *Mind, Self and Society* (1934) he wrote that 'when a self does appear it always involves an experience of another. There could not be an experience of a self simply by itself' (p. 195). Elliott, in his broad overview of the progress of psychoanalytic theory observes that:

> For many modern theorists, social relationships do more than just influence the development of subjectivity. Rather, the human subject's inner world is *constituted* through these relations. That is, the nature and meaning of a person's subjective and sexual experiences are actually formed in relationship with others.
>
> *(Elliott, 1994: 19)*

Marcuse made a political point about the situatedness of psychoanalytical theorizing:

> Psychology could be elaborated and practiced as a special discipline as long as the psyche could sustain itself against the public power, as long as privacy was real, really desired, and self-shaped; [but] if the individual has neither the ability nor the possibility to be for himself, the terms of psychology become the terms of the societal forces which define the psyche
>
> *(Marcuse, 1956/1987: xi)*

> psychoanalytic categories do not have to be 'related' to social and political conditions – they are themselves social and political categories
>
> *(Marcuse, 1973: 44)*

Both of the paradoxes I have referred to thus disappear once we allow ourselves to entertain the possibility that the self may have different origins and functions. We may want to start off with a more literally Freudian/Meadian view of the self, as an entity that is elicited only in its confrontation with one or more alters, that is, as a *relational construct*, whose effects and concreteness are manifest only within a social world as such. Since relationality posits an important external origin to selfhood, it constitutes a corrective to the strong and monadic subject of Geertzian constructionism. In this chapter, I expand on an anthropologically useful psychoanalysis that begins with this assumption.

To do so, I will perforce be making an argument that psychoanalysis, as opposed to *psychology*, is a *social science*, perhaps even 'the human science par excellence' (Lacan, 1977a: 144–5; Macey, 1988: 88). From this viewpoint, the difference between psychoanalysis and psychology is much vaster than that between psychoanalysis and anthropology. When I say it is a social science, I call attention to the following characteristics of psychoanalysis:

1 The making visible of the reflexivity of social encounters. By this I mean the bringing to awareness of how the perceiving subject both constitutes and is constituted by those others with whom the subject engages. Freud spoke about introjection as the manner in which the agency and subjectivity of one's parents was sedimented within the child's developing self. The bringing to the patient's awareness the history of this deposition of exogenous agency was construed by Freud to be the primary goal of psychoanalysis.

2 The role of language, and of symbolic objectivation in general, in making visible these exogenous origins of the self, considered as a locus of speech. In the speech of the subject, Freud found the manifestations of this history of sedimented social interaction, most characteristically in jokes, slips of the tongue, and in artistic and literary expression, but more generally in the overall pattern of negation and repudiation which provided the contours of the patient's verbal awareness.

3 Because both the psychoanalyst and anthropologist therefore must, as Devereux put it, provide an elicitory disturbance for the patient to respond to with speech, the task of the analyst is to provide his or her own gloss on the verbal response so elicited: this makes of the work of interpretation one of the core existential projects of human social life and language.

4 The resulting temporality and historicity of analysis, in the ontological sense as delineated by Heidegger (1962). Because analysis, whether anthropological or psychoanalytical, requires a considerable passage of time for the analyst and interlocutor to establish their own modelling discourse, the temporality of self-formation is, as it were, mimicked in the form of the temporal, narrative sequence of question and response between them. One of the legacies of the post-war neo-Freudian revision which Lacan originally posed as a foil for his own 'return to Freud' was a view of the psychic structure of the individual as static and ahistorical, a product of a universal and primordial Oedipal configuring. But the establishment of this configuration is very much dependent upon the psychic traumas produced by relational conflicts that are events in a subject's life

and which punctuate his or her consciousness and memory. Analysis itself is a social relation, occurring through time, through which these punctuating traumas can be dialogically reconstituted and revisited.

I will now consider each of these topics in turn. In these four dimensions, I outline an anthropological psychoanalysis congruent with the versions detailed most persuasively by Crapanzano (1992a and 1992b),
Obeyesekere (1990) and Ewing (1992). All of us begin with Ricoeur's
reading of Freud (1970) which identifies the hermeneutic dimensions of
psychoanalysis, that is, its position within the social life made possible
through language, but there is an important way in which this reading of
Freud also relates to Heidegger's notions of the historicity of human being and finitude. As against the open-endedness of dialogism, the Lacanian-
inspired psychoanalytic anthropology I advocate here sees the punctuating
of discourse as a means of precipitating interpretative meaning. This punctuation makes both the subject and the temporality of the discourse visible at one and the same time. Further, along with this punctuation comes
the reassertion of distanciation between analyst and interlocutor that has
been criticized in contemporary dialogic anthropology. But it is a
distanciation that is asserted in the face of the ontological primordiality
of the self's relationality. The act of distanciation thus makes the relation,
rather than the discreteness of individuals, visible.

Objects, selves and reflexivity

When I say that psychoanalysis is a social science, do I mean that it recognizes some central, foundational social arrangement: the nuclear family and its Oedipal configuration, say? No. To call it a social science is to
recognize that *its procedure makes use of the social relationships that are
its subject matter* – the phenomena of repetition, deferral, repression are
at once items of analysis and characteristics of the mode of inquiry. Like
ethnography or linguistics, it uses its own subject of study as the medium
of that study. The anthropologist engaged in long-term ethnographic fieldwork has to willy-nilly form and sustain social relations with those people
who are her objects of study. She is therefore unavoidably cast as both
object and subject of study at one at the same time.

The realization of this reflexivity is found specifically in the technique
of both psychoanalysis and ethnography, what Freud called the *transference*, and in the *resistance to transference*.[1] Freud found that his patients
inevitably came to act towards him in the same way they acted towards
the persons who were the focus of their anxiety and who were the sources
and subjects of their self-narrative . He noticed that the analytical dia-

logue did not just stand as external commentary on the patient's relational history, but was playing a constitutive role in it. Freud called this the transference – in effect, the analytic encounter came to model the person's own relational topography. For psychoanalysis, then, transference occurs when the analytical model *becomes* or *takes over* the thing modeled.[2] Lacan's 'return to Freud' refocuses psychoanalysis upon the radical intersubjectivity implied in the transference, the realization of the essential relational constitution of all the components of the self – the ego, the drives, object attachments, the subject – and in so doing, restores psychoanalysis as the study of the history of a subject's *relations*. The language of psychoanalysis and anthropology is also the language of its theory, which is to say that its technique, theory and object of analysis are all given simultaneously.[3] As Ricoeur stated, what is 'audacious' about psychoanalysis is its way 'of treating the intersubjective relationship as *technique*' (1970: 406).

Anthropology until recently has always struggled against the relativization of the transference through an appeal to a methodological objectivism and to a variety of descriptive and analytical languages that allowed the anthropologist the privilege of outside observer. As the anthropologist Roy Wagner put it (1981), we attempted to study the social relations of our hosts as if our own were not also implicated. In an analogous fashion, what the revisionist ego psychology as it developed in the United States after the Second World War[4] accomplished was to repress or repudiate the radically anti-Cartesian view of the subject towards which Freud had laboured. Neo-Freudian doxa stipulated that the analyst always acts as a point of stability and rationality; that there is a corresponding core of rationality hidden within the disturbed patient that it is the analyst's duty to make contact with and draw out, so that it can overpower the pathological part of the patient's personality; that the transference procedure that effects this struggle goes one way, from patient to analyst, but not back again.[5] This was made possible, as was the case in anthropology, by a view of the self and its origin as distinct from the relations into which it entered.

Lacan wished to take a much more radical view of Freud, one which he felt was more faithful to the subversiveness of Freud's original message. The autonomous ego which is thought to pre-exist all psychological defences is itself a defence. There are only defences played off against each other to give particular ones the illusion of pre-existent personality. There is not the ego and his or her alter, only types of alter – the subject is, after all, constituted from the same acts of speech and perception as all other objects and relations, and the subject takes its place among these things, in the space created between them rather than prior to them.

With this view of the self, anthropologists can proceed to examine the ritualization of these object relations. This strategy contributed prominently to the making of psychoanalytic anthropology in Géza Róheim's classic analyses of Australian Aboriginal initiation (e.g. Róheim, 1925 and 1945) and also in Nancy Munn's analyses of object relations in the myths of the Walbiri and Pitjantjatjara in Central Australia (Munn, 1970 and 1973). Central Australian myth centres importantly around the process by which ancestral creators detached pieces of themselves, including emissions and extrusions from within their body, and used them to mark the landscape or create its notable physical features. The relation between these acts of inscription or naming are also pronounced, so that we can say that the verbal dimension of these processes of corporeal extrusion and extrojection is integral to them in Central Australia.

> In Walbiri ideology an ancestor singing his songs is, in effect, putting his ground marks, or making his country. As one of my informants put it, *guruwari* [iconographic designs], *yiri* [songs], and *walya* [soil, or ground] are all 'one thing' [*djinda-djugu*].
>
> (*Munn, 1973: 146*)

According to Munn, individuals construe an intimate corporeal relationship between themselves and their birthplaces and the sedimented traces of their associated ancestral beings.

> For example, a [Pitjantjatjara] woman explained that a marking upon an ancestral rock at her birthplace was also on her body. The rock was the transformed body of the ancestor lying down and the marking was originally his hair.
>
> (*Munn, 1970: 146*)

In merely journeying across the landscape in the course of life activity, the Pitjantjatjara and other Central Australians confront the spatial extrusion of their own selves, the territorial laying-out of their own interiority. This occurs not just by way of bodily substance, but also in terms of the agency and will which are attributes and preconditions of this historical world of place-creating marks. As Munn concludes, the Central Desert person attempts to establish his or her own autonomy by reintegrating these external nodes of agency and bodily regeneration (ibid: 159), and we could interpret this as the moment when Central Desert persons make visible their own form of reflexivity.

Central Desert subjectivity is thus predicated on a relation between a self which is incomplete and an exterior world littered with the self's bodily and onomastic deposits. For the analysts of the British object relations school, Klein (see Mitchell, 1986) and Winnicott (1974), this decentring of the subject was empirically observable as an effect in the behaviour of

Western children, against which the establishment of the centred, complete individual is a later development. We should then be cautious of our common contrast between *subjectivity* and *intersubjectivity*. The addition of the prefix 'inter' to the noun stem 'subjectivity' makes it appear as if the latter were a derivatory form of the former, that subjectivity comes first and that intersubjectivity is dependent upon it. But from my point of view, the opposite is more nearly the case: we should call subjectivity *intrasubjectivity*, to signal the way in which our relational encounters with other persons and with objects are deposited in the identity structure of the speaking subject. Let us then proceed as if intersubjectivity is the semantic primitive, the fundamental orientation towards others that is primordial and originary, and that *intrasubjectivity*[6] is a derivative, analytic isolate.

The Dialectic of Language and Body

At the beginning of this chapter I noted that Freud first phrased his psychoanalytic principles in biological terms, and throughout his career as analyst he never endorsed an antinomy between the psychoanalytic and the biological. Another aspect of Lacan's 'return to Freud' was an attempt to resite the biological within the interpretational. For example, Lacan's paper on the mirror-stage (in Lacan, 1977a) was an attempt to demonstrate how the constitution of the self was dependent on particular types of external imaging. This nature of this imaging for Lacan was very much tied up with the physical, biological and corporeal aspects of the perceiving organism. Further, since this image arises only within the confrontation with an other, then it itself is relationally constituted at its inception (see Muller and Richardson, 1982: 29):

> the total form of the body by which the subject anticipates in a mirage the maturation of his power is given to him only as *Gestalt*, that is to say, in an exteriority in which this form is certainly more constituent than constituted . . . this *Gestalt* . . . symbolizes the mental permanence of the *I*, at the same time as it prefigures its alienating destination; it is still pregnant with the correspondences that unite the *I* with the statue in which man projects himself.
>
> (*Lacan, 1977a: 2–3*)

Lacan saw the bounding function of this *Gestalt* as having extremely important implications in early life. The mirror-image is an everted pregnancy, where the child recognizes the *contingency*, that is the social origin, of its corporeal boundary.

The identification of oneself with another being is the very process by which a continuing sense of selfhood becomes possible, and it is from successive assimilations of other people's attributes that what is familiarly called the ego or the personality is constructed (Bowie, 1991: 30–1). In much the same vein, Wagner has said: 'The self is an effect that we perceive indirectly in the reactions of persons, creatures, or objects around us. . . . We become a self through the mediation of things other than that acting, perceiving self' (1977: 147).

One first identifies one's self only in another person who him/herself is also a desiring subject. And hence our relation to all others and objects is mediated by such desire. Marilyn Strathern's observation of Melanesian personhood can thus be read in more general terms: 'Intention and motivation have physiological consequences. The person is vulnerable, so to speak, both to the bodily disposition of others toward him or her and to their wills and desires' (Strathern, 1988: 131–2).

These characterizations by Lacan, Strathern and Wagner show quite definite corporeal materialism as a component of their interpretational theories of relationality. What Lacan referred to as the *Imaginary* refers then not just to the imaginative capacity, but to the *image* of one's body that grows out of the subject's visual confrontation with an encountered other. In the Imaginary, one draws forth the limits of the body, an image of the body's outline, a projection of a body schema in imaginary space. As Wilden (1968) put it, 'the Imaginary is the area of the biological maturation through perception' (p. 175). Insofar as Lacan seized upon the common biological phenomenon whereby physiological and hormonal changes are set off by a sensory stimulus, he recognized, as did Marilyn Strathern, the role of form and of the aesthetic contours of the image as elicitory trigger (Strathern, 1988) in the constitution of relationality. 'I use "image" to refer both to the sense impression of perception and to the conceived, elicited forms of sense impressions such as "a figure" or "a pattern"' (Strathern, 1991: 129 n. 49).

But as Wagner suggested, the notions of embodiment and corporeality find their most organic expression in the actual human body, and should be broadened to include any perception which calls forth its own external bounding, any articulation which calls forth the whole of which it is part.[7] These include the ways in which we assemble a framing 'skin' around the things we isolate, the way in which a space or frame is constructed in anticipation of certain events, acts, performances whose effects are also anticipated. The words of another thinker for whom the elicitation of its own limits was the core feature of human being are relevant here: 'form, *forma*, corresponds to the Greek *morphe*. It is the enclosing limit and boundary, what brings and stations a being into that which it is' (Heidegger, 1979: 119).[8]

In other words, the delimitation of these relational processes does not proceed solely within the domain of the body image, the specular image of the other. For Lacan, the accession to language, which in his view ontogenetically follows the acquisition of body image, introduces an entirely different relational register to the subject. It is language, the domain of the *Symbolic,* as Lacan terms it, that provides this more encompassing embodiment, for it brings to the specular field of body image the expansive properties of metaphor, and the enchainment of signifiers that metaphor makes possible.

As Freud described in *Beyond the Pleasure Principle*, the child first experiences relationality through the withdrawal of the maternal body from the orbit of its corporeality, within which it is at first unable to distinguish between itself and the other body. What language affords is the possibility of labelling the gaps and detachments that constitute object loss as the first experience of embodied relationality. The loss of the maternal breast, its absence, becomes, through the act of signification, as much a positivity as its presence. Words and signs come to fill the spaces that are created through the detachments that make relationality possible.

What results is a hermeneutic of the embodiment of language, and this is what is captured by Lacan's contrast between the Imaginary and the Symbolic. If language has hitherto been seen as exclusively part of the conceptual function, then Lacan's reformulation means that we have to come to terms with the embodiment of linguistic and cultural meaning – that is, the fact that in the realm of the Symbolic, it is language itself which is revealed as the outer limits or skin of the subject, as the boundary within which a subjective history can unfold as a discourse, a discourse between, for example, patient and analyst, or between informant and anthropologist. Through language, the Imaginary becomes recast as a myth of origin of the body. In the Papua New Guinea context, as Wagner put it, 'This is the fractality of the Melanesian person: the talk formed through the person that is the person formed through talk' (1991: 166).

Wagner and Lacan thus make a case for the embodiment of the visual image as a vital constitutive process of *language*. They phrase this embodiment of language in sexual terms through what Wagner calls the trope of embodiment: language is the figure-ground reversal of thought, and the reproductive body becomes the microcosmic embodiment of the socialized body:

> The counterpart of the brain's synthesis of collective cultural image through language is the body's reproductive synthesis of another body. As the brain contains the microcosm of the mind within the macrocosm of the body, so the loins – particularly the uterus – contain the macrocosm of the body, as fetus, within a reproductive microcosm.
>
> (*Wagner, 1986: 138*)

Relationality is thus a capacity shaped by the body's spatial, motile and sensorial contours, all of which are themselves aspects of something analogous to the 'total social fact' and which Freud called *die ganze Sexualstrebung*, the 'total sexual tendency' (Lacan, 1977b: 199). And by this I mean not some narrowly defined range of erotogenic drives or posited instincts but a consideration of how body schema, language, desire and world emerge together within a total cultural order (cf. Bourdieu, 1977).[9]

Because we depend upon our presence in a social field for the making visible of conventional meaning, and because, as we have seen, this social field is delimited by the domain of body image and its perceptual register, we must understand that for Freud, Lacan and Wagner, meaning is itself a function of perception. The sensoriness of the sexual capacity, its functioning at the superficies of the body, is already embodied by the conceptual capacity of the brain. Freud himself made a phylogenetic argument for the evolution of conceptualization out of imagistic sensation: 'the central nervous system originates from the ectoderm. The grey matter of the cortex remains a derivative of the primitive superficial layer of the organism and may have inherited some of its essential properties' (*SE*, xviii [1920]: 26). Freud here posits a developmental sequence that is counterintuitive from the perspective of the received Cartesian view of human consciousness: thought, perception and cognition are *not* processes restricted to the interior of the body's brain centre, to which the sense organs at the body's borders transmit sensations originating from the outside world. Rather, thought, perception and symbolization occur amidst the external world of objects, persons and sensations; in a phenomenological sense, they *draw out* the body's cognitive capacities rather than passively feed into them.

The Australian Central Desert also provides examples of how such an externalized perception is recognized and the kinds of motivation it provides for actors. It is the case for the Walbiri that the ancestors created the landscape by first visualizing it in a dream. The features of the landscape then are objectifications which 'are conceived as external projections of an interior vision' (Munn, 1970: 145). But the dream experience of living Walbiri reverses this assumed originary act of externalization. A person's dreams are the effects of ancestral intervention originating from certain externally emplaced objects and sites; hence 'for the living individual the object is prior, and the initial direction of movement must be ... from object to subject, from outside to inside' (ibid). Hence, Munn concludes: 'the country is an experiential "given", a pre-ordained structure which as "homeland" or "birthplace" (or both at once) provides a stabilization of "self" in object form' (Munn, 1970: 147).

The symbolic capacity is thus as much a part of our *perceptual* apparatus as our eyes, ears and voice. Hence, without the symbolic limits that language places on the world, there would be no body, in the sense of a notion of encompassing limit, to our actions or thoughts. We are forced to conclude that in order to make these limits visible, the function of bodies of language such as myths is more to cut off or obviate explanatory expansion than to facilitate it. What productive actions ensue from such a discursive bounding?

If I have maintained that it is untenable to see the self as separate from its relations, so, in a similar way, I argue that the self is not external to the language by which it is captured and which it uses both as a generalized mode of projective communication and communicative projection. The one thing we can say about the self in the social world is that it is mediated: though it is most thoroughly concealed from us in our day-to-day lives, our sense of self-identity and personality is dependent upon the confirming presence of others, the reflection and assessment of our efficacy on others. In speaking, we direct our wishes, desires and anticipations to others. It is thus the answering, responding speech of the interlocutor, whether analyst or other, that constitutes us as subjects. All this is summed up in Lacan's now famous dictum that: the unconscious is the discourse of the other (see Wilden, 1968). Insofar as we are inclined to see the unconscious as a space within our mental terrain, it is a space made possible by the euphemizing, concealing properties of language, for what is characteristically hidden from us within our unconscious is the meaning of our acts to which only language can give us access. Battaglia has similarly spoken of the self as a 'representational economy' (1995: 2), 'a reification continually defeated by mutable entanglements with other subjects' histories, experiences, self-representations'.

As Bowie has remarked (1991: 48), because processes like repression, the unconscious and relationship are not things we can put our fingers on, psychoanalysis and the social sciences have to infer their nature from their effects on behaviour, chiefly verbal behaviour. Our everyday experience is surely that we cannot always know what we say, nor can we be sure that what we say is what we mean. Nor do we always understand what others say. Meaning is not a function of purely subjective construction, intention, deliberation or cognition, and any theory, like Chomsky's, that locates meaning chiefly within an already cognitively sited grammar and lexicon would miss the essential property of meaning: that it is a matter of negotiation between subjects. The attribution and agreement on meaning is something we very much arrive at after the fact of speaking and signing.

These considerations are necessary in confronting the Foi of Papua New Guinea, with whom I have conducted research since 1979; much of Foi communal assessment and meaning-production takes place within their rich field of public discourse. Speaking and interacting in Foi is very much, from a Western viewpoint, a matter of the positioning of bodies, and of the gesturing power and capacities of bodies in the act of speaking. Speaking is considered more as a physical than a cerebral activity by the Foi, a function of the body's musculature and vigour. Words, or talk, are material things, and issues from the mouth are ranged alongside other fluid emissions of the body. And like these other fluid emissions, the Foi consider that talk has fertile, economic properties: it can be 'sent along paths'; it can pierce bodies and have hard impacts; it can be passed along from person to person; in the case of secret magic formulae, it can be sold and bought. All these metaphors for the materiality of talk are constantly referred to in the course of public debate. Indeed, the most common subject of public talk in New Guinea is talk itself (see Rumsey and Merlan, 1991). Every sentence in a public forum is uttered as if what is said is less important than the conditions under which the words were uttered and the effects they had as they are sent on their unwitting paths by the utterer. Just as the procreative substances blood and semen literally form the physical body, so do words and speech flow from the body, adhere to people, and contribute to forming the social shape and body of persons.

Interpretation

But more than that: public discourse in Papua New Guinea centres on those events that produce conflict and on which judgement must be passed: adultery, sorcery, insult, homicide, all of which demand a thoroughgoing and public excavation into people's intentions and putative motives and interests, which are not normally publicly revealed or generally known. Foi public discourse is always an occasion for retrospective examination of the context of incidents of conflict, and is founded on the assumption that people do not reveal their intentions at the time and often misrepresent or deceive others about them. To put it simply, the moments when the sociality of the community becomes most visible are in these collective attempts at retrospective negotiation through discourse.

If it is assumed that there are gaps or holes in meaning of this kind in any arena of social activity we might care to isolate – exchange, production, ritual, language and so on – these gaps cannot be exposed with the resources of that particular activity alone; the exposure must come by way of another outlook that is deliberately situated in a relationship of externality to it. We could say that the making visible of social meaning and social knowledge becomes possible when some external perspective is attained on that activity. Social life then becomes the ceaseless attempt to fashion different languages, different analytic perspectives that allow the actor to uncover the concealments of conventional thought and action.

It is significant then that Ricoeur chooses to characterize psychoanalysis as follows: 'analytic experience unfolds in the field of speech and . . . within this field, *what comes to light is another language, dissociated from common language*' (1970: 366–7; my emphasis).

Psychoanalysis works by inventing a new language for the patient, one that replaces or glosses the language that is her symptom. And here I am identifying the following parallel questions for anthropology: what else do people do for their social life when, for example, they tell a myth?; what else do we attempt as anthropologists when we provide the gloss on those myths or rituals?; and if this is so, do not all these glosses play their role in creating the possibility of meaning within myth and social behaviour?

Let us recall the theme of one of Freud's most powerful papers on technique, 'Remembering, Repeating and Working Through': what cannot be remembered is repeated in behaviour (see Lacan 1977b: 129). Freud's theory, as I have just noted, was that certain childhood experiences of a traumatic nature are *repressed*; they are consigned to a region of subjectivity that Freud called the unconscious. Once there, they are insulated from language and discourse. But they are not insulated from representation and symbolism *tout court*. They resurface during the life of the subject in disguised form, in dreams, slips of the tongue and so forth. Most importantly, their presence is marked in the subject by what he or she *cannot remember*. In those instances where words and memory fail us, we confront the *limits* of our representational practice. What psychoanalysis offers social science, what it makes prominent, is the necessity to make the elucidation of such limits part of the technique. If we see the subject as constituted by relationships, then Lacan's psychoanalysis views social relationships as themselves limited by the language and the repression of language available to the subject.

What cannot be remembered is repeated in behaviour. The subject reproduces the force of the action which accounted for the memory by repeatedly *acting it out*. And the subject does so most explicitly in the analytical situation, and with the analyst as object of the action. So Freud observed: 'the patient does not say that he remembers that he used to be defiant and critical towards his parents' authority; instead, he behaves that way to the doctor' (*SE*, XII [1914]: 150). Or, a woman does not admit that she harboured sexual feelings towards the father; instead, she finds herself falling in love with the analyst. Freud said the following, and there is no other passage in twentieth-century social theorizing which so powerfully illuminates the limits of language:

> When one has announced the fundamental rule of psycho-analysis to a patient with an eventful life-history and a long story of illness and has then

asked him to say what occurs to his mind, one expects him to pour out a flood of information; but often the first thing that happens is that he has nothing to say.

(*ibid*)

Let us not fail to notice that Freud, like Heidegger, accords a central and important role to silence in characterizing human language. And when we consider what it is we elicit and demand from our informants, is it not true that we rarely know how to leave room for the silence of the repressed and the foreclosed? 'Above all, the patient will *begin* his treatment with a repetition of this kind. . . . As long as the patient is in the treatment he cannot escape from this compulsion to repeat; and in the end we understand that this is his way of remembering' (ibid).

What cannot be said must be acted out. Hence, what is in behaviour is not the same thing as what is in language; in fact, what is in behaviour competes with or negates what is in language, and what is in language forecloses or repudiates what is in behaviour. But it is in the fact of this negation, foreclosure or repudiation, that the possibility of meaning lies, the possibility of the meaningful resolution or interpretation of that repudiation through language. In other words we are led to conclude that *what is seen to lie beyond language must be included in a description of it*. What is negated by language, and what language negates, is part of language. The repetition, the acting out, is made necessary by language's repressive possibilities; it is a function of language, and does not originate or become possible outside it. Ritual, as the anthropological example *par excellence* of acting out, is a part of language, not as another form of it, but as the articulation of its defining limits, as the repetition which is the beyond of language.

Transference is just a piece of repetition, Freud went on to say. The analyst wants to encourage such transference, to get the patient to act out such memories, and to aid the patient in transferring the actions themselves to the realm of discourse so that the patient can understand them. But what happens when this is attempted? The patient *resists*. He or she resists the transference. And what is more, 'the greater the resistance, the more extensively will acting out (repetition) replace remembering' (ibid). The stronger the resemblance of the situation to the repressed incident, the more strongly will resistance occur – the more strongly will the subject assert the gaps in discourse. It is only in the analytic encounter with resistance that we can consider the temporality of self-formation, to which I now turn.

Temporality

Ricoeur places dreams and their interpretation at the centre of the Freudian project, because in this critical engagement of disguised desire and interpretation he saw posed the central questions of psychoanalysis: 'How do desires achieve speech? How do desires make speech fail, and why do they themselves fail to speak?' (1970: 6).[10]

Now desire is a complex term, especially in Lacan's formulation. It is not synonymous with need, demand or sheer focusing of erotic attention. It is born in the space created between the self and the language system in which the self is embedded and through which it must mediate itself. For Lacan, the self can encounter itself only through the misleading and euphemizing ambiguities of a signifying system in which he or she is represented chiefly through the pronominal 'I'. Thus, 'mediated by language, the subject is irremediably divided, because he is at once excluded from the signifying chain and "represented" by it.' (Lemaire, 1977: 68). Language occludes and conceals need and demand, and desire arises in that space 'beyond', *au delà* in Lacan's terms, what is revealed through signification.

As Bowie lucidly discusses in his Bucknell Lectures of 1993, desire then must always speak to us of anticipation, of the futurial orientation which Freud and Heidegger saw as the primordial human temporal orientation, for a desire is defined by a moment of satisfaction that is beyond, that will always not-yet come to pass. As Freud said, 'Past, present and future are strung together, as it were, on the thread of the wish that runs through them' (*SE*, IX: [1959] 148), to which he added, 'the wish makes use of an occasion in the present to construct on the pattern of the past, a picture of the future' (ibid).

The speech of the patient then is oriented forward against the resistance posed by the analyst. Our desire, insofar as it precipitates itself in and through speech, is captated and punctuated by the speech of others, whether analyst or other interlocutor – their speech interrupts our own and forces us into a temporary suspension of or satisfaction of that desire. It is thus at the point of its interruption that the origin of desire makes itself momentarily visible. This sets up a counter-movement, a reversibility of perceived cause and effect engendered by the resistance of social encounters, and this reversibility is a fundamental feature of the temporal horizon modelled or mimicked in the psychoanalytic encounter. Forrester thus observes that: 'Psychoanalysis starts with, and always works within, an original intersubjectivity; it then works *backwards*, to earlier states, whose reality and significance is only conferred on them retrospectively' (1990: 203).

Resistance is central to Freud's notion of *Nachträglichkeit*, 'deferred action' or retroactive motivation (*SE*, I [1895]: 356). Freud suggested that sexual experiences that occurred at a very young age were incapable of being understood, owing to the subject's lack of sexual maturity. They are therefore 'deferred' until a later date, when, after having become capable of understanding sexual motivation, desire and its drives, the subject can reconstruct the events as meaningful, and 'it is this revision which invests them with significance and even with efficacy or pathogenic force' (LaPlanche and Pontalis, 1988: 112). A crucial feature of language so conceived is that it includes repression, denial and forgetting as integral components of its meaning-giving function, without which the perception of temporality would not be possible.[11] The perceived efficacy of past events, in other words, is a function of insights arrived at in the subject's own present.

The capacity for revision and retroactive grounding is itself constitutive of human temporality. But this temporality is itself embodied, made possible by the configuration of the human body's own physical and sensory make-up that I have already described. Freud, Lacan and Wagner all make a key issue out of the long period of post-partum physical immaturity of humans. The drives exercise themselves within the specular bounds of the body image, where the outline of the body emerges within the field of objects of desire. But it remains for the later acquisition of language, the symbolic capacity, to fix the history of these drives within the narrative of the subject, a narrative that retains and makes visible, albeit in disguised form, the other that is its source. This ontogenetic sequence became the framework for Freud's most powerful case studies (e.g. the 'Wolfman', in Freud, *SE,* xvii [1918]).

Nor can we refuse to consider that such retroactive motivation is at work in the excavations of subjectivity that anthropologists label the 'analysis of culture' or 'cultural symbolism' and the forms in which we usually locate it – primarily in art, myth and ritual. We have already seen that Walbiri life is thought to be a 'backtracking' of the originary actions and journeys of the ancestors. The ancestors were self-creative: they both dreamed and objectified their own tracks, marks and names. Present-day living people can only 'submit' to this already created world and reintegrate a self by retracing these external tracks. In Papua New Guinea, men give pearl shells and other wealth items as bridewealth in exchange for brides. Insofar as men's attention is focused on the political dimension of social life created through the endless transfer and passing on of these items, they must perforce turn away from the counter-flow of feminine reproductivity that is enabled by this flow of wealth items. Female productivity, childbirth and life itself thus move in a direction opposite to that of men's anticipations and strivings in the social world (Wagner, 1986). This reverse orientation, this projection of a prefigured past that is revealed only by looking ahead, is also a significant theme of Foi myth, where protagonists have to journey beyond the domain of human habitation and confront the origins of things – in the form of things like pearl shells, flowers, or the true source of a drum's voice.

There is great variation in gross scale of time in the forms of speech and action that anthropologists study – the narration of a myth, the performance of a ritual, the early years of a person's life. Nevertheless, it is precisely Wagner's observation that humans construct and perceive interval and causality, deferral and retroactive motivation in a way that occupies their time: 'What matters in the working out of a [motivational] sequence, or in the transformation from one sequence to another, is a matter of relationship among points – opposition, mediation, cancellation – rather than arbitrary interval' (1986: 81).

To phrase it in the most paradoxical way possible, history also takes place in its own time. History, Lacan said, is not about past events. History is about how a subject views and reconstructs the past and brings this perceived pattern of events into a relation with a current state of affairs (1991: 12). And this process can be studied at the level of a single individual subject or the shared subjectivity of a community of language speakers. The meanings generated in either case are not of different scales; they are perceived as different because they are articulated through different discursive modalities.

Conclusion

I wish to make two arguments for why I think psychoanalytic principles are fundamental to any social science including anthropology. First of all, I do not think it is a coincidence that Freud built his image of the human psyche on what could be called the specimen myth of Western culture – that of Oedipus the King, wherein the whole human drama of temporality, denial, concealment, revelation and retroactive motivation is depicted. That Freud should resort to this essentially anthropological and cultural analysis indicated that he did not dissociate the mechanisms by which the psyche was formed from those involved in the making visible of cultural symbolism in general. In *The Question of Lay Analysis*, Freud included the following disciplines in what he conceived of as a Faculty of Psychoanalysis: 'the history of civilization, mythology, the psychology of religions, literary history, and literary criticism' (*SE*, xx [1926]: 246). But this is not to repeat the mistake of conventional psychological anthropology and view a myth as a collective version of an individual neurosis. Rather, it is to reaffirm Ricoeur's critique of the original Freudian antinomy between analytic and genetic interpretation. Instead of accepting this antinomy, Ricoeur asked:

> Should not a distinction be made between levels of actuality in symbols? In addition to the commonplace symbols, worn with use, at the end of their

course, and having nothing but a past; and even in addition to the symbols in use, useful and utilized, which have a past and a present and serve in the clockwork of a given society as a token for the nexus of social pacts, are there not also new symbolic creations that serve as vehicles of new meanings?

(1970: 102)

In the subjective perception of life situation, all symbols, collective and 'private', are ranged alongside each other and do equivalent work in the patterning of meaning. The original Freudian antinomy asserts the self-evidence of the distinction between individuals and their relations. Rephrasing this as a dialectic in Ricoeur's terms takes this very contrast as a product of the differential proportions that meaning and interpretation take in social life. An example of an ethnography that demonstrated such a dialectical account of symbolic life patterning is Michael Young's *Magicians of Manumanua* (1983). Drawing upon the notion of 'living myth' which Leenhardt articulated for the Canaques of New Caledonia (Leenhardt, 1979), Young observed that in Kalauna (Massim area, Papua New Guinea):

A man's relationship to his myths . . . is neither arbitrary nor contingent, and it is colored by the fact of inherited ownership. They are things he carries around within himself as a singer carries a song or, more aptly, a magician his spells . . . his thought mediates the lives of his ancestors or heroes dwelling within him. The individual notionally becomes the vehicle for their lives: they live through his thinking and telling them. In this view, such myths are more than practical charters for ritual acts . . . ; they are constituents of selfhood, which affect a person's psychological stance and thereby his social behavior.

(Young, 1983: 18–19)

Secondly, and more specifically, because of Freud's and Lacan's understanding of the centrality of language, and their identification of language as the constituting mechanism of the unconscious, I view the psychoanalytic notions of repression and denial as intrinsic consequences of the metaphoric and metonymic dimensions of language itself in its entirety. And because this language is at once the tool and the object of study, we return to the characterization I posed earlier: that both psychoanalysis and anthropology become possible when the analytical model becomes or takes over the thing being modelled.

As is clear in the use of the term 'work', Freud, Heidegger and Marx all converge on a dimension of human being which places struggle, anticipation and resistance to energic discharge at the centre of human self-consciousness and its form of temporality. Anthropologists, too, have made use of the terminology of resistance and work in describing the task of penetrating to beneath the surface appearances of human speech and life. This is buttressed by our own fabricated economy of information – field notes, negotiable data, the objectifications without which we feel that we have not made our own relationality visible. These products attest to the duration and temporality of our field stay, and hence stand as a measure of the social relationships we have established and the depth of our commitment. As Ewing (1992) made clear, depth of penetration is still a persuasive metaphor for the 'work' of ethnographic analysis. The perception of depth is a consequence, however, of the manner in which a community imposes form on its social life and its imagery by recognizing the limits reached by its articulatory media. As anthropologists we struggle against these limits, the resistance of the subject, and against the opacity and unremarkability of everyday life. We struggle to elicit a gloss on behaviours which are problematic to us. But in our own struggle to understand, we must not refuse to concede a positive function to repression or denial.

This discrediting of repression is also the difference between transference and certain contemporary form of dialogicity, which could be glossed as transference without negation. One of the mainstays of post-modern anthropology is a focus on retaining the 'dialogic moment' of the anthropological encounter. The 'voice of the other' should not be obliterated by the anthropologist's constructed, authoritative text, but should retain visibility and retain its status as the source of anthropological insights. A great deal of textual skill has been brought to bear to render these conversations between anthropologist and informant in some of these dialogically constituted ethnographies and they undoubtedly represent a more sophisticated understanding of the variety of ethnographic techniques now available to late twentieth-century anthropology. But the conversations do not get us any closer to the real problem of the transference: the manner in which one's voice and subjectivity internalize and model or take over another's. In these terms, dialogicity is only a *faux*-transference. Kevin Dwyer makes just this point, as against the more adamantine textualism of Geertz:

> contrary to Geertz's view, the anthropologist, in practice, does not simply overhear or eavesdrop upon an informant's interpretation that would have been expressed no matter what the context; instead, the anthropologist's actions clearly provoke those interpretations and help structure them and give them context.
>
> (1982: 262)

But even as he or she accords a position to the voices of both interrogator and respondent, the dialogician must focus on what is constructed through speech at the expense of what is concealed or misdirected. This was brought out with extreme pathos in the last phases of Dwyer's interviews with his Moroccan informant, upon which Crapanzano has commented:

> K.D.: And what do you think that I think about you? What might I say to myself about you?
> F.M.: You're the one who understands that. Why, am I going to enter into your head?
> K.D.: But you can't enter the sheik's head, or Si Hassan's, yet you said something about what they might think of you.
> F.M.: I don't know. That – I don't know about it. I don't know about it.
> K.D.: All right.
>
> *(Dwyer, 1982: 219)*

As Crapanzano noted, the Moroccan interlocutor seems less interested in acceding to an epistemic positioning or definition of himself as a subject and more interested in sustaining the exchange as a vehicle of his relation with Dwyer (1982: 225–6).[12] The Moroccan informant tried to tell Dwyer what he did not know, which by definition cannot then contribute to the self-conscious fashioning of a subject position. Yet the entextualized dialogic version of this self must necessarily engage in just this act of fabrication.

Bakhtin insisted that dialogicity was characterized by 'unfinalisability' (see Morson and Emerson, 1990). There is no reason why we cannot see the novel in the same way we must anthropologically view myth and dream, as a symbolic form that grows out of and relates to the relational life of humans and which, like myth and dream, reveals the dependence of relationality upon speech for its form. Perhaps because the novel as text was so obviously a bounded world of finishing, Bakhtin chose to focus on the novel as a genre, that is as a process, rather than as a work whose most important feature is its 'sense of an ending' (as Frank Kermode put it). But the conclusion we must approach from a social science perspective is that room must be made to consider both effects simultaneously: any interpretative framework which focuses on the life of speech between people, as well as those constructed within objectifying forms such as ritual, myth and art, including the novel, must contain within themselves mechanisms for their own limitation.[13] For the Foi and people like them the process of interpretation is more a narrowing down of the expansive tendencies of trope than it is an exercise in proliferating alternative readings. The use of terms that refer to concealment, cutting-off, covering over, and so forth in the public speech of the Foi and other Papua New Guinea peoples attests as much to this restrictive power of trope as to its capacity to enhance meaning and multiply possible glosses. What Freud urges us to do is to annul 'the times for understanding in favour of the *moments of concluding* which precipitate the meditation of the subject towards deciding the sense to attach to the original event' (Wilden, 1968: 18).

A final point comes to mind, as a way of returning to Marcuse's point about the co-equivalence of social and psychoanalytical categorizations. In the psychoanalytic encounter, the analyst is perceptive to the likelihood that the patient is 'fabricating' an identity or a personal history in order to rationalize and justify a present behaviour pattern or dilemma. In the case of psychoanalysis the analyst can 'deconstruct' the fabrication, based on the psychoanalytic principles of denial, repudiation, repression and negation, what the 'true' (i.e. causal) state of affairs is that is determinative of the patient's discourse.[14] This does not seem much different from the task that confronts us in the anthropological study of contemporary indigenous 'invention of tradition': to bring the historical-causal analysis of behaviour to bear to de-naturalize the internalization of such nationalist and primordialist sensibilities, and in so doing, restore temporality and historicity to the human sciences. The repressive mechanism, because it conceals the historical sequence of enchained signification that emerges around traumatic events, constantly works against historicity and coevality. Seen as a more broadly situated human *existentielle*, the repressive mechanism is visible in the strenuous efforts of some of our indigenous interlocutors to re-establish contact with their own primordiality. But through analysis, repression serves as the motivation – both in terms of action and in terms of symbolic positioning – for reasserting historicity. Handler (1985) has remarked that in the face of these dehistoricizing essentialisms, one must bring to bear a Sapirian 'destructive analysis', a term which is appropriate to both anthropology and psychoanalysis. As Foucault said:

> In relation to the "human sciences", psychoanalysis and ethnology are rather "counter-sciences": which does not mean that they are less "rational" or "objective" than the others, but that they flow in the opposite direction, that they lead them back to their epistemological basis, and that they ceaselessly "unmake" that very man who is creating and re-creating his positivity in the human sciences.
>
> (1970: 379)

Psychoanalysis will always serve as a bulwark against a recent trend in contemporary social science, the view of the world in which meaning is produced through the articulation of hypersubjectivity, in which any signs can be juxtaposed and meaning can be extracted from any montage or concatenation according to the will of the articulator. In this respect, the dialogism of Dwyer seems to me more sophisticated and humanly scaled than my characterization of it. At the end of his monograph Dwyer criticizes a *faux*-dialogism that assumes:

that communication may be severed from its timing and sequence, that segments may be recombined and reordered and some eliminated, with no vital loss of meaning. [This] fiction promote[s] a view in which Self and Other are only provisionally different, a view that posits an Other that can be tamed and captured, at some point, for good.

(1982: 276–7)

And yet the Lacanian version of psychoanalysis I am advocating here sees endings as very important, sees the analyst in a position to bring the dialogic exchange to a halt in order to draw attention to a particular pooling of meaning in the history of that dialogue. To make visible through the act of severing and cutting, rather than constructing through acts of joining or concatenating. Psychoanalysis can lead anthropology out of this abyss of constructionism and voluntarism yawning before it by returning to anthropology a consideration of how the unconscious processes of erasure and repudiation inflect all regimes and processes of meaning and action, and are at work in the speech of all participants in a dialogue, and in so doing make human temporality, morality and destiny possible. In making the end or limit of meaning one of its significant features, we reassert the gaps between the very selves which strive to differentiate themselves against others, and in so doing also secure the possibility of perspective on these selves that is the goal of both anthropology and psychoanalysis.

Notes

This chapter is largely excerpted from chapters 1 and 8 of my book *The Lost Drum: The Myth of Sexuality in Papua New Guinea and Beyond* (Weiner, 1995). I am grateful to the University of Wisconsin Press for permission to reprint passages from that book here. My thanks also to Henrietta Moore and Gananath Obeyesekere for their valuable commentary on the material presented here.

1   See, for example, Freud, *SE*, xii [1912]: 104; *SE*, xii [1914]: 154.
2   See also Devereux: 'Since the existence of the observer, his observational activities and his anxieties (even in self observation) produce distortions which it is not only technically but also logically impossible to eliminate, ... [a]ny effective behavioral science methodology must treat these disturbances as the most significant and characteristic data of behavioral science research' (1967: xvii).
3   Robert Paul acknowledges this when he says simply that 'the essence of psychoanalysis is its method' (1987: 84).
4   As represented in the work of Erikson (1963) and Anna Freud (1937). Anthropological appropriations of this framework include Marsella, DeVos and Hsu, eds. (1985) and more recently Paul (1994). Marsella, DeVos and Hsu write in the introduction to their book: 'This volume assumes ... that ...

[t]he self can and must be considered apart from one's social role. Behaviour is often a result of continuous conflict between experiences of self and one's social role expectations. . . . Behaviour is judged consciously as adaptive or maladaptive in reference to social expectations' (1985: 6,7).

5   'It appears incontestable', Lacan wrote in his famous Rome Discourse, 'that the conception of psychoanalysis in the United States has inclined toward the adaptation of the individual to the social environment, toward the quest for patterns of conduct, and towards all the objectification implied in the notion of "human relations"' (Wilden 1968: 7).

6   See Wilden, 1968: 174 for a similar appeal to intrasubjectivity.

7   Including, as Lévi-Strauss first made clear in *The Savage Mind* (1966), temporal and spatial sequences, the idea of species as an operation of perception rather than a physical feature of the Classified World.

8   'We know by now perhaps a great deal – almost more than we can encompass – about what we call the body, without having seriously thought about what *bodying* is. It is something more and different from merely "carrying a body around with one"; it is that in which everything that we ascertain in the processes and appearances in the body of a living thing first receives its own process-character' (Heidegger, 1982: 79).

9   In Merleau-Ponty's words: 'the libido is not an instinct, that is, an activity naturally directed towards definite ends, it is the general power, which the psychosomatic subject enjoys, of taking root in different settings . . . of gaining structures of conduct. It is what causes a man to have a history. Insofar as a man's sexual history provides a key to his life, it is because in his sexuality is projected his manner of being towards the world, that is, towards time and other men' (1962: 158). And Ricoeur similarly notes: 'between sexual behaviour and total behaviour there can only be a relationship of style, or, to put it another way, a relationship of homology. Sexuality is a particular manner of living, a total engagement towards reality' (1970: 383).

10   Juillerat also begins his examination of the West Sepik Ida Ritual by saying that 'Of all the productions that human genius and the unconscious have been pleased to present to the observer, often in figurative language, ritual and myth have perhaps proved to be the most resistant to interpretation' (1992: 1).

11   'The general precondition of repression is thus clearly deemed to be in the "delaying of puberty" which is characteristic, according to Freud, of human sexuality: "Every adolescent individual has memory-traces which can only be understood with the emergence of sexual feelings of his own' [*SE*, I: 356]. *The retardation of puberty makes possible posthumous primary processes*' [*SE*, I: 359]"' (LaPlanche and Pontalis, 1988: 112).

12   I acknowledge Crapanzano's thoughtful critique of these passages (1992a: chapter 8).

13   Crapanzano thus says that: 'All hermeneutical systems are threatened with an interpretive swirl and must provide ideologically supported conventions that arrest it. Such conventions . . . require a forgetting' (1992a: 121).

14   '*The complete real pattern of a culture is a product of a functional interplay between officially affirmed and [un]officially negated patterns*' (Devereux, 1967: 212).

Bibliography

Battaglia, D., ed., 1995. *Rhetorics of Self-Making*. Berkeley: University of California Press.

Bourdieu, P., 1977. *Outline of a Theory of Practice*. Cambridge: Cambridge University Press.

Bowie, M., 1991. *Lacan*. London: Fontana.

—— 1993. *Psychoanalysis and the Future of Theory*. Oxford: Blackwell [Bucknell Lectures].

Crapanzano, V., 1992a. *Hermes' Dilemma and Hamlet's Desire*. Cambridge, Mass.: Harvard University Press.

—— 1992b. 'Some Thoughts on Hermeneutics and Psychoanalytic Anthropology', in *New Directions in Psychological Anthropology*, ed. T. Schwartz, G. White and C. Lutz. Cambridge: Cambridge University Press.

D'Andrade, R., 1990. 'Culture and Personality: A False Dichotomy', in Jordan and Swartz, eds, op. cit.

Devereux, G., 1967. *From Anxiety to Method in the Behavioral Sciences*. The Hague: Mouton.

Dwyer, K., 1982. *Moroccan Dialogues: Anthropology in Question*. Baltimore: Johns Hopkins University Press.

Elliott, A., 1994. *Psychoanalytic Theory*. Oxford: Basil Blackwell.

Erikson, E., 1963. *Childhood and Society*. New York: Norton.

Ewing, K., 1992. 'Is Psychoanalysis Relevant for Anthropology?' in T. Schwartz, G. White and C. Lutz, eds, op cit.

Forrester, J., 1990. *The Seductions of Psychoanalysis*. Cambridge: Cambridge University Press.

Foucault, M., 1970. *The Order of Things*. London: Tavistock.

Freud, A., 1937. *The Ego and Mechanisms of Defense*. London: Hogarth Press.

Freud, S., 1953–74. *Standard Edition of the Complete Psychological Works*, trans. James Strachey. London: Hogarth Press and the Institute of Psychoanalysis [*SE*].

Handler, R., 1985. 'On Dialogue and Destructive Analysis: Problems in Narrating Nationalism and Ethnicity', *Journal of Anthropological Research* 41: 171–82.

Heald, S., and A. Deluz, eds, 1994. *Anthropology and Psychoanalysis: An Encounter through Culture*. London: Routledge.

Heidegger, M., 1962. *Being and Time*. London: SCM Press.

—— 1979.*Nietzsche*, vol. 1: *The Will to Power as Art*. New York: Harper and Collins.

—— 1982. *Nietzsche*, vol. 3: *The Will to Power as Knowledge and Metaphysics*. New York: Harper and Collins.

Jordan, D., and M. Swartz, eds, 1990. *Personality and the Cultural Construction of Society*. Tuscaloosa and London: University of Alabama Press.

Juillerat, B., ed., 1992. *Shooting the Sun: Ritual and Meaning in West Sepik*. Washington: Smithsonian Institution Press.

—— 1997. 'Yangis, Lacan and Caducity: A Reply to James Weiner'. *Social Analysis* 41(2): 35–54.

Lacan, J., 1977a. *Écrits: A Selection*, trans. A. Sheridan. London: Routledge.
—— 1977b. *The Four Fundamental Concepts of Psychoanalysis*, ed. By K.-A. Miller and trans. A. Sheridan. Harmondsworth: Penguin.
—— 1991.*Seminar Book I: Freud's Papers on Technique*, ed. J.-A. Miller and trans. John Forrester. New York: Norton.
LaPlanche, J., and J.-B. Pontalis, 1988. *The Language of Psychoanalysis*. London: Karnac Books and the Institute of Psychoanalysis.
Leenhardt, M., 1979. *Do Kamo: Person and Myth in the Melanesian World*. Chicago: University of Chicago Press.
Lemaire, A., 1977. *Jacques Lacan*, trans. David Macey. London: Routledge and Kegan Paul.
Lévi-Strauss, C., 1966. *The Savage Mind*. Chicago: University of Chicago Press.
Macey, D., 1988. *Lacan in Contexts*. London: Verso.
Marcuse, H., 1973. *Five Lectures: Psychoanalysis, Politics and Utopia*. London: Allentane.
—— 1956/1987.*Eros and Civilization*. London: Ark Paperbacks.
Marsella, A., G. DeVos, and F. Hsu, eds, 1985. *Culture and Self: Asian and Western Perspectives*. London: Tavistock Publications.
Mead, G. H., 1934. *Mind, Self and Society from the Standpoint of a Social Behaviorist*. Chicago: University of Chicago Press.
Merleau-Ponty, M., 1962. *The Phenomenology of Perception*. London: Routledge and Kegan Paul.
Mitchell, J., ed., 1986. *The Selected Melanie Klein*. Harmondsworth: Penguin.
Morson, G., and C. Emerson, 1990. *Mikhail Bakhtin: Creation of a Prosaics*. Stanford, Calif.: Stanford University Press.
Muller, J., and W. Richardson, 1982. *Lacan and Language: A Reader's Guide to "Écrits"*. New York: International Universities Press.
Munn, N., 1970. 'The Transformation of Subjects into Objects in Walbiri and Pitjantjatjara Myth and Ritual'. in *Australian Aboriginal Anthropology*, ed. R. Berndt, Perth: University of Western Australian Press.
—— 1973. *Walbiri Iconography*. Ithaca, NY: Cornell University Press.
Obeyesekere, G., 1990. *The Work of Culture*. Chicago: University of Chicago Press.
Paul, R., 1987. 'The Question of Applied Psychoanalysis and the Interpretation of Cultural Symbolism', *Ethos* 15 (1/2): 167–95.
—— 1994. 'Recruitment to Monasticism among the Sherpas', in Jordan and Swartz, eds, op. cit.
Ricoeur, P., 1970. *Freud and Philosophy*. New Haven: Yale University Press.
Róheim, G., 1925. *Australian Totemism*. London: George Allen and Unwin.
—— 1945. *The Eternal Ones of the Dream*. New York: International Universities Press.
Rumsey, A., and F. Merlan, 1991. *Ku Waru*. Cambridge: Cambridge University Press.
Schwartz, T., G. White, and C. Lutz, eds, 1992. *New Directions in Psychological Anthropology*. Cambridge: Cambridge University Press.
Spiro, M., 1951. 'Culture and Personality: The Natural History of a False Dichotomy', *Psychiatry* 14: 19–46.

Strathern, M., 1988. *The Gender of the Gift*. Berkeley: University of California Press.

—— 1991. 'One Man and Many Men', in *Big Men and Great Men*, ed. M. Godelier and M. Strathern. Cambridge: Cambridge University Press.

Young, M., 1983. *Magicians of Manumanua: Living Myth in Kalauna*. Berkeley: University of California Press.

Wagner, R., 1977. ' "Speaking for Others": Power and Identity as Factors in Daribi Mediumistic Hysteria'. *Journal de la Société des Océanistes* 56–7: 145–52.

—— 1978. *Lethal Speech*. Ithaca, NY: Cornell University Press.

—— 1981. *The Invention of Culture*. Chicago: University of Chicago Press.

—— 1986.*Symbols that Stand for Themselves*. Chicago: University of Chicago Press.

—— 1991. 'The Fractal Person', in *Big Men and Great Men*, ed. M. Godelier and M. Strathern. Cambridge: Cambridge University Press.

Weiner, J., 1995. *The Lost Drum: The Myth of Sexuality in Papua New Guinea and Beyond*. Madison: University of Wisconsin Press.

—— 1997. 'The Unspoken Myth: A Reply to Juillerat',*Social Analysis* 41(2): 55–65.

Wilden, A., 1968. 'Lacan and the Discourse of the Other', in J. Lacan, *Speech and Language in Psychoanalysis*, trans. A. Wilden. Baltimore: Johns Hopkins University Press.

Winnicott, D., 1974. *Playing and Reality*. Hardmonsworth: Penguin.

10 Becoming Undisciplined: Anthropology and Cultural Studies

Nicholas Thomas

The objects of anthropological knowledge – society, culture, belief, gender, law and so on – have never been exclusively anthropology's own. The discipline has always shared ground – or disputed ground – with neighbouring disciplines such as sociology, law, psychology and religious studies. This chapter traverses the most recent manifestation of this cross-disciplinary sharing and disputation. The ground of overlap is that of 'culture', and the tension is that between anthropology and cultural studies. I do not offer anything like a survey of either field, or of all the issues raised by the intersections and contentions between the two. I am concerned, in part, to acknowledge contrasting approaches to culture and politics that prevail in anthropology and cultural studies, but I am also concerned to question the terms of the operation of disciplinary juxtaposition that such a project involves. While it is important to be specific about the particular commitments particular disciplines entail (such as the canonical orientation toward ethnographic fieldwork in anthropology), I argue for a more hesitant approach to the characterization of discipline-based methodologies. This hesitancy is, to some extent, a product of the present: disciplines are increasingly heterogeneous, hence their reification tends to be increasingly invidious, increasingly a matter of evoking caricatures to be dismissed or defended. But my unwillingness to trade in reifications has another basis, and this lies in a sense that much scholarship now occupies interstitial locations. If not exactly 'interdisciplinary' in the sense that has been established since the 1960s, a good deal of research now has intellectual lineages, methodologies, modes of address and audiences that arise from political commitments (to feminism, for example) that are neither contained by disciplines nor constitutive of new disciplines. Hence the interest of the question of the relationship between anthropology and cultural studies lies as much in what is patently problematic about its terms, as in the issues that it indeed raises.

Culture is at once anthropology's most vital and most discredited concept. If it was marginal over most of the life of the British school of social anthropology, it became increasingly significant as the tenets of that school were diversified during and after the 1960s; it was central from the beginnings of Boasian American anthropology, and has been equally important in European anthropological thought and in anthropological traditions in other parts of the world. Culture, notoriously resistant to specification or definition, has not been so much an object of study as the ground upon which other issues can be addressed. Classically, seemingly odd or irrational practices and beliefs could be culturally contextualized; any aspect of Western behaviour, identity or knowledge could be shown not to be natural, but to be culturally distinct. Other peoples' views of personhood, economics or reproduction could be revealed through the diagnosis of cultural difference, and empowered, as critical devices that drew attention to the specificity and cultural particularity of beliefs and practices that were thus identified as merely 'Western'. Culture, in this guise, enabled such prominent (and only latterly controversial) anthropological interventions in public debate as Margaret Mead's juxtaposition of Samoan and American sexualities. It also enabled Clifford Geertz's evocations of the distinctiveness of Indonesian and North African behaviours, traditions and polities, that did much to define the promise of anthropological 'local knowledge', not for a broader public, or so much for anthropologists themselves, as for the American humanities. Anthropology, as a discipline understood and drawn upon by influential American historians such as Simon Schama (1991) and Robert Darnton (1984), owes much to this culturalism.

At the same time, the notion of culture has been vigorously disputed. It has been identified as an idealist reification, and one that lacks credibility on psychological or cognitive grounds; its predicate of shared meaning has been rejected by those calling for a greater recognition of diversity in knowledge, values and orientations among members of 'the same' culture. Most recently, its essentialism has become routinely questioned. Almost by definition, a notion such as Samoan, American or Japanese culture has become as untenable as it was once axiomatic: it is now apparent (perhaps too apparent) that, on the one hand, Samoans, Americans and Japanese share a good deal and that, on the other, any such ethnic group will differ a good deal among themselves, to such an extent that it becomes facile to speak of 'the Samoan view of' any particular notion or relation (cf. Thomas, 1994).

Despite the extent to which the concept of culture would seem preju-diced by an anti-essentialism that now pervades the humanities as a whole, and is perhaps especially strong in anthropology in particular, the concept nevertheless retains great salience, indeed a pivotal role in much anthropo-logical talk and analysis. For example, consumption has become a key topic for contemporary anthropology, in part because consumption practices mediate between global processes of production and circulation and the local societies which anthropologists have conventionally studied (and which ethnographic fieldwork is best adapted to study). The very alignment of the articulation between the global and the local in this particular kind of prob-lem is conducive to a particular anthropological response, which character-istically (and no doubt appropriately) emphasizes the local distinctiveness of the appropriation of global phenomena, and this is typically if not in-variably expressed as cultural difference. In diverse ways, even when the most overtly post-modern issues are addressed, anthropologists thus tend to return to culture and cultural difference, as context and principle respec-tively, through which phenomena are located and explained.

If 'culture' has long been susceptible to critique from within the disci-pline of anthropology, it has become increasingly problematic for reasons that emerge from without. The word and the idea have, of course, never been exclusively the property of anthropology, but have always had wider lives. If, for a long time, 'culture' in common parlance referred mainly to high culture, and thus did not overlap much with anthropological usage, the situation has changed dramatically and irreversibly. If culture in the broader sense has in fact long been an object of administrative regulation and manipulation, the word itself has increasingly been used in an an-thropological sense, in government policy formation, in business and com-mercial discourse, in the context of multiculturalism, in a whole range of legal contexts, and in oppositional activism, by communities affirming their cultures and demanding their recognition (cf. Turner, 1994).

On the one hand, this could be seen as a positive development for an-thropology – if it is not too facetious to suggest that the discipline's sub-ject matter is multiplying before our eyes, as 'cultures' are explicitly identified in an ever-increasing range of locations, and as the efforts of museums, tourist industries, educational bureaucracies and a host of other agencies to define and present culture proliferate. Yet at the same time all this makes us uncomfortable. We can draw no fine line between 'our' use of the term and the usages that circulate more generally. Given that much public debate turns precisely on notions of cultural difference, the distinc-tiveness of professional discourse is elusive. And, more negatively, from the point of view of the discipline, anthropological authority is perforce challenged. There is no self-evident sense in which a cultural question requires an anthropological expert to answer it.

'Threats' to anthropology

The expansion of cultural discourse, and the associated proliferation of claims to speak authoritatively about culture, has had a particular impact on anthropological research in certain regions. In the Pacific, in Amazonia, in Native North America and in many other places, the people studied no longer simply and unreflectively live out their lives (if they ever did); they are increasingly concerned to define their own cultures and be the authors or at least the joint authors of public representations of those cultures. In much of the South Pacific, for example, local discourses of *kastom* (custom, culture, tradition) have emerged over a number of decades and figure as a kind of 'auto-anthropology'. Perhaps initially generated by the circumstances of labour migration, through which people from particular areas came into contact with other Melanesians and with whites and were prompted to reify and describe their particular ways of life, these characterizations acquired greater, supra-local significance in the 1970s and 1980s. In most Melanesian nations this was during the lead-up to independence and, as movements for sovereignty acquired momentum elsewhere, in places such as New Caledonia and Hawaii, which remained under colonial control. Much of the contention around these reifications of culture has primarily been of local significance; where, for instance, men attempt to impose particular patterns of behaviour on women on the grounds that they are customary. However, anthropologists and anthropological authority have frequently been challenged; the project of anthropology is seen to exemplify colonialism in the intellectual domain (Jolly and Thomas, 1992; Trask, 1989; Keesing, 1989).

Such conflicts between indigenous intellectuals and anthropologists have been intensified rather than ameliorated by recent theoretical trends. Anthropologists are now broadly concerned to emphasize the mutability of culture, and have employed the notion of 'invention' to address innovation in meaning, and to deconstruct ideas of stable traditions (e.g. Hanson, 1990; Thomas, 1997). However unobjectionable these propositions may appear to be in general, they can be construed and have been construed to subvert indigenous claims in settler societies such as New Zealand and Australia. In these contexts, both the legal purchase and the public credibility of indigenous claims regarding land and other resources tend to depend on the demonstration of continuity – that present claimants are substantially connected with people who once held land and culture. In this context, and given that the word 'invention' has connotations of concoction, anthropological argument, especially as it is represented in the media, can collide directly with indigenous investments in 'culture'.

Anthropological discourses on culture are thus diversifying and vigorous yet profoundly beleaguered; they are challenged in different ways in different places. The debate with indigenous authorities is of far greater moment within countries such as Australia, Canada and New Zealand than it is within Europe, though distinct but related issues concerning the 'right to represent' certainly arise in non-indigenous contexts. If there are threats to anthropology from outside the academy, the emergent discipline of cultural studies has appeared to constitute a threat from within. A challenge has been registered as such within both American and British anthropology – witness for instance the fact that the Group for Debates in Anthropological Theory, based at the University of Manchester, staged a discussion in 1996 on the question of whether 'Cultural studies will be the death of anthropology'. And there is indeed a threat of sorts, not only because of the overlap of subject matter, but also because of the sheer popularity of cultural studies, or rather of the cultural studies that has emerged most recently, which differs in a number of respects from the field as it was established in Britain in the 1960s and 1970s. It is important to recall that academic disciplines are not merely conceptual entities, but also institutionalized ones; they consist of teaching machines, sectors of the publishing business, professional associations, criteria of advancement and employment and so on. In at least some of these domains, cultural studies has become, after a period of limited growth in the 1960s and 1970s, a rapidly expanding field (in a context in which most arts disciplines have been 'downsized' dramatically; although circumstances vary in different countries, the position of universities generally, and humanities and social sciences within universities, has broadly been in decline). There can be no doubt that among students, in English, history and in other fields in the humanities as well as in anthropology, cultural studies has far more cachet than the more 'mainstream' or 'conventional' areas of research within those disciplines. But what, in this context, does 'cultural studies' mean?

The formation of cultural studies

The cultural studies 'boom' of the 1990s has little connection with the earlier body of British writing associated particularly with the Birmingham Centre for Contemporary Cultural Studies. That work drew upon sociology but was more strongly influenced by Marxism (if always in a problematic and critical relationship with its orthodoxies and reductionism), and by the cultural-historical materialism of Raymond Williams and other contributors to *New Left Review* such as Perry Anderson. It was conspicuously eclectic, sometimes leaning toward the ethnographic and empirical (Hall and Jefferson, 1976) and sometimes toward the theoretical, in work on ideology for example (CCCS, 1978). One of the Birmingham Centre's most sustained bodies of work focused on youth subcultures, and could be seen to have approached those subcultures in terms that were, in some respects, consistent with the anthropological theory of the period, even though reference was made to sociological rather than anthropological literature, and 'ethnography' was understood sociologically rather than anthropologically.

The concern was to establish that the behaviour of groups such as Teds and skinheads was not simply 'deviant' (as it remained for the mainstream sociology of deviance), it was rather a collective response to particular economic and class circumstances that was culturally expressed. Subcultures consisted in shared meanings, distinctive dress, style and focal concerns that amounted to a singular way of life. There was a concern to map out the rules that structured particular subcultures, to identify what had to be done, what was never done, what the rituals were. And these attributes of behaviour were explained in somewhat functionalist terms; the 'touchiness' of Teds, for example, reflected their jealousy to defend what little status those traditonally lacking in status possessed; hence fighting to defend territory served the broader need to defend space (Jefferson, 1976). Whatever theoretical affinities might be noted between this critical, sociological ethnography and the social anthropology of the time certainly should not be exaggerated. The politics of cultural studies was certainly conspicuously different to that of anthropology. Whereas the former was linked with the new left, and with a broadly oppositional attitude to the British state and class structure, anthropology had all the eclecticism that one would expect to be associated with an established discipline. Although post-war anthropology could be seen generally to be basically opposed to racism, and generally supportive of the shifts toward decolonization in various arenas over the 1960s and 1970s, the political orientations that individual anthropologists' work gave rise to were perforce as globally dispersed as the situations of research. While a peripheral group (represented in British and European circles by the journal *Critique of Anthropology*) adopted an engaged stance, particularly in relation to the critique of colonialism, this sort of activist orientation was constitutive of, rather than marginal to, the proto-disciplinary endeavour of cultural studies, as it was manifested in the Birmingham group.

Whatever cultural studies was in the 1960s and 1970s, the post-boom, primarily American, field (which is very much alive elsewhere, in Australia and New Zealand, for example) diversified extraordinarily. While the Birmingham Centre had begun to engage with feminism and race, while retaining an overarching emphasis on class, questions of ethnicity, gender, sexuality and race were to become central largely to the exclusion of class. These issues were, of course, also being increasingly explored by sociologists and by anthropologists: the distinctiveness of the work that emerged in cultural studies arose from the emphasis on representation and textual politics, which followed from an engagement with post-structuralist and deconstructive theory, especially in the key writings of the post-colonial canon of Homi Bhabha (1994) and Gayatri Spivak (1987), with which cultural studies was sometimes virtually conflated. Although this canon has become salient, almost a *de rigueur* point of citation for much art-world practice as well as more strictly academic work within the 'new humanities', it is vital to remember that there is a great deal more than this to cultural studies: witness for example the work of Tony Bennett and his colleagues on cultural policy, which ranges over the forms of civic education propagated by museums since the nineteenth century, to broadcasting law, copyright, indigenous intellectual property and a host of other issues, many with very broad political and commercial implications (e.g. Bennett, 1995). It is difficult to put forward any generalization that is not misleading, but it could be suggested broadly that cultural studies began from a dialogue between sociological orientations and methods and Marxist theory, and moved toward one between literary orientations and post-structuralist theory. There are important exceptions, such as the work of Bennett, just mentioned, but it is reasonable to assert that cultural studies, as a movement that has become popularized, is primarily textual in orientation.

The shortcomings of 'cultural studies'

The dialogue between the disciplines has involved a good deal of mutual stereotyping. Anthropology has been regarded by cultural studies practitioners primarily as a remnant of colonial ideology, as a voyeuristic discourse of exoticism. Marianna Torgovnick's treatments of both Leiris and Malinowski exemplify this reductionism (1990). And although Trinh T. Minh-Ha's films are challenging and open-ended, her writings subjected anthropologists to over-familiar critiques, making easy use of Malinowski's diary (Trinh, 1989; Moore, 1990). Anthropologists might have felt that they were being subjected to similar critiques to those that had been generated largely from within the discipline and substantially aired in the late 1960s and 1970s (notably in Asad, 1974) and that critics were oblivious of shifts in orientation in the discipline. These responded to critiques of imperialism, including the work of Edward Said, and made colonialism and the formation of anthropological knowledges objects of anthropological investigation (Cohn, 1987; Comaroff and Comaroff, 1991; Thomas, 1994).

Bearing in mind the need to avoid producing reciprocal distortions, a number of features of current work in cultural studies appear problematic, and it is worth identifying these, if only to highlight areas in which anthropological theorizing may offer greater potential, not only to anthropologists, but to those working in interstitial areas of contemporary culture and cultural history. With this qualification in mind, I would like to suggest that there are a number of significant shortcomings in the popularized project of cultural studies: (1) a textual and semiotic orientation; (2) a preoccupation with the contemporary; (3) an approach to questions of identity that tends to reinstate the essentialisms that are overtly the targets of critique; and (4) a paradoxically US-centric approach to cultural difference. To address these points in turn:

1 Cultural studies, like many other disciplines and fields, was profoundly influenced by structuralism and semiotics, and indeed exemplifies the degree to which the humanities as a whole has been pervaded by the model of language, and the use of linguistic analogies in interpreting countless social and cultural phenomena. Roland Barthes' work (1972) was thus inspiring and profoundly influential for work on a host of topics in popular culture: it both drew attention to phenomena such as magazine covers that warranted attention, and suggested ways in which they might be approached. Vital as this was in opening up a field, the perspective in hindsight appears to be fundamentally flawed. As Norman Bryson, himself an influential exponent of semiotic perspectives within art history was to note: 'Barthes' failure [in his study of fashion] to consult either fashion designers or fashion wearers, as a check to his analysis, vitiates and discredits all the generalizations he proposes . . . though the bracketing out of competence as a criterion can be taken as symptomatic of the structuralist strategy' (Bryson, 1983: 73). This lack of interest in engagement with the producers and consumers of particuar cultural forms was linked with a 'screening out of practical and operational determination within cultural life' (ibid). The tendency remains, in a great deal of work, including much work that is not specifically committed to structuralist interpretative strategies, to take the meanings and political significances of a text to be accessible through critical reading; analysis is routinely equated with 'reading', when for instance we speak of a critic's reading of a film, an exhibit or a monument, equating these operations with the more specifically literary-critical effort of reading a novel.

What this leads to is an indifference to the history of a text's or an object's uses. Torgovnick, for example, finds it sufficient to draw attention to Leiris's conflations of eroticism and primitivism. The questions of how his writings were received, what they were perceived to lend support to, what distinct uses they might have now, are passed over. There is a basic difference of orientation between a purely literary critique, and one which aims to grasp the significances of texts in their historical contexts. There is also an equally vital difference between the textual and the artefactual. Though it is certainly important to address the meanings and significances of public objects such as monuments, it is necessary in doing so to acknowledge that these objects are not simply texts, but entities with a distinct physical, architectural and environmental presence. Like clothing and other fashion objects, their uses are embodied. This is not the place to go into theories of embodiment; my point is simply that language-based theories of culture will perforce impoverish the non-linguistic domain (Appadurai, 1986; Miller, 1987). Accordingly, insofar as cultural studies remains committed to language-based theories, such as semiotics, its address to a whole range of phenomena – fashion, architecture, the cinema – is likely to be less adequate than approaches which foreground practice, embodiment and materiality, or those which see these terms as complementing the terms of linguistic interpretation. In this context, the important exceptions include Gilroy's work on music (1993: ch. 3).

2 Cultural studies has been defined by work on contemporary culture, and particularly contemporary mass culture and youth culture. There was obviously point to this orientation in the early Birmingham studies: these areas had been neglected. But the legacy of the paradigm is arguably problematic in a number of ways. For example, the bias toward the new, oppositional, urban and fashionable has meant that a whole series of common cultural practices which appear to be conservative and middle class, such as gardening, are never addressed, though they are obviously expressively significant in many ways. The intellectual scope of the field is thus narrower than might generally be acknowledged. A lack of engagement with history is also conspicuous, although here again there are many exceptions, such as Tony Bennett (whose work has addressed nineteenth-century museums) and Paul Gilroy. This lack of historical engagement has different ramifications in different contexts. Given that many theoretical discussions of particular topics, such as globalization, are predicated on the novelty of specific cultural conditions, many general claims are thus rendered insecure: one cannot make a claim for the distinctiveness of a particular situation in the present, without having demonstrated that what is supposedly novel was in fact absent from the past. Hence, although there are no doubt many grounds upon which the nature of contemporary cultural interaction is in fact singular, much commentary on globalization blithely ignores the various forms of transregional culture that existed in the past, associated with earlier phases of the world system, mass migration and world religions. This lack of attention toward history is perhaps of particular importance in the context of work on colonial culture, which I discuss further below.

3 There has been a preoccupation with challenging the 'politics of identity', but much of the literature does this in terms that seem doggedly attached to categorical constructions of identity (as race, sexuality, ethnicity and so on) that are problematized only insofar as they are shown to cross-cut one another. Identities are therefore exhibited as pluralized and fractured rather than singular and integrated, yet a notion of identity as given by categorical location (straight/gay and so on), and as fixed possession rather than historical and biographic contingency, thus seems to haunt current discussion, to be strangely reinvigorated by the proliferation of essays that disavow it. This is one of the areas in which theorizing within cultural studies has failed to engage with more radical critiques of personhood, such as those developed on the basis of Melanesian anthropology by Marilyn Strathern (1988). In her work, and in Debbora Battaglia's broader inquiry (1995), categories such as the self and identity are displaced far more creatively, and to a far greater extent, than they are in the literature of identity politics.

4 The above epitomizes the extent to which 'difference' is cited in principle, and is a key term for cultural studies in the present, while the *content* of cultural difference is rarely investigated or taken to be of interest. Anthropologists who remain concerned to study topics such as those addressed by Strathern – Melanesian notions of the person – may be derided for retaining an anachronistic interest in the representation of the exotic, while cultural studies exhibits no engagement with the diversity of perceptions of culture, history, attachment to place, self and so on, that flourish in various parts of the world despite 'globalization' (Thomas 1996a). Where globalization indeed enables new flows of representations, it is rarely appreciated that many of these (e.g. transnational Hindi cinema) are independent of 'the West' and indifferent to products such as those of Hollywood.

There is, moreover, a residual attachment, as Pnina Werbner (1997) among others has pointed out, to the Manichean oppositions and the theme of resistance that was characteristic of the Birmingham school work. In whatever situation is being analysed, it is presumed that one group occupies a subaltern position, which analysis seems to possess a will to validate, often proceeding by authenticating various forms of style, consumption practice and so on as 'resistance', or at least as the expression of identity. However adequate this was in the context of British subcultures, it became increasingly problematic in the case of colonial histories, which loomed larger as cultural studies became increasingly identified with postcolonial theorizing. Here, again, the tendency was for analysis to be curiously self-defeating, in the sense that the theme of subversive mimicry and ambivalence that was rendered central as a result of Bhabha's stimulating essays (1994) presumed that colonial representations were pervasively salient: the colonized, in other words, might be distorting and deflecting their address, and exposing their instabilities and ironies, but were not able to produce meaning and representation autonomously.

Post-colonial theory could, indeed, be seen to distil and accentuate the various problems that much writing in cultural studies has exhibited. It needs first to be acknowledged that post-colonial theory has – if Ranajit Guha's subaltern histories (1983) and Edward Said's *Orientalism* (1977) are retrospectively identified with this body of work – produced insights of foundational importance for the humanities in the late twentieth century. We are now far more attuned to the interplay between questions of knowledge and power in the theatre of colonial culture than we were previously; we are conscious of the strained interplay between gender, emancipation and writing in metropolitan and colonial situations, and we are attuned to expressions of doubleness and ambivalence in colonial texts. Yet there are multiple points at which these insights have stopped short, and somehow failed to deliver nuanced accounts of the cultures of either colonizers or colonized. Said cannot himself be blamed for the partiality of his enterprise: given that he was by training a literary critic, albeit one who has ventured beyond literature to interrogate constructions of the Orient in the discourses of area studies and the media, we can hardly expect him to have approached the question of colonial representation in a more ethnographic or historically localized fashion. While Said was in fact to some degree sensitive to the particular authorial imprint upon the various texts he explored, the more basic and more enduring problem has been that critics have remained concerned primarily with Western texts about the non-Western world. Whereas, for instance, a huge body of writing on travel literature has emerged, the question of travel on the part of non-Europeans has scarcely been broached. Yet there were of course many Asian, African, Native American and Middle Eastern travellers who both moved about within their own regions (as tax collectors, pilgrims, as well as travellers in one modern mode or another), and travelled to Europe. In many cases their writings have been published or are accessible archivally; their responses might be compared with European travel writings about their own regions, and about Europe itself. Insofar as this kind of topic is explored, it is by area-studies scholars whose work tends not to be incorporated or acknowledged within the wider cultural studies sphere.

The underlying problem to which this particular example points is a lack of interest in engagement with cultural expressions that lie beyond the imperial net. The texts of imperialism themselves, and those that are enunciated in direct opposition to it, such as those of the avowedly post-colonial literatures, are taken to constitute a field in which identities, claims to authority, racial stereotyping, and their various subversions, are subjected to critical reading, while cultural practices that may lie beyond these texts and counter-texts also lie beyond the vision of the analyst. Hence, even if the aspiration is to demonstrate the limitations or the failure of colonial power, the critic's very standpoint necessarily amplifies that power, because the materials engaged with are essentially limited to those produced by the colonial archive itself. In particular situations, much local representation may be unaware of or indifferent to the notional hegemony of 'the West'. As Christopher Pinney has demonstrated in his study of Indian popular photography (1997), a colonial visual technology was appropriated by a subject population and turned to ends that were neither prescribed by nor subversive of Western visual cultures. They were, rather, extensions of Hindu practice into the use of images produced in new ways. What is distinctive to these practices can be accessed only ethnographically, through methods that attend to practices, to the materiality of objects and behaviours, that are in other words not limited to textual interpretation.

In this sense, there may remain a profound difference between the orientations of those strands of 'cultural studies' that stand in awe of post-colonial literary theory and the work of anthropology, which tends to ground itself in local ways of engaging with things. Pinney's work typifies an anthropology that has radically distanced itself from the objectifying exoticism with which critics such as Torgovnick continue to charge the discipline. My assertive comments here – in defence of anthropology, as it were – resonate with a number of anthropological interventions in debate about cultural studies. Signe Howell has claimed that:

> (1) They [practitioners of cultural studies] focus upon cultural representations to the exclusion of presenting contextualized indigenous views and practices. (2) Despite frequent assertions that they conduct ethnographic and qualitative research, it is difficult to accept these claims at face value. The prevailing strength of social anthropology is precisely the extended fieldwork and the use of empirical data in theorising. (3) They frequently operate on a highly abstract, jargon-ridden, meta-level. Not being an academic discipline, their theoretical vocabulary is necessarily borrowed. This means that they frequently use it idiosyncratically (not necessarily a bad thing) while claiming generality. (4) Cultural studies focuses on the modern western world. Social anthropology focuses on both alien and familiar sociocultural formations and is comparative in its aims. (5) Despite claims to the contrary, those working in cultural studies are not reflexive about their own theories and assumptions. (1997: 107)

My interest in citing this text is not in endorsing or, necessarily, dissenting from this set of comments. It is rather to draw attention to their tone, to the aggrieved and defensive posture, which in its discomfort, comfortably evokes an unlocated set of people: 'them'. While I naturally believe that my own complaints, in the previous paragraphs, are more defensible than Howell's, I have to concede that these sets of statements are of much the same order. What is telling, in relation to my own comments rather than Howell's, is that many of these points have been made repeatedly by cultural studies theorists themselves, perhaps most notably by such prominent figures as Stuart Hall (1992) Paul Gilroy (1992) and John Frow (1995). Conversely, it might be pointed out that if one surveys the scholars who subscribe to the tenets I have contested, one finds that in many cases they are *not* figures within cultural studies, but literary scholars, art critics or anthropologists. The tendency to validate forms of popular consumption as authenticating projects of identity, has, for instance, been as central to the anthropology of consumption as it has been to work in the same area within cultural studies. In other words, if anthropologists are irritated by the tendency for cultural critics to represent the critique of anthropology's ambivalent connections with colonialism, that was substantially elaborated within anthropology thirty years ago, practitioners of cultural studies might be perturbed with as much justification, to be criticized in terms that have been extensively aired within the field.

The limits of juxtaposition

We have more to lose than to gain by conducting a debate that centres upon juxtaposed reifications. The terms of such debate presume from the start that the most productive way to conduct it is to evoke two 'neighbouring' disciplines, whose overlapping interests represent conflicts of interest, and whose perspectives are readily characterized and assessed. What we need to do instead is particularize such argument, by reviewing the various methodologies that have emerged in their analysis; this is not necessarily a discipline-specific issue, nor necessarily one in which the competitive economies of disciplines need be invested. For example, it can be argued that particular colonial formations, such as the anthropologically informed governmentality associated with the British projects of 'indirect rule' in Fiji, Nigeria and elsewhere, could not be seen as a purely discursive entity, but needed to be addressed as a practically transformative endeavour: agents, imaginings of past and future, constructions of existing and potential social orders, and strategies through which social forms, habits and subjectivities could be reformed. It needed to be acknowledged, however, that these projects were prone to fail, not because of any general logic that inheres in 'mimicry' or in the operations of stereotyping, but because particular strategies of colonial government were inefficient and insufficient to circumscribe and neutralize indigenous resistance; moreover, they actually empowered and enabled new forms of indigenous action, notably those that appropriated aspects of the colonial state, missionary Christianity and similar impositions (see Thomas, 1994 for fuller discussion). The post-colonial approach, which resorts to such terms as 'the general text of colonialism' (Young, 1990: 151), is unable to grasp or specify why some colonial projects succeed and fail in different ways and different proportions.

The aim of this critique of post-colonial approaches was not a critique of theorizing *per se*, nor of cultural studies; objection might equally have been made to the formerly ahistorical anthropological orthodoxies, and the forms of history that were insensitive to culture, or that neglected the stimulating questions around governmentality raised by Foucault's later work. The aim was rather to negotiate issues within arguments that had emerged both from cultural studies and anthropology, toward a set of terms that seemed more apt to an account of colonial projects that were at once global and local. The question could not be addressed by lining up one discipline against another.

My objection to discipline-based argument is not motivated primarily by a sense that the reifications in which we trade are misleading, even though this is true and has characterized earlier phases of interdisciplinary debate involving anthropology, for example the debate around history and anthropology. In that instance, 'anthropology' was easily caricatured as ahistorical functionalism and 'history' as linear causal narrative insensitive to culturally various historicities (as Cohn demonstrated with great wit; 1987: ch. 2). Neither these typifications nor those emergent in current discussion of anthropology and cultural studies do justice to the heterogeneity of the work that the labels supposedly evoke. There is, then, an issue of empirical complexity, and the diversification of disciplines makes characterization still more problematic than it once was. However, my more specific motivation arises from an interest in the interstitial location of much scholarship in the present. My stake in the 'interstitial' is partly personal, in the sense that all of my own work has been either between anthropology and history, or anthropology and art history; the institution which I was involved in establishing and currently run is not discipline-based, but is rather a centre 'for cross-cultural research'. If my own trajectory has been singular, the situation of being inside and outside particular disciplines and milieux in turn is rather less so. The point that feminist anthropology/anthropologically minded feminism may involve such a relation of interiority and exteriority, a complication if not a confusion of intellectual and political loyalties, has often been made (Moore, 1988).

The most complex problem that arises from scholarship in the interstices is not, perhaps, a purely intellectual or methodological one, but a problem of writing, namely the problem of audience. Much writing that is engaged with the problematic and inchoate objects that constitute the field of cultural politics potentially addresses not only broad, but also disparate constituencies. Much anthropological writing will now be consumed not only by anthropologists, but also by 'natives' or at least by a few members of the communities with whom the anthropologist has worked. One's address to those people is perforce distinct in many senses from one's address to students, and to the cantankerous colleagues who may be asked to referee an article submitted to a journal. There are also many cases when a text, on art for example, will be read by art-world professionals, who are themselves heterogeneous (artists, curators, administrators, journalists) but who share a distance from the arena of university based scholarship. For example, much of my own writing in recent years has appeared not in anthropological journals or in scholarly books directed at anthropologists, but in exhibition catalogue essays and art magazine essays. Writings of this kind are, like the reports that emerge from development anthropology and various other 'applied' expressions of the discipline, complicit in systems of value from which anthropologists might otherwise aim to stand back, to describe rather than reproduce. An essay about a particular contemporary artist cannot avoid contributing something to the valuation of that artist's work; it will be photocopied by their dealers, submitted with CVs and portfolios in fellowship and grant applications; it will be passed on to private collectors, institutions and prospective buyers. Particular arguments concerning the relative values of 'traditionalist', diasporic or 'hybrid' art forms may influence curators designing exhibits; arguments concerning history, identity and place may well influence the practice of artists themselves. There is nothing unexpected or remarkable about this process, through which research has diverse outcomes and diverse ramifications inside and outside scholarship (Thomas, 1996b).

I am not concerned particularly to *advocate* interstitial knowledge or to argue that work which entails these extra-academic engagements is necessarily more worthy than work that does not. It is a matter of personal preference that I engage in the kinds of projects that I do, rather than something that either warrants or requires special theoretical justification. Something may be gained, however, from *acknowledging* the interstitial character of the working and writing situations that already exist, but that writing about disciplinary theory almost invariably passes over. The very banality of the point that many anthropologists have long worked, for example, as development consultants, in health care, in legal contexts or in museums and the art world is in itself telling. The seeming matter-of-factness of this observation indexes the degree to which anthropology does not theorize its own situation. To be sure, it has consistently pretended to do so, by adumbrating the epistemological correlates of the centrality of fieldwork, and latterly exploring the singularity of anthropological writing (Clifford and Marcus, eds, 1986; Geertz, 1988). But, however vital and energizing both fieldwork and 'writing up' have been, there is much more to the question of what anthropologists do than either.

Anthropologists are also social actors who are implicated, to a greater or lesser degree, in the reproduction of a discipline and, as I have suggested, often in projects that lie beyond that discipline, and commonly enough beyond academic disciplines altogether. The 'politics of difference' is not only about ethnicity and sexuality. It also needs to be about the heterogeneity of scholarly practice and the ways in which that heterogeneity creates a host of divided loyalties, distinct constituencies and multiple audiences. The example of work on art reminds us that anthropologists, like many others in the social sciences and humanities, do not simply analyse culture but also produce it, or at least are implicated in its production and presentation, often for broad museum-going and television-viewing audiences. 'Anthropological' practice thus entails these engagements, the problem of the translation of research into forms other than conventional scholarly publications, such as the report, the exhibit and the fifty-minute programme, with all their complex compromises – with one's materials, one's constrained resources – in addition to compromises of the more straightforwardly political or commercial kind. The most vital questions to address are perhaps not: what do we need to preserve or defend in particular disciplinary frameworks? or, what are the respective strengths of anthropology and cultural studies? but: who are we writing or creating representations for? and what do we want to tell them?

Bibliography

Appadurai, A., ed., 1986. *The Social Life of Things*. Cambridge: Cambridge University Press.

Asad, T., ed., 1974. *Anthropology and the Colonial Encounter*. London: Ithaca.

Barthes, R., 1972. *Mythologies*. London: Paladin.

Battaglia, D., ed., 1995. *Rhetorics of Self-Making*. Berkeley: University of California Press.

Bennett, T., 1995. *The Birth of the Museum*. London: Routledge.

Bhabha, H., 1994. *The Location of Culture*. London: Routledge.

Bryson, N., 1983. *Vision and Painting*. London: Macmillan.

CCCS [Centre for Contemporary Cultural Studies], 1978: *On Ideology*. London: Hutchinson.

Clifford, J., and G. Marcus, eds, 1986. *Writing Culture*. Berkeley: University of California Press.

Cohn, B., 1987. *An Anthropologist among the Historians*. Delhi: Oxford University Press.

Comaroff, J., and J. Comaroff, 1991. *Of Revelation and Revolution*. Chicago: University of Chicago Press.

Darnton, R., 1984. *The Great Cat Massacre and Other Episodes in French Cultural History*. New York: Basic Books.

Frow, J., 1995. *Cultural Studies and Cultural Value*. Oxford: Oxford University Press.

Geertz, C., 1988. *Works and Lives*. Cambridge: Polity Press.

Gilroy, P., 1992. 'Cultural Studies and Ethnic Absolutism', in *Cultural Studies*, ed. L. Grossberg, C. Nelson and P. A. Treichler. New York and London: Routledge.

Gilroy, P., 1993. *The Black Atlantic*. London: Verso.

Guha, R., 1983. *Elementary Aspects of Peasant Insurgency in Colonial India*. Delhi: Oxford University Press.

Hall, S., 1992. 'Cultural Studies and its Theoretical Legacies', in *Cultural Studies*, ed. L. Grossberg, C. Nelson and P. Treichler. New York: Routledge.

Hall, S., and T. Jefferson, 1976. *Resistance through Rituals*. London: Hutchinson.

Hanson, F. A., 1990. 'The Making of the Maori: Cultural Invention and its Logic', *American Anthropologist* 91: 890–902.

Howell, S., 1997. 'Cultural Studies and Social Anthropology: Contesting or Complementary Discourses?', in *Anthropology and Cultural Studies*, ed. S. Nugent and C. Shore. London: Pluto.

Jefferson, T., 1976. 'Cultural Responses of the Teds', in *Resistance through Rituals*, ed. S. Hall and T. Jefferson. London: Hutchinson.

Jolly, M., and N Thomas, eds, 1992. *The Politics of Tradition in the Pacific*. Special issue, *Oceania* 62 (4).

Keesing, R., 1989. 'Creating the Past: Custom and Identity in the Contemporary Pacific', *The Contemporary Pacific* 1: 19–42.

Miller, D., 1987. *Material Culture and Mass Consumption*. Oxford: Blackwell.

Moore, H., 1988. *Feminism and Anthropology*. Cambridge: Polity Press.

—— 1990. 'Anthropology and Others', *Visual Anthropology Review* 6 (2): 66–72.

Pinney, C., 1997. *Camera indica*. London: Reaktion Books.

Said, E., 1977. *Orientalism*. New York: Viking.

Schama, S., 1983. *The Embarrassment of Riches: Dutch Culture in the Golden Age*. Berkeley: University of California Press.

Schama, S., 1991. *Dead Certainties: Unwarranted Speculations*. New York: Knopf.

Spivak, G., 1987. *In Other Worlds*. London: Routledge.

Strathern, M., 1988. *The Gender of the Gift*. Berkeley: University of California Press.

Thomas, N., 1994. *Colonialism's culture*. Cambridge: Polity Press; Princeton: Princeton University Press.

—— 1996a, 'Cold Fusion', *American Anthropologist* 91: 9–16.

—— 1996b, 'From Exhibit to Exhibitionism',*The Contemporary Pacific* 8: 319–48.

—— 1997. *In Oceania: Visions, Artifacts, Histories*. Durham, NC: Duke University Press.

Torgovnick, M., 1990. *Gone Primitive*. Chicago: University of Chicago Press.

Trask, H.-K., 1989. 'Natives and Anthropologists: The Colonial Struggle', *The Contemporary Pacific* 3: 159–67.

Trinh, T. Minh-ha, 1989. *Woman, Native, Other*. Bloomington: Indiana University Press.

Turner, T., 1994. 'Anthropology and Multiculturalism', in *Multiculturalism: A Critical Reader*, ed. D. T. Goldberg. Oxford: Blackwell.

Werbner, P., 1997. '"The Lion of Lahore": Anthropology, Cultural Performance, and Imran Khan', in *Anthropology and Cultural Studies*, ed. S. Nugent and C. Shore. London: Pluto.

Young, R., 1990. *White Mythologies*. London: Routledge.

Index